WAR AS PARADOX

McGILL-QUEEN'S STUDIES IN THE HISTORY OF IDEAS
Series Editor: Philip J. Cercone

1 Problems of Cartesianism
Edited by Thomas M. Lennon, John M. Nicholas, and John W. Davis

2 The Development of the Idea of History in Antiquity
Gerald A. Press

3 Claude Buffier and Thomas Reid: Two Common-Sense Philosophers
Louise Marcil-Lacoste

4 Schiller, Hegel, and Marx: State, Society, and the Aesthetic Ideal of Ancient Greece
Philip J. Kain

5 John Case and Aristotelianism in Renaissance England
Charles B. Schmitt

6 Beyond Liberty and Property: The Process of Self-Recognition in Eighteenth-Century Political Thought
J.A.W. Gunn

7 John Toland: His Methods, Manners, and Mind
Stephen H. Daniel

8 Coleridge and the Inspired Word
Anthony John Harding

9 The Jena System, 1804–5: Logic and Metaphysics
G.W.F. Hegel
Translation edited by John W. Burbidge and George di Giovanni
Introduction and notes by H.S. Harris

10 Consent, Coercion, and Limit: The Medieval Origins of Parliamentary Democracy
Arthur P. Monahan

11 Scottish Common Sense in Germany, 1768–1800: A Contribution to the History of Critical Philosophy
Manfred Kuehn

12 Paine and Cobbett: The Transatlantic Connection
David A. Wilson

13 Descartes and the Enlightenment
Peter A. Schouls

14 Greek Scepticism: Anti-Realist Trends in Ancient Thought
Leo Groarke

15 The Irony of Theology and the Nature of Religious Thought
Donald Wiebe

16 Form and Transformation: A Study in the Philosophy of Plotinus
Frederic M. Schroeder

17 From Personal Duties towards Personal Rights: Late Medieval and Early Modern Political Thought, c. 1300–c. 1650
Arthur P. Monahan

18 The Main Philosophical Writings and the Novel *Allwill*
Friedrich Heinrich Jacobi
Translated and edited by George di Giovanni

19 Kierkegaard as Humanist: Discovering My Self
Arnold B. Come

20 Durkheim, Morals, and Modernity
W. Watts Miller

21 The Career of Toleration: John Locke, Jonas Proast, and After
Richard Vernon

22 Dialectic of Love: Platonism in Schiller's Aesthetics
David Pugh

23 History and Memory in Ancient Greece
Gordon Shrimpton

24 Kierkegaard as Theologian: Recovering My Self
Arnold B. Come

25 Enlightenment and Conservatism in Victorian Scotland: The Career of Sir Archibald Alison
Michael Michie

26 The Road to Egdon Heath: The Aesthetics of the Great in Nature
Richard Bevis

27 Jena Romanticism and Its Appropriation of Jakob Böhme: Theosophy – Hagiography – Literature
Paolo Mayer

28 Enlightenment and Community: Lessing, Abbt, Herder, and the Quest for a German Public
Benjamin W. Redekop

29 Jacob Burckhardt and the Crisis of Modernity
John R. Hinde

30 The Distant Relation: Time and Identity in Spanish-American Fiction
Eoin S. Thomson

31 Mr Simson's Knotty Case: Divinity, Politics, and Due Process in Early Eighteenth-Century Scotland
Anne Skoczylas

32 Orthodoxy and Enlightenment: George Campbell in the Eighteenth Century
Jeffrey M. Suderman

33 Contemplation and Incarnation: The Theology of Marie-Dominique Chenu
Christophe F. Potworowski

34 Democratic Legitimacy: Plural Values and Political Power
F.M. Barnard

35 Herder on Nationality, Humanity, and History
F.M. Barnard

36 Labeling People: French Scholars on Society, Race, and Empire, 1815–1849
Martin S. Staum

53 Nature and Nurture in French Social Sciences, 1859–1914 and Beyond
Martin S. Staum

54 Public Passion: Rethinking the Grounds for Political Justice
Rebecca Kingston

55 Rethinking the Political: The Sacred, Aesthetic Politics, and the Collège de Sociologie
Simonetta Falasca-Zamponi

56 Materialist Ethics and Life-Value
Jeff Noonan

57 Hegel's *Phenomenology*: The Dialectical Justification of Philosophy's First Principles
Ardis B. Collins

58 The Social History of Ideas in Quebec, 1760–1896
Yvan Lamonde
Translated by Phyllis Aronoff and Howard Scott

59 Ideas, Concepts, and Reality
John W. Burbidge

60 The Enigma of Perception
D.L.C. Maclachlan

61 Nietzsche's Justice: Naturalism in Search of an Ethics
Peter R. Sedgwick

62 The Idea of Liberty in Canada during the Age of Atlantic Revolutions, 1776–1838
Michel Ducharme
Translated by Peter Feldstein

63 From White to Yellow: The Japanese in European Racial Thought, 1300–1735
Rotem Kowner

64 The Crisis of Modernity
Augusto Del Noce
Edited and translated by Carlo Lancellotti

65 Imprinting Britain: Newspapers, Sociability, and the Shaping of British North America
Michael Eamon

66 The Form of Politics: Aristotle and Plato on Friendship
John von Heyking

67 War as Paradox: Clausewitz and Hegel on Fighting Doctrines and Ethics
Youri Cormier

WAR AS PARADOX

Clausewitz and Hegel on Fighting Doctrines and Ethics

Youri Cormier

McGill-Queen's University Press
Montreal & Kingston • London • Chicago

ISBN 978-0-7735-4768-1 (cloth)
ISBN 978-0-7735-4769-8 (paper)
ISBN 978-0-7735-4849-7 (ePDF)
ISBN 978-0-7735-4850-3 (ePUB)

Legal deposit fourth quarter 2016
Bibliothèque nationale du Québec

Printed in Canada on acid-free paper that is 100% ancient forest free (100% post-consumer recycled), processed chlorine free

This book was first published with the help of a grant from the Canadian Federation for the Humanities and Social Sciences, through the Awards to Scholarly Publications Program, using funds provided by the Social Sciences and Humanities Research Council of Canada.

McGill-Queen's University Press acknowledges the support of the Canada Council for the Arts for our publishing program. We also acknowledge the financial support of the Government of Canada through the Canada Book Fund for our publishing activities.

Library and Archives Canada Cataloguing in Publication

Cormier, Youri, 1980–, author
War as paradox: Clausewitz and Hegel on fighting doctrines and ethics/ Youri Cormier.

(McGill-Queen's studies in the history of ideas; 67)
Includes bibliographical references and index.
Issued in print and electronic formats.
ISBN 978-0-7735-4768-1 (cloth). – ISBN 978-0-7735-4769-8 (paper). – ISBN 978-0-7735-4849-7 (ePDF). – ISBN 978-0-7735-4850-3 (ePUB)

1. Clausewitz, Carl von, 1780–1831. Vom Kriege. 2. Hegel, Georg Wilhelm Friedrich, 1770–1831 – Criticism and interpretation. 3. War – Moral and ethical aspects. 4. War (Philosophy). I. Title. II. Series: McGill-Queen's studies in the history of ideas; 67

B105.W3C67 2016 172'.42 C2016-904702-4
C2016-904703-2

This book was typeset by Marquis Interscript in 10/12 New Baskerville.

To my parents, pedagogues, pacifists, who encouraged critical thinking and did not allow toy guns into the family home. May this book contribute to sharing your values, now mine, far beyond the household.

Contents

Acknowledgments

Special thanks to Dr Jan Willem Honig and Prof. Mervyn Frost of King's College London, whose invaluable feedback, generosity, and keen understanding of the authors formed the backbone of this project's development. Prof. Philippe Constantineau at the Royal Military College of Canada was also instrumental in helping me shape certain arguments in the book. I also wish to thank Prof. Beatrice Heuser (Reading) and Prof. Barrie Paskins (KCL) whose difficult but highly insightful critiques strengthened many of the arguments. I should also mention my debt to Christopher Bassford, in particular for his advice, and more generally for editing www.clausewitz.com, a high-quality website of great utility to anyone intent on studying Clausewitz. Andreas Herberg-Rothe provided excellent suggestions with regard to the chapters on the converging elements of Hegel and Clausewitz. My thanks also go out to various other scholars who helped me along the way, either by answering a quick question or by offering comments or feedback relative to specific sections of the book: Prof. Vivienne Jabri (KCL), Prof. Azar Gat (Tel Aviv University), Prof. Danic Parenteau (Royal Military College Saint-Jean – Canada), Luc Haché (CEGEP de St-Jérôme), and Prof. Charles Taylor (McGill). And finally, I wish to thank the editorial boards of the *International History Review*, the *Journal of Military and Security Studies*, and McGill-Queen's University Press.

Note

For reasons that will become more apparent throughout this book, my primary source for Clausewitz's *On War* is not the Howard/Paret translation – despite the fact it has generally become the norm amongst scholars. Rather, I will be referring to the Graham translation. In my view, this older translation is far better suited to a study of the philosophical aspects of Clausewitz since it is a more literal replica of the original. While not always the most practical for everyday use, it is more helpful in uncovering word choices and concepts that Clausewitz borrowed from philosophical literature.

WAR AS PARADOX

Introduction

ON WAR BY CARL VON CLAUSEWITZ is without a doubt the most impressive and most significant book ever written about war. It has shaped the strategies and tactics of every major military conflict since it was published (section by section) from 1832 to 1835. General Moltke, the architect of the German victory during the Franco-Prussian War (1870–71) was one its first adepts. He cited it as one of only two books he always kept handy, alongside the Bible. On the left, Karl Marx, Friedrich Engels, Vladimir Lenin, Leon Trotsky, and Mao Zedong referred to it. During the two World Wars, it was central to French strategy under Maréchal Ferdinand Foch, as well as the famous German Schlieffen Plan, and was read by officers and strategists on all sides including J.F.C. Fuller, T.E. Lawrence, George S. Patton, Erwin Rommel, and Dwight D. Eisenhower. Whether the Cold War, the Vietnam War, or more recent engagements – in every case Clausewitz had something to offer strategists and practitioners alike. Today, the book lines the shelves of every military academy on the planet and those of any good department of politics and international relations. Perhaps all the more interestingly, a copy of *On War* was also recently found in an Al Qaeda hideout. At all ends of the spectrum, left to right, secular to religious, warmonger to pacifist, for those who are thinking about war or developing strategies to fight it or avoid it, *On War* represents the common item they all seem to agree upon.

And yet, the book's single most original contribution is at times lost in seeking out its many applied uses. Beyond shaping tactics and strategies, *On War* reinvented something far more important: the way in which we wrap our heads around the very concept of war. Clausewitz elevated the paradoxical nature of war and the dynamic elements within the idea of war that determine how it unfolds. He also investigated the social and political underpinnings of war. This represented a shift from seeing war as a fact of nature or the unleashing of the wrath of gods and the fulfillment of scripture, in order to arrive instead at a truly modern, humanistic theoretical foundation that centralizes the responsibility for warfare directly on mankind itself as opposed to something abstracted or separated from man. From this secularization of war there is truly no going back – and we will discuss later how this is even true for those claiming to be fighting "holy" wars.

Much has therefore been written about Clausewitz's famous book, both with regard to how it came about as well as how it should be interpreted. There remains, however, much controversy. *On War* was published posthumously and, from two editorial notes the author wrote (one in 1827 and the other undated, but likely in 1830), we know that he considered the work incomplete and unsatisfactory in its form. Clausewitz intended to completely overhaul the book in order to integrate his recent ideas and make the book more coherent from cover to cover. But he never got around to it, because he died a sudden death during a cholera outbreak in 1831. In a surprising act of prophecy, Clausewitz wrote in the second note: "Should the work be interrupted by my death, then what is found can only be called a mass of conceptions not brought into form; but as these are open to endless misconceptions, they will doubtless give rise to a number of crude criticisms."[1]

Since *On War* took over a decade to write (approximately 1815[2]–1830) during which Clausewitz's thinking evolved considerably, there are indeed aspects of the work that are not perfectly coherent, and – as will be discussed later – even words and ideas that change in meaning from one chapter to another depending on when it was written. That being said, though, interpreters have exaggerated the internal conflicts in the book – most of which are actually planned dichotomous pairs that serve a methodological purpose. We can't undo the fact that the book was incomplete, but knowing the direction in which Clausewitz's thinking was evolving can help readers better understand the most salient features of the book. Most importantly, understanding the structure of his thought – the underlying philosophical systems he was building upon – allows us to see the trend in his intellectual path, which led to this crisis point in 1827, which in turn set Clausewitz on a path to completely overhaul the book from cover to cover. Grasping the nature of the sudden turnaround in Clausewitz's mind helps explain what problems the older Clausewitz saw in the work of his younger self, and this is indeed a powerful tool for improving our interpretation of the whole.

1 Clausewitz, *On War*, xxxviii.

2 Paret, "The Genesis of *On War*," 3.

Another reason for all the controversy and commentary regarding the book is just how difficult it is to read. *On War* has been described by one commentator as a text that surrounds the reader with a "metaphysical fog."[3] Another suggested it should be presented to students as mere "poetry" instead of a manual for understanding war, because it is full of contradictions.[4] These issues, however, can be resolved by developing a better understanding of the book's methodology and its effective use of contradictions to heighten the paradoxical elements of war. What makes *On War* difficult to read for practitioners in the military is that they are rarely reading it with a full knowledge of the concepts Clausewitz was directly borrowing from the philosophical systems that were being developed in his country, during his lifetime. These philosophical systems ground his book as a whole and explain how he organized and proved his various arguments. Once we understand the philosophical methods and context that give rise to this complexity, the fog quickly dissipates and the reader can grasp Clausewitz more intuitively, thereby calming the most common frustrations with the book.

If a central element in the coming lines is indeed to improve the precision with which we interpret Clausewitz by using an angle that has been underappreciated by past commentators, this is nonetheless not the main purpose of the book, but rather the fortunate outcome of asking another wider set of questions regarding the philosophical systems that made up important aspects of the work. Clausewitz plays the role of the main character, in a plot that focuses on the commonalities between his work and that of his contemporaries (Immanuel Kant, G.W.F. Hegel, Johann Gottlieb Fichte) so that we may uncover what I will refer to as "dialectical war theory," which provided not only Clausewitz, but Hegel as well, with a powerful framework upon which to synthesize conclusions on the subject that are so widespread that we often know little about where they came from and how. Having uncovered, in both authors, the implications of this wider dialectical war theory, it will be possible to critically assess its implications in history as well as current relevancy. With so many people turning to Clausewitz for advice on political violence, it is not only fair to ask, but imperative that we should ask, whether this 200-year-old theory still offers much to strategic thought, knowing just

3 Hubert Camon, *Clausewitz* (Paris: R. Chapelot, 1911), vii. Cited by H. Rothfels, "Clausewitz," in *Makers of Modern Strategy*, ed. E.M. Earle (Princeton: Princeton University Press, 1943), 93.

4 Bruce Fleming, "Can Reading Clausewitz Save Us from Future Mistakes?," *Parameters* (Spring 2004): 76.

how dramatically war has evolved since it was fought by lines of tens of thousands of musket-laden men.

Clausewitz was born in 1780, and first experienced battle at the age of thirteen, when the Prussian Army (i.e. Germans), which he had joined at age twelve, took part in the First Coalition to push back the French Revolutionary Army from the Rhine. A few years after this campaign, he suffered the "catastrophe" at Jena-Auerstadt in 1806, when the Prussians were crushed by the French. Clausewitz, who was serving as a tutor to the crown prince at that time, was captured with him and the two were held by the French until 1808, when the Peace of Tilsit allowed them to be repatriated. For the rest of his life, this humiliating experience would fuel Clausewitz's bitter resentment of the French. In fact, his patriotic zeal was so strong that when Napoleon marched towards Moscow and the subjugated Prussian monarchy agreed to reinforce the French expedition, Clausewitz crossed to the other side and fought with the Russians against the Franco-Prussian forces, until the Prussian army surrendered at Tauroggen and joined the Russian effort against Napoleon in part thanks to Clausewitz, who negotiated the terms.

If these three great moments during the Revolutionary/Napoleonic Wars shaped Clausewitz viscerally, it is important to understand how the times when he was not fighting shaped him intellectually. After the 1795 Treaty of Basel, Clausewitz's unit was garrisoned in Neuruppin, where Prince Henry kept a rich library that all officers could use. Clausewitz devoured it. His interest in military studies and education was noted by his superiors, and in 1801, he was sent off to the brand new War College in Berlin where he would meet General Gerd von Scharnhorst, who founded and commanded the college. He became a mentor, and Clausewitz would one day refer to him as the "father of my spirit." Among the most important lessons Clausewitz would take from Scharnhorst was his insistence on the idea that the strength of the French revolutionary army was "closely connected with the transformation of the society,"[5] but also how he "discounted the authority of theoretical systems; whether classic works or the product of contemporary revolutionaries, all were fit objects for critical and historical analysis."[6] Scharnhorst insisted on critical thinking and historical proof. He had a true distrust for commonly held, supposedly foolproof tactical doctrines.

Clausewitz's bookishness has been observed by many authors, and Beatrice Heuser uncovered excellent citations from people who wrote

5 Howard, *Clausewitz*, 7.
6 Paret, *Clausewitz and the State*, 70.

about their first-hand interactions with him. The descriptions are contradictory, no doubt, from "endearing" to "totally unpalatable," but most seem to agree that he was very scholarly, if at times cold and quiet. He was also quick to either take offence or react abruptly. A man of few friends, those he had were close and reliable.[7] Clausewitz was extremely well-read and intellectually curious, which explains why and how he made such good use of such a wide mix of methods: he looked to political thinkers like Niccolò Machiavelli and Montesquieu; he borrowed from the fields of physics and thermodynamics to provide his writing with heuristic and metaphorical tools; he was influenced as well by philosophers like Kant (in a variety of ways) and Fichte (in developing the notion of "absolute war"). Clausewitz was also extremely well versed in works of military science and had read practically every single major work of interest on the matter, including, but not limited to Raimondo Monteccuccoli, Maurice de Saxe, the Marquis of Puységur, Henry Lloyd, Jacques Antoine Hippolyte Guibert, Adam Dietrich Heinrich von Bülow, and Antoine-Henri Jomini. These, however, he was far more critical about. Throughout the book, it is not only the references he makes that are vast, but also his own way of thinking, which at times is based on critical analysis, battlefield history, geometry, and logistical analysis, set out in a way that systematically embarks on a pedagogical path: the reader is being engaged to think critically about war theory. As a result, the book is deep and rich throughout – and often for different reasons, not the least, its many "instances of sharp observation, biting irony, and memorable phrases that have given a long series of readers … a treasure trove of quotes and insights."[8]

The description of his personality is important, because it explains the kind of intellectual drive that would push a man to writing as ambitious a book as *On War*. Furthermore, it explains his various appointments. The reason he was appointed to serve as the tutor to the crown prince was that he had graduated top of his class at the War College and had been recommended by Scharnhorst for the post. Later in his career, he was held back from promotions in the army, for a variety of reasons, including the fact that he had turned his back on the king to join the tsar, and he had tense relations with some of the higher brass, as a result of being critical, surely, but also because he hailed from the middle class at a time when senior military functions were deemed aristocratic. On this subject, Clausewitz was engaged in a process of trying to reform the army

7 Heuser, *Reading Clausewitz*, 5.

8 Jan Willem Honig, introduction to Clausewitz, *On War* (Barnes & Noble), xv.

from its old aristocratic ways, which may have contributed to some of the frictions he experienced within the officer corps. He had in fact served as an integral member of the Military Reorganization Commission, which Scharnhorst had set up towards those objectives.[9]

Clausewitz yearned for autonomous command, but it was never granted. He never reached full generalship, but peaked in his career at the rank of major general, which was a sour element in his professional path, though he nonetheless had a remarkable career, including serving in the prestigious role of commander of the War College and chief of staff to the eastern front when, in 1830, there was a risk that the Polish revolution would spill over westward. And yet, Clausewitz remained unsatisfied: he was rebuffed in his attempts to use the college as a tool for reforming the forces as he had intended, and was for the most part simply given administrative duties when he served there. It was, however, a blessing in disguise since the type of work he had is what allowed him to engage in theoretical and historical contemplation and to write major historical works on the Napoleonic Wars as well as his magnum opus, *On War*.

Though a few metaphors from this masterpiece have become common parlance, such as the "fog of war" (the difficulty one has in properly gauging, measuring, and predicting anything in war) and "friction" (the impression that everything in war is slower, more complicated, and less effective than one expects), his more important theoretical contributions were at a higher level. First of all, Clausewitz differentiated between tactics and strategy in a way that was altogether novel, developing the first ends-means definition of their relation, where tactics are subordinate to strategy and represent the methods for winning a specific battle, whereas strategy is how one orchestrates a series of battles towards winning the war. Secondly, he put forward a dual nature of war, which consists of conceptualizing, on the one hand, what war could be if it were entirely left to its own limitless escalatory logic, war in an "absolute" form, and on the other hand, what war actually is, when counterbalanced with the more limited aims of those waging it, coupled with those elements that slow down this escalation, namely, the "fog" and the "friction." This real/absolute divide as intellectual device is meant to exaggerate the idea of war, to purify war's potential if pushed to an all-out war-to-the-finish, in order to provide a more complete frame of analysis for what war actually looks like in the real world: straddling somewhere between its potentiality and its materiality. Clausewitz asks what actual or "real" war looks like as a result of it having such an "ideal" underlying logic, but framed within a material context that has inherent limiting

9 Waldman, *War, Clausewitz and the Trinity*, 4.

features. The dual nature of war has caused a lot of ink to be spilled, because many erroneously equate the totally conceptual "absolute war" to the actual twentieth-century reality of "total war." This problem we will consider in greater detail further below.

Most importantly, Clausewitz provided us with the undeniably best definition of war there is: the "continuation of policy by other means." What is particularly important about it is that it effectively links war to the political realm. From this perspective war is no longer to be understood as an inevitable fact of nature or curse from the gods, but an "instrument" in the hands of political entities. It is a social device and as a result, war's ethical dimension should be guided by humanistic values as opposed to theistic dogma. Clausewitz's definition clarifies that war is a human construct and that we are responsible for its every excess and cruelty as well as its nobility when waged on just grounds. Though Clausewitz did not believe in the idea that peace and justice could be firmly founded on mere paper treaties, the intellectual legacy of his secular, modern definition of war nonetheless sets the stage for holding the agents in war responsible for their actions, which has since become central to our modern judiciary concepts of war crimes, genocide, and crimes against humanity.

The culmination of Clausewitz's philosophy of war is described in the final section he wrote before sealing the document and heading off on the mission that would take his life – establishing a sanitary cordon to ward the spread of cholera, where he caught the disease and died soon thereafter. Having started off by describing war as an "act of violence intended to compel our opponent to fulfill our will,"[10] which he explains has an internal logic that leads to extremes, he nonetheless arrives at an opposite argument: that reason instrumentalizes (or at least attempts to instrumentalize) war. This paradoxical relationship between the irrational and latent forces and the rational will to instrumentalize it forms two of the three sides of a "wondrous trinity" at the heart of the notion of war, to which he adds a third interacting element, chance, which further complexifies the paradox. The three are: "the original violence of its elements, hatred and animosity, which may be looked upon as blind instinct; the play of probabilities and chance, which make it a free activity of the soul; and the subordinate nature of a political instrument, by which it belongs purely to reason."[11] He explains that these "mostly concern" the

10 Clausewitz, *On War*, bk 1, ch. 1, 1.

11 Ibid., 19. Please note: for clarity I have removed the word "of," which precedes each of the three clauses. Also, the Graham translation ends on "pure to the reason" – here the word "the" is superfluous and perhaps even slightly misleading, since Clausewitz uses the word "Verstand," which is not a specific reason but "Reason" itself.

following three groups in their respective order: 1) the people, 2) the army; and 3) the government, and what gives "life" to war, ultimately, is how violence, chances, and reason play out and become manifest. Whereas it is clear that the trinity is the abstract portion of the idea, and "mostly concerns" different elements of society, the error of interpretation that has come about is to overstate the importance of the groups of people involved – suggesting these groups actually form the trinity, as opposed to being merely in relation to it. This interpretation has led some writers to focus their argument on this secondary trinity as opposed to the true trinity, and then complain that it is too state-centric a device, but this is only because they have detached the relational and conceptual element from the concrete example of what or who it influences.

The state-centrist argument is the foundation of a series of claims that Clausewitz is no longer relevant today, because it doesn't properly consider, as Kaldor coined them, "new wars" – intra-state wars, insurgencies, interconnected with criminal organizations. Others such as Keegan and van Creveld also held similar arguments regarding the fact that Clausewitz placed too much importance on the state. While these points of views from the 1990s have been effectively challenged by scholars ever since,[12] the truest testimony regarding their demise is that, as I mentioned in the first paragraph above, a copy of *On War* was found in an Al Qaeda hideout. If even the main protagonists in these so-called "new wars" are reading up on Clausewitz, we can hardly claim that his ideas are out of date on these very same grounds. Actually, Clausewitz had much to say on the subject of "small wars," as insurgency warfare was called in his day. This we will consider in chapter 1, when I explore and counter the state-centric argument in greater detail.

The missing link today in how authors such as Keegan, van Creveld, and others attack Clausewitz is that they do so from a perspective that is completely devoid of a methodological understanding. The problem is far-reaching among supporters and detractors alike. Colin Fleming is enthusiastic about the legacy of Clausewitzian thought, but is disappointed to find that *On War* doesn't have a "clear methodological structure."[13] Actually, the bulk of the methodology is spelled out quite explicitly by Clausewitz in Book II of his opus, and it is also implicitly rendered from cover to cover in *On War*, through a variety of concepts and arguments borrowed from philosophy, as we shall explore in the pages to come.

12 See Christopher Bassford, "Tip-Toe through the Trinity," http://www.clausewitz.com/mobile/trinity8.htm, 31 March 2016; Echevarria, *Clausewitz and Contemporary War*; Heuser, *Reading Clausewitz*; and Strachan and Herberg-Rothe, *Clausewitz in the Twentieth Century*.

13 Fleming, *Clausewitz's Timeless Trinity*, 34.

In order to correct this situation, the chapters below build a genealogy of the method in order to re-found the study of Clausewitz upon a more serious grounding, from which we can then extend our analysis to more complex questions about the method and its utility – not on a snippet-by-snippet basis, but from a more holistic perspective. The appearance of contradictions that frustrate so many readers of *On War* can easily be made intelligible when they are understood as a methodology that elevates the paradoxical aspects of war in order to enhance our understanding of the phenomenon. Meanwhile, knowing that Clausewitz wrote the book over a long period of time, during which his ideas evolved, we should always keep in mind when these different parts were written. This is important, because, as Herberg-Rothe has noted, the most vindictive criticisms against Clausewitz, written by van Creveld and Keegan, not only suppress the second clause "by other means" in the famous maxim "war is the continuation of policy by other means," thereby altering the paradoxical element in the idea, but also focus on ideas from either the young Clausewitz or the mature Clausewitz, but exclusively so. Herberg-Rothe rightly explains: "Keegan's criticism could be answered with reference to the later Clausewitz, while the early Clausewiz can respond to van Creveld's criticism."[14] It is essential to tell them apart if we are to understand the author properly, which is to say, read his ideas in the adaptive language he uses, rather than countering, sentence by sentence, word by word, Clausewitz's overarching theory by superposing words and concepts as we understand them today, to how he wrote about them so long ago. There is more fluidity to it.

In the final passage that Clausewitz wrote, before sealing up the manuscript for the last time, he described war as a "chameleon." War changes, adapts from one place to another, from one era to the next. To effectively theorize about war means that theory as well must be adaptive. That is the greatest strength of Clausewitz's analysis – it sets a framework for critical analysis rather than doctrinairism on the subject of war. A larger question, therefore, that we should ask in wondering about the relevance of Clausewitz today is whether the paradoxes he exposes have in fact become all the more paradoxical today, in which case a method that builds upon these would be all the more pertinent than the opposite: which is to treat war as something clear, simple, and unchanging. That is the dream of many a practitioner and theoretician of war, but it is as fleeting as it is inconsistent with experience.

Framing *On War* within its methodological and philosophical underpinnings will mean at times looking into how the author was influenced,

14 Herberg-Rothe, *Clausewitz's Puzzle*, 5–6.

not for the sake of proving that this or that author was necessarily the source of Clausewitz's thought, but rather to bring out the commonalities for the sake of developing better interpretative models based on the parallels drawn from noting the common methods. Whether Clausewitz's genius was to generate independently the same systems of thought as Hegel and Kant without having read either, which I doubt, the commonalities are there to be found. It makes little difference anyway how he got there, but what matters is what this convergence means and does. Whenever Clausewitz's ideas converged with those of Kant and Hegel, the effect was to generate some of the very most effective passages in his work. The more we understand these, the better we can grasp the mechanics or underlying logic and methods that created many of the most powerful passages in *On War*. The goal is therefore not to prove beyond all doubt this, that, or another influence, but rather to limit the question to better understanding Clausewitz. Let us cut to the chase: what are the similarities, what are the differences, and why does it matter?

This process will clarify the system of logic upon which dialectical theories of war emerged. However, as we begin this exploration by focusing on the works of Clausewitz, it will be necessary to recognize that this evolution of a new method was happening in parallel. Even though we will take the time to consider in what sense Clausewitz apparently borrowed from the work of Hegel, it will be essential to present Hegel's own work on the subject of war, which converges methodologically with Clausewitz but diverges considerably in its conclusions. The two side by side allow us to draw larger conclusions regarding dialectical war theory.

Hegel and Clausewitz have been described as "*the* two great thinkers on war,"[15] an exclusive title that is by no means an exaggeration. The success of these two German writers, who lived during the same era in Prussia's capital city Berlin and died only a few days apart, has much to do with the time and place in which they lived. Indeed, Prussia was a major intellectual centre at the time: the works of Kant, Fichte, F.W.J. Schelling, and J.W.V. Goethe had set the bar high amongst contemporaries, while also stimulating a true golden age in philosophy. Furthermore, only decades earlier, Prussia had been at the height of its glory under the reign of Frederick the Great (1740–1786), and was suddenly reduced to a status one might compare to that of a puppet regime of the French, as a result of the formidable wars Napoleon brought eastward. The experience of war that the nation lived through undoubtedly served as a catalyst for

15 Girard, *Achèver Clausewitz*, 77, emphasis added to reflect the original French grammar, in which exclusion is implied.

Prussians to think about and write about war. Yet, beyond this context, something more contributed to raising Hegel and Clausewitz above all other war theorists, a shared method, closely connected to the works of Kant, which often has been missed in the interpretations of each, and has been altogether disregarded as a feature of both.

Both authors used highly specialized philosophical language and methodology, and as a result they may be well known, but are often poorly read. Unfortunately, it is more often the norm than the exception in the field of war theory to make very broad claims about what they meant, based on truncated phrases and snippets that have been entirely removed from the philosophical and methodological frameworks that provided the original, intended meaning, as opposed to the meaning that is tacked onto these cropped maxims. These famous one-liners are often assumed to be starting points or subjective assertions made by both authors, but if we take the time to uncover their underlying arguments, we find that the reality is diametrically opposed: in fact, these statements are, for the most part, conclusions reached by Hegel and Clausewitz after very thorough and objective processes of argumentation and historically based critical analysis.

Beyond the complexity of both authors, another source of concern regarding the two stems from the fact that they were studying the very worst wars mankind had known until then, the Napoleonic Wars, and consequently did not hold back their words in how they presented war in all its brutality. Some therefore perceived the authors as warmongers, suggesting that war "should" be this way, but the other way one can read them is to see their aim being objectivity, and far from "prescribing" how war should be, they are offering posterity what war "has been" as a warning rather than a goal. The works of Hegel and Clausewitz have been labelled as a source of self-fulfilling prophecy: describing war in coarse terms leads war to be all the more coarse. This problem will be discussed in the first chapter so that we may clear the controversy at least enough to justify furthering the inquiry.

Very few commentators seem to have read beyond Book 1, chapter 1 of *On War*, where we find Clausewitz's "Trinity" and his most famous one-liners – even if they have read beyond it, rare are those who quote beyond it. Focused on dissected one-liners, detractors and supporters alike have written very long and ambitious books about very short passages in Clausewitz. The same is true of those who refer to Hegel, especially in the field of war theory. This has led to excruciatingly long and convoluted arguments and claims that ultimately fall short when it comes to convincing the reader, especially in the case of the detractors, because they take aim at mere parts while claiming to undermine the whole. In the coming lines, my goal is to do the total opposite: to write a shorter piece about a wider set of longer passages, to seek out an analysis of the whole, while making far more modest claims. Ultimately, this has the potential to open up a higher-level argument that encompasses many of the smaller contentions that have fuelled controversy in the field. The question is not directly whether or not these "rational" theories of war from the late Enlightenment, written at a time of hand-to-hand combat, line formations, formal declarations of war, and state-to-state political violence, continue to be pertinent when framing wars that are not so chequered and predictable. It encompasses this by going beyond it and asking: how are we to rationally frame a subject that seems at times completely devoid of reason? If political violence has changed over time in how it is practised, this forces us to wonder whether or not its "essence" also changes in time or if there is something eternal to it. Today, the threat of nuclear annihilation stands at one conceptual pole of warfare, and opposite this, we find decentralized and barbarous acts of terrorism, characterized by lone wolves and small pockets as was the case in the Charlie Hebdo attack at one end, and using drones in extra-judicial targeted killing at the other. Scattered between all this, how do we make sense of the Rwandan genocide, Ex-Yugoslavia, the Syrian civil war, Boko Haram, ISIS, and Al Qaeda? The extent to which we can integrate such distinct forms of political violence into a single idea may seem to defy the very notion that we can frame war in a theoretical "system" of analysis to begin with. If there is something irrational to any of it, or at least visceral rather than rational, in the logic that gives modern political violence its shape, then what use would rational tools of analysis be, if merely superimposed rather than derived from the object of study?

This book will make no attempt to settle whether today's wars are more rational or less rational than those of the past, but it will propose that rationalist theories of war are extremely pertinent in either case, because they help us uncover underlying paradoxes that are fixed neither in time nor in technology, but evolve, and build upon themselves larger possible answers to larger questions and problems we may encounter with regard not only to the nature of political violence itself, but its tactics, strategies, and systems of justification – even if these tend towards unreasonable propositions, including, for example, fighting towards immaterial and ever-fleeting objectives or sustaining violence on premises of circular logic. One particularly interesting aspect of this exploration will be the surprising metaphysical similarities that connect the justification processes for fighting wars in the name of a secular concept, "freedom," and fighting for the sake of religious doctrine and the glory of god.

However, before bringing the discussion to these later points, we rebuild the rationalist theories from the ground up and reclaim the method that gives meaning and life to the famous maxims found in Hegel and Clausewitz. This forces me to make this book rather lopsided, because while the end goal is to eventually compare the ethical ramifications of Hegel and Clausewitz's theories of war, the bulk of the book is about Clausewitz, and, meanwhile, I will only introduce Hegel in the second half. The reason for this is that I wish to cover all three dimensions of war theory, namely, the questions *what is war* (ontology), *how is it fought* (strategy, tactics, logistics), and *why is it fought* (ethics). Doing this imposes a particular order to the exploration of the topics, but it is not the order one might expect.

If the order above appears to be the logical sequence to follow – what, how, why – there is nonetheless a flaw to it. If we were to start by asking "what," we would find ourselves with only a vague or incomplete idea of what war "is," because without an analysis of the observable characteristics of war (i.e. the battle, its strategies and tactics), conclusions on the matter would be subjective. The second question informs the first considerably and forces us back to the "what" again, allowing our subjective ideas about war to be reconsidered objectively based on the experience of it. Consequently, I start with the how, then move into the what, and finish with the why. This explains why Hegel comes later. The difference between the two authors is that Clausewitz studied strategy/tactics and ontology, without explicitly making claims regarding ethics. It is not absent from his work, but is latent within it and must be extracted through analysis. Meanwhile, Hegel did not write about military strategy – he was not an officer like Clausewitz, but a university professor who dedicated his life's work to philosophy. The subject of Hegel's analysis is first and foremost the ethical dimension of war, which can be shown to ultimately have tactical, strategic, and ontological implications as well, but he stays clear of these dimensions in his writing. Hegel was a philosopher who considered the topic of war among other things, whereas Clausewitz was a war theorist, who referred to philosophy as a means to better understand and analyze his central topic. Since Clausewitz's work touches specifically on the first two dimensions of war theory, this explains why we should begin with his work, but the fact that his theory touches more directly all three dimensions explains why the book is so lopsided in favour of analyzing his work, its development, and its impact on the field, before culminating with a comparative analysis between the two authors on the question of ethics.

Hegel and Clausewitz are rarely considered in tandem, and have never been presented as the co-founders of a single tradition in war theory.

Whenever we do find both authors side by side in textbooks and articles, it is primarily to argue, as D.B. Creusinger, Walther Malmsten Schering, Michael Howard, and Azar Gat have, that Hegel influenced Clausewitz, or as Raymond Aron and Peter Paret argued, that he was not at all influenced by him. The opposite influence, that is, Hegel being influenced by Clausewitz's writings, is not apparent in Hegel's works, and would have indeed been rather unlikely since Clausewitz's major works were published after Hegel's death. While, admittedly, many other profound influences in the works of Clausewitz must be acknowledged in order best to appreciate Clausewitz's analyses, namely Montesquieu,[16] Machiavelli,[17] and Scharnhorst,[18] this book will nonetheless argue in the same spirit as those in the first group who hold that the convergence with the Hegelian way of thinking was important to the development of Clausewitz's later works.

If Kant and Hegel's influence on Clausewitz is often contested, this stems principally from a lack of systematic study and the reliance on impressions of an influence on the one side, and the dogmatic belief that unless one finds the smoking barrel – a direct quotation – there's no point bothering at all to seek out gunshot holes and other demonstrations of someone having fired. There are two extreme positions on the matter. On the one hand, finding a specific quote that demonstrates the influence can be a superficial discovery if it is a mere one-liner or fragment especially if it is offset by a much larger lack of unity or coherence, which would suggest a lack of influence rather than a sure sign of it. On the other hand, failing to find a specific one-liner should not be assumed to mean there is no link, since while minor ideas can be spelled out in short fragments and phrases, larger convergences cannot because they are overarching. They can in fact spell a far more potent type of influence, without there being any full certainty to the claim, for lack of the phrase or line it is common for academics to seek. One is either stuck

16 Aron, *Penser la guerre*, 23–4.

17 Clausewitz took the time to write about Machiavelli and also makes numerous allusions to his works in *On War*, particularly on the issues of militias and the people's war. There is also undoubtedly much to be said about their similar concepts of art as means. In a letter written in 1809, Clausewitz explains with regret that Machiavelli's *Art of War* lacks the liberty and independence of judgment that characterized his political writings. Clausewitz also questions Machiavelli's nostalgia for the wars of the Ancients, explaining that the solution is rather to revive the spirit of war. Clausewitz, Letter to Fichte, annexed in Fichte, *Machiavel et autres écrits philosophiques et politiques*, 197–203.

18 In a letter to his fiancée, 28 January 1807, Clausewitz refers to Scharnhorst as the "father and friend of my Spirit." Clausewitz, "Carl und Marie von Clausewitz, Ein Lebensbild," 85.

with weak influence that appears much more certain, or a strong influence that appears much less certain. Either scenario is less than ideal.

Exploring the various links between Clausewitz and either Kant or Hegel, however, means going up against a very credible and erudite expert who stood on the opposite side of the argument. Raymond Aron, a twentieth-century pillar of French philosophy, wrote a thorough reflection on the works of Clausewitz in which he makes a convincing case regarding the lack of influence that links Clausewitz to either Hegel or Kant, but one that has many flaws nonetheless. Proposing a counterargument, however, is no easy task, because it cannot be achieved without a deep reading of all three of the above Prussian thinkers. One must tease out not only general similarities, but quite specific terms, language, and methods, which travelled from the two philosophers into the works of the war theorist. Peter Paret may have argued that "relating Clausewitz to Kant or Hegel almost necessarily results in forced and unconvincing historical constructions,"[19] but in reality, these are only unconvincing insofar as they are forced.

As long as this book's argument sets as its limit to expose rather than force conclusions, then this task may yet have some serious merit: to help us understand both the origin and the meaning of various concepts in international relations that are often taken for granted and misrepresented. The problem with our knowledge of the works of Kant, Hegel, and Clausewitz on war and state is that these are so influential in the field of war theory and international relations, their impact so sweeping, that we often fail to notice their contributions at all. That is, we take for granted what their theories provided in posterity, because they permeate every aspect of our international political life and appear to us as common sense, when in fact these ideas and conclusions were not always known: they were observed, developed, and written. They include, among so many others, civil society, state interest and state rights, escalation in war, the distinction between strategy and tactics, absolute war and real war, the fog of war, friction in warfare, and the oft-cited adage "war is the continuation of policy by other means." These are Clausewitzian and Hegelian ideas. And if we turn to the philosopher who fathered the bases of their shared system of logic, Immanuel Kant, then we would also have to add a few more concepts to the lot: perpetual peace, the League of Nations, and the United Nations. And finally, since we are using a family analogy, we might also add communism, anarchism, and class warfare, since Marx, Engels, Mikhail Bakunin, and Peter Kropotkin might

19 Paret, "Education, Politics and War," 395.

be described as the troublesome offspring of this revolution in thinking. Kant, followed by Hegel, provided the initial philosophical context, the method, and a system of logic that took shape in the words of the former, and was further developed in the words of the latter. Years later, the four revolutionary writers would found economic and sociological theories derived from this method of reasoning, whereas Clausewitz and Hegel lit the flame of its application to the study of war and state. Altogether, this single family of thought, split into three generations of theorists, played such an overwhelming role in shaping and defining our current conception of world affairs that we might be surprised to find that it could possibly originate in one single idea uniting them all, namely, the dialectic.

Once we have uncovered the dialectic as the source of these concepts, a second and more problematic issue comes up, which again justifies further inquiry into the depth and meaning of dialectical reasoning among these authors. If Paret saw this as inconsequential, probably because he perceived dialectics to have been no more than "standard equipment"[20] in nineteenth-century German thought, what he missed is that dialectics might have been widespread, but they definitely were not standardized. There were distinctions in method from one author to another; and today, when the dialectic is no longer "standard equipment" among scholars, it is useful to remind ourselves of the method's origins, subtleties, and complexities if we wish to see what impact it had on the study of war. Both reasons for pushing ahead are in themselves legitimate, more so given just how elusive dialectics can be. The dialectical method, or methods rather, are difficult to grasp, and far more difficult to define. Scholars readily admit confusion with regard to its exact nature.[21] Schneider proposes that there are in fact seven distinct and potentially unrelated "meaning-clusters" regarding the dialectic.[22] It is surprising that "thinking in twos," if you will, though it might at first appear quite simple, does in fact generate much complexity. This has everything to do with the fact that we are dealing with a system of paradoxes by definition. The word "dialectic" comes to us from the Greek, where the first element, "dia," means "two," and the second, "logos," literally means "speech" or more broadly "reasoning." Thus dialectics are the study of pairings, specifically oppositions, and the attempt to find truth at their intersection. The method has its origins in the ancient Greek dialogues, where interlocutors clarified objects of contention by the process of taking opposite stances, in order to uncover or extract higher truths.

20 Paret, *Clausewitz and the State*, 84.
21 Ball, "The Dialectical Method," 785.
22 Ibid.

However, when we speak of dialectics today, it is usually with reference to their more recent embodiment, inspired by the ancients, but reinvented by the later rationalists of the eighteenth and nineteenth centuries, in the context of debates that will at first appear quite far removed from war studies.

Indeed, to find the origin of modern dialectics, one must turn to the origin, that is, the metaphysical debates of the Enlightenment and the quest to prove scientifically the existence of god, miracles, and the human soul. In the context of these debates dialectics were not constructed as mere exchanges of divergent opinions between dialoguers, but instead as the process of uncovering deep paradoxes, contradictions, and mutually exclusive categories of human knowledge, which emerge from our attempts to *know* the immaterial world. Could anything be further removed from the very real and concrete manifestations of war? What might "speaking in twos" provide to the field of war theory? To answer this, one must begin by searching for the commonality in war and god, or rather by trying to discover order in the disorder of war, using the methods philosophers had tried in order to find cosmos and god in the chaos of the universe.

The context for the method is holistic. In response to questions about god and the universe, the method was an attempt to frame the whole, as opposed to the empiricists and rationalists who attempted to build a theory of the whole merely as a sum of its parts, and the causal relations that united them. As a result, some of the language borrowed from spirituality reappears in the works of Hegel and Clausewitz, most notably in Hegel's concept of "spirit" to describe the advance of history and Clausewitz's description of war as a "wondrous trinity."[23] Mimicking the concept of a Christian god, these theories attempt to uncover war's eternal and universal essence.

Yet, can dialectical logic actually provide an eternal and universal theory of war? Are there limits to its claims? If self-contradictions in the theory can be shown to have existed since its very inception, or have since appeared historically as a result of changes in weapons or political evolution, to what extent would such findings undermine its logic and conclusions? That being said, an antithetical question must be asked, in taking this exploratory path: Even if we were to come to a positive conclusion on the matter, that there are self-contradictions, in either of the two forms suggested above, would we be forced to admit that dialectics are invalid? Not necessarily. If a contradiction bears fruit, that is, resolves

23 Clausewitz, *On War*, bk I, ch. 1, 19.

itself in new and more complex questions and paradoxes, then the process of exposing end points to logic can be, in fact, a very powerful means of heightening our understanding. If it can be demonstrated that a final breakdown in the logic of the dialectics of war does indeed emerge, we may find ourselves exasperated to discover that it is precisely dialectical thinking which allows us to make sense of such contradictions, that is, the more we turn the dialectics of war onto itself and study it through its own lens, the more we may uncover its inherent weaknesses, but only as a result of the power of dialectical reasoning, which allows us not only to assess the subject critically, but also the very method for studying it. Turning the dialectic onto itself is a means to shed light on the method's greatest benefit, which is to expose its own internal contradictions and build upon them. The strength of the method is its weakness and vice versa. It is a frustrating paradox.

Towards this end, the coming chapters will present three different levels of dialectical war theory. The first and second levels are the subject of the first few chapters of this book, and derive exclusively from the works of Clausewitz. The third involves both Hegel and Clausewitz, and will be featured in chapters 6–11. Roughly speaking, they represent three interrogations mentioned above in the following order: "How is war to be fought?"; "What is war?"; and "Why war?" The first is about method, the second is ontological, and the third deals with ethics, agency, and responsibility.

With regard to method, or strategy and tactics, Clausewitz categorically refuted the works of Enlightenment war theorists, who had proclaimed various grand "principles of war" or "positive doctrines" which were meant to provide generals with foolproof systems to "cause" victory, with a physical or mathematical form of certainty. Clausewitz's refutation of these methods borrowed heavily from Kant. It was by no means a fruitful dialectic, which opens discourse and ideas, but rather one that shut down a certain way of thinking. His argument effectively destroyed the very principle of there being such "principles of war," and this refutation was total, irreversible, and therefore sterile or dead in its tracks. Since then, attempts to salvage principles of war have succumbed to a mix of circular logic and self-defeating reductio ad absurdum forms of logic.

To make this case will require an overview of the metaphysical debates of the Enlightenment, which I will limit, however, to only the successive works of René Descartes, George Berkeley, David Hume, and Kant. Evidently, choosing such a narrow set of philosophers to discuss the wide field of metaphysics is a conscious editorial decision to sacrifice exhaustiveness for the sake of expediency. Indeed, we must return as quickly as possible to the question of war theory, more specifically, how Clausewitz represented a culminating point, the coming together of the military and metaphysical enquiries. Using these four philosophers nonetheless provides the basics: first, the origins of the method in Descartes, second, the fulfilment or apogee of its claims in Berkeley, followed by a counterbalancing appearance of scepticism and limits in Hume representing a certain end, and ultimately, the achievement of a new and distinct plateau of analysis in Kant's system of categories, representing a new beginning. This leaves out much, but nonetheless sheds a reasonable light upon the central themes and questions of this important philosophical journey.

For similar reasons, the theorists chosen to represent Enlightenment thinking on war do not form an exhaustive list either, but certainly represent among the best known and most widely read in the tradition: Raimondo Montecuccoli, Marquis de Quincy, Maurice de Saxe, Marquis de Puységur, Joly de Maizeroy, Prince de Ligne, Comte de Guibert, Dietrich Heinrich von Bülow, Antoine-Henri Jomini. Chosen first and foremost because they were among the theorists that Clausewitz himself had read (with the possible exception of Quincy and Maizeroy, who do not appear in Clausewitz's notes),[24] another consideration was to match and distinguish theorists who wrote concurrently, as well as to showcase the evolution in the cleavages that marked earlier rationalism from later rationalism in the theories themselves, showing a progression over time from a more nuanced debate on the principles of war to a black-and-white opposition between those who held ambitious, all-encompassing positive doctrines in the highest regard and those who mocked these as pure folly.

It is the other two "moments" of Clausewitz's dialectical theory that are fertile. The second moment is his exploration of the real war/absolute war dichotomy. It is a fertile creation because, unlike with his first level of dialectic, it is not merely refuting something that is illogical, it is positing a method of analysis regarding war, which must necessarily be flexible in time because weaponry and aims in war are not fixed, but progress historically. Thus, real and absolute wars are not forced to take on the same form at all times and for all time.

With regard to the third question, "why," the angle I am taking in order to analyze it is not so much the "causes of war," where the "why" is directed at this or that specific war or battle, but the larger, overarching question "why," where we are seeking an answer to what grounds wars ethically, why do we release this "evil," how is war "rational" within a system of "greater good" and "lesser evils," or alternatively, how do we "rationalize" such violent social behaviour?

24 Paret, *Clausewitz and the State*, 81n.

As we enter the question of ethics, there is an underlying stability to any rational attempt at theorizing war: it is impossible to put forward a rational (or rationalist) theory of war without having a firm and inherent ethical framework upon which to edify it, for the simple reason that unjustified violence is inherently irrational, and irrational violence is inherently unjustified. This means that any rational theory of war that cannot clarify or generate a logically sound ethical system that frames it cannot be a legitimate method for understanding war. It fails the surest test of its own validity.

It is within this third level of dialectical analysis that we find in the works of Hegel and Clausewitz their most challenging and fruitful interrogations. When applied to modern war, they are even more interesting because the paradoxes they engage with are at the very crux of war's historical development, the threshold of its own capacity to be rational or rationalized. The nineteenth and twentieth centuries gave rise to technologies, ideologies, and fighting doctrines that were founded on seemingly absurd, irrational premises based on circular logic, concepts such as the "war to end all wars" and "mutual assured destruction," which might arguably have been carried out as rational policy, despite the deep irrationality at the heart of their propositions. Can the ethical constructs developed in the dialectical theories of war help clarify our ideas of war even at this very threshold between the rational and the irrational?

The way to approach the question will be to determine where the limits of these theories are to be drawn, precisely on the question of ethics, because it is the larger picture, that which encompasses all of war; it is developed in a way that mimics god in part because it represents the whole, but arguably also because of its claim to provide judgment on "good" and "evil" in war – a secularization process, the usurpation of what once belonged exclusively to the powers of gods.

The problem we encounter, in hoping to provide some analysis on these grand questions, and how they relate to dialectical war theory defined as a single tradition, is that no single, complete dialectical theory of war exists proper. The two we encounter in Hegel and Clausewitz are in fact only partial dialectical theories of war. In Clausewitz, we find that the work is generally not dialectical in construct and that the method applies principally to a few sets of concepts, most notably in his discussion of the dual concepts of war as both "real" and "absolute." From this dichotomy emerges the idea that the political nature of war is inherent to both forms and thus serves as an explanatory outcome of this contradiction. So Clausewitz has generated a concept of war that is dialectical in itself, but it floats in a universe of other considerations which are not dialectically constructed. While his theory attempts a holistic concept of war, it builds it up in a non-holistic thought environment, which limits this holism.

Hegel does the inverse. His universe is dialectical and contains within this logic historical and social processes that produce the ethical framework in which war resides. That being said, he does not break down war itself, as Clausewitz does, as a dual concept. This is not to say that Hegel's notion of war is not deeply paradoxical – indeed it is, as we will consider this later in the book. However, its paradoxical elements are apparent at a different level of analysis than Clausewitz's – not in the thing itself, but rather its raison d'être. Hegel's analysis takes place at the "why" rather than the "what" and the "how." There is no discussion of tactics, strategies, or the sliding scale that separates types of wars from the limited to the all-out. As a result, his discussion on ethics focuses on how peoples and states invest their social structures with an inherent right to wage war, regardless of the form it takes. This analysis is in fact deeply grounded in the dialectical system analysis at the heart of Hegel's concept of state, but what is central in Hegel's discussion of war is not so much that war should be understood as a dual concept, but as existing in a dialectical universe that gives war its material life and ethical logic. This holism surrounds war, and encompasses it, but unlike Clausewitz's absolute/real war division, Hegel does not break down war itself into contradictory conceptual parts.

As a result of this distinction, it would be an overstatement to claim that the coming chapters are a proper or complete study in "dialectical theory of war." In fact, the exploration is a substratum of this: to consider the building blocks of such a theory, two methods of it, which are at times similar, at times distinct, but in both cases fragments of what a whole dialectical theory of war might encompass. Luckily, this task has been made simpler by what appears to be a fortuitous coincidence: while neither Hegel nor Clausewitz is purely dialectical in his methodology, where they use the method and where they do not are perfectly symmetrical and reciprocal. Their distinctions make it possible to clarify the methodology, while also shaping one of its apparent foundational contradictions, which appears when the ethical dimensions of war from each of the two authors' perspectives are considered.

If the study of Clausewitz and Hegel together is facilitated by the symmetrical way in which both authors were using and not using the dialectic, the major conundrum appears in the question of ethics, where the conclusions of each author regarding the justification of war are mutually exclusive and in direct contradiction. Any attempt to bring together Clausewitz and Hegel methodologically into a single dialectical theory of war can only lead to a hopeless dead-end if by the same process we cannot reconcile an ethical dimension that encompasses the divide. We would wind up with an inapplicable theory of war, methodologically coherent, but contradictory in its ethical conclusions. And this would indeed fail the test mentioned above regarding ethics and rationality in war theory.

The purpose of this essay is not to reconcile the two fragments, but perhaps to provide the necessary groundwork that might allow such a project eventually to take shape. The task here is limited to showing the origins and development of the method by starting with a genealogy and ending with the ethical impasse between the two. Though later chapters will describe in greater detail how both authors arrived at opposite ethical perspectives into the nature of war, it is worth briefly describing the disagreement, at this early stage in the argument, as something to keep in mind throughout. Hegel portrays war as a self-justifying expression of "right" and a necessary aspect of the survival of the idea of a people, whose independence and existence are otherwise "mortal and transient."[25] He also suggests that war allows societies to maintain themselves and better themselves, as is made evident in the following two lines from the *Philosophy of Right*: 1) "Successful wars have checked domestic unrest and consolidated the power of the state at home,"[26] and 2) "Just as the blowing of the winds preserves the seas from the foulness which would be the result of a prolonged calm, so as corruption in nations would be the product of prolonged, let alone 'perpetual' peace."[27]

Alternatively, Clausewitz distinguishes the political actor from the concept of war, and subordinates war as a tool of the political will, which he refers to as "the intelligence of the personified state."[28] In that sense, war is not imbued with any self-justification or inherent right. While most academics who quote Clausewitz on this topic quickly skim the introduction and reach for what they assume is a founding maxim of the entire work, that "war is a continuation of policy by other means," it is rather in Book VIII that we learn that the idea is a conclusion, a synthetic reconciliation of real war and absolute war, in which the "unity is that war is only part of political intercourse, therefore by no means an independent thing in itself."[29] Furthermore, this relationship is hierarchical: war is not an expression of a people's collective being in itself; rather, the

25 Hegel, *Hegel's Philosophy of Right*, 209.
26 Ibid., #324, 210.
27 Ibid.
28 Clausewitz, *On War*, bk I, ch. 1, 18.
29 Ibid., bk VIII, ch. 6B, 674.

"all-overpowering element of war" is made out into a "mere instrument" of their political will or government.[30]

In the final lines of this text, we will explore whether or not such a distinction between war understood as an instrument and war understood as a right actually has any bearing in real life. If it did not have measurable, tangible impacts, then this book as a whole would serve little purpose. It would wallow in the miseries of academic futility. By isolating a historical example to showcase the divide, it will indeed be possible to conclude that the breakup is extremely important and determinant of how strategy is developed and propagated (and consequently can be predicted by others and/or countered). Fortunately, the work of isolating such an example is already done, since history provides us with one particular context where both ethical approaches existed concurrently and in opposition to one another: the anti-bourgeois revolutions. Though the communists and anarchists most probably did so without being fully conscious of the distinction, they were in fact embodying in their fighting doctrines this very ethical division. Although the two groups were fighting a single war, they diverged entirely on the political or anti-political purpose and methods of their revolution. As a result, the Marxists would become heavily indebted to Clausewitz, while the anarchists would shun him and bring their strategic thought more closely in line with Hegel. The very concrete set of examples that we uncover in the revolutionary left provides clear opportunities to understand in what sense the ethical divide splitting Clausewitz and Hegel had measurable effects on how war and revolution would be carried out, be it as an instrument or a right. What is observed, ultimately, is that even within this converging methodology, these fathers of dialectical war theory bequeathed a very fruitful contradiction with real and tangible impacts on how wars are fought and how these are framed within a fragile and paradoxical secular ethical system.

This final contradiction opens up a whole new realm of analysis, because it brings to the surface something that was hiding much deeper behind the veil of dialectical war theory's attempt at a holistic theory of war: there is indeed a potential for irrationality that continues to reside at the very centre and intersection of these apparently rational twin justifications for war. We thereby arrive at a very fragile ethical system that can indeed break down under certain conditions. By furthering the inquiry into this fragility, it becomes possible to understand better the forms of justification for today's wars, especially as it relates to the

30 Ibid., 675.

universalistic quest to expand so-called freedom in the world and human development and security, and the opposite, particularistic call for religious war and decolonization. This speculative discussion, which appears in the epilogue, is meant to deconstruct and rebuild our understanding of the scope and limits of legitimacy in applying force, but also to introduce a path forward to understand the new and ever more complex paradoxes of modern war and how we can not only wrap our heads around these, but also how we can further peace and order within a framework that, while it legitimizes the existence of a threat of force, nonetheless contributes to its systematic defusing and rarefaction of political violence.

1

How to Approach Claims That Hegel and Clausewitz Generate Self-Fulfilling Prophecies and War Mongering

THERE ARE MANY REASONS TO BE WARY and concerned with how Hegel and Clausewitz understood war. And it is worth dealing with some of these problems before diving ahead too quickly. To engage with Hegel and Clausewitz can be controversial,[1] especially if the end goal is to legitimize and elevate their ideas. It has been said of Clausewitz that he "glorified war … and was obsessed by a cruel passion."[2] To avoid being branded with similar criticisms it is necessary to tread carefully and provide the proper context and clarification – otherwise one might quickly be brushed off as siding with authors who were apologists for bloodshed and potentially even the intellectual backbone for twentieth-century totalitarianism, total war, and genocide. In the case of Hegel, this conclusion is also widespread, as Shlomo Avineri has argued citing Hermann Heller, William Montgomery McGovern, Karl Popper, and John Bowle as examples.[3]

In his introduction to Clausewitz, Rapoport wrote that, "regardless of how he pictured war 'carried out to its logical conclusion, in the present political and technological environment the actualization of Clausewitz's absolute war is total war, that is, genocide."[4] Van Creveld went further yet and more or less blamed Clausewitz specifically for Auschwitz.[5] But are these severe judgments warranted? To make that call, one must go

1 Avineri rightly suggests that "While one can be lukewarm about Locke and objectively detached even about Kant or Rousseau, Hegel brings out the partisan in everyone: one is either for or against, and in a rather extremist fashion." Avineri, "Hegel Revisited," 133.

2 Rapoport, introduction to *On War*, 79–80.

3 Avineri, "Problem of War in Hegel's Thought," 463.

4 Rapoport, introduction to *On War*, 62.

5 van Creveld, *Transformation of War*, 65.

through a long and arduous process of working through the ethical dimensions of the whole, and not merely quotes plucked here and there. When the dialectical method is properly contextualized in the works of Hegel and Clausewitz, it becomes simpler to refute these particular claims, but that alone is not enough to pass an alternative ethical judgment on the question. This short chapter is meant to clear enough space in the controversy so that we can move the debate on ethics and methodology away from context and deeper into the content itself.

It is indeed a severe jump from claiming that Hegel and Clausewitz are amoral philosophers, in the lineage of Machiavelli and Hobbes before them, to then construing this as an opportunity to forgo the neutrality of amorality and brand them all simply as "immoral." Morality, amorality, and immorality are products of the larger ethical systems that define what is good and evil, and what is a lesser evil or a greater good. The deeper we consider the origin and complexities of the systems put in place by the two authors upon which to make their claims, the more we shall be forced to abandon the tempting move to "brand" the two philosophers of war into such a small box. It will become clearer that they were not unethical philosophers at all, but rather philosophers whose judgments on the subject of war were anchored in a modern, secular ethic. From a theological standpoint, they might be seen as "immoral" simply because they are "godless," but from a philosophical perspective, that is an unfair judgment, if we assume that a secular morality is possible within a secular ethical system, and perhaps more specifically the modern ethical framework that society has built into statehood.

Interestingly, the reason the two authors have been brushed aside quickly (though not effectively) by authors keen on discrediting them the easy way is built into two lines of argumentation that are very closely linked, though they might not appear so on the surface: the question of statehood and of ethics. In the Hegelian tradition, as we shall see later, these two are one and the same, where the state is nothing more than the institutionalizing of an ethical system. The reader must keep in mind that it is important to distinguish the definition of ethics from the institutions that are built in its name, the form ethical concepts take when they are manifested, be it as a family unit, a group, a state, etc. The best way to achieve this distinction is provided in fact by Hegel's work, which firmly grounds the matter on a dialectical process that allows these functions, outcomes, and definitions to coexist.

THE STATE ARGUMENT

The word "state" will come up often throughout this book and it is worth taking a minute to qualify the term. We will consider what the term meant for Hegel briefly in chapter 8 and will return to the question in full detail in later chapters. For now, however, let us first consider how it relates to Clausewitz, since he bore the brunt of the "state-centric" argument. This argument follows a typical route: since Clausewitz made his observations and prescriptions in the context of inter-state wars in the nineteenth century, these are necessarily tainted and inapplicable outside the state model. The recurring claim is that since non-state actors play a more important role today, or since there are multilateral organizations through which supranational norms and laws are established, a theory built on the state model cannot be adapted. Such a black-and-white breakdown of political actors into types is often a rhetorical tool of academicians, rather than a legitimate way to treat complex subject matter. There are far more grey tones to uncover.

Perhaps the most convincing attempt to shift the paradigm away from a Clausewitzian perspective on war in post–Cold War literature was Mary Kaldor's *New and Old Wars*, in which she makes the argument that classical interstate war (the old) has been replaced in the context of the state's relative decline, the rise of privatized violence, the growing roles of warlords and mercenaries, and a resurgence of irrational violence.[6] That being said, we can question just how new some of these ideas are, considering for example that "widespread atavistic and vernacular violence were prominent features of the Chinese civil war, the Russian civil war, the Armenian genocide, and many more episodes of 'old war.'"[7] It is in fact all the more surprising to speak of this as a novelty of the post–Cold War era, when we consider the very origin of the Cold War itself as the product of the communist revolutionary movement, which was infused with guerrilla tactics and terrorism from its onset in the nineteenth century.

Later in this book, I will complete the circle by returning to the question of how the communists and anarchists justified their use of revolutionary violence and what contradictions emerged in the process, but what is important to keep in mind is that whether political violence is waged by the state or against the state, it nonetheless has commonalities that cannot simply be tossed aside because of surface differences. In fact, the in-depth commonalities are greater than we expect, especially with regard to objectives and justifications, regardless of how such groups

6 Kaldor, *New and Old Wars*.

7 Andreas Herberg-Rothe, "Clausewitz and the Democratic Warrior," in Herberg-Rothe, Honig, and Moran, *Clausewitz*, 154. Citing Chojnacki, "Wander der Kriegsformen"; Martin Kahl and Ulrich Teusch, "Sind die 'neusen Kriege' wirklich neu?," *Leviathan* 32, no. 3 (2004): 382–401.

institutionalize themselves or instrumentalize violence or claim their right to its use.

Clausewitz did not equate policy to statehood by any stretch. He wrote, "the aim of policy is to unify and reconcile all aspects of internal administration as well as of spiritual values, and whatever else the moral philosopher may care to add. Policy, of course is nothing in itself; it is simply the trustee for all these interests against the outside world."[8] By this definition, any group that perceives itself as having interests that are external or contrary to those of another has a claim to policy-making for itself and fighting towards its objectives within a state or without.

The other two main proponents of categorically dismissing Clausewitz as a state-centrist are Martin van Creveld and John Keegan, who use a variety of different angles to question the political nature of war, and emphasize its cultural, individual, and historical aspects. Van Creveld argues that individual soldiers who gain from war, be it by capturing enemy soldiers for ransom, gaining the spoils of war, or pleasing the gods, have a vested interest in the war, and this undermines the idea of war as a political end of the state.[9] Keegan adds, throughout his book, a similar confrontation of the Clausewitzian theory by suggesting that primitive warfare had no political ends but only cultural ones. "Primitive peoples accorded a high degree of ceremony and ritual to combat, the spur to and ends of which bore scant relation to the causes and results which modern man perceives in the wars he fights."[10]

In both cases, the authors attempt to invalidate "continuation of policy" not by providing a direct hit to the centre of its idea, but with skirmishes at the flank: they showcase the existence of parallel determinants and motives in war, but they do not clarify in what sense these are in contradiction or for that matter mutually exclusive to Clausewitz's argument. Are they make-or-break arguments, or merely a sub-level of interesting considerations from which to enrich our understanding of war? It would be foolish not to agree that the rituals of combat and the personal objectives of the soldier can play a role in determining the form war will take, and will likely inform the deliberations, one way or another, regarding where a battle might take place, and when, and why, but this very process of deliberation is in fact war's social element, its collective and political element. If this process of deliberation exists in a state, or in a church, or in a tribal council, so be it, but this does not equate to an

8 Cited by Andreas Herberg-Rothe, "Clausewitz's Concept of the State," in Herberg-Rothe, Honig, and Moran, *Clausewitz*, 20.

9 van Creveld, *Transformation of War*, 66–72, 150, 151.

10 Keegan, *History of Warfare*, 114.

alternative formula where war is the continuation of religion by other means, or the continuation of tribalism by other means, it is in fact that instrumentalization of violence towards the policy aims of church, state, tribe, etc. Clausewitz's formula is not undermined, only qualified further. In that sense, Keegan and van Creveld have made a useful contribution to the debate, by providing additional insight, but have not offered an effective refutation.

Clausewitz was well aware of the differences between modern and primitive warfare and actually made the argument in *On War* that "Half-civilized Tartars, the republics of ancient times, the feudal lords and commercial cities of the Middle Ages, kings of the eighteenth century, and, lastly, princes and people of the nineteenth century, all carry on war in their own way, carry it on differently, with different means, and for a different object."[11] He then provides the example of how the Tartars marched as a whole nation – bringing their wives and children to the battlefields.[12] In this section of the book, Clausewitz, perhaps for cultural reasons or for the sake of consistency, speaks of these various "states" but his concept of the state is clearly not static or unchanging, as it is represented in the Keegan's analysis.

Let us keep this in mind when considering how Keegan attempts to discredit Clausewitz on such a technicality, when he writes: "Clausewitz's thought is incomplete. It implies the existence of States, of State interest and of rational calculation about how they may be achieved. Yet war antedates the State, diplomacy and strategy by many millennia."[13] Van Creveld's approach is similar to Keegan's. He writes, "That organized violence should only be called 'war' if it were waged by the State, for the State, and against the State was a postulate that Clausewitz took almost for granted."[14] From this, van Creveld suggests that "the dictum that war is the continuation of politics means nothing more or less than that it represents an instrument in the hands of the State, insofar as the State employs violence for political ends."[15] The two make the assumption that only the modern state can be understood as the source of policy, but clearly from the above passage, there is no reason to take such a narrow stance, since Clausewitz's own words show him to be very flexible not only on the concept of the state itself, but also how wars are fought at

11 Clausewitz, *On War*, bk VIII, ch. 3, 650.
12 Ibid.
13 Keegan, *History of Warfare*, 3.
14 van Creveld, *Transformation of War*, 36.
15 Ibid.

different times and in different social contexts, whether in "semi-barbarous" nations, commercial cities, or ancient republics.

Though Rapoport does not take the argument as far as van Creveld and Keegan do, it is nonetheless worth considering the subtle deviation he makes of Clausewitz's writing in order to make the "state" argument. He conditions the words "instrument of policy" by tagging on the word "national" to make his point.[16] It is misleading, because while a state is necessarily a group infused with a political will and capable of generating and enacting policy, policy and political will are not necessarily the product of statehood, nor does the formula "instrument of policy" make that claim. That claim is not Clausewitz's, but only Rapoport's, who takes the formula and rewrites it in a new and misleading way: "instrument of national policy." The state, or the nation-state if we want to take the idea further, is but one of many manifestations of coordinated and materialized political will, one institution out of many others capable of monopolizing violence and applying it towards its ends.

It is also true of Kaldor's analysis of the role of the state in Clausewitz. The passages she uses from *On War* to claim that Clausewitz speaks of states and only states are in fact devoid of the word state. Clausewitz writes that war "is an act of violence intended to compel our opponent to fulfill our will," to which Kaldor adds two modifications, first, that statehood is implied in the "we" and the "our opponent," and second, that this statehood requires a will that is clearly defined.[17] Both are quite external not only textually but, if we look at the question deeper, contextually in Clausewitz's experience of the state.

The central counterargument to the distinction of "New" and "Old" wars as a way to exclude a Clausewitzian approach in the context of terrorism, guerrilla, and non-state actors is to remind the reader that not only did Clausewitz teach the subject of small wars and peoples' wars at the War College, he also wrote extensively about it in texts that have not been translated to English, but also in Book VI of *On War.* Clausewitz advocated a "Spanish civil war in Germany" as opposed to the Prussian king's decision to ally himself with Napoleon. Clausewitz was referring to the guerrilla tactics that the people of Spain had used against Napoleon's invasion. He perceived this as a means of mobilizing formally unused resources.[18] Clausewitz's decision to fight on the Russian side against his own king finds itself justified in the section of *On War* entitled "Arming

16 Rapoport, introduction to *On War,* 50, 52.

17 Kaldor, *New and Old Wars,* 15.

18 Christopher Daase, "Clausewitz and Small Wars," in Strachan and Heberg-Rothe, *Clausewitz in the Twenty-First Century,* 190.

the Nation" in which he argues that even the loss of a great battle (we can imagine that Clausewitz must have Jena-Auerstedt in mind) is no reason to believe that its fate is sealed or that there is an "urgent haste to die." There can be a change of fortune or help from abroad, he explains (again, we may assume here that Clausewitz is hinting at Russia), but without this last effort, Clausewitz feared that a nation would have no soul left to it.[19]

In his article *Clausewitz and Small Wars*, Daase notes that Clausewitz understood small wars as "the application of organized and unorganized violence by non-state actors against military forces to harass and exhaust the enemy's army in order to change his policy."[20] Referring to examples such as Vendée and Tyrol, on top of the central example he referred to, Spain, Clausewitz argued in his *Lectures* that "small wars are waged strategically in the defence, but tactically in the offence."[21] In this sense, small wars are not to be understood as conceptually different from "big" wars or "old" wars, but simply as being fought using a distinct tactical and strategic paradigm.

If we understand the state, as Hegel and Clausewitz did, as a living thing, an embodiment of political will rather than a sort of machinery stuck in time, that is fulfilled, permanent, and static, then it becomes easier to understand how the political nature of war is not identical or dependent on a state-centric concept of war. There is room in the concept of war as the continuation of policy formula for stateless insurgents on one end, and multilateral UN peacekeepers on the other. That being said, it would be fair to argue that both Clausewitz and Hegel hoped that war would indeed be absorbed into the state, because they perceived the state as a desirable way to conduct rational policy in the interest of the people who resided within it. At the time of writing, this state, or better yet, this ideal, rational state that both authors imagined was not a done deal. That is precisely why they could idealize it in the first place. Nowadays we do not have that luxury. We see the state as what it is or has become, for better and for worse, instead of what it could in fact be.

The ideas of statehood and the political vigour of one's society were indeed central to Clausewitz's thought.[22] Clausewitz's life's work was geared towards shaping and strengthening and unifying his nation. He even wrote, in a letter to his fiancée, "I sense within myself a specific striving after a noble purpose; in me – as in a well-administered state – all

19 Clausewitz, *On War*, bk VI, ch. 26, 522.
20 Daase, "Clausewitz and Small Wars," 187.
21 Ibid., 189.
22 Paret, *Clausewitz and the State*, 6.

energies shall obey and serve this striving."[23] However, his notion of State was not and could not have been static and absolute in the way it is presented by van Creveld and Keegan.

The reason for the discrepancy can be attributed to historical differences. Van Creveld and Keegan are products of a time where states have for the most part been stable in their constitution and infused with internal coherence for decades, and in some cases centuries. This is particularly true in the Western world. During the revolutionary period, this was not the case at all. The entire political realm of Europe was fragile and in constant flux. Clearly, the authors are indeed using the term "politics" in a "very modern sense," as Roxborough has argued, because "Prior to the modern secularization of discourse, which produced an autonomous sphere of politics, conflict about power ('politics') were not absent; political contention, rather, was often expressed in religious or tribal vocabulary."[24] I would not go so far as Roxborough to then claim that war as a continuation of politics by other means itself depends on how the terms are defined,[25] but rather that one can build a convincing, though inaccurate argument based on that premise.

Clausewitz had a fluid understanding of the nature of states which have, much like war itself, its own set of moral factors. His concept of nation was one that "achieves independence and unity, only to disappear once again" and is infused with the metaphysical and temporal idea of Will.[26] "Even a disarmed and defeated France, as a homogenous, unified, well-situated, well-protected, wealthy, warlike and Spirited nation, contains within herself the means of securing her long-term integrity and independence."[27] In discussing the demise of the Kingdom of Poland, he argued that sentimental grounds were insufficient to justify its restoration. He explained that it was impossible to grasp how or why nations come and go, but nonetheless warned the Germans against weak political structures and a divided sense of direction.[28]

Clausewitz's experience in war adds more to this impression. He could not have viewed the State as the one and only embodiment of political will. The first campaign in which he fought was against Revolutionary

23 Clausewitz to Marie v. Bruhl, 29 March 1807, *Correspondence*, 102.
24 Roxborough, "Clausewitz and the Sociology of War," 627.
25 Ibid.
26 Clausewitz, *Historical and Political Writings*, 372–3.
27 Ibid., 376.
28 Ibid., 372–5

France in 1792–93[29] before the revolution's political Will was institutionalized as a state proper. The first Revolutionary War was declared against Austria by the French Assembly on 20 April 1792, five months before the monarchy was abolished in France on 21 September 1792 and the First Republic was proclaimed the next day. This was also nine months before France's absolute monarch Louis XVI was executed for treason 21 January 1793. There was a complexity in the political situation in France that could not be simplified into a single concept of state. Many political forces were at play, and all had access to the implements of war, be it through conscription, loyalists, or foreign armies.

What then was the state for Clausewitz? It was a means of "placing heavy demands on its citizens since it served cultural and national ends and thus enabled both the individual and society to achieve their innate potentials."[30] Clausewitz's notion of the state was built up on a classification of means and ends: a tool by which peoples achieve national and its cultural ends. It was not an end in itself. Immobility and lack of vitality were what Clausewitz loathed. During his captivity after the fall of Jena, he wrote about his compatriots. "With whips I would stir the lazy animal and teach it to burst the chains with which out of cowardice and fear it has permitted itself to be bound. I would spread an attitude throughout Germany, which like an antidote would eliminate with the destructive force the plague that is threatening to decay the Spirit of the nation."[31] In this phrase again he hammered on the separation between political will and statehood. His own interpretation of his role in embodying the national political will was in opposition to people in his own state, even though he understood them as his own people. He even went so far as to fight alongside the Russians against his own king because he was appalled that Prussia had sided with the French, against its own national interest.[32] This is the ultimate proof that his concept of politics and state was complex rather than simple: he committed treason in order better to serve his country; out of patriotism, he crossed the line so as to free his homeland from those who conquered it and placed the king under tutelage. Clausewitz was in effect carrying out a "policy" of the state that was in fact not at all concordant with the state itself. He was in effect that stateless insurgent, the freedom fighter who carries with him a strong

29 Howard, *Clausewitz*, 6–7.
30 Paret, *Clausewitz and the State*, 6.
31 Ibid., 129.
32 Howard, *Clausewitz*, 9–10.

political ideal, which serves him to justify and instrumentalize the use of violence towards this goal.

With this in mind, it is worth reconsidering the argument that would discard Clausewitz on the grounds that the state has evolved or that non-state and international actors have come to the fore. Honig reminds us that the "Clausewitzian idea of all military effort as being driven by an interaction between the trinity of government, military and people may have been based on the idea of the state, but it is adaptable to forms of warring social organization that do not form states. Any community has its leaders, fighters and common people."[33] The same applies to Hegel, and I am tempted to take the argument one step further. Statehood is power *legitimized*, both internally and externally, whereby its territory, population, international voice, as well as the right to bear arms collectively are recognized. We should be capable of distinguishing groups whose objective is commercially driven from other "non-state" actors that aspire to statehood in one form or another. Even though pirates and other organized crime groups and narco-states sometimes straddle a fine line, because the criminals are closely affiliated to political causes or attempt to usurp state power to benefit their criminal transactions, it remains that the proper measure of statehood, regardless of whether this state is achieved or emerging, is nothing more than its professed universality, that is to say, its legitimacy in the eyes of its people as a tool of their human development, coupled with its command of territory, a political system, and eventually, a likely result of the previous items, external recognition. Once we capture this distinction, it becomes clear that many, if not most, non-state fighters have state aspirations, that is, aspirations to legitimize their political claims and rest them on territory, people, and the monopoly of force. Far from excluding emerging or willed states, these aspiring states are perhaps even more state-like in their expression, more concrete and powerful in the minds of their would-be citizens who believe in them and who are willing to die for them, than those states that have achieved their independence and may have succumbed to complacency and political apathy. Is this very political apathy not a result, at least in part, of having something that one has not fought for, or that one would not be willing or able to fight for in their role within the realm of being a citizen of this established, bureaucratized, and professionalized political will? In the case of Clausewitz, he would have whipped these people, while he carried on their work of defending the nation with every means at his disposal, even revolt against the state.

33 Honig, "Strategy in a Post Clausewitzian Setting," 109–10.

When we consider Clausewitz as a rebel himself, who fights against his king, it becomes difficult to offer full credit to Rapoport's argument that "revolutionary wars are not 'Clausewitzian' wars of sovereign states."[34] Sovereignty is not so clear-cut in Clausewitz's mind, and in fact if we truly want to take this discussion to its crux, it is all the more impossible that revolutions should be "non-Clausewitzian" when we consider that Clausewitz's main example throughout *On War* is precisely that, the revolutionary wars of Napoleon. As we shall see later in this work, revolution is the very root of Clausewitz's interrogation on the nature of war, and his development of the concept "absolute war" was in fact a term borrowed from Fichte to describe revolutionary wars, which Clausewitz further developed and defined.[35]

If we return now to Hegel, his concept of the state as an embodiment of an ethical system is far more significant than whatever shape or form its institutions might take, he is not proposing a traditional definition of state as some settled or immobile and fixed thing, but a process that creates itself, asserts itself, renews itself, etc. In fact, he regards the independence and existence of a people as something "mortal" and "transient."[36] Far from resting his idea of state on firm and immortal instruments, bureaucracies, constitutions, etc., for Hegel the state is a far more fluid thing; it is the "actuality of concrete freedom."[37] Though cryptic when we encounter it at first, this central idea in Hegel's notion of the state sheds much light on the rest of his observations on the subject. However, it is too complex an idea to introduce properly so early in the text, and we shall consider it in full in later chapters. At that point, it will become clear that the ethical system that governs our times, and which defines the range of activities which we allow the state to carry out, including war, is deeply intertwined with how we define freedom, and why some hold it as something so primordial to individual and collective development. Hegel teaches us that rights, both state rights and individual rights, are not natural or god-given, but created and developed as a process within an ethical community, which explains why these rights and liberties are constantly at risk and in flux. While Hegel was not an apologist for war, he nonetheless stood opposite those who hold that all wars are by definition evil and unethical, because he held this idea of freedom to be a greater good worth fighting for.

34 Rapoport, introduction to *On War*, 53.
35 The full discussion is found in ch. 4 of this book.
36 Hegel, *Philosophy of Right*, #324, 209–10.
37 Ibid., #260, 160–1.

If we consider the question of totalitarianism and Auschwitz in this context, we are forced to admit that, as the total negation of freedom, both would be worth fighting against, if we stick word for word to what Hegel wrote. The association of Hegel to Nazism is for the most part an obscuration of facts at best, but actually, it is no more than a silly argument based on the superposition of ideas that share no relation. "Hegel was rarely cited in the Nazi literature, and, when he was referred to, it was usually by way of disapproval. The Nazis' official 'philosopher,' Alfred Rosenberg, mentioned, and denounced, Hegel twice in his best-selling *Der Mythus des Zwanzigsten Jahrhunderts*."[38] It is not surprising since totalitarianism was the antipode of Hegel's idea of the state as the actualization of individual freedom. The two were irreconcilable.

How one defines the greater good is necessarily impacted by a variety of factors, such as culture, religion, and community, but it is important again to make the distinction between what it means to define this greater good and to institute it. War does not fit in the context of the former – no one defines war as a good thing in itself – but it relates to the latter. To instate one's definition of the greater good is a political act. And it is within this aspect of the equation that war may be legitimized, for Hegel and Clausewitz alike. Boxing in "politics" into meaning state and only state elevates a straw man and results in a refutation that is superficial at best. Bassford hit the nail on the head when he expressed the fact that Keegan was making use of "naive and one-dimensional definition of the word politics."[39] The same can be said of many other interpreters of Clausewitz.

THE SELF-FULFILLING PROPHECY ARGUMENT

The most damning and significant argument made by Keegan and van Creveld is that following Clausewitz's system of thought leads to a self-fulfilling prophecy of "total war." If such conclusions were proven true, then all copies of *On War* would best be gathered up for a book burning of massive proportions, as a safeguard for generations to come. That is, unless we perceive the opposite possibility: that writing the brutal reality of what war is can be the very safeguard against war going too far, becoming too extreme, and being fought for the wrong reasons.

The self-fulfilling argument was best spelled out by Keegan, who wrote: "In the post-primitive world, human ingenuity ripped ritual and ceremony, and the restraints they imposed on warmaking, away from warmaking

38 Kaufmann, "Hegel Myth and Its Method," 88–119.

39 Bassford, "Grand Tradition of Trashing Clausewitz," 325.

practice, empowering men of violence to press its limits of tolerability to, and eventually beyond, the extreme. 'War,' said Clausewitz the philosopher, 'is an act of violence pushed to its utmost bounds.' Clausewitz the practical warrior did not guess at the horrors toward which his philosophical logic led, but we have glimpsed them ... Unless we unlearn the habits we have taught ourselves, we shall not survive."[40] The reality is that one's interpretation is completely dependent on whether or not we attribute to the authors a prescriptive purpose or a warning, or perhaps a mixture of both. In his reply to Keegan, Bassford draws our attention to this important passage in *On War*: "Let us not hear of generals who conquer without bloodshed. If a bloody slaughter is a horrible sight, then that is a ground for paying more respect to war, but not for making the sword we wear blunter and blunter by degrees from feelings of humanity, until some one steps in with one that is sharp and lops off the arm from our body."[41]

To Keegan's presentation of Clausewitz as a Napoleonist and Shaka as a Clausewitzian, and his argument in favour of greater ritualization, Bassford retorts:

> In actuality, then, Shaka, like Napoleon, was exactly what Clausewitz was warning us against, just as Keegan warns us against "ethnic bigots, regional warlords, ideological intransigents, common pillagers and organized international criminals." Unfortunately, Keegan then goes on to tell us that "there is a wisdom in ... symbolic ritual that needs to be rediscovered." Perhaps he has forgotten the elaborate diplomatic dances that preceded the Gulf War and surround the problem in Bosnia. The danger in Keegan's suggestion, as Clausewitz pointed out, is that one side will substitute ritual for action while the other side acts decisively. Or does Keegan think his criminals will join in the ritual and submit to its restraints?[42]

A first aspect of these false interpretations can be attributed to the fact that one can accord far too much significance to the historical taints and the excessive word choices found in the texts, rather than the lessons proper. Some of these word choices are indeed quite maddening, but they should not blind us to the rest. It is important to keep in mind that both Hegel and Clausewitz lived through the very worst wars humanity had seen to date, and on top of that they were writing on the subject of war from the perspective of a conquered people, they were on the losing

40 Keegan, *History of Warfare*, 385.

41 Clausewitz, *On War*, bk IV, ch. 11, 232. Note: Bassford uses the Howard/Paret translation, but for the sake of consistency I have referred to the Graham translation.

42 Bassford, "Grand Tradition of Trashing Clausewitz," 332.

side throughout most of the Napoleonic Wars, and both philosophers saw with their own eyes the French Revolutionary Army push forward into Jena-Auerstedt, site of the greatest Prussian defeat. How else were they to describe war? In soft and tender words meant not to offend?

With a short list of excerpts, we can indeed make up a damning portrait of the authors as heartless warmongers, but having read these we must then question whether or not such distillations and dilutions are fair and accurate representations of the whole. Clausewitz did write some brutal lines, such as: "Self-imposed restrictions, almost imperceptible and hardly worth mentioning, termed usages of International Law, accompany it without essentially impairing its power. Violence, that is to say physical force (for there is no moral force without the conception of states and law), is therefore the means; the compulsory submission of the enemy to our will is the ultimate object."[43] He also wrote that "philanthropists may easily imagine there is a skilful method of disarming and overcoming an enemy without causing great bloodshed, and that this is the proper tendency of the art of War. However plausible this may appear, still it is an error which must be extirpated; for in such dangerous things as war, the errors which proceed from a spirit of benevolence are just the worst."[44]

Hegel has his fair share of apparently sinister quotes, including, for example, writing that "by the agency [of war], the ethical health of peoples is preserved in their indifference to the stabilization of finite institutions; just as the blowing of the winds preserves the seas from foulness which would be the result of a prolonged calm, so also corruption in nations would be the product of prolonged, let alone 'perpetual' peace."[45] He also refers to the "ethical substance" of war residing in the fact that it offers systems of property, personal independence, and the preservation of this whole.[46] For Hegel, therefore, "war is not to be regarded as an absolute evil and as purely accidental."[47] It is there to provide security to the state which otherwise would be "mortal and transient."[48]

Having read these widely quoted extracts, used primarily by those who seek to dismiss the two authors quickly, rather than meaningfully, the next step is to ask whether these actually provide proof that there is something either immoral or illogical at the core of Hegel and Clausewitz's

43 Clausewitz, *On War*, bk I, ch. 1, 1–2.
44 Ibid., 2.
45 Hegel, *Philosophy of Right*, #324, 210.
46 Hegel, *Phenomenology of Spirit*, #475, 289.
47 Ibid.
48 Hegel, *Philosopohy of Right*, #324, 209.

philosophizing. If war is a brutal thing, then should an honest representation of war's nature not be "brutal" in order to be accurate? By giving us an honest and frightening glimpse into the coarse nature of war, Hegel and Clausewitz provide posterity with the clarity required for self-restraint and self-control when brandishing the beast that is war. While some may perceive the language as a call to arms, we may equally choose to read these passages as warnings. That decision resides in the reader far more than the writer.

In the case of Clausewitz, failing to understand the dialectical constructs is problematic, because one such contradiction is the difference between a hypothetical "absolute" war and war in the real world. Unless we catch the dichotomy, we are bound to make the most basic misinterpretation: where either pole of the dichotomy is removed and considered in isolation. This would be like insisting to be served either a Ben's or a Jerry's ice cream cone, when in fact it is only Ben *and* Jerry's that can provide you with your treat. It is the same when we consider that Clausewitz described war having a conceptual, "absolute" form, and a "real" material form, where the former represents its unlimited potential for reciprocation towards extremes, and the latter frames war as something limited by its purpose, aim, and scope, as well as the material realities of battlefield (friction, fog of war, etc.). The two poles only exist as a relation to one another. It is only because Clausewitz has conceptualized an "absolute" that he must counter this conceptual and ideal formula with its opposite, a concrete manifestation, a real embodiment of the concept, which by the very process of being posited is a demonstration that the ideal is *not* real. The ideal is meant to help us better conceptualize war, by freeing the inner logic from that which constrains and limits it.

By forgoing this analysis, we perceive two singular poles, unrelated and equally attainable as objectives. However, the problem here is that at either of these poles, war becomes nonsensical. Fully real war would be so bogged down by limited objectives, insecurities, uncertainties, and material considerations that it would reach a point of complete immobility, a long wait where no force comes into play: a non-war war. At the other end of the spectrum, a fully "absolute" war would be so brutally fuelled by the reciprocation of extremes that it would eventually destroy everything one could possibly be fighting for in the first place, undermining its very own raison d'être.

This failure to appreciate the dialectics of Clausewitz has been the norm, not the exception amongst scholars and soldiers alike. In fact, the very best example we have comes from Ferdinand Foch, who as both a soldier and a scholar cherry-picked only the most extreme snippets one can find in Clausewitz's *On War* and contributed to the doctrine of *attack à outrance* during the First World War. Foch's interpretation of Clausewitz was built on a distillation process, whereby the passages he prioritized in *On War* were those in which Clausewitz referred to Napoleon as the closest anyone had ever gotten to embodying the "absolute" form of war. Indeed, in the chapter on modern war found in *Principes de guerre*, Foch quoted Napoleon once and Clausewitz seven times, and of these seven quotes, only one was not an elevation of Napoleon and the concept of absolute war. In Foch's version of Clausewitz, the only parts of *On War* worth quoting are those that amplify war's brutality, and Foch attempts even to amplify these further. Thus, when he quotes Clausewitz as having said "blood is the price of victory,"[49] he unsurprisingly forgets the rest of the sentence in which Clausewitz writes, "it is not merely reciprocal slaughter, and its effect is more a killing of the enemy's courage than of the enemy's soldiers."[50] And elsewhere he continues to focus on the excerpts that amplify the extremes of war, rather than any principle of limitation, such as fog of war, friction, and limited aims. So we find also among his chosen extracts: "The French Revolution by the force and energy of principles and the enthusiasm which with it inspired the people, threw the weight of the people and all the forces into the balance"; "Napoleon relentlessly sought opportunities to engage in battle"; and, "In war everything is submitted to decision by arms."[51]

Fuller described Foch's interpretation as that of "a Clausewitz drunk on violence" and a "tactically demented Napoleon,"[52] which strikes me as rather close to the mark. Foch's focus on the Napoleonic character of war should not come as a surprise; Foch himself was a devout Napoleonist. When France celebrated the hundredth anniversary of the emperor's death at the Arc de Triomphe, Foch delivered a glowing eulogy. The first line sets the tone: "Napoleon! If the prestige of this name conquered the admiration of the world, it is less certain that its luster continues to grow, as time casts a shadow on the greatness of the task accomplished."[53] Foch may have admired Clausewitz, but it is not so clear that he actually understood him that well, given that "his own writing is totally different in character."[54] While Clausewitz stressed two important concepts in war, its political nature and the superiority of the defence, by the turn of the

49 Foch, *Principes de la guerre*, 33.
50 Clausewitz, *On War*, bk IV, ch. 11, 230.
51 Foch, *Principes de la guerre*, 21–44.
52 Fuller, *Conduct of War*, 128.
53 Foch, *Eloge de Napoléon*, 21.
54 Brodie, "Continuing Relevance of *On War*," 50.

century these two features had become somehow excluded from the analysis.[55] If Foch was "dreadfully wrong and it took a sea of blood to prove it,"[56] we must admit that many others at the time were equally off-track in their interpretation of Clausewitzian thought. Across Europe and in North America as well, war theorists and generals had fallen victim to this form of distillation, "totally imbued with oversimplified neo-Clausewitzian ideas."[57]

It is therefore not without reason that Liddell Hart reacted harshly to this Clausewitz, but in reality, what he was reacting to were these bad interpretations of Clausewitz. Liddell Hart famously gave Clausewitz the nickname "Mahdi of mass and mutual massacre," on the grounds that Clausewitz, in his opinion, "was the source of the doctrine of 'absolute war,' the fight to a finish theory which, beginning with the argument that 'war is only a continuation of state policy by other means,' ended by making policy the slave of strategy."[58] Liddell Hart spelled out the most damning criticism of Clausewitz that had yet been written. He was suggesting that Clausewitz's theory was a self-fulfilling prophecy: that by defining strategy and war in a certain way, they were making war take that form ever more so. But this argument was only admissible insofar as it was an answer to misinterpretations of Clausewitz to begin with. If Clausewitz had been taken at his word, rather than his conceptual poles ripped apart from one another, then his writings would have maintained their strength of paradox, rather than taken on the weak form of isolated extremes. Liddell Hart's reactions were against a pseudo-Clausewitzian doctrine, which Clausewitz had never actually written.

The pseudo-Clausewitzians of the turn of the century were not the true inheritors of Clausewitz, but undoubtedly the first to misread him so thoroughly badly as to generate self-fulfilling prophecies with regard to pre-empting war's rise to extremes by starting off with one's fullest national ability to produce extremes. By excluding half the concept, within a dialectical whole, one effectively destroys the root of the system before even engaging with it. Consequently, this does not pose a true problem to our analysis or reading of Clausewitz, because the problem is not with Clausewitz, but faulty interpretations of his work.

With regard to Hegel, the question of war as "the moral health of peoples" is a complicated one, which will be considered in greater detail later in the coming chapters. However, with regard to the issue of

55 Howard, "Influence of Clausewitz," 37–41.
56 Brodie, "Continuing Relevance of *On War*," 50.
57 Howard, "Influence of Clausewitz," 37.
58 Liddell Hart, *Ghost of Napoleon*, 120–1.

self-fulfilling prophecies, we have not completely solved the problem by eliminating it from our discussion of Clausewitz. There exists a far more compelling argument regarding self-fulfilling tendencies in the works of Hegel, who speaks of "necessity" as though history is following a set path. In this case, we are no longer dealing with the particular absolute/real construct of war, but rather war within Hegel's dialectics of history, and the materialization of the evasive concept – which we will be studying in greater depth in chapter 8 – of "world Spirit" or *Geist*.

Hannah Arendt questions the notion of history in Hegel's philosophy, arguing that it commits a fallacy that "consists in describing and understanding the whole realm of human action, not in terms of the actor and the agent, but from the standpoint of the spectator who watches the spectacle ... the truth inherent in it, being that all stories begun and enacted by men unfold their true meaning only when they have come to their end, so that it may indeed appear as though only the spectator, and not the agent, can hope to understand what actually happened."[59] A self-fulfilling prophecy argument is implied in that if events can be proclaimed as destiny, and the agents in the action perceive themselves as an active part of historical necessity's fulfilment, then they are turning Hegel around from studying the past into predicting the future, and setting the course to fulfilling it.

Arguably, this fault is more a product of Marxism than Hegelianism per se, and it would be difficult to deny that throughout the nineteenth and twentieth centuries, this idea of "historical necessity" served as a justification and perhaps even the theoretical backbone of the ideological struggles against capitalism. However, while it was taken from Hegel's system, historical necessity was not constructed in a way that could be pushed forward into the future, implying "necessary" courses or directions for history and society. It was a misuse of Hegel's method. In fact, Hegel was quite clear about how his system was not endowed with any claim about the future or the path that destiny was to take. In the preface to the *Philosophy of Right*, he wrote, "The owl of Minerva spreads its wings only with the falling of the dusk,"[60] by which he meant, in reference to the Roman goddess of wisdom, "that philosophy understands reality only after the event. It cannot prescribe how the world ought to be."[61]

59 Arendt, *On Revolution*, 42–3.

60 Hegel, preface to *Philosophy of Right*, 13.

61 Peter Singer, "Owl of Minerva," *The Oxford Companion to Philosophy*, ed. Ted Honderich (Oxford: Oxford University Press, 1995), 638.

Just as we saw with Clausewitz, Hegel's system is not self-prophetic in itself, but was used by ambitious interpreters to generate a self-fulfilling prophecy in his name. Both Hegel and Clausewitz were used and abused to provide clout and credibility to doctrines that they would never have acknowledged as their own. Arendt was right to suggest that historical actors made use of Hegel by proclaiming self-fulfilling prophecies: projecting "historical necessity" forward onto the future that one's ideology is attempting to build. In many ways, the distillation of Clausewitz is a parallel phenomenon. In either case, one cannot blame the words in the text, if the fault clearly lies with the reader. Again, it is necessary to stress that with Hegel and Clausewitz alike, the only way properly to dispel the claims regarding self-fulfilling prophecies is to enhance our understanding of their dialectics and the origin and logic of their systems.

With this short caveat, an open mind, and academic rigour, it is possible to deepen our understanding of both authors, and extract extremely potent lessons regarding war and peace. Much would be lost were we to stop our analysis on account of an offensive line or a quick and superficial dismissal. There are, as we shall see, true problems with the historical evolution of the Clausewitzian and Hegelian systems, which are far more complex and significant than the non-problems above. Yet, to perceive them, we must start by understanding them well, and in the context of when they were written.

If we arrive at end points in the logic that generates the contradictory systems of ethics at the heart of Hegel and Clausewitz, then it will be possible to make judgments not on the perceived "self-fulfilling prophecies" of their conclusions, but rather on the conclusions themselves. And instead of teasing out historical abnormalities in how states and non-state actors have evolved with regard to their conclusions, or how weapons and technology have changed over time, we will be able to consider in broader terms, ethical terms, the problems at the heart of these, in ways that apply not merely to the state, the faction, or the revolutionary, but to the very abstractions that generate a sense of greater good and lesser evil that gives rise to the justification of political violence, its rationality and rationalization alike, and the form political violence takes, when the framework of ethics we attach it to changes.

However, before we can hope to even approach this level of discussion on the dialectics of war without falling into the trap of oversimplification and superficial judgments on the subject, we must start from the ground up. It means going back a few hundred years and understanding the philosophical context that gave rise to the dialectical method and its application to the question of war.

To speak of a Hegelian and Clausewitzian ethic on the subject of war may appear counterintuitive to those who perceive both authors as amoral or immoral. However, through our exploration of the Kantian revolution in thinking and its impact on these two authors, the notion of "instrumentality" and "right" will lose their opacity. We will rest our understanding of these not only on their inception, development, method, and ultimate clash, but also in action, where history provides a critical demonstration of its significance. From this process, it will be possible to understand and pass judgment not merely on the conditioning elements, what the context provides, but also on those features of the dialectical theories of war that are unconditioned and synthetical.

2

Perfection and Certainty in Metaphysics and War Theory

BEFORE THE ENLIGHTENMENT systematized the study of war, the Western world had not been in any way devoid of literature on the topic. Homer and Thucydides provided us with the histories of Greek wars. Plato, Xenophone, Vegius, Caesar – to name only a few – brought in a mix of political and strategical considerations. Later, theological explorations regarding the possibility of war being "just" before the eyes of god were developed in the works of Saint Augustine and Saint Thomas Aquinas, which shaped not only the way our ancestors thought about war, but how today's international laws are formulated. The introduction of the Chinese masterpiece *The Art of War*, by Sun Tzu, to Europe at the beginning of the seventeenth century, on top of the sixteenth-century contribution to the field by Machiavelli, no doubt also stimulated new interest in writing about the battlefield in the following decades. Perhaps more importantly, the Enlightenment was characterized by a universal interest in systematizing the study of phenomena and uncovering universal truths about the world, which was fuelled by increased literacy and access to printing, but also influenced by a cultural push in the direction of scientific inquiry.

To understand war – or better yet, to develop foolproof strategies and methods that could translate to military supremacy – was an objective of political and military figures alike, and this contributed not only to increasing the readership of military theses and manuals, but also their production. New books on the subject of war were published with increasingly ambitious claims – systems that appeared convincing on the surface, but where the validity was built on indemonstrable and untestable propositions. When, ultimately, all-out revolutionary war broke out at the end of the eighteenth century, the inherent weakness of such theories became all too evident.

Fuelled by an optimistic quest to unearth true, immutable, and fundamental "principles" for the military arts, writers of the Enlightenment were falling into a "Pythagorean obsession,"[1] as they aimed for but never actually succeeded in achieving a proper "military science," which would provide practitioners with the predictability and certainty of a Newtonian or Galilean science. To that end, war theorists became increasingly didactic and pedantic in their use of geometry, mechanistic notions of the engagement, mathematical formulae, ballistics, clockwork, and time management. Ultimately, however, their schemas and systems never achieved anything near a proper science. Even though they were built on examples and practice from the battlefield, these attempts to extract unconditional truths regarding war that could be applied universally towards achieving victory in war hit a brick wall, not long after their glory and effectiveness seemed to have been confirmed by history.

By many accounts, it was this very science of war that had been the source of Prussia's greatness under the reign of Frederick the Great. The king had indeed had numerous successes on the battlefield and had grown the size of his kingdom considerably as a result. But how central was method to these successes? Could other factors have been equally contributing to Prussia's military successes? Perhaps, but rarely are theories critically assessed until they fail. And this was just around the corner: the Revolutionary and Napoleonic wars.

How could it be that even in the hands of the best veteran armies in Europe these principles could not contain the rise of Napoleon's *Grande armée*, composed of mere conscripts – young and inexperienced revolutionaries with little training and little or no experience in battle? If this was the first "big" question, there was also the case of Napoleon's demise, which demanded further explanations since it also had elements that were counterintuitive in the minds of strategists and tacticians of the day: why did the conquest of Moscow, instead of leading to the capitulation of the Russians, according to the "principle" by which the fall of any capital was decisive, instead lead to the demise of the great general? And why did Napoleon, this *genius* of war, fail at the Battle of Waterloo, despite having applied almost word for word the prescriptions of perfected "principles" regarding attacking key points and operating from internal lines?

If the principles of war were meant to provide ready-made answers regardless of context, it was in fact context itself that had brought them to their final impasse. Whereas warfare between absolute monarchs had

1 Fernández Vega, *Las guerras de la política*, 64.

inherent limiting features, that is, a risk aversion based on the need to protect the institution of monarchy itself from self-destruction, the types of risks people were willing to take in their revolution against this institution were of a higher scale. Hence the surge of intensity during the French Revolution, which, as Clausewitz described, "beggared all imagination."[2] The size of the engagements, the passions of the new citizen-soldiers, and the distances travelled by the troops – from one end of Europe to the other – would undermine the conceptual bases of military thinking. The social element of war had been unleashed, and no scientific theory that claimed to provide the sure method towards victory could stand up to the sheer power and disturbances of the masses. The principles of war might have had some value to them, but only so long as all the players were abiding by the same rules and playing the same game. Nevertheless, in the context of revolutionary fervour the chessboard of European warfare – with its predictable moves and inherent limitations – had been tossed to the floor, its principles dispersed so that even a "genius" like Napoleon who applied perfected "principles of war" was incapable of "causing" victory, let alone avoiding total defeat.

The relationship that theorists had developed to the notions of "genius" and "principles" allowed Enlightenment war theory to support its claims regarding perfection in method – but in fact it was pure sophistry. Since the two concepts were inherently fixed and immutable but reciprocal by definition, when good or right principles failed one could blame the lack of genius in how these were applied – and when bad or wrong principles succeeded, one could credit the genius of the general who nonetheless made them work, against nature. These two absolute concepts sustained one another thanks to the sophistry that linked them, coupled with an underlying expectation regarding the scientific method and its universal applicability and validity. So long as the scientific method as an approach to the military arts went unquestioned in its fundaments, this relationship between genius and principles was enough to justify failure and success. But when the revolutionary wars struck their intensity so overwhelmed war theory that even this old stopgap – this easy solution to counter any scepticism – proved insufficient.

It is easy to say, looking back, that Napoleon failed at Waterloo despite his genius, and despite his observation of the principles regarding how to make use of such military concepts as "key points" and "internal lines," because of many other aspects of the battle: he was heavily outnumbered and he was forced into a battle rather than having the opportunity to

2 Clausewitz, *On War*, bk VIII, ch. 3., 592.

fight at a time and place that would have been more advantageous. Similarly, the Russian expedition failed, despite the principle of capturing a capital, because his enemy simply *decided* not to concede after losing their capital. If the context can drive the principle, then the principle is only valid insofar as it is being applied at the right place at the right time – which means it is neither universal nor absolute. Napoleon's rise and fall had brought to light the fact that "truths" found in the various doctrines of war were only as powerful as the ink and paper upon which they had been decreed in the first place. From this angle, it was unnecessary to claim that Frederick the Great possessed such thing as a "perfected" military art. In fact, in debates that pitted highly divergent views on Frederick the Great's strategy by Delbrück and Wilhelmine against each other, as to whether it rested on war of attrition or acts of desperation, one consensus did emerge: that the "execution of his strategy was far from perfect."[3] Rather Frederick had likely developed some relative gains in discipline and efficiency that gave Prussia a competitive advantage in warfare – an advantage that was compounded by Berlin's rise as a European political, cultural, and economic centre, and by a high level of conscription in the male population. There was nothing magical to any of it. There was no higher power residing in these principles that accorded them any inherent certainty and universality. All there was were the right conditions that allowed superiority in this particular context.

This was the great realization. But what it doesn't clarify is: why did war theorists come to believe that absolute principles were possible in the first place? There had to be some underlying expectations regarding validity and certainty in the way theorists were conceiving military thought. The first part of this answer can be found in Delbrück's *History of the Art of War*, where he notes that during this time "it was believed that one could turn completely away from the decision by battle, and the method of pure manoeuvre was developed."[4] This first degree of separation and elevation of a single aspect of war simplified the possibility of generating principles since it cleared the field, so to speak: it eliminated the dynamic element itself, the soldiers using their weapons, focusing instead on fixed values such as terrain, geography, angles, and the predictable speed and movements of armies that are not in battle.

The idea that a war could be won merely on manoeuvre changed the focus of war theory, making it more in line as well with the risk-aversion of princes and kings who sought relative gains in strength and holdings,

3 Ecchevaria, *After Clausewitz*, 184.
4 Delbrück, *History of the Art of War*, 387.

rather than significant socio-political change. Delbrück notes that in the army regulations of the Elector of Saxony in 1752, it was written: "A battle is the most important and most dangerous operation of war. In open country without a fortress the loss of a battle can be so decisive that it is seldom to be risked and never to be recommended. The masterpiece of a great general is to achieve the final purpose of a campaign by alert and safe manoeuvres without danger."[5] It was this abstraction that allowed the "science of war" to truly take off.

The Enlightenment was underscored by an expectation that scientific inquiry could be transferred from the natural sciences (i.e. physics, mathematics, etc.) into other areas of human understanding – such as the social sciences, the military arts, and philosophy. If the breakdown in Enlightenment war theory can be described as the rise in a new form of scepticism, one that dug to the very core of methodology and could not be suppressed simply by balancing genius against principle, it was only made possible because some legwork had already taken place towards this deep form of scepticism in the philosophical world, from which Clausewitz would borrow.

Only through dialectical reasoning and its implications for the study of human understanding and the scope of possible knowledge – inspired by the works of Kant and his disciples – could Clausewitz explain in what sense the methodology of the Enlightenment had, by incorrectly elevating observations that were conditioned by context to the rank of unconditional truths, failed and was necessarily predisposed to such failure. Skipping from the analytical to the synthetical created an illusion of progress that was always tainted by an impression of unfinished business, because theories and principles could easily be extracted through causal inferences – but they could also easily be refuted using the same method and different examples. The surplus of contradictory historical material feeding into war theory provided an infinite source for the development of "rational" principles and counter-principles, but intuitively, something was missing.

This chapter is complementary to the thorough research by Azar Gat in *A History of Military Thought*, but I explore a dimension that Gat himself accepts was outside the scope of his own research, and which he only "roughly outlined":[6] to study in greater detail the intellectual context and the philosophical, rather than the purely historical, aspects that gave rise to Enlightenment and German Idealist treatises on war. I don't intend to

5 Ibid., 315.
6 Gat, *A History of Military Thought*, 28.

suggest military writers all read philosophy, or to determine whether direct philosophical influences are to be found. A positive or negative answer to this question would not change in any way the similarities. Arguably it was the overall culture itself that was infused with science and certainty, and which explains the parallel development in both fields. More importantly, we must consider the reflected argument that comes out of this observation: the fact that these theories were written in this same spirit allowed Clausewitz to borrow a set of philosophical arguments, conceived as a reply to the metaphysics, directly in his case against the Enlightenment military thinkers.

Suggesting that the abstract theorizations of metaphysics would have any bearing on war theory may at first seem like quite a tenuous and unlikely argument. How can the quests to understand concepts such as "being," "time," "knowing," "mind," or the proof of god's existence and of supernatural events, or the form, immortality, and indissolubility of the soul – any of these – apply to the dramatic, real-life, tangible enquiries into the military arts? It is not so much the topics at hand as the type of arguments and methods that provide the link. Specifically, the moment war theorists broke away from the materiality of proclaiming maxims and best practices in war, and sought instead fundamental, objective, and immutable "principles of war," they replicated the formula of the metaphysical quest to prove and define the spiritual and the immaterial. It was this overlap that allowed Clausewitz to juxtapose the methods of refutation found in metaphysics and apply them to his refutation of the scientific principles of war, which he referred to as "positive doctrines."

If Clausewitz's dialectics of war emerged as the synthesis of the metaphysical debates pitting Kant and Hume against Berkeley and Descartes, and the breakdown in military theory that the Revolutionary Wars had wrought, this however was not achieved as a single process, but in two separate moments of development. In a first moment the dialectics of war were a negation, a refutation of the Enlightenment's "positive doctrines" on the strategic/tactical plane of analysis or a reply to the question "how is war to be fought?" In this case the movement away from the metaphysical was with regard to methodology and validity expectations.

The second moment in the development of Clausewitz's dialectical war theory takes shape as a result of the first. As was mentioned earlier, the chessboard of warfare – the rules of the game – having apparently been tossed out during the Revolutionary Wars, people began to question preconceived notions of how wars are fought. But eventually this also begged the question: what are the true rules of the game, if what was taken for granted no longer applies? This second moment is less about methods and systems, and more about understanding war's nature – a question that had until then been relegated to the metaphysical, whether god's will or punishment, or else human nature: something simple, unitary, taken for granted, and unchangeable. However, upon closer and more systematic scrutiny, Clausewitz would consider war's paradoxical "real" and "absolute" forms, and this would lead him to an objective observation of war's political nature, which meant that war was not in fact fixed according to some divine or natural law, but dualistic, dynamic, and changing. As such, this second moment, focused on a higher level of analysis, which moves us from the "how" in war to the "what is war," also represented a breakaway from the traditional deistic or naturalist assumptions regarding war's nature and its causes.

Kant's method did not undermine in any way Clausewitz's attachment to Scharnhorst, Fichte, Machiavelli, and Montesquieu. None were excluded in the process of integrating Kant. In fact, they were arguably enhanced as a result. The method allowed him to clarify, amplify, substantiate, and *objectively* demonstrate through a sceptical and critical analysis what he had already come to hold as intuitively true, based on a wide range of readings.

As we explore how and why Clausewitz first introduced dialectics into war theory, and later developed it further from one chapter to the next over time, we eventually find ourselves face to face with the problem he would ultimately come across. The more clearly defined and mutually exclusive his categories and dichotomies became, the more the system was overtaking what had previously been written. When he wrote his final editorial note, after having completed writing Books VII and VIII, he had come to realize that he would need to re-edit the entirety of Books I to VI in order to integrate what he had recently written.[7] It suggests that the more Clausewitz deepened his use of dialectics, from the end of Book VI onwards, the more overwhelming its effects on the rest of the project. In writing Book VIII Clausewitz quipped: "A small jump is easier than a large one, but no one on that account, wishing to cross a wide ditch, would jump half of it first."[8] In this case, we might wonder if there was not some personal truth to this line. When he had started *On War*, Clausewitz had in fact jumped halfway into dialectics, not knowing the full scope of where its chasms would eventually land him by the end of the book. And now that he had water up to his neck in dialectics and was making plans to start all the way back from chapter 1, Book I – maybe he was in fact feeling a bit overwhelmed by the consequences of jumping halfway in.

7 Clausewitz, *On War*, "Notice," xxxviii.
8 Ibid., bk VIII, ch. 4, 666.

If Clausewitz's preliminary use of dialectical reasoning is found not in what his theory posited, but in what it negated or refuted, then we should therefore begin our exploration by looking at the Enlightenment theories of war that were the subject of Clausewitz's reply. Despite their different subjects of inquiry, the relationship between science and reason as it was conceived during the Enlightenment was nonetheless identical in both fields. Without this parallel, it would have been impossible for Clausewitz to make such good use of Kant's reaction to the metaphysicians in his own reply to the military theorists. However, before we can engage in this larger question, we must ask ourselves: what were these grand proclamations with regard to god, miracles, angels, strategy, and tactics – and in what sense did they overlap?

The two fields shared a common starting point in wanting to elucidate what makes cosmos out of chaos, which was assumed in both cases to be some external form of intelligence rather than some inherent logic to the thing itself or simply a chaos that is naturally chaotic. Unlike phenomenology, for example, which posits existence as essence, rationalist philosophy starts with the expectation that existence must emerge causally from essence. It is from this initial premise that the Rationalists and Empiricists sought god by observing that which he created, the effect to his cause. Similarly military theorists sought this external intelligence as it might appear through observation of the causes and effects that linked factors of war together – whether combat to victory, terrain to superiority, or angle to advantage. And so, just as the metaphysicians Descartes and Berkeley were looking for order in the apparent chaos of the universe and the logic that made it intelligible in its creation, so too would military writers from Montecuccoli to Jomini claim that one could synthesize order from the apparent chaos of warfare.

In either case an aesthetic of perfection surrounded the project and its methodology, and the higher knowledge sought was assumed to exist – simply requiring of intellectual explorers that they should find or discover it, like America or the curvature of the Earth. And secondly, the method for discovering it would be, as in the natural sciences, to remove layers of confusion that surrounded the isolated question: what are the true, immutable, and eternal causes of victory? Causality appeared to these explorers as a concept or thing external to the human mind and therefore possessed by some higher intelligence or ordering idea to the material world. For the metaphysician, the form of external knowledge was an omnipotent and eternal god; while for war theorists, it took the form of an omnipotent and eternal set of principles of war, theories whereby such things as "decisive points," "the key to a country," and "base lines" – among many other simple concepts – were assumed to have universal and absolute power to generate victory in war, regardless of the overall context. This was only tenable so long as the "decisive," "key," or "base" idea represented by the expectation that causality in itself was a form of absolute truth held strong; but should it begin to waver, the whole edifice that linked certainty to causal inductions and deductions would crumble in metaphysics and war theory alike.

War theorists and metaphysicians failed to see the problem of validity they were creating all around, by which they reached a single impasse though for opposite reasons. On the one hand, the metaphysicians could not prove their conclusions intuitively, because these were all based on immaterial concepts that could not be materialized for proper testing or validation. Meanwhile the war theorists also met up with the problem of never achieving intuitive certainty – not because they lacked material proof, but as a result of the sheer surplus of it. Whenever a principle succeeded, history could provide a number of counter-examples of where it had failed – and this provided content enough to encourage debate amongst war theorists. The fact that one could make arguments for and against each and every principle of war stimulated the quest in the first place because it encouraged the expectation that these eternal truths were out there, just waiting to be uncovered.

EARLY ENLIGHTENMENT WAR THEORISTS: THE QUEST FOR PRINCIPLES BEGINS

Our first clue into the nature of Enlightenment thinking in general, and more specifically into its thinking on the military arts, comes from breaking down the meaning of this word "principle," which appeared to be so central to the purposes of the theorists. Making its first appearances in the early 1600s, the word would soon spread across the field of war theory, both in terms of the scope of what it represented or what it could mean, and in the overall number of references to the word that we find in the later years of the Enlightenment.

"Principle" is by no means an insignificant little word. Its claim to fame is none other than being the Bible's opening phrase, a word that invokes the divine power of creation. Whereas in English we are familiar with the phrase "In the beginning" from the King James translation of Genesis, the word choice loses the flavour of St Jerome's Latin translation, the Vulgate, which reads "In *principio.*" Etymologically the word "principle" is from the Latin root "princeps," sharing its etymology with the word "prince," whereby the first syllable "prin" or "primus" means "that which is first," and the second comes from "capere," meaning "to take."[9] Together, they represent the idea of that which is "first" in the sense of "original," as well as the power that the origin bestows. Hence the word principle implies causality in two mutually enhancing ways: first, it brings forth the notion of *Causa Prima*, or creation as consequence of a divine act, and secondly, the very formulation of the concept is a causal idea, where an idea has power *because* it is original or first. There is a certain self-contained logic that binds principle to causality, and both to the divine. That is to say that causality might be unearthed by human inquiry, but it exists outside of the human mind as an absolute form of truth.

As such, "principle" is distinct in its connotation from other synonyms that we use in various theories. "Groundings" and "fundamentals" imply their stability from being fixed from below. They have an earthly origin, or as the French say, "terre à terre" or "down to earth," which is closer in meaning to "common sense" or that which is "firmly" established. Meanwhile "maxims" can be translated from the Latin as the "big" idea or the "big" picture. "Adages" and "theory" are distinctly human in their connotation, the former derived from "speaking" and the latter from "looking." Only the word "principle" implies a powerful, absolute truth derived from the primordial nature of things and of god.

In the natural sciences, this spiritual connotation was reinforced by the fact that uncovering causality in the physical properties of objects generated formulae that had the power to predict events in the material world, thereby fulfilling the premise that causality was providing a glimpse into god's creation and the laws which govern it. However, it was not so clear that this same power of prediction and understanding could in fact take proper form outside physics, mathematics, and geometry. But that did not stop the metaphysicians and war theorists from dreaming up ways to deploy physics, mathematics, and geometry into their respective fields. In fact, the most colourful example of this in war theory was to be found in Dietrich von Bülow's *Geist des neueren Kriegssystem*, in which he went so far as borrowing directly the theory of gravity to describe the agency of military energies with mathematical certainty, arguing that they become weaker in "an inverse ratio of the square of its distance."[10] Yet this extreme form of scientific theorizing would only come later in the game. Before such precise principles could be expounded, the question that was on the minds of war theorists was whether or not principles of war were even possible in the first place. In fact

9 *Merriam-Webster Online*, s.vv. "prince," "principle," accessed 31 March 2016, http://www.merriam-webster.com.

10 von Bülow, *Esprit du system de la guerre moderne.*

among early Enlightenment war theorists the word principle was avoided. The word itself was not associated with dictates of tactics and strategy, but with questions regarding how such a universal theory might eventually form through systematized inquiry. There was hope and confidence in the method, but there was not yet a sense of having achieved this end.

The Enlightenment's quest for principles of war progressed vigorously, fuelled by growing literacy and access to printing presses, two defining characteristics of the time. While the seventeenth century had produced some seventy publications on the subject of the military arts, a century later the rate of publication had increased fourfold.[11] Among these works, the two schools of thought had reached an irreconcilable distance from one another: on the one side, the principles of war were becoming more precise and grandiose, while on the other, a few counter-current authors pressed harder and used harsher criticism in questioning the claims to absolute certainty.

To find the origin or the foundations of the quest for principles, we must go back to the early and mid-seventeenth century, a time when Galileo and Descartes were publishing their works. Montecuccoli was among the first to embark upon the quest for organizing a systematized and scientific study of war. Writing in roughly the same years, Montecuccoli did not generally use the word "principle." However, the methodology he proposed framed war in the necessary didactical frame, upon which would emerge the formulation of principles. Using a tight set of calculations, measures, concepts, and subdivisions, Montecuccoli flirted with narrower and more systematic notions, while never actually expounding principles. Interestingly, while the title of his major work, which he wrote between 1649 and 1654, was *Dell'Arte militarea*, the French translation in 1734 would insert the word principle into the title, in the process changing it from "The Military Arts" to "Principles of Military Art" – a rather evident demonstration of just how central the word principle had become in the field of war between the time the manuscript was originally written and when the French translation came about.[12]

Montecuccoli's work set the foundations for a systematized study of war by introducing a smaller set of ideas, which aligned key items to a single, ultimate goal: victory. Of course, this may appear trivial from a modern perspective, but as Moran explains, this "seemingly unexceptional claim" was a challenging idea "because it elevated an illusive military abstraction above traditionally, socially defined concerns with honour, glory, plunder

11 Cited by Gat, *A History of Military Thought*, 27. J. Pöhler, *Bibliotheca Historico-militaris* (Leipzig: G. Lang, 1887–97).

12 Montecuccoli, *Memoires de Montecuccoli.*

and prestige."[13] Montecuccoli was giving war theory a far keener intellectual shape, which involved the relationship between ends and means, as well as a reduced framework for analyzing and achieving "victory," which in fact depended on one's mastery over each element in a set of only three categories of actions.

La guerra è un'azione di eserciti offendentisi in ogni guisa, il cui fine si è la vittoria.[14] (War is an action of armies which clash between themselves in every way, and for which the end goal is victory.)

La vittoria si conseguisce per mezzo dell'apparecchio, della disposizione e dell'operazione.[15] (Victory follows by means of preparations, dispositions and operations.)

Despite the fact that this formulation at first appears to have absolute claims, when one proceeds to the description of these aspects of war, it becomes evident that their parts consist of variables, not immutable maxims. To give an example, regarding "dispositions" Montecuccoli explains that one must "consult slowly, execute with speed … accept the role of chance … take profit from unforeseen situations … remember that one who thinks of everything does nothing, and one who thinks of nothing succumbs to error."[16] These are not the words of a person who would profess an absolute faith in the power of science or geometry to overwhelm or undermine the uncertainties of war. Rather, Montecuccoli embraced these uncertainties and looked to enlightened leadership to profit from them.

Well into the eighteenth century, this was generally the case. The word "principle" had still not yet made complete headway into the field of military arts, even though certain scientific principles were finding their way through. The relationship between science, method, and the military arts was becoming tenser but the former two had not yet overtaken the latter. Marquis de Quincy, writing in 1728, systematically avoided the use of the word "principle" and spoke rather of "maxims," "art," and "tactics" to make his arguments. Given that the term was known to the military arts and widely used in other fields of study by that time, this avoidance was without a doubt a conscious decision. Science was meant

13 Daniel Moran, "Strategic Theory and the History of War," in *Strategy in the Contemporary World*, ed. John Baylis et al. (Oxford: Oxford University Press, 2002), 21.

14 Montecuccoli, *Opere*, 81.

15 Ibid.

16 Montecuccoli, *Memoires de Montecuccoli*, 62. My translation.

to serve the general, not dictate his every move. In his book *L'Art de la guerre: Ou instructions sur l'art militaire*, Quincy allowed for a coexistence between the art of leadership and adaptation to situations, and certain geometrical and mathematical imperatives of the type of warfare being fought at the time, given its lines and fortifications. And so, far from dismissing science as a tool in the quest for improving war's outcomes and techniques, Quincy effectively applied scientific models to specific features of war but made no claim to apply them as an ontological whole or a model by which all of war's many intricacies could be understood. Thus, in his introductory comments, Quincy placed the subject of geometry among the four intellectual disciplines in which a general must excel in order to succeed in the battlefield. He offered a compelling example of why that is later in his treatise, in his exploration of the difficulty involved in aiming one's guns from afar at the right angle required to strike through the embrasures in the fortifications behind which soldiers shot at the approaching army: "I have seen otherwise very competent officers fall into this trap, for having marked the terrain at night. One must take measures, in order to be precisely parallel to that which he seeks to attack. Without this, he weakens his ability to clear the embrasures on the side we are firing at, and we find it difficult to undo such a disadvantage, which may cause a considerable delay."[17]

Yet, far from turning these questions of angles into foolproof systems of conduct, Quincy also included moral factors in the way troops were to be led to victory, emphasizing such things as recompense, glory, leadership, and inspiration: "One must unite all the forces, and examine the advantages of terrain, the wind, the sun and choose a field which will accommodate size of one's troops ... and through strong speeches, showing one's countenance, firmness, tranquillity and assurance, inspiring the strength of one's army, and showing them their certainty of victory and reminding them of their duty, the necessity, the glory, the booty, the recompenses, and coming end of their fatigue, so that they may recall the great actions they have accomplished in the past."[18]

In the case of Maurice de Saxe, writing in roughly the same years (1732 to be precise), the relationship between principles and the art of war was a somewhat confused one. In the introduction to his *Reveries*, he clearly states: "All sciences have principles and rules. War has none."[19] From this categorical stance, he manages to pursue an argument that leads him, in the final chapters, to spell out his own set of "principles."

17 Quincy, *L'Art de la guerre*, 193–4.
18 Ibid., 199–200.
19 Saxe, *Reveries on the Art of War*, 17.

This inconsistency, he would probably reply, was likely caused by the feverish disposition he was in when he wrote the book in the first place,[20] but it is nonetheless telling that this paradox should appear in the years in which it did – right before the quest for absolute principles of war truly took off.

By the end of the eighteenth century the care that went into managing the paradox or uncertainties of principles and the military arts ceased. There were, on one side, people like Prince Charles-Joseph de Ligne, a field marshal under the Holy Roman Empire, who were categorical in their "anti- principles" stance. De Ligne argued that the infinity of situations in war negates the very possibility of principles. "My fundamental principle in war is to not have any principles … Are any two situations perfectly identical? It is so of combat like of faces, when two are alike, that is already quite a lot."[21] On the other side stood Guibert, Puységur, Maizeroy, Bülow, and Jomini, whose works we shall consider further below, who revelled in all kinds of mathematical and scientific generalizations and systematization on war. What separates the early Enlightenment from the five I have enumerated is precisely this willingness to accept uncertainty in their theorizing, moving away from Quincy's moderation, through Saxe admitting the paradox, and onwards to the final *gravitations* of Bülow.

While we can easily see how optimism in the sciences might have contributed to this, what is missing from the analysis is the jump from "scientific inspiration" to "scientific certainty." Among the early Enlightenment war theorists, there is no doubt that "causal" inferences were at the centre of all their theorizing: the induction of principles was based on the premise that isolation and observation caused principles to emerge; and reciprocally, once such principles were found, should they be found, they would permit the deduction of logical stratagems based on the premise that applying a principle to a situation causes a series of effects that would generate the conditions of victory. We find that there was a confidence in the premises and the method involved in generating and using principles of war, but in exchange there remained some flexibility and perhaps uncertainty about the nature and form such principles would take. To understand where this specific point in war theorizing is analogous to the metaphysics, we must turn to Descartes. He also had developed a total confidence in the method, which he would use to uncover the truth about god, and he concluded that one could know scientifically that god

20 Ibid., epigraph.

21 Prince de Ligne, *Fantaisies militaires* (Kralovelhota: printed by author, 1780), 188. Cited in Coutau-Bégarie, *Traité de stratégie*, 279.

existed – though he had not gone so far as trying to extrapolate the form and substance this god would take, the details behind the veil.

DESCARTES: A SCIENTIFIC APPROACH TO THE IMMATERIAL

The year was 1641. The Church had suffered many setbacks to its official dogma, from Columbus to Magellan, and Copernicus to Galileo. Science was on the rise, but luckily for the Church, science's interest in *demonstrating* god was not fuelled by questions of atheism, but rather an interest in heresy, in improving our knowledge of the divine.[22] The arguments were not altogether new. Ideas found in the works of Saint Anselm of Canterbury almost 600 years earlier resurfaced in Descartes's proof of god's existence, as a deductive argument that used god's perfection as a starting point.[23] Descartes also followed in St Thomas of Aquinas's footsteps in suggesting that god's existence cannot be derived in and of itself, but must result from our experience of his effects becoming manifest to us.[24] What was truly original in Descartes was not so much the conclusion or even the argumentative path he used to get there but rather the method itself: Descartes was not a trained theologian or philosopher, he was a mathematician and physicist cum philosopher. Consequently, Descartes's approach to the question was grounded in the scientific method. He assumed that one could analyze the world in the same way one could analyze numbers and figures to prove geometrical concepts, i.e. by making demonstrations using "long chains of reasoning,"[25] but this depended on a high level of belief in the certitude of causality as the linking element that allows our minds to connect our experience of the world to the universe and to the divine.

Descartes defended "a position in which it is true both that god is the total efficient cause of everything and that created substances have a real efficient causal role in each and every effect after the initial creation. This was aided by a conception of cause that treats any proposition that occurs as a premise in a scientific explanation as a cause."[26] Later philosophers including Hume and Kant would come to challenge the idea of causation as the standalone centre of certitude in theories of human understanding, bringing a new scepticism to the forefront, but before

22 Gaukroger, *Blackwell Guide*, 4.
23 Vaysse, *La stratégie critique de Kant*, 10.
24 Ibid., 11.
25 Gilson and Langan, *History of Philosophy*, 57.
26 Clatterbaugh, "Cartesian Causality," 199.

that occurred, it was another approach to scepticism that had generated a kind of belief system regarding causality.

Paradoxically Descartes's sense of certitude was built upon an extreme form of doubt. In Descartes's "First Meditation" he establishes an "intense sceptical doubt." Unlike the type of doubt already known to ancient sceptics, his was not meant as a way of life or philosophy, but rather as a tool of abstraction – a radical doubt that is not meant to be practical, but which was nonetheless useful for the purpose of his treatise.[27] Descartes was in fact working to refute traditional scepticism using an extreme form of scepticism that would allow him to settle a firm concept of certainty. He actually boasted, in a letter to Bourdin, that he was the only one to have adequately refuted the sceptics of his day.[28] The argument begins by questioning perceptual information, which can deceive the perceiver both in dreams and our waking hours. While this argument can be traced back to those of the Ancients, what followed was an original form of doubt: the assumption, for the sake of the inquiry, that god is not the source of all truth, but rather a "malignant demon, who is at once exceedingly potent and deceitful, and who has employed all his artifice to deceive me."[29] In this hypothetical context everything in the universe, as perceived by the human mind, is false. But a beacon of light exists for the mind even in this hypothetical place of total falsehood: "But there is I know not what being, who is possessed at once of the highest power and the deepest cunning, who is constantly employing all his ingenuity in deceiving me. Doubtless, then, I exist, since I am deceived; and, let him deceive me as he may, he can never bring it about that I am nothing, so long as I shall be conscious that I am something. So that it must, in fine, be maintained, all things being maturely and carefully considered, that this I am, I exist, is necessarily true each time it is expressed by me, or conceived in my mind."[30]

If we recall our earlier discussion of principles we are reminded of the power of a truth that comes from the origin, or the fundament. Descartes's "cogito ergo sum" is the outcome of this reflection and takes this form because it exists in and of itself, it does not depend on some other higher truth in the universe. That is why Descartes would go so far as to refer to it as the "first principle of philosophy."[31] This conclusion, though it claimed not to rest on any other higher truth, did nonetheless

27 Gaukroger, *Blackwell Guide*, 2.

28 Grene, "Descartes and Skepticism," 557.

29 Descartes, "First Meditation," *Meditations*, 27.

30 Ibid., 30.

31 Peltz, "Logic of the Cogito," 257.

rest on something more fundamental – a total belief in the method and the power of causal inferences. Even beyond the method that leads to this conclusion, the conclusion itself is a set up as a causal relation between thinking and being, "ergo."

This conclusion is only the first half of a larger argument that moves from this initial certitude to another: the inference of god's existence from the perception of god's effect in the physical universe and the certainty of our relation to it. In the "Third Meditation" Descartes confronts the possibility of there being a malignant demon, arguing that it would be wrong to assume that god is a deceiver before even considering the larger question of whether god actually exists or not.[32] Having asked us to put aside the hypothetical construction that allowed the cogito in the first place, he reconsiders the existence of god in relation to the cogito and thereby establishes a new basis for certainty:

> since I am a thinking thing and possess in myself an idea of god, whatever in the end be the cause of my existence, it must of necessity be admitted that it is likewise a thinking being, and that it possesses in itself the idea and all the perfections I attribute to Deity. Then it may again be inquired whether this cause owes its origin and existence to itself, or to some other cause. For if it be self-existent, it follows, from what I have before laid down, that this cause is god … and thus there can here be no difficulty with respect to them, and it is absolutely necessary to conclude from this alone that I am, and possess the idea of a being absolutely perfect, that is, of god, that his existence is most clearly demonstrated.[33]

Scholars generally refer to the line of reasoning that links Descartes's absolute doubt to his demonstration of god's existence as the Cartesian circle, because "the criterion of clear and distinct perception depends on the assumption that god exists, which in turn depends on the criterion of clear and distinct perception."[34] It generated in metaphysics a doctrine of knowledge independent of any metaphysical guarantee or proof.[35] Method had in effect been elevated to the point where it had generated its own, internal sense of self-certainty. And this lack of material demonstration, which would provide an intuitive sense of certainty rather than an analytical one, became an important cultural grounding upon which to elevate the study of war since it also had problems with

32 Descartes, "Third Meditation," *Meditations*, 44–5.

33 Ibid., 59, 60–1.

34 *Encyclopedia Britannica Online*, s.v. "Cartesian circle," accessed 31 March 2016, http://www.britannica.com/topic/Cartesian-circle.

35 Gewirtz, "Cartesian Circle," 372.

the issue of material proof. Examples from the battlefield, though they may at times follow certain patterns, were not necessarily defined by a pattern or another. The existence of proofs and counter-proofs for each and every situation in war kept the possibility of universality always one step removed from theory, and also kept theory stuck in the realm of observation and speculation rather than intuitive certainty.

The arguments about god and about principles of war evolved in tandem. Montecuccoli was not seeking out specific examples of principles because the time for it had not yet arrived; this was still in the phase of asking whether or not principles could even exist in the first place. First the premises for their emergence needed to be set, the foundations for the coming military science. This was equally the place of Descartes in history. He was not trying to demonstrate god's form and substance, but arguing that there could be certainty in our knowledge of god's existence. It was after these preliminary conclusions, and indeed only afterwards, that Enlightenment war theorists began to settle on the premise of there being principles of war, and then went about on a quest to unearth their scientific details, their form and substance.

Not until this new inquiry had been developed in metaphysics did it trickle down into the military arts. During the roughly one hundred years that separated Monteccucoli from Maurice de Saxe and Quincy, the existence or not of principles remained somewhat of a mystery – where we could imagine the potential for a future military science, but we could not yet assume to possess it fully. This explains why Quincy might opt for a compromise while Saxe chose a paradoxical approach. There was a clear impasse in war theory's relationship to principles, but a new and more ambitious philosophical age was dawning, in which the goal would be to study the form and substance, the details and depth of our knowledge of the divine, as opposed to merely the yes or no of its existence. There was enough confidence in the "yes" to justify moving onwards and upwards. And so too would some war theorists soon thereafter take on the quest to uncover the form and substance of principles, because they too stopped questioning the underlying premise of whether or not these did in fact exist.

BERKELEY: THE FORM AND SUBSTANCE OF GOD

The impetus to begin questioning Descartes's logic did not come so much from a reply directed at Descartes as from those aimed at his disciple George Berkeley, who would take the Cartesian method to a whole new level. His major work *A Treatise concerning the Principles of Human Knowledge* was first published in 1710, and in it he developed a far more ambitious demonstration of god. It is worth noting that the title takes on the word "principle" which should not come as a surprise, given its scope to go beyond mere methodology and into the measurement of divine attributes. Berkeley did not make use only of the scientific method; he also – as we shall soon see – added to scientific analogy and terminology a modification and enhancement, which was equally relevant to the field of war theory.

Berkeley's system has been described as "the most consistent development of Descartes's fundamental thesis of the priority of self-consciousness, coupled with a theistic conception of god and a subordination of mechanistic physics to idealistic metaphysics."[36] Indeed the Cartesian influence on Berkeley was considerable, and in fact easily confirmable thanks to notes Berkeley took in his diary.[37] Furthermore, if one takes the time to analyze where he stood on various arguments that had pitted Hobbes against Descartes, Berkeley almost systematically stood in agreement with the latter, against the former.[38] Berkeley adopted the Cartesian project as his own and tried to clarify and improve upon its argumentation in a way that would allow him to propose more ambitious conclusions, about not only the existence of god but also the form and substance of spirit. His purpose was to uncover "those doctrines or principles which somehow lead to scepticism and atheism. He thinks he can specify which principles have these consequences, an important matter unto itself since these principles were all accepted by one or more of his predecessors. However, Berkeley also wants to refute scepticism and atheism; he claims to vindicate commonsensical views about knowledge and certainty and in the process establish the existence of God, thereby discharging two tasks at one blow."[39]

In his *Treatise* Berkeley introduced scientific methodology and analogy in a way that Descartes had not. Berkeley's text did not limit itself to the existence of god but went further, attempting also to elucidate the substance of divinity and thus integrating concepts from the physical world and the natural sciences, such as indivisibility and indissolubility, into his metaphysics.

> We have shown that the soul is indivisible, incorporeal, unextended, and it is consequently incorruptible. Nothing can be plainer than the motions, changes, decays, and dissolutions which we hourly see befall natural bodies (and which is

36 Kantonen, "Influence of Descartes on Berkeley," 483–500.
37 Ibid.
38 Ibid.
39 Pappas, "Berkeley and Scepticism," 133.

> what we mean by the course of nature) cannot possibly affect an active, simple, uncompounded substance; such a being therefore is indissoluble by the force of nature; that is to say, the soul of man is naturally immortal ... Hence, it is evident that god is known as certainly and immediately as any other mind or spirit whatsoever distinct from ourselves. We may even assert that the existence of god is far more evidently perceived than the existence of men; because the effects of nature are infinitely more numerous and considerable than those ascribed to human agents.[40]

Yet regardless of the new tools and precision in the exposition, once again, the crux of the argument fell back on the older arguments of Aquinas and Descartes, whereby god's existence is inherent to the concept of causality, the *Causa Prima*, the explanation for human perception of the natural world.

What is remarkable, when we transfer back to the field of war theory, is that its evolution went through the exact same process. Let us recall from the above section on the early Enlightenment war theorists that their purpose was to find principles and to prove that such principles were possible. Like Descartes they were after the thing itself. The later Enlightenment military thinkers, convinced that they already possessed it, like Berkeley, went on to describe what they already possessed in much greater detail, leaving behind any scepticism regarding the method or the proof or demonstration of its conclusions. The greater the reliance metaphysicians and war theorists put on the "certainty" of causal inferences, the more their conclusions became dependent on the validity of this very concept. This therefore meant that they were at a high risk of becoming destabilized by anything that might cast doubt on causality itself, and its claims to certitude. Could causality lose its luster as the basis of all human understanding? And if it did, what would be the consequence for the theories of war that were constructed entirely on this edifice? This will be the topic of the next chapter. However, before this discussion, it is important to observe just how far the theories of war would go, in their analytical claims, before they began to break down intuitively as a result.

THE LATER ENLIGHTENMENT WAR THEORISTS: THE FORM AND SUBSTANCE OF PRINCIPLES

What connects this upcoming section to the preceding one is not that philosophers were becoming war theorists or that war theorists were

40 Berkeley, "Principles of Human Knowledge," 209–12.

becoming philosophers, but rather that the quest for principles of war was in fact taking on a form that was increasingly mystical and metaphysical in its essence. As the principles were perfected and broken down into their minute parts they became increasingly removed from any material reality, and their capacity to be proven empirically was further eclipsed by the ambition to be universally applicable and certain. By the mid-eighteenth century, the quest had indeed broken with the past, and taken a path that began with Puységur and Maizeroy and finally culminated in the acclaimed works of Bülow and Jomini.

The first representative of this new generation of military theorists was Puységur, who wrote *Art de la guerre par principe et par règle* in 1743. Inspired by the famed French fortifications expert Sébastien Le Prestre de Vauban,[41] Puységur hoped to convey the spatial and geometrical advances in the science of fortification to the art of war in the battlefield. It is indeed no surprise that the initial impetus should come from the art of fortification, because if there was one place in the military arts where formulas and mathematics were essential, this was it. Again, we are reminded of what Quincy had to say about embrasures and angles with regard to this particular form of warfare. Geometry and science could indeed generate very tangible tactical ramifications in this case, but the question remained whether the principles would carry from this fixed environment to the very mobile environment of the open battlefield.

As an interesting side note, however, while one might expect that because of this immobility and constancy, the art of fortifications would have been the most logical place to begin speaking of principles, this was actually not the case at all. This doesn't mean that Vauban was not scientific in his calculations. His improved design on the "poudrerie" – the powder magazine – remained the official one in France for the following 200 years, replaced only in 1874.[42] Everything was counted and organized systematically and meticulously, and Vauban was also known to "work out sets of tables, which related the garrison, armament and interior space to various numbers of bastions."[43] And yet regardless of this the word principle was not on his mind. In *La defence des places*,[44] Vauban's most important text, even though he makes very precise observations regarding the methods of fortification he does not use the term principle once. This was clearly a thought-out word choice, since Vauban was quite familiar with the term principle and made regular use of it in his

41 Gat, *History of Military Thought*, 37.
42 Duffy, *Fortress*, 74.
43 Ibid.
44 Vauban, *Les Oisivetés*.

political and economic writings, such as in *Les Oisivetés*.[45] Vauban, who died in 1707, wrote in a way that was perfectly in line with an early Enlightenment war theorist, even though he would became the inspiration for the principles of the later Enlightenment war theorists.

Puységur best describes his concept of principles in his discussion entitled *Comparing Caesar's oblique lines at Pharsalus with those we should have taken at Nordlingen: reflection on the errors we commit for lack of principles.*[46] In it Puységur explains that principles are a system of analysis based in geometry that will automatically lead the general to the best course of action, insofar as the situation has been properly gauged:

> Among the methods used in combat by the great Roman and Greek captains, those that were not considered, because they were unknown of, since truth in the science of war (as I have said before) cannot be acquired until practice in armies is the result of theory founded on principles of geometry, which consist of comparing the moving forces which are acting against one another … After having recognized the numbers and the orders of battle of the enemy, this comparison of your forces with his offers your imagination all the different approaches one can take, whether to attack or defend; and once these have been weighed, it will make you chose the best option.[47]

Whereas it is easy to gauge a situation when attacking or defending a fortress, because the situation is generally unchanging, what is not so clear, and did in fact depend on a great leap of faith, was that the lessons learned from siege warfare could be adapted to battlefields, where angles and motion – everything – was so variable. The pedantry in Puységur seemed to have no limit – for example, through mathematical formulas he would break down complex, possibly even daylong manoeuvres not to the hour or the minute but to the precise second.[48]

A few years after Puységur, this direction towards perfection continued to be felt in Lieutenant-Colonel Joly de Maizeroy's work, which had the stated goal of building "a theory on the science of war based on solid and invariable principles."[49] In his treatise entitled *Mémoire sur les opinions qui partagent les militaires,* Maizeroy wrote: "We begin with the well-known and invariable principle of combat, which consists of bringing

45 Vauban, *Œuvres.*

46 Puységur, *L'Art de la guerre*, 379.

47 Ibid., 119–20.

48 Ibid., 379.

49 Joly de Maizeroy, *Theorie de Guerre* (Nancy: Chez la Veuve Leclerc, 1777), xxiv. Cited by Coutau-Bégarie, *Traité sur la stratégie*, 279.

the strong against the weak, vanquishing the enemy's flank, and turning him – robbing him, as much as possible, of the ability to make movements to this end."[50] The language of war theory had indeed evolved, away from the uncertainties and exploratory nature found in the works of Montecuccoli or Quincy. Now, in Maizeroy, war's methods and concepts had acquired a language that posited strategies and tactics that were infallible.

This new faith continued to hold true in the works of General Guibert, who wrote *Essai général de tactique* in 1770. In this text he complained that military thought had not yet managed to generate the types of scientific truth that physicists and astronomers had discovered in their fields. By contrast he hoped to develop tactics that "would constitute a science at every period of time, in every place, and among every species of arms; that is to say, if ever by some revolution among the nature of arms which it is not possible to foresee, the order of depth should again be adapted, there would be no necessity in putting the same tactics in practice to change either manoeuvre or constitution."[51]

Guibert did not mince his words. His science showed no fear. At one point, he would go so far as to claim that he could "*perfectly* develop a theory regarding obliques orders."[52] Fond of demonstrating things with unquestionable certainty, Guibert was also of the opinion that, "surrounded by tumult and danger, in an environment where there are many wrong options and only one good one, this is where 'coup d'oeil' shows its wisdom, the judgment that wins battles ... The science of 'coup d'oeil' and the knowledge of terrain being intimately linked to tactics, we can see how many false and useless illuminations military colleges will give, which will not be constituted on this fundamental principle."[53]

Guibert's science was to be a set of principles whereby he would "demonstrate the grand combinations of the interior mechanisms that must be weighed by an army in its transition from marching orders to combat dispositions."[54] Here the use of the words "demonstrate" and "must" are of interest, because they are categorical. In fact, Guibert prided himself on having proclaimed a "perfect theory," in which his principles were meant to be of the "dogmatic" order![55] Typical of the later Enlightenment

50 Maizeroy, *Memoire*, 66.
51 Gat, *History of Military Thought*, 56.
52 Guibert, *Essai*, 75, emphasis added.
53 Ibid., 245–6.
54 Ibid., 64.
55 Ibid., 75.

war theorists, Guibert had altogether given up on doubting any of his own claims.

The word dogmatic is wonderfully ironic in that on the one hand, Guibert took pride in his own dogmatism yet in hindsight one might say that that dogmatism was exactly his flaw: Guibert's conclusions were merely dogmatic. It is here that the parallel between Enlightenment metaphysics and war theory becomes most tangible. This professed certainty stood on tightrope, but the theorists appeared blind to the fact their shaky edifice could fall to the ground. Given that method had been elevated and material proof relegated to a somewhat subservient role, their pretensions were only valid insofar as they could not be properly questioned. Whereas this lack of materiality in metaphysics had rendered hypotheses impossible to disprove for lack of material evidence, the opposite occurred in the art of war: there was so much material evidence with contradictory outcomes that no single principle could be elevated to certainty because each rule had a counter-rule, each example had its opposite.

The answer to the riddle or problem of certainty in war theory was everywhere to be found among Enlightenment war theorists, but it seemed a surprisingly unconscious one. In what each of them had to say about the other, they regularly decried one thing in common: a thorough dissatisfaction with all the preceding theories and principles written by others. Rarely building upon the works of others, they seemed intent on starting from scratch, as though the work of the previous authors had not, in fact, brought us any closer to the goal of finding immutable principles. This trend was best shown in the works of Jomini, as he wrote that even those who had served as his greatest influences and guides early on, Lloyd and Guibert, they had achieved only "more or less complete," "imperfect," and "deplorably contradictory" theories.[56]

The same people who wrote grandiose principles of war were inadvertently agreeing with Prince de Ligne's argument stating that no true principle of war could exist, or at least that there had not yet been any *better* principles (until their own, of course) to suddenly shine light upon the Enlightenment's darkness. It was precisely this optimism and lack of scepticism – despite the repetitive incompletion of the project and the dissatisfaction it wrought – which serves as the parallel we find with the metaphysical project. Here too, the professed certainty of the project was proportional and growing alongside the further application and reliance on the power of the scientific method and its languages and

56 Jomini, *Précis de l'art de la guerre* (Anselin), 16.

precepts. This explains equally why Berkeley's claims had eclipsed the scope and range of those of his predecessors. But the closer one got to the final truth, the more it became evident that an inherent weakness at the centre, at the first cause, was collapsing on itself.

THE ANTINOMIAN PROBLEM

The next chapter will explain in greater detail the nature of the breakdown in Enlightenment thinking, and how the arguments made by Hume and Kant would eventually find their way into Clausewitz's approach to the principles of war. But before this more substantial discussion it is worthwhile to first introduce the way in which Clausewitz exposed the inescapable weaknesses of the writings of the most ambitious and perhaps also the most tragic figure of all Enlightenment military theorists, Dietrich Heinrich Bülow.

Bülow's successful piece entitled *Geist der neuern Kriegssystem*, which was briefly mentioned earlier for its discussion of the theory of gravity in describing the movements and forces involved on the battlefield, would become Clausewitz's favourite target for mockery. The main thrust of Bülow's argument, however, was not about these forces of repulsion and attraction but rather the very different subject of bases and lines of operations. Bülow claimed that the need for a regular supply of ammunitions to succeed in war required a geometrically calculable base upon which to rely. Using simplistic geometric formulas, he argued that a right-angle triangle represented a critical point or cut-off, after which any angle more acute would not allow enough cover to protect the base. Obtuse angles, on the other hand, offered the added advantage that any attempt by the enemy to penetrate the base would leave their own bases undefended. Thus obtuse angles were most advantageous.[57] In his concluding remarks, Bülow argued that beyond the ninety-degree cut-off one could "undertake an offensive operation against the enemy with safety."[58] He also argued that all retreats, in order to be successful, had to be accomplished using exocentric formations.[59] His system excluded the possibility of exceptions or circumstances where these hard rules could not be applied or could be less efficient than alternatives.

With regard to Bülow's concept of base lines, Clausewitz argues that, "as far as history is concerned, we have decidedly not been led to any

57 von Bülow, *Esprit du system de la guerre moderne*, section 2.
58 Ibid.
59 Ibid.

deductions of that kind through constantly recurring forms."[60] He then proceeds to explain how different contexts generate different best practices: "What Daun did by the extent and provident choice of positions, the king did by keeping his army always concentrated, always hugging the enemy close, and by being always ready to act extemporally with his whole army. The method of each general proceeded not only from the nature of the army he commanded, but also from the circumstances in which he was placed."[61]

Similarly, in Book IV Clausewitz countered Bülow's argument regarding exocentric retreats by providing two examples that were absolutely contrary to the stated rules, which was enough in itself to invalidate the rule's claim to universality:

> Now and again it has been suggested to divide for the purpose of retreating, therefore to retreat in separate divisions or even eccentrically ... The idea of harassing the enemy by separate corps on both flanks at the moment when he is following up his victory, is a perfect anomaly; a faint-hearted pedant might be overawed by his enemy in that manner, and for such a case it may answer; but where we are not sure of this failing in our opponent it is better let alone. If the strategic relations after a battle require that we should cover ourselves right and left by detached corps, so much must be done, as from circumstances is unavoidable, but this fractioning must always be regarded as an evil, and we are seldom in a state to commence it the day after the battle itself.
>
> If Frederick the Great after the battle of Collin, and the raising of the siege of Prague retreated in three columns, that was done not out of choice, but because the position of his forces, and the necessity of covering Saxony, left him no alternative. Buonaparte after the battle of Brienne, sent Marmont back to the Aube, whilst he himself passed the Seine, and turned towards Troyes; but that this did not end in disaster, was solely owing to the circumstance that the Allies, instead of pursuing, divided their forces in like manner, turned with the one part (Blucher) towards the Marne, while with the other (Schwartzenberg), from fear of being too weak, they advanced with exaggerated caution.[62]

Having demonstrated the opposite stance, Clausewitz was not completely satisfied, nor would he use this to propose an alternative and opposite set of absolute principles replacing one set of doctrines with another. In fact, Clausewitz generally agreed that bases and lines were useful concepts – he simply insisted that one could not derive war plans

60 Clausewitz, *On War*, bk XI, ch. 30, 566.

61 Ibid.

62 Ibid., 246–7.

from them.[63] What he sought was to *challenge the very principle of principles, and create doctrine against doctrines.* If Clausewitz had only wanted to refute Bülow at the same level of analysis that Bülow was himself writing, he would have stuck to a direct refutation; but instead, if we look to other sections of *On War*, the scepticism that Clausewitz makes use of is not merely a scepticism regarding specific facts and types of analysis, but scepticism as itself an entire method of analysis.

The reason why Clausewitz could eventually go beyond mere direct refutation and question positive doctrines on a methodological or higher level was in fact the underlying unity, which we set out to explore in this chapter, linking the metaphysics to the Enlightenment war theories. What was illogical in Bülow's attempts to turn a few examples of exocentric retreats into a principle of retreats was not the reasoning itself, which provided examples from past battles and deduced causal relationships between actions and military success. The problem was rather the absolute certainty that was allocated to the deduction, followed by the inference, based on this, of an absolute principle. One could argue a logical stance both for and against exocentric retreats, and by extension any single positive doctrine, because of war's many forces and possibilities, reciprocal actions and contradictions. And so, while Clausewitz could provide proof showing the opposite of Bülow's conclusion, he could not demonstrate, and indeed knew not to even attempt to demonstrate, that a counter-example such as the battle of Brienne could provide an opposite doctrine. In different contexts, there can be distinct, logical deductions that are mutually exclusive and opposite one another, that are nonetheless *equally true* – which is to say that the study of war had the ability to generate antinomies of pure reason, or mutually exclusive *conditional* truths that fail to demonstrate themselves or their opposites as *unconditional* truths in the process of being compared or analyzed jointly.[64]

The result of this "irreconcilable opposition between such a theory and practice" was, according to Clausewitz, the necessary outcome of any "endeavour to establish maxims, rules, and even systems for the conduct of war," because it meant attempting to circumscribe or place into a system something that had no definite limits.[65] This is the source of the contradictions that appear in history, and the antinomies that emerge as so many examples both prove and disprove every positive doctrine. By

63 Delbrück, *History of the Art of War*, 453.

64 We will be breaking down this complex Kantian argument in the upcoming chapter.

65 Clausewitz, *On War*, bk II, ch. 2, 74.

bringing forward the paradox itself, rather than tying himself down to merely agreeing or disagreeing with Bülow's conclusions, Clausewitz cut the underlying basis of the argument. He was escaping the endless circle of agreeing or disagreeing with any single principle of war, and moving his analysis to a higher level that encapsulated the debate and could thereby supersede it.

A parallel evolution occurred in war theory and metaphysics during the Enlightenment. In the former case, the seed took root in the works of Montecuccoli, where victory was isolated as the only objective in battle, and a simplified list was drafted regarding how one could generate victory as a result of actions. Following this method, which linked causes to effects, an early rationalist tradition in war theory began asking whether or not it was possible to generate absolute principles of war, and finding themselves uncertain they sought instead a moderate coexistence between art and science in the study of war. Meanwhile in metaphysics, thanks to Descartes's methodology the quest for proving god's existence would eventually branch out into the far more ambitious question of god's form and substance. After this process had been completed – and not before – a similar transition occurred in the science of war, where method was assumed to provide the basis upon which to unearth those principles that could deliver victory with predictability and certainty. The problem, however, was that this certainty in knowledge became detached from material proof, precisely because of the faith in the methods in both philosophy and war theory. Any deduction and induction could be proclaimed binding and absolute, from the study of causes through isolation, as though each causal relationship possessed something divine to it.

If Clausewitz noticed within the many existing theories of war a common failure to actually attain the certainty they claimed, it was because he understood that refuting one doctrine or another was an insufficient process: the very antinomies that produced distinct and opposite principles were the basis of a higher, negating truth. Whereas the metaphysical debates were indemonstrable because they were immaterial, the "principles of war" were indemonstrable because there was simply too much material contradictory evidence, too much confusion, too much chaos for the cosmos to ever emerge. However for him to see this – the antimonies, the causal breakdowns, and the reciprocity of action that made war too dynamic to be intelligible in static constants – Clausewitz had to have been well introduced to and very conscious of Kant's system. It was Kant who demonstrated the problem of antinomies in pure reason. It was Kant's sceptical method that Clausewitz turned to in order to build his final refutation of positive doctrines.

3

Clausewitz's Scepticism: The First Dialectical Moment

SCHOLARS HAVE ARTICULATED various views regarding the origins of Clausewitz's theory of war. Some focus on his personal history and relations, others on his experiences in battle – and some attempt to ground *On War* in a simpler and perhaps more easily manageable framework. While each different approach may have some merit, none can individually surpass the importance of understanding how Clausewitz organized his thinking within the framework of a Kantian sceptical method. To exclude this central feature of Clausewitz's way of philosophizing severely muddles how we interpret his work, because it means taking the substance of the work out of its vessel.

A recent example, which illustrates the problem quite well, can be found in Antoine Bousquet's *The Scientific Way of War*. The author avoids the philosophical origins of Clausewitz's thought in order to make space for an argument on metaphors, which elevates the significance of thermodynamics in *On War*. Bousquet does all this by citing Clausewitz's occasional use of concepts such as "friction," "perfect explosion," and "discharges," and then by suggesting that they come together as a foundational or ontological backdrop.[1] In order to push forward his metaphorical analysis, the author makes use of a clever division that allows him to agree with Gat's discussion of influences in Clausewitz, while sidestepping the question altogether: "While Azar Gat has made a persuasive case for the influence of romanticism and anti-rationalist impulses on the writings of Carl von Clausewitz … it would be misleading to view Clausewitz himself as anti-science or anti-reason."[2]

1 Bousquet, *Scientific Way of War*, 85–91.

2 Ibid., 85.

Bousquet is right in placing Clausewitz on this side of *this* divide, but he is wrong in suggesting that such a divide exists in the first place. While *On War* provides a careful refutation to the scientific certainties and claims made by Enlightenment war theorists, the either/or presentation, which places German Idealism against or opposed to science, is false. In the context of Kantian thought, science is in no way dismissed, but rather elevated by its distinction from the metaphysics. It was precisely because of the philosophical debates that had proclaimed and disclaimed grand, absolute truths about abstract, intangible objects such as god and miracles that Clausewitz could, by an analogous process, reclaim the scope of what science could afford war theory, and what it could not. In his first note regarding the project to write *On War*, Clausewitz explained that he was frustrated by the "unscientific spirit" of the existing theories in the military arts, suggesting that those who wrote them tried "so hard to make their systems coherent and complete that they were stuffed with commonplaces, truisms, and nonsense of every kind."[3] Clausewitz was not "anti-science" or "anti-reason," nor is that what a philosophical reading would claim. Rather, Clausewitz was simply being *reasonable about science,* because he was integrating into his works Kant's theory of human understanding, which was, in fact, nothing else than a *scientific inquiry into reason itself.*

The distinction is an important one. Enlightenment thinkers had confused reason and science to the point where their quest for science had become unreasonable. Modern dialectics came about as a remedy to this situation, offering an alternative way to conceive human understanding and allowing certain limits and inherent contradictions to be exposed. The outcome of this would be that the science of knowledge became more interested in the question of its own scope than in the question of its depth. Specifically, in the case of metaphysics – which was at the centre of these inquiries – the question transitioned from how to prove the existence of god to an exploration of the proof itself: whether there could be any certainty to this demonstration. In order to be "reasonable about science," the first requirement was a healthy dose of scepticism with regard to the scope of human understanding and the relationship between observation, deduction, and certainty.

Clausewitz makes use of scientific analogy in a manner diametrically opposed to how Enlightenment thinkers had made use of it. Whereas the latter did in fact make science an ontological feature of their work,

3 Clausewitz, "Author's preface to an unpublished manuscript on the theory of war written between 1816 and 1818," *On War*, ed. and trans. Howard and Paret, 61. Note: this early preface is unavailable in the Graham translation.

the basis upon which they hoped to edify their systems, Clausewitz did no such thing. Clausewitz does use thermodynamics in *On War*, in a scattered and non-systematized way, but it has a purely heuristic – not ontological – purpose. Clausewitz himself makes that very clear. He explains that the use of scientific analogies and metaphors are "nothing more than ornamental flourishes,"[4] which is to say that even when Clausewitz used metaphors in his own discussion he did not attribute any serious value to them. His use of thermodynamics was not actually scientifically derived, it was merely borrowed from science and attached as an "ornament" to help the reader understand. In *On War* thermodynamics is used as an image, and was actually derived from a mix of philosophy, war history, and critical analysis.

To understand the centrality of philosophy in Clausewitz's method requires a much deeper reading, which does not limit itself to extracting various snippets and proclaiming a whole. Indeed, as Fernández Vega notes, it cannot be boiled down to being anti-Enlightenment or not, since Clausewitz was writing at a time that was characterized by a combination of trends (*Sturm und Drang*,[5] Kantianism, idealism, historicism, romanticism, and nationalism).[6] Trying to pick and choose among influences in his work is a completely self-defeating approach to understanding Clausewitz. We should be doing the very opposite, finding ways to analyze the various influences in ways that make room for them to coexist intellectually and logically. Even if the overarching system was in fact Kantian, this did not exclude other sources, arguably it helped Clausewitz improve and enhance the proof of their conclusions in a more objective way.

The one concept that allows us to appreciate the complexity of Clausewitz's frame of mind and the influences that shaped it is without a doubt also his most defining characteristic as a scholar: he was profoundly sceptical. It is plain to see. In fact Clausewitz's visceral scepticism is well illustrated in a letter written in 1827:

> I hate the sort of technical language that leads us to believe we can reduce the individual case to a universal, to the inevitable. Strategists manipulate these terminologies as if they were algebraic formulae, whose accuracy has long been

4 Clausewitz, *On War*, bk II, ch. 5, 117.

5 This German phrase, which means "Storm and Urge," refers to a philosophical and artistic movement in the second half of the eighteenth century, which took place in Prussia and elevated the ideas of individual subjectivity and the free expression of individual emotion in response to the perceived constraints of rationalism.

6 Fernández Vega, *Las guerras de la politica*, 72.

established, brief formulae that may be used as substitutes for the original reality. But these phrases do not even represent clear and definite principles. Rather they are nebulous, ambiguous expressions, whose true meaning remains open to question. This is no accident. Their vagueness is intended, because they did not derive from what is essential and could be presented as universal truth. Consequently the inventors of these terms found it natural to allow a certain latitude in their meaning.[7]

That being said, it is not enough to state that Clausewitz was a sceptic. The proper question thereafter should rather be: what kind of a sceptic was he? And to answer this one must be far more thorough. The specific kind of scepticism we find in Clausewitz first appeared in Hume, and it culminated in Kant's *Critique of Pure Reason.*

THE KANTIAN LINK: KIESEWETTER

No interpreter of Clausewitz has weighed in against the role of Kant in the formation of Clausewitz's thought more aggressively, and with more authority, than Raymond Aron in *Penser la guerre.* It is worth noting a few of his concerns here, in order to keep them in mind, but ultimately I will return to his overall argument only in later chapters, so that I may discuss his dual dismissal of both Hegel and Kant at once. With regard to Kant, specifically, Aron starts off by suggesting that Clausewitz never actually read Kant, but was merely introduced to his works indirectly. This argument, which is stated but not backed up in any serious way, is thereafter followed by a blatantly weak ad hominem argument against the person who represents this indirect link: Prof. Kiesewetter. Aron writes that Kiesewetter was reputed as providing Kantian doctrines in "homeopathic doses."[8] Before even engaging with the question of a Kantian influence in Clausewitz, Aron has cast an unfounded doubt on the question.

It is worth taking a bit of time to dismiss this line of argument right away, so that we may quickly move into Aron's more serious points. Even though Aron may have considered Kiesewetter in such a negative light, Kant himself did not share the impression, as he corresponded with Kiesewetter regularly and went so far as to ask his publisher in Berlin to hire Kiesewetter as the proof editor for the *Critique of Practical Reason.*[9] There is therefore no reason to give credence to Aron's attack on Kiesewetter in the first place. But even if there were ... the argument

7 Clausewitz, "Letter to Roeder, 22 December, 1827," in *Two Letters on Strategy*, 198.
8 Aron, *Penser la guerre, Tome I*, 362.
9 Arendt, *Lectures on Kant's Political Philosophy*, 7.

remains mere diversion: why limit ourselves to placing Kiesewetter on trial to determine whether Clausewitz had good knowledge of Kant, when we can analyze how well Clausewitz integrated Kant directly?

A way to determine this is to gauge whether or not when Clausewitz made references to Kant, he was paraphrasing the original or rather the textbooks and distillations written by Kiesewetter, which he would have had access to while studying under him. That being said, when we consider, as Aron does, that Kiesewetter was a "vulgarisateur" (meaning someone who simplifies ideas in order popularize them),[10] it is not a huge step to jump over Kiesewetter, especially if it simply means Clausewitz was paraphrasing a person who was paraphrasing Kant. The fact is that Clausewitz was applying Kant, and in all likelihood, and mostly, given the depth of his appreciation, it seems to be a near-certainty that Clausewitz would have read the originals, first because he was clearly interested in them, and secondly because as a student, then a professor, and finally as the commander of the War College, there is no doubt he had access to copies of the philosopher's works if he wanted them – especially in a time when Kant was all the rage across Prussia, and had been published in Berlin.

That being said, there is an argument to be made which strongly suggests that Clausewitz had in fact read and understood Kant directly. Echevarria provides us with the right place to find it, by having noticed that the paragraph below, written by Clausewitz, was very similar to one penned by Kiesewetter: "Every educated person knows that a formal truth is the condition sine qua non of all truth and that it can only exist in the correct form ... By formal truth we mean the agreement of a concept with respect to the laws of thought logic. These laws are the same for all humanity; consequently, logical truth must also be the same for all humanity."[11]

Echevarria rightly argues that the similarities with Keisewetter's version of this are "too obvious to ignore,"[12] but if we step back and consider the original version of this idea, written by Kant in the *Logic*, there is no reason to believe that Clausewitz was paraphrasing Kiesewetter and not the original. In fact, the extra words in Clausewitz's version, which do not appear in the quote Echevarria uses from Kiesewetter's *Outline of Logic*,[13] render additional elements, including the "agreement of a

10 Aron, *Sur Clausewitz*, 44–5.

11 Echevarria, *Clausewitz and Contemporary War*, 22. Citing Clausewitz, "Ueber den Zustand der Theorie," in *Schriften-Aufsätze-Studien-Briefe*, 28, 34.

12 Echevarria, *Clausewitz and Contemporary War*, 22.

13 Ibid. Citing Kiesewetter, *Grundriss*, I, 110–11.

concept" and the concept of "universality" which is implied in Clausewitz's mention of "all humanity." These two extra points do appear in the passage from Kant to which both were referring.[14] It suggests, quite frankly, that Clausewitz understood the argument better – or at least summarized it better – than Kiesewetter had.

Aron acknowledges the fact that elements of Kant can be found in Clausewitz, but he minimizes them. Enumerating various examples, namely, reciprocity of action, synthetic/analytic knowledge, genius – all of which we shall discuss further below – he relegates these to something quite superficial, going so far as to say that Clausewitz, at best, could formulate phrases and expressions that "sounded Kantian."[15] Though it is a good start to find areas in Clausewitz that have a "family resemblance"[16] to Kant, as Fernández Vega does, there is much work that remains to be done to go beyond these similarities, and analyze how the whole of their use comes together into a far more systematized understanding and convergence with Kant's philosophy. Sounding is one thing, but what Clausewitz was doing was quite another. Granted, he did not integrate the whole of Kant systematically into his work, but this does not imply the reverse, that Clausewitz was not systematically and wholly Kantian in his own work. Clausewitz made good and proper use of those elements of Kantian thought that he needed, where he needed them, and at times this shows up in a superficial way, but that should not be construed as meaning a minor influence, let alone a complete lack of it. As we shall see, Clausewitz was very precise in his use of Kant. When he did refer to Kantian phrases and expressions, he used them in ways that were accurate, as we saw above, but more importantly, very well chosen and relevant, as we shall see below.

In exploring the Kantian elements in the works of Clausewitz, a frustrating element becomes increasingly apparent. On most occasions where Clausewitz borrows almost word for word from Kant, he does so in very limited and precise ways that apply to a specific item, and these examples can be easily identified because they are so clear and concise. However, as we shall explore later, in chapter 5, the larger Kantian influence, the one that underpins the intellectual and philosophical context of *On War*, cannot be found in one quote or another. It must be appreciated on the whole and this means in a somewhat abstracted way. It is impossible to merely distill this overarching framework. Rather, it must

14 Kant, *Logic*, 69.

15 Aron, *Penser la guerre, Tome I*, 368.

16 José Fernández Vega, "War as 'Art': Aesthetics and Politics in Clausewitz's Social Thinking," in Strachan and Heberg-Rothe, *Clausewitz in the Twenty-First Century*, 129.

be shown that *On War* converges methodologically with the *Critique of Pure Reason*. The minor examples serve to remind us of the links, but the true influence is more significant, albeit less tangible. It would be a rather pointless endeavour to pick out Kantian influences for its own sake, were it not framed within this larger question, because it is this approach to human understanding itself, the scope of what can be known to the human mind, that allows Clausewitz to refute the Enlightenment's positive doctrines with a system of scepticism.

THE NEW SCEPTICISM: FROM HUME TO KANT

If Hume delivered a serious blow to the works of Descartes and Berkeley, this was not achieved by applying a whole new system of analysis so much as by turning rationalism onto itself. He accepted the theory of ideas developed by Descartes, but "followed it to its logical conclusions, or, that is, to the point that he denied genuine knowledge, basic realities (for example, causes, a substantial self), and real values."[17] Hume undermined the conclusions of empiricism using its own argumentative techniques, salvaging the basis at the cost of the conclusions. He effectively brought the metaphysical debates of the past century to a discomforting standstill. On the one hand, certain features of empirical reasoning such as the origin of ideas and the distinctions between factual and relational knowledge were elevated and improved, but in exchange claims to absolute knowledge of the divine, of miracles, and of supernatural events were relegated to intellectual oblivion. However the complete effect was to instill in the empirical system a new form of scepticism that seemed impossible to remedy. The new scepticism found in Hume can be understood as having two widely accepted but divergent outcomes: "The first is to see Hume as having advanced a radical scepticism which devastated the very possibility of scientific knowledge. The other regards Hume as having introduced a healthy scepticism prompting philosophers and scientists to abandon the rash claims of modern rationalists and to embrace humbly the fact that non-trivial knowledge is after all only probable."[18]

Either way, reason was forced to engage in a discussion about itself, its scope and depth, from which certainty in the world of ideas would never remerge entirely. This introspection would begin with a categorization of all knowledge as belonging to one of two forms. Customarily referred

17 Norton, *David Hume*, 4. This represents an elaboration of comments first written by Thomas Reid in *The Works of Thomas Reid*, 2 vols, 7th edition, ed. William Hamilton (Edinburgh: MacLachlan and Stewart, 1872).

18 Butts, "Hume's Scepticism," 413.

to as "Hume's fork," his breakdown of human understanding generates two distinct types of knowledge: "relations of ideas" and "matters of fact." Here, he is proposing that one must separate human understanding into two mutually exclusive planes, and consider as inadmissible any form of knowledge that claims to exist outside of the two:

All the objects of human reason or enquiry may naturally be divided into two kinds, to wit, relations of ideas, and matters of fact. Of the first kind are the sciences of geometry, algebra, and arithmetic … Matters of fact, which are the second objects of human reason, are not ascertained in the same manner; nor is our evidence of their truth, however great, of a like nature with the foregoing. The contrary of every matter of fact is still possible, because it can never imply a contradiction, and is conceived by the mind with the same facility and distinctness, as if ever so conformable to reality.[19]

The significance of these two paragraphs is difficult to ascertain at first, but it marks a pivotal moment in philosophy, the beginning of modern dialectical reasoning, where an inherent contradiction serves as the basis upon which to explore the scope of human understanding. It is in direct opposition to the Cartesian tradition, where knowledge was understood as "global and unitary" in that "all cognizable objects are knowable in the same way and follow an order similar to that of the terms in a mathematical demonstration, the whole body of human knowledge is necessarily one."[20] Hume understood knowledge as having two separate and mutually exclusive realms, an approach which would find its finality in the works of Kant, where this seed is cultivated to its ultimate purpose, with the introduction of the synthetic/analytic division of knowledge, which was a derivative of this initial argument.[21] This, however, is a discussion to be had later when the text transitions to a discussion of Kant's philosophy.

For now, we must focus on how Hume cast doubt on the certitude of causality. Was Hume interested in the question, because he recognized that causality was at the central weakness of metaphysical exploration? Or did he stumble upon it in an attempt to save empiricism from itself? Either way, saving the empiricist doctrine regarding the origin of ideas had the unfortunate cost of discrediting our ordinary idea of causation.[22] The two were inherent to one another. In his *Enquiry Concerning Human*

19 Hume, *Enquiries*, 25.
20 Gilson and Langan, *History of Philosophy*, 58.
21 Rey, *Analytic/Synthetic Distinction.*
22 Langsam, "Ordinary Concept of Causation," 629.

Understanding, Hume was not seeking to challenge certainty outright, but rather to characterize certainty in knowledge, which required that he study the problems of evidence and justification.[23] Ultimately, this process uncovered that even the one thing that science took most for granted – and which was at the centre of not only its origin, but also each subsequent discovery – remained a limited concept, subject to scepticism. Causal effects could no longer be construed as the absolute manifestation of truth, and consequently could not serve as the methodological template upon which to edify the types of inferences that Berkeley and Descartes had made. Hume wrote:

> When we look about us towards external objects, and consider the operation of causes, we are never able, in a single instance, to discover any power or necessary connection; any quality, which binds the effect to the cause, and renders the one an infallible consequence of the other. We only find, that the one does actually, in fact, follow the other. The impulse of one billiard-ball is attended with motion in the second. This is the whole that appears to the outward senses. The mind feels no sentiment or inward impression from this succession of objects: consequently, there is not, in any single, particular instance of cause and effect, any thing which can suggest the idea of power or necessary connection.[24]

"The thrust of Hume's analysis was directed toward showing that our causal inferences are neither intuitive, nor demonstrable, nor based on perceptions of causal connections or rational inference from past experience."[25] In the end, he brought to light a firm doubt of necessary connections and therefore causality itself. His conclusions were extremely damaging not only to the Cogito itself, which posits a causal inference regarding thought and being, but also in the entire method that used it as a starting point for further inferences. Indeed, if we return to the paragraphs taken from Descartes and Berkeley above, we find further demonstrations that entirely depend on causality being free from any scepticism: god's existence is made evident as nothing more than a circular thought process based upon a set of inverse causal relations, where I think ergo I am, and since being and sentience are combined as causal, it becomes logical to induce the god's existence as merely I am ergo god thinks. Therefore, to doubt the experience of causality is no small matter, but forces scepticism upon the entire metaphysical project, not merely in its conclusions, but more importantly, at every point in the

23 Butts, "Hume's Scepticism," 414.
24 Hume, *Enquiries*, 63.
25 Norton, *David Hume*, 228.

method, from the inference of god as the *Causa Prima* of the universe at one end to the Cogito at the opposite end. Only one causal inference remains certain: if causality is no longer anointed with an immortal or supernatural certainty, then it appeared that certainty itself had died.

Clausewitz's scepticism, though it does not show itself to be in any particular way informed directly by Hume, nonetheless fits into to the tradition of thought bequeathed by Hume. This can be explained by the fact that Clausewitz's knowledge of Kant would have introduced him to the central argument of the *Critique of Pure Reason*, which is in fact to build upon, while also refuting Hume by using critical reasoning to bypass or rather go beyond this initial state of scepticism in causality. Kant's work was a transition from pure scepticism to sceptical method, but nonetheless served to engage directly with the problem of certainty and causality. In *On War*, Clausewitz positions himself clearly in this tradition of questioning causality, and eventually transitioning from pure scepticism to sceptical method as well. In this passage from Clausewitz's "Kritik," in Book II, he expresses scepticism with regard to causality in a way that places him squarely in the intellectual lineage of Hume and Kant:

> From the simple narration of an historical occurrence which places events in chronological order, or at most only touches on their more immediate causes ... As respects the tracing of effect to cause, that is often attended with the insuperable difficulty that the real causes are not known. In none of the relations of life does this so frequently happen as in War, where events are seldom fully known, and still less motives, as the latter have been, perhaps purposely, concealed by the chief actor, or have been of such a transient and accidental character that they have been lost for history. For this reason critical narration must generally proceed hand in hand with historical investigation, and still such a want of connection between cause and effect will often present itself, that it does not seem justifiable to consider effects as the necessary results of known causes.[26]

Even though he proposes that one can and should study causality in war, or at least attempt to do so through the many interfering layers of possible causes and effects, Clausewitz nonetheless ends the paragraph with a caveat: even if you have done this perfectly well, there should remain some doubt. The investigation does not lead to *necessity*, which means that on the subject of causality, its study, and its implications, Clausewitz clearly stands with Hume and Kant as opposed to their predecessors.

26 Clausewitz, *On War*, bk II, ch. 5, 100–1.

This scepticism regarding causes and effects leads Clausewitz to systematize his study in the form of a critique found in Book II. It is worth briefly mentioning here that the title of this section can be understood as an allusion to Kant, whose three major works were also titled as Critiques. This method was essentially Kant's remedy to the problem of uncertainty. In the *Critique of Pure Reason*, Kant explains this succinctly: "The dogmatical use of reason without criticism leads to groundless assertions, against which others equally specious can always be set, thus ending unavoidably in scepticism."[27] This sentence sums up exactly what Clausewitz tried to resolve in his own chapter entitled "Kritik."

In response to the uncertainty he found in studying causality in war, Clausewitz's solution was to make no claim to provide the soldier with absolute truths regarding what can be done in battle to guarantee victory. Instead, he offered a "limited theory" of war, one which replaced such laws, rules and principles, for adaptable concepts, designed to meet "the most probable cases"[28] instead of all cases, for all time and with absolute certainty. This limited approach would nonetheless allow him to generate a practical guidebook for the soldier, but without falling again into the antinomies of reason that were the product of positive doctrines.

PRELIMINARY FEATURES OF THE KANTIAN METHODOLOGY IN CLAUSEWITZ

The more we attempt to unearth the Kantian element in Clausewitz's works, the less we can draw simply on quotes and details that link the two. Instead, we must consider the larger picture regarding how one resolves problems of reason. And while in many cases the two overlap, which facilitates the exploration, there are some areas where the links are intellectual and not necessarily linguistic. This makes it slightly more difficult to demonstrate, but should not stop us in our tracks. For example, with regard to antinomies of reason, Clausewitz never in fact used the term "antinomy" in his writings at all, but he nonetheless exposed and analyzed the problem of antinomies in a Kantian way. Arguably, he probably chose to keep his language simple, because unlike Kant, his readers would not be philosophers, but practitioners.

In the *Critique of Pure Reason*, Kant uses the antimonies of pure reason to show that there are problems of reason that cannot be resolved without paradoxical conclusions. Using four distinct examples, he shows the

27 Kant, *Critique of Pure Reason* (George Bell & Sons), 14.

28 Clausewitz, *On War*, bk III, ch. 5, 143.

reader that certain mutually exclusive and opposite ideas are nonetheless equally demonstrable and valid in pure reason. In one of these, he makes the parallel argument that: a) the universe is finite in time and space, and b) the universe is infinite in time and space. Kant then proceeds to argue that both views are perfectly tenable and logical.[29] The relationship between these two ideas is that the validation of either one necessarily invalidates the other; it is impossible to prove both at once. Also, the invalidation of one does not necessarily validate the other, since the possibility that both are false remains. If it were demonstrated that the universe is not determinable, not a thing in itself but conditional and incomplete, then it could very well be neither finite nor infinite.[30] The effect of this sceptical form of thinking is that unlike Hume, who fell into blanket scepticism, here Kant explains that it leads rather to a useful sceptical method. Instead of being bogged down by scepticism regarding each proposition, we achieve a level of thinking about both propositions at once that offer us better intellectual guidance on the subject. "The transcendental dialectic, therefore, does not favour scepticism, but the sceptical method, which can point to the transcendental dialectic as an example of its great utility. For when we allow the arguments of reason to oppose one another with perfect freedom, something useful and serviceable for the correction of our judgement will always result, though it may not always be what we were looking for."[31]

Clausewitz mimics the argument when, having discussed what appears to be a series of contradictions and antinomies in the science of war, he asks whether when faced with the "uncertainty of all knowledge and all of science" it should not make "him doubt himself and others." But he eventually concludes like Kant that scepticism can be made *serviceable*:

When the discernment is clear and deep, none but general principles and views of action from a high standpoint can be the result; and on these principles the opinion in each particular case immediately under consideration lies, as it were, at anchor. But to keep to these results of bygone reflection in opposition to the stream of opinions and phenomena which the present brings with it is just the difficulty. Between the particular case and the principle there is often a wide space which cannot always be traversed on a visible chain of conclusions, and

29 Kant, *Critique of Pure Reason* (George Bell & Sons), 263–89.

30 Ibid., 310–16.

31 Kant, *Critique of Pure Reason* (Penguin), 447. I've used this translation because the word choice brings out a similar idea. To be clear, though, the two authors are not using the same term, but are making a similar argument with synonyms that mean "beneficial" or "serviceable." Clausewitz uses "wohltätig" whereas Kant is using "grossen Nutzens."

where a certain faith in self is necessary, and a certain amount of scepticism is serviceable.[32]

If Hume's *Enquiry* sought to salvage aspects of the empirical method at the expense of certainty we could say that Kant, in trying to repair the damages of Hume's scepticism, and to salvage at least our empirical knowledge of the natural sciences, was willing to expend elements of the empirical method towards that end, exchanging its linear and straight path to unmanageable certainty and scepticism, for a dialectical path that leads to manageable paradoxes. Thus, Kant wrote *Critique of Pure Reason* with two objectives in mind: first, positively, to defend the possibility of scientific and everyday knowledge (common sense), and second, negatively, to show that traditional metaphysics are impossible.[33]

To this end, Kant started the *Critique of Pure Reason* by developing a set of categories of knowledge based on two dichotomous pairs: the synthetic/analytic and the a priori/a posteriori, meant to include all possible forms of knowledge. With regard to the first of the two dichotomies, he explained: "Either the predicate B belongs to the subject A, as somewhat which is contained (though covertly) in the conception of A; or the predicate B lies completely out of the conception A, although it stands in connection with it. In the first instance, I term the judgement analytical, in the second, synthetical."[34] Kant provides the reader with two straightforward examples of these two categories of knowledge. With regard to analytical judgments, he cites the notion that "all bodies are extended" for the former, because extension is a feature inherent to the definition of a "body." A synthetic judgment, on the other hand, would be "this body is heavy," which cannot be inherently known, but which must connect the notion of body to that of gravity. The synthetical is in this sense relational – it is the combination of knowledge.

With regard to the a priori/a posteriori the former represents a knowledge that emerges as self-evident for having been thought, whereas the latter depends on a process such as experimenting.[35] When superimposed, these two dichotomies generate four quadrants. The analytic/a priori and the synthetic/a posteriori pose no problem, because we can easily conceive them. The analytic/a posteriori is nonsensical. This leaves the synthetic/a priori as the central problem of the inquiry. Kant

32 Clausewitz, *On War*, bk I, ch.3, 45.
33 Dicker, *Kant's Theory of Knowledge*, 6.
34 Kant, *Critique of Pure Reason*, 7.
35 Ibid., 7–8.

formulates his thesis question for the *Critique of Pure Reason* in the fewest terms: "How are a priori synthetic judgements possible?"[36]

Kant explains the nature of synthetical judgments a priori by referring to mathematical principles: while an equation does not require experimentation to prove, solving it is nonetheless a synthetic process because it requires intuition and the outcome is not self-evident, but is the coming together of two or more other concepts. Using the example 7 + 5 = 12, Kant explains that one cannot by analysis deduce that the number 12 is inherently the sum of 7 and 5. The same is true of various geometrical and physical principles. Whenever tested, these intuitive ideas become materially evident. And Kant adds that metaphysics are in the same category, because they are synthetic propositions (i.e. god is not inherent to the definition of the universe), but ones that cannot be tested because they "leave far behind us the limits of experience."[37]

Kant was unsatisfied with Hume's conclusion, arguing that Hume "stopped short at the synthetical proposition of the connection of an effect with its cause, insisting that such propositions a priori were impossible. According to his conclusion, then, all that we term metaphysical science is a mere delusion if that were the case there likewise could not be any pure mathematical science."[38] Kant's answer to Hume on this question is found most unambiguously in his Second Analogy,[39] in which he stood in "complete agreement with Hume that our knowledge of causal connections between specific events is a posteriori not a priori, synthetic, not analytic, inductive not logical, probable not certain … He agreed with Hume in disagreeing with the rationalists who thought that logical insight into causal connections was possible."[40] However, even though they agreed on this premise, Kant's conclusions were quite different.

Using his own terminology, Kant described the problem of causality as a synthetic proposition, which must be dealt with using a transcendental argument or one where the truth of the principle is a necessary condition of experience.[41] In answer to Hume's scepticism towards causality, Kant explained that the problem of cause and effect, its subjective validity as a universal idea, can be overcome with the objective validity it takes on when limited to the scope of what is observable. He states: "causality in the succession of phenomena is therefore valid for all objects of experience,

36 Ibid., 12.
37 Ibid., 9–12.
38 Ibid., 12.
39 Dicker, *Kant's Theory of Knowledge*, 163.
40 Beck, *Essays*, 134.
41 Dicker, *Kant's Theory of Knowledge*, 163.

because it is itself the ground of the possibility of experience."[42] The universal validity of causality in the material world or for experimentation comes from our ability to perceive alterations of the state of substance over time, and our ability to synthesize this, using our imagination, into a coherent "continuous determination of the position in time of all phenomena."[43]

What did this mean? Kant had set causality free from Hume's grip, insofar as it applied to certain areas of knowledge for which we could be satisfied with it as a process of imagination. But that also meant that for other areas we could not be satisfied, and that even when we were satisfied with it, this was not some holy certainty, but a mere human acceptance of it. Causality had lost not only its divinity, but also its universality: it had been forced into a compartment of human knowledge. This created a chasm between that area of knowledge where causality is admissible – as a result of being experienced, which allowed it to be intuitively demonstrable in the mind of man – and the plane of analysis where human intuition is excluded. Kant had effectively broken apart man's knowledge of the world from the world itself, the distinction between phenomena or how things appear to the human mind, and noumena, the things in themselves.[44] Within the a posteriori/synthetic category, Kant's approval of causality's validity in the context of the observational sciences rehabilitated natural sciences and mathematics from Hume's complete scepticism, but in doing so also cut the last standing leg of metaphysics. Now, the material world would become infused with a type of certainty, but its own self-contained certainty limited causality to the scope of that which is measurable and tangible the world of objects. The world of ideas could be isolated from this, thereby clarifying reason itself. In the end, both "reason" and "science" re-emerged from the Kantian process, but in the context of the two spheres: the ideal and the material, floating in a paradoxical stasis. This is the very same conceptual splice upon which Clausewitz would eventually build up his analysis of the ideal and real forms of war in his absolute war/real war dichotomy, which is the subject of chapter 5.

POSITIVE DOCTRINES IN WAR THEORY AS SYNTHETICAL JUDGMENTS A PRIORI

Clausewitz's objective was to invalidate strict formulas, models, and schematics, because he thought these blinded the judgment of officers and

42 Kant, *Critique of Pure Reason*, 150.
43 Ibid., 141–55.
44 Rohlf, "Immanuel Kant."

... them a false impression of the true difficulties of winning.[45] However, making this argument required that he go beyond his intuition that positive doctrines of Enlightenment military theory were flawed, and proceed to uncover the false logic that generated them. Luckily for him, Kant's *Critique of Pure Reason* had set the groundwork for such a task.

If Clausewitz never actually wrote, word for word, that *positive doctrines are synthetical judgments a priori,* he nonetheless constructed his arguments in ways that made this point for him. In fact, he went further than this. He took for granted that positive doctrines were equivalent concepts to metaphysical propositions, and his refutations did not innovate upon or improve Kant's system, but simply made use of it in direct refutation, as though the two forms of reasoning were not merely analogous, they were in fact congruous to one another, identical in form and logic. This form of analysis appears throughout *On War,* but it is systematized in Book II, chapter 5, entitled "Critique," which is fitting, since the very term critique in the Kantian tradition is a method by which to stop conditioned, empirical reason from constituting in and of itself the basis for universal principles[46] – which is in fact what Clausewitz is also trying to accomplish here.

A preliminary way to gauge this is to look at how either synthetical judgments a priori or positive doctrines are expressed in form and language. The only way to represent them as simple and fundamental truths is that they be compressed or contained in a way that conveys their universality in the simplest form (i.e. 7 + 5 = 12). Kant had in fact concluded that: "In all theoretical sciences of reason, synthetical judgements a-priori are contained as principles."[47]

Interestingly, Clausewitz makes the exact same observation with regard to positive doctrines: "Principles, rules, prescriptions, and methods (*Grundsätze, Regeln, Vorschriften, und Methoden*) are conceptions indispensable to a theory of the conduct of war in so far as the theory leads to positive doctrines, because in doctrines the truth can only crystallise itself in such forms."[48]

Beyond exposing the common form which they take, Clausewitz also intellectualized the problem of positive doctrines using the Kantian separation of categories in human understanding, as he attempted to clarify

45 Carrias, *La pensée militaire allemande,* 201.

46 Vaysse, *Le vocabulaire de Kant,* 87. Note: the author here is referring more specifically to principles as they apply to "will."

47 Kant, *Critique of Pure Reason,* 9. "In allen theoretischen Wissenschaften der Vernunft sind synthetische Urteile a priori als Prinzipien enthalten."

48 Clausewitz, *On War,* bk II, ch. 4, 95.

where and how exactly the inconsistency emerges in their claims, relative to the question scope of human understanding. Having already described them with blunt criticism as "useless," a "whirl of opinions, which neither revolved on any central pivot nor according to any appreciable laws, could not but be distasteful to people's minds," and finally as simply unable to "gain ascendency in the real world,"[49] Clausewitz goes on to demonstrate his objection to these in a more objective way: "All these attempts at theory are only to be considered in their analytical part as progress in the province of truth, but in their synthetical part, in their precepts and rules, they are quite unserviceable."[50]

Clausewitz not only borrows the synthetic/analytic divide from Kant's method, but he goes on to substantiate it by making a very clever merger between the arguments which Kant makes regarding what exactly makes knowledge "synthetical" in the first place. As we saw above, while analytical knowledge is inherent to the object itself, synthetic knowledge is a product of experience or observation of relations between objects. Kant makes use of three "analogies of experience" in order to show that there are some preconditions that exist in how we understand relations that allows us to achieve synthetic knowledge as a process. A process necessarily implies time, and so Kant presents to his reader three possible notions of time: permanence, sequence, and simultaneity, in which our concept of experiment and thus synthetic knowledge is different. In the first, he argues that to perceive change this must happen in relation to something that is permanent. So, if I can tell the difference between when my bicycle is dirty and when it is clean, it is also because I can recognize that both the dirty and the clean object before my eyes is the same, and that it is in fact still my bicycle, as opposed to a different one. The second analogy, briefly alluded to earlier in this chapter, deals with Hume's problem of establishing causation in the context of sequential events, and how through imagination, we may be satisfied with the validity offered by objects of experience. Finally, the third analogy considers the objects that coexist in time. Kant argues that for two objects to be perceived simultaneously by a single observer, they must be in relation of complete reciprocal action (*Wechselwirkung*) to each other.[51] This, for example, gives perceptual logic to the theory of gravity, as one observes how the sun and the planets interact in their orbits. Together, all three analogies complete the cognitive premises upon which we then edify our synthetical knowledge of the world, upon which we are sufficiently

49 Ibid., ch. 2, 73–5.
50 Ibid., 75.
51 Kant, *Critique of Pure Reason*, 156.

satisfied with the credibility of our observations as to build knowledge upwards and beyond mere analysis.[52]

Right after Clausewitz writes the above passage in which he claims that the positive doctrines are analytic, not synthetic, he goes on to explain in three reasons why that is the case, and unsurprisingly, these three reasons proceed in perfect order: the first with regard to substance and change over time, the second with regard to causality, the third, reciprocal action. What is very original, however, is that he uses this intellectual background as the base, but he applies it very concretely to the question of war. First, he writes that while Enlightenment theorists sought determinate quantities, they failed to see that *everything* in war is variable. Secondly, they forgot to consider the *actions and effects* of moral and intellectual factors in war. And finally, in the third, Clausewitz adds: "they only pay regard to activity on one side, whilst war is a constant state of reciprocal action (Wechselwirkung), the effects of which are mutual."[53] While these three different bases upon which synthetical knowledge is constructed are completely distinct and separate, because they exist on three different concepts of time, Clausewitz aptly makes the case that all three issues are relevant to our understanding of warfare and in every single one, the positive doctrines fail to show themselves as admissible as a synthetical knowledge. The passage is not a long one, nor does it show a very dense or thorough read of the three analogies, but it nonetheless fulfills its task – which again shows Clausewitz being pragmatic. He is interested in framing war with a Kantian structure, but he will not go so far as to swamp his reader with the full explication. Is this because Clausewitz himself had a limited understanding of Kant, or was it instead that he knew that those he identified as his target readers, military professionals might be lost if he did not keep it simple? Either way, he has taken his argument to its fullest effect, because having shown that positive doctrines do not achieve a synthetic outcome in any of the three possible forms that synthesis can take, he has cut the entire basis of their claim to being synthetical.

The positive doctrines are necessarily stuck in the analytical level because they fail to elevate themselves above at least one of the premises – substance, causality, and reciprocal action – in which they could ground themselves as synthetical. And as of the moment that they nonetheless try to present themselves as synthetical even though they are not, they are doomed to produce contradictions, tensions, and paradoxes. Clausewitz

52 Ibid., 132–6.

53 Clausewitz, *On War*, bk II, ch. 2, 75–6.

embraced this problem with principles of war and in fact would go so far as to demonstrate this paradoxical tension by bringing out similar examples in his own works. As W.B. Gallie explains:

> Clausewitz discusses a number of "principles of war," but it is notable that he nowhere tries to deduce these principles from any single source or to establish relations of logical priority and subsequence between them. Moreover, in this connection he displays a curious and at first sight irritating habit. He will lay down some principle which immediately commends itself to common sense, that of constancy in one's objective, or of the concentration or economy or security in the use of forces, for example; but he thereupon proceeds to show how some other principle of war commonly interferes with it, to modify or even cancel its authority in certain situations.[54]

Clausewitz generally avoids using the word "principle" altogether, though it regularly appears from cover to cover in the translations. In the above case, for example, Gallie uses the word "principle" because he is citing the Howard/Paret translation as his primary source,[55] in which the word "principle" is used in ways that are inconsistent.[56] The problem is that Clausewitz uses two distinct German words, *Prinzip* and *Grundsatz*, which can both be translated to "principle" but have distinct connotations that Clausewitz recognizes in his usage of them that the translators have missed. As we saw in chapter 2, the etymological difference is quite important. While Grundsatz is derived from earthly roots, meaning that something is firmly grounded, Prinzip is the true German translation for the word principle, derived from the concepts of primacy and power. The latter of the two has an absolute and abstract connotation, whereas the former is relative and tangible. Clausewitz uses the word Prinzip very scarcely. It comes up, for example, when he argues that war is not imbued with a "principle of moderation,"[57] or else when he speaks of the "principle of polarity" that exists between either the victor and the defeated or the different and opposite objectives in battle.[58]

54 Gallie, *Philosophers*, 44.

55 Ibid., Notes, 145.

56 Jan W. Honig has also shown other items on which the H/P translation is inconsistent in its use of terms, noting, for example, in the case of "Politik," that it was translated in to "politics," "policy," "statesmen," "statecraft," and "political conditions," and that the adjective "politische" is translated into a noun the five times it appears in conjunction with the words "Akt," "Handlungen," "Instrument," and "Werkzeug." See Honig, "Clausewitz's *On War*," 70.

57 Clausewitz, *On War*, bk II, ch. 2, 76.

58 Ibid., bk I, ch. 1, 2.

An example of where the translation problem becomes flagrant is the title of Clausewitz's second-most widely read book, *The Principles of War*,[59] which is a rendition of a textbook he had written while serving as the crown prince's tutor. The original German title of Clausewitz's book is *Die Wichtigsten Grundsätze des Kriegführens.* This title literally means "main grounding," and would be more properly translated as *The Fundamentals of War* because foundations are ground up, whereas principles are top down. The problem also appears in the Howard/Paret translation of *On War*, where they make absolutely no distinction between Grundsatz and Prinzip. A good example of this can be observed by comparing the Graham and Howard/Paret translations in Book IV, chapter 13, where Prinzip occurs once and Grundsatz occurs five times. The Howard/Paret translation uses the word "principle" for each "Grundsatz," and simply omits the word "Prinzip" altogether from the sentence in which it is written. Meanwhile, perhaps even more confusingly, Graham generally translates Grundsatz to "maxim," which is a far more accurate word choice – but it is not always consistent. He does so for four of the five occurrences in Book IV, chapter 13, and also uses the word "principle" appropriately in the case of Prinzip. However, he then goes on to use the word "principle" for one of the Grundsatz occurrences, which completely muddles the lot. In reality, Clausewitz saw an important difference between the two terms and he never used them interchangeably: Grundsatz is what a soldier may use to frame his decisions on the battlefield; Prinzip is for the higher conceptual sphere. The former has many examples, the latter is rarely used, and neither implies certainty in the link between the conceptual and the practical.

To return to Gallie's point, these oppositions and contradictions are the very centre of Clausewitz's contention with regard to positive doctrines. In the same way that Kant used a discussion of the antinomies of reason to outline the structure of human understanding, so too did Clausewitz need to build up antinomies regarding the inherent contradiction regarding any single Grundsatz, in order to make evident the problems of reason one finds in positive doctrines. Clausewitz, enacting what Gallie subsequently described as an "irritating habit," was in fact building a *serviceable* system of scepticism – as opposed to falling simply into the sterility of pure scepticism. This is the role of dialectical reasoning, through which one does not get bogged down by contradictions, but elevates understanding from a false sense of absolute certainty to a set of true paradoxes.

59 Clausewitz, *Principles of War.*

Clausewitz's conclusion on positive doctrines was categorical: what leads a generally good maxim in the field to become a false principle when elevated to that level is the intellectual "emptiness" that separates the two, the very process of attempting to transition from the analytical to the synthetical. His best demonstration of this can be found in his discussion of "key points," which among Enlightenment theorists were thought to convey absolute advantages, so much so that they were in fact referred to as "decisive points." While Clausewitz recognized that high terrain can be tactically beneficial, he refused to assume that high terrain is necessarily beneficial, or that even when it happens to be beneficial it should be taken to mean that this factor will be *decisive*:

Thus the highest point on a road over a mountain is always considered to possess a decisive importance, and it does in fact in the majority of cases, but by no means in all. Such points are very often described in the despatches of generals by the name of key-points; but certainly again in a somewhat different and generally in a more restricted sense. This idea has been the starting point of a false theory (of which, perhaps, Lloyd may be regarded as the founder); and on this account, elevated points from which several roads descend into the adjacent country, came to be regarded as the keypoints of the country – as points which command the country.[60]

Earlier in *On War*, in the concluding remarks to Book V, Clausewitz had already made the argument regarding the absolute strategic value of terrain, in which he brings forward an important discussion of the "emptiness" or "hollowness" of their meaning, which again, as we shall soon observe, resonates with ideas that Kant described. Clausewitz wrote:

But nevertheless the expressions "commanding ground," "sheltering position," "key of the country," in so far as they are founded on the nature of heights and descents, are hollow shells without any sound kernel. These imposing elements of theory have been chiefly resorted to in order to give a flavour to the seeming commonplace of military combinations; they have become the darling themes of learned soldiers, the magical wands of adepts in strategy, and neither the emptiness of these fanciful conceits … they are drawing water in the leaky vessel of the Danaides. The conditions have been mistaken for the thing itself, the instrument for the hand. The occupation of such and such a position or space of ground, has been looked upon as an exercise of power like a thrust or a cut … is nothing

60 Clausewitz, *On War*, bk VI, ch. 23, 490–1.

but the lifeless instrument, a mere property which can only realise itself upon an object, a mere sign of plus or minus which wants the figures or quantities.[61]

In this paragraph, he shows once and for all just how well versed he is in fact in the works of Kant. The argument is taken from a short, lesser-known text that Kant wrote in the final years of life,[62] specifically chapter 3 and the appendix of *What Real Progress Has Been Made by Metaphysics in Germany since the Time of Leibniz and Wolff?* That work was a clarification of the subject of noumena (thing in itself) and phenomena (thing as it appears) in his earlier and far more widely read *Critique of Pure Reason.* Clausewitz not only drew from the main argument of *Real Progress,* he also borrowed – candidly – the exact same analogy that Kant used with regard to the Danaïdes from Greek mythology. Kant explains that metaphysics is stuck in either theoretical or practical dogmatism, but nonetheless gives the illusion of being demonstrable thanks to the antinomies of pure reason, which it creates. The impression of truth that we perceive when presented with antinomian arguments is an illusion. Truth is not in fact demonstrated in itself, but merely assumed on the grounds that its opposite has been shown to be false. It is not unconditional knowledge, but merely the sum of all coordinated conditions, where the antinomy of pure reason results in the confusion between the apparent and the thing itself. And it is this very dialectic that shapes the invitation to pass from reasoning regarding the sensible (material things) to the super-sensible (immaterial things).[63] Having earlier written that "materialism can never be employed as a principle for explaining the nature of our soul,"[64] Kant adds: "It was a vain labor that it traditionally gave itself, to reach the super-sensible by way of speculation and theoretical knowledge, and thus that science became the leaking sieve of the Danaïdes."[65] There is an illusion of progress, of arriving at the goal, but it is only achieved through trickery of the mind, where abstract conceptualizing cannot be rendered intuitive, because it is not positively demonstrable, but only to be deduced by the deceptions of contradiction and double negatives.

61 Ibid., bk V, ch. 18, 353–4.

62 This discovery adds to José Fernández Vega's observation that Clausewitz made much use of Kant's "later philosophy," including elements from the *Critique of Judgement.* See "War as 'Art,'" 122. It is worth noting that in this text, I do not spend much time referring to the *Critique of Judgement,* because I consider that much of the work has already been done by others including Fernández. Also, to understand the methodological rather than the substantive similarities, I perceive the *Critique of Pure Reason* as a better tool for this specific task.

63 Kant, *Theoretical Philosophy after 1781,* 397.

64 Ibid., 395.

65 Ibid., 396.

In fact we learn in the *Critique of Pure Reason* that "the effort to acquire metaphysical knowledge through concepts alone, however, is doomed to fail, according to Kant, because (in its simplest formulation) 'concepts without intuitions are empty.' (A52/B76)"[66] Kant is not only interested in showing that the metaphysical arguments are fallacious, he is also trying to unearth where their illusion of validity comes from. And this comes down to a concept that Clausewitz is referring to in the paragraph above, the distinction between what is conditioned and unconditioned, or the conflation between noumena (the unconditioned thing in itself) and phenomena (the conditioned thing, as it appears). The "supreme principle of pure reason" that provides the background assumption under which the metaphysician proceeds, is that "If the conditioned is given, the absolutely unconditioned … is also given. (A308/B366)" That is to say that, the decision or justification for *seeking* the unconditioned offers a metaphysical principle that tells us that the unconditioned is *already given* – it is there to be found.[67]

This is the crux of the case. Clausewitz could use the metaphysical arguments against the Enlightenment war theorists precisely because of the three layers of analysis we have here exposed. First, the principles of war were assumed to exist prior even to being sought out, let alone found. Secondly, antinomies of pure reason were the source of the illogical formulations at the heart of positive doctrines. That is, one could argue for and/or against virtually any positive doctrine, which reinforced the expectation that positive doctrines did in fact exist: i.e. *why else would we be arguing about them?* But that meant that every inch we got closer to them, they seemed to slip one or two more inches away. And finally, as this last quote from Clausewitz reminded us, when he speaks of the hand versus the tool, the material examples theorists referred to were merely conditions, the context of a demonstration, but not the demonstration itself, or the demonstration of an unconditional truth. If each element of certainty was indeed fixed to a single event in which it produced an outcome, then there was in fact nothing absolute or universal to it. It was this realization that allowed Clausewitz to pinpoint the role of critical judgment, and its only objective measure, *victory in battle*, as opposed to some peripheral object or quantity.[68]

To achieve this conclusion, Clausewitz had to peer into the problem through the lens of dialectical reasoning. He had to uncover the antinomies of pure reason – and thereby perceive the positive doctrines as mere replicas of metaphysical speculation – to know that pursuing the

66 Grier, "Kant's Critique of Metaphysics."

67 Ibid.

68 Clausewitz, *On War*, bk VI, ch. 30, 354.

Kantian argument against their perceived validity would work. Otherwise, these quotes he uses from Kant would all appear vague and out of context. In fact they are extremely well used, and uncover the central weakness of Enlightenment thinking as well as how this weakness found its ways into the works of military writers.

By asking the question "what kind of sceptic was Clausewitz?" we find that his way of thinking follows the path cleared by Hume and Kant, especially as it pertains to the link between causal relationships and certainty. In his refutations of the positive doctrines, Clausewitz shows a very significant indebtedness to Kant, especially to the *Critique of Pure Reason*. He was not merely "sounding Kantian," he was applying the method in clear and logical way, which had a demonstrable effect on the power of his refutation. Clausewitz was not countering any single positive doctrine, he was demonstrating why their contradictory nature made them inescapably invalid. And this he achieved by referencing various ideas and demonstrations found in Kant's major works, as well as minor works.

This process depended on dialectical thinking. Clausewitz's appreciation of Kant allowed him to perceive, though he did not state it clearly, that the contradictions that existed between different sets of equally valid positive doctrines – albeit valid only in certain contexts – formed antinomies of reason, which Kant's *sceptical method* could uncover and discredit. If, as we saw above, these antinomies were caused by a surplus, rather than by a lack, of material proof, they nonetheless operated according to an identical form of logic, expectation, and validation, built not only on the premise of their assumed existence, but also further encouraged by the very quest for them, which generated arguments and analyses in which the principles were in fact residing. The principles existed only in these debates, and that is why they appeared so real to those who were busy arguing for and against each of their many forms.

We should recall, however, what was said regarding the dialectic in this book's introduction: it is not a single method or concept, but rather implies various meaning clusters. This is also true in Clausewitz's work, and is best exemplified not in any single case but in his overall comfort with divisions, contradictions, and paradoxes, which he did not shun but actually elevated. In his refutation of the positive doctrines, Clausewitz did use a variety of different dialectical tools. He brought forward the analytic/synthetic division of knowledge; he exposed the antinomies of reason in contradicting positive doctrines; he distinguished noumena from phenomena and the conditioned from the unconditioned. In all of these, he was showing that he could be *reasonable about science, because he was making use of a science of reason*, built on dialectics and scepticism.

4

The Decay and Resilience of Positive Doctrines from Jomini to the Twentieth Century

WE ENTER NOW A SECTION of the text where the purpose is to study the opposite of our topic, in order to shed more light on the topic itself. Clausewitz demonstrated very credibly that positive doctrines were not theoretically or practically sound, and yet years after this argument was made many nonetheless continued to hold on to – and publish – their own positive doctrines. Was Clausewitz wrong? By exploring how those who held on to positive doctrines did so by committing themselves to deep forms of illogic, we can uncover in a very clear and crisp way just how right Clausewitz had been to begin with.

In fact, Clausewitz's refutation of the positive doctrines was so successful that it converted even the master of positive doctrines, Jomini, albeit kicking and screaming, until his new writings were mere shadows of his previous work. And Clausewitz's method did even more than that: it created a way of thinking about war that showcases to what extent those who refuse to let go of positive doctrines, even today, fall into a whirlwind of circular logic and a *reductio ad absurdum* way of thinking that is self-defeating. Given how bad logic has such a broad uptake in some of the most well-read and appreciated textbooks, it is perhaps not too surprising that positive doctrines did so well after they had been so effectively refuted, because it seems that those who read and write such books want to believe in them: they want principles to exist at the intersection of their debates, because it justifies their work, at least in their own eyes.

This chapter comes down to two geometrical ideas: the angles 180° and 360°. The effect of dialectics on war theory's positive doctrines is analogous to what physicists call "torque," the moment of force which sets an object into rotation. Whereas Jomini's discovery of Clausewitz forced him to "pull a 180" and effectively renege on almost everything he had once proclaimed in earlier works, later war theorists accumulated so much spin that they found themselves caught in a hopeless circular logic that descended into *reductio ad absurdum* illogic.

Despite this, not only did the positive doctrines not fade away immediately and entirely, they came back in force. Though intellectually these were moribund, practitioners had apparently not received the memo. By the twentieth century, instead of fading out, they continued to progress, albeit in an increasingly simplified and tight list consisting of mainly offence, manoeuvre, concentration, economy of force, liberty of action, certainty, and initiative.[1] Unaware of the irony of their quest, theorists were in fact attempting to salvage the idea of "principles of war," by applying these very principles onto themselves: concentrate them, make an economy of them, etc. These attempts to codify the non-codifiable had ended up completing a full circle. And Coutau-Bégaries compares it to a larger problem that affects scientific argumentation, where we "transform that which we are attempting to explain into a principle of explanation."[2]

SWAYING JOMINI

Jomini was the last true enlightenment war theorist. His theories were "characterized by a highly didactic and prescriptive approach, conveyed in an extensive geometric vocabulary of strategic lines, bases, and key points."[3] Scattered graphics, charts, and maps were regularly used in his writings to "demonstrate" and "prove" various maxims, principles, and positive doctrines. Yet, despite his techniques and argumentative approach, which were of an earlier time, when we compare Jomini's first books to his later works, it becomes evident that something dramatic changed.

It is necessary to be categorical with regard to the argument made by various scholars suggesting that Clausewitz and Jomini were more often in agreement than not.[4] This is not by any means universally true. It is a consequence of Jomini having read Clausewitz. The foremost proponent of this view, Handel, only came to this conclusion because he was citing exclusively from Jomini's *Précis sur l'art de la guerre*,[5] Jomini's last major work, and not from his early works such as the *Traité*, published decades

1 Dominique Terré, *Les dérives de l'argument scientifique* (Paris: Presses universitaires de France, Paris), 287, cited by Coutau-Bégarie, *Traité de stratégie*, 280.

2 Coutau-Bégarie, *Traité de stratégie*, 280. My translation.

3 Bassford, *Clausewitz and Jomini.*

4 Ibid.

5 See Handel, *Masters of War*, 74, 122, 126,127, 249, 370, 373.

earlier. This is significant, because Jomini before and after Clauswitz is clearly a different war theorist. When scholars claim that Jomini and Clausewitz think alike, they must absolutely distinguish between the young and the old Jomini in order to clarify their stance because the similarities appear only in Jomini's later works, as a result of a significant turnaround in his point of view.

In the *Précis*, for example, Jomini suddenly accords more importance to the moral and political factors of war, going so far as to make them the opening sequence of his book. Prior to reading Clausewitz, he had never placed any discussion of these matters so prominently. More dramatically still, his views and ideas about the "principles of war," which were the heart of his systems, were fully warped in the process. For example, we know that in a late reprint of the *Traité*, Jomini "dropped his insistence on interior lines, acknowledging à la Clausewitz – though without actually mentioning it – that the value of interior or concentric lines depended on the situation."[6] Colson has argued that maturity alone can explain how Jomini's ideas evolved from more extreme to more moderate. "The later Précis is an attempt to distil what can be learned from the Napoleonic Wars into considerations marked with a will to return to a more prudent strategy, where the objective is to occupy territory rather than destroying the enemy's army … The earlier Treatise reflected his admiration for Napoleon, Jomini arrived at a more methodical and territorial conception of strategy … Having matured with age and witnessed the changing times, Jomini now opted for prudence and moderation."[7]

The maturity argument does not account for what is altogether new – such sudden insistence on moral and political factors – nor does it account for the severity of differences with regard to the positive doctrines found in the *Traité de la grande tactique*, written in 1802–07, and the lack of them in his later treatise *Précis de l'art de la guerre*, written in 1838. The younger Jomini believed in the perfectibility of war theory, whereas later he would backtrack and attempt to fortify a few of his most cherished principles at the cost of sacrificing many others he had once claimed.

Gauging where and how Jomini changed his arguments around over time is quite a difficult task, given that he was re-editing his old works, republishing them, and not making any mention, footnote, or explanation with regard to what these corrections were and where in fact he was making them. It is a puzzle. That being said, one can nonetheless get a

6 This is the case in an 1865 version of the *Traité*, translated by Holabird (New York: Nostrand, 1865). Noted in Bassford, *Clausewitz and Jomini.*

7 Colson, "Présentation," 21.

partial picture by looking at passages from a relatively early print of the *Traité* and the much later *Précis*. The distinction is evident:

1 (Traité de la grande tactique, 1805) L'idée de réduire le système de la guerre à une combinaison primitive dont toutes les autres dépendent, et qui ferait la base d'une théorie juste et simple, présente une foule d'avantages; elle rendrait l'instruction bien plus facile, le jugement des opérations toujours sain, et dès-lors les fautes moins fréquentes. Je crois que les généraux ne sauraient assez s'en pénétrer; qu'elle devrait diriger tous leurs projets, toutes leurs actions.[8]

The idea of reducing systems of war into its primary combinations on which all others depend, and which would establish as a base an exact and simple theory, presents numerous advantages; it would improve instruction, improve judgments during operations, and consequently, lower the frequency of errors. I think generals could not make enough use of learning and applying it, that it should guide all their projects, all their actions.

2 (Précis de l'art de la guerre, 1838) Et si l'on rassemblait, sous la présidence de l'archiduc Charles ou de Wellington, un comité composé de toutes les notabilités stratégiques et tactiques du siècle, avec les habiles généraux du génie et de l'artillerie, ce comité ne parviendrait pas encore à faire une théorie parfaite, absolue et immuable, sur toutes les parties de la guerre, notamment sur la tactique!! [*sic*].[9]

Even if we were to form a committee, presided by the Archduke Charles or by Wellington, composed of all the notable strategists and tacticians of the century, with the most competent generals of engineering and artillery, this committee would still not achieve a perfect, absolute, and immutable theory on the different aspects of war including tactics!!

We might expect that maturity would cause one to perfect one's argument, clarify its structure, enhance its demonstration, and perhaps make minor adjustments or concessions. What we see here is nothing of the sort, but rather a 180-degree turn-around in perspective. How did this change come about? Colson gives us two hints. Longevity had much to do with it, as well as the "changing times" that he mentions in the above quote. Jomini lived to the ripe age of ninety, which allowed his writing career to both precede and outlive Clausewitz's. While Clausewitz

8 Jomini, *Traité de la grande tactique*, 536.
9 Jomini, *Précis de l'art de la guerre* (Anselin), 33.

was surrounded by new methods of dialectical reasoning simply due to being at the right place at the right time – the academic circles of Germany at the turn of the century – Jomini did not experience the radical change in how metaphysics had altered the way perfectibility and immutability of concepts should be conceived. In fact, it is said that Jomini was not particularly well-read beyond military textbooks. He would have been somewhat familiar with Montesquieu, and he had read Puységur, Lloyd, and Guibert in great detail, but he was unfamiliar with philosophy in general, and even less so with the current movements.[10]

As such, the method of reasoning he discovered in *On War* must have been quite shocking, perhaps even overwhelming. He was in fact "deeply wounded"[11] by what he discovered. These feelings are easily detected in his writing style, which breaks away from his typical didactical style, suddenly emboldened with anger and awe directed at Clausewitz. Seeming to accept that his earlier ideas now stood on wobbly grounds, Jomini began seeking out ways to reinforce key points, while delimiting or deleting others. That he began writing the *Précis* immediately after having come across Clausewitz should not come as a surprise. He had been personally attacked in it, and his reaction was clearly embittered. Within single paragraphs in which he discussed *On War*, he integrated a melodramatic and frantic mishmash of praise, insults, and hints that he hoped to find reconciliation with the work of Clausewitz, even though these three goals were thoroughly contradictory. He described Clausewitz and *On War* within a wide spectrum of qualifiers: "luminous ideas," "greatly instructed," "well written," "vagabond," "pretentious," "savant labyrinth," "sophism," "frequently logically faulty," etc.[12] Uncertain of where he stood on Clausewitz, Jomini nonetheless wanted to protect his own works and arguments from this new theory, and tried to fix his ideas in reaction to Clausewitz. Pretentious to the finish, Jomini wrote in this new book that if only Clausewitz had lived long enough to read the *Précis*, he would have "accorded it some justice."[13] Jomini offered some mild refutations regarding Clausewitz's stance that positive doctrines were invalid, but he did not try to undo the latter's argument as a whole, probably because he recognized it not as an entire truth, but at least a partial truth. Jomini ultimately turned his back on his old influences, Bülow and Lloyd. In the *Précis*, Jomini recalls the fact that these two authors had been so formative and important to his view regarding war that after reading them for

10 Langendorf, *Faire la guerre*, 77–90.
11 Bassford, *Jomini and Clausewitz*.
12 Jomini, *Précis de l'art de la guerre* (Perrin), 9, 126, 137.
13 Ibid., 21.

the first time, in his youth, he thereafter burned all his previous essays, to start anew.[14] Yet many years later, after reading Clausewitz, his exaltation suddenly wavered and he started distancing himself from the two. Indeed, in the same chapter of the *Précis* where he recalls this story of his youth, he also writes that Bülow and Lloyd had in fact only produced a few minor interesting elements, surrounded by dogmatic and wrong ideas. With regard to the latter, Jomini wrote: "Lloyd raised interesting questions about strategy, which he unfortunately buried in a maze of minute details on tactics and formations, and on the philosophy of war. While the author resolved none of these questions in a way that could provide a system, we can at least say that he would point us in the right direction to take. The way he relates the Seven Years' War, of which he only completed two campaigns, was more instructive (to me at least) than all his dogmatic writings."[15]

As to the former, Bülow, Jomini also found new and tough words for him, stating that "he builds upon an inexact foundation, and his works thus necessarily contained at times erroneous maxims."[16] Clearly we find that if Jomini had in fact "matured," this had little to do with age and much more to do with method and renunciation. Jomini had turned his back on the works that marked his youthful optimism in the power of scientific methods in war. In fact, by the end of the transition, Langendorf notes that Jomini not only "attenuated his views,"[17] he also "no longer proposed absolute rules."[18] The turnaround was complete.

FUNDAMENTAL PRINCIPLES

The most dramatic aspect of Jomini's 180° is his transition with regard to principles and fundamental principles. Whereas the *Traité* had a number of them scattered throughout, only a selected few remained in the *Précis*. The concentration of principles after Clausewitz therefore happened first in Jomini, but it is a strategy that would be repeated well into the twentieth century, as we shall see further below.

The idea that war had a plural set of "fundamental principles" was first written in the *Traité*: "The Fundamental principles upon which rest all good combinations of war have always existed ... These principles are unchangeable; they are independent of the nature of the arms employed,

14 Jomini, *Précis de l'art de la guerre* (J.B. Petit), 8.
15 Ibid., 6.
16 Ibid., 79.
17 Langendorf, *Faire la guerre*, 290.
18 Ibid., 88.

of times and places ... For thirty centuries there have lived generals who have been more or less happy in their application ... While comparing the causes of the victories of ancient and modern times, we are greatly surprised to discover that the battles of Wagram, Pharsalia and Cannae were gained from the same original cause."[19]

When he wrote the *Précis* he did not forget entirely the concept of fundamental principles, but he might have suffered from partial amnesia. Suddenly, the indeterminate number of fundamental principles had been qualified to being "few" and further along, a single overarching fundamental principle of operations would tower above all others. Jomini was trying to recoil to safer argumentative grounds by pruning so many branches of his tree that he found himself with a sapling: "I agree that the absolute rules are few ... I concur in good faith with this truth, but should this mean that there can be no theory? If out of forty-five articles, one has ten positive maxims, the other has one or two, is it not enough to have 150 to 200 rules to form a respectable body of strategic or tactical doctrine? And if you add to this the multitude of precepts that have occasional exceptions, would you not have more dogmas than necessary to fix your opinions on all the operations of war?"[20] A few pages later, Jomini adds: "My 20 years of experience, have fortified my conviction of the following: There exist a small number of fundamental principles in the art of war, which one could avoid only at his own peril, and quite to the contrary, application of these principles have practically always been crowned with success."[21]

Among the remaining true fundamental principles, Jomini held on to the existence of one single "fundamental principle of all operations in war."[22] This fundamental principle consisted essentially of "bringing forth, through strategic combinations, the bulk of the forces of an army, successively upon decisive points in a theatre of war ... and manoeuvring against fractions of the enemy army."[23] Jomini concedes that the difficult part, of course, is to identify the "decisive points" that he relegates to genius in war, or in this particular case, the "art." As he writes later in this subsection: "It will be up to the talent in execution, the know-how, the energy, the *coup-d'oeil,* to complete that which good combinations will have prepared."[24] And finally, as an extra fortification around his

19 Jomini, *Treatise of Grand Tactics,* 445.
20 Jomini, *Précis de l'art de la guerre* (Perrin), 22.
21 Ibid., 26–7
22 Ibid., 157.
23 Ibid., 158.
24 Ibid., 161.

principles, Jomini will gladly point to "exceptions" to various rules on six different occasions.[25]

Though Clausewitz also speaks of key points in his works, he delimits their pretensions very clearly, then submits his analyses to critique and at no moment does he make any claim to provide fundamental principles. For this reason alone – lack not only of critique but even the possibility of critiquing – one might be tempted to dismiss Jomini's argument above for having no proper theoretical test for its validity. Nevertheless there are a few examples from the Napoleonic Wars that we can turn to in order to isolate both of these variables at once, and demonstrate that not only was the one, single fundamental principle sophistical, it was in fact demonstrably wrong.

In fact, Jomini himself provides us with the very elements required to proceed to isolate the principle of "decisive points" for empirical testing. Two examples appear in Jomini's *Précis*: the first, individual commanders whose coup d'oeil and genius are unquestionable: Caesar, Frederick the Great, and Napoleon;[26] and secondly, the question of state capitals, where Jomini writes: "All state capitals, since they are at the centre of a country's roads, would be decisive, strategic points, not only for this reason, but also for statistical and political motives, which add to this importance." Hence, in certain cases, we can indeed find ourselves dealing with the principle itself, denuded of its expectations regarding genius and the nature of a "decisive point." In Jomini's own words, the capital is necessarily decisive, and Napoleon is necessarily a genius. Thus the objective principle itself is separated, isolated from its subjective components.

Clearly, the capture of Moscow is as damning a counter-argument as there can be. It did not prove to be a decisive event: it did not force political capitulation, nor did it break the enemy's base, communications, or reinforcements. In fact it precipitated the deterioration of France's imperial power. Taking the capital became a decisive point of defeat rather than victory. Jomini, who was there at the time when it happened, may have considered Moscow as an exception to the rules – but one cannot have it both ways, either a fundamental principle is universal or else there is nothing fundamental about it.

JOMINI'S GENIUS

Jomini mastered like none other the "genius" sophistry, a tenuous and circular argument that went as follows: absolute rules exist, but to know

25 Jomini, *Précis sur l'art de la guerre* (J.B. Petit), 36, 53, 72, 92, 114, 272.
26 Jomini, *Précis sur l'art de la guerre* (Perrin), 12–13.

how to make use of such absolute rules takes genius, and a genius is one who does not act contrary to these rules. The problem, however, is that if the rule is indeed so absolute, then it should be equally applicable regardless of genius. As it stood in Jomini's work, "genius" played the role we saw above, as the ultimate theoretical stopgap for safeguarding absolute principles that were inherently flawed. Instead of admitting a flaw in the theory, one could usually always shift blame away from the theory by striking at the artist or the tactician as opposed to the art or the tactic. The formulation Jomini makes of it is carefully constructed to even further enhance the sophistical relationship between genius and the principles of war: "Genius has a great deal to do with success, since it presides over the application of recognized rules, and seizes, as it were, all the subtle shades of which their application is susceptible. But in any case, the man of genius does not act contrary to these rules."[27]

There are many highly confounding problems with the above statement, as it places genius both above the rules, presiding over them, yet also implies that one should submit to them. So which is it? How is a rule supposed to be on the one hand binding and formal, while on the other hand remain variable so that it can be interpreted differently according to context? One may be tempted to see in this great erudition even a taste of dialectical complexity, but it is nothing of the sort. The double set of contradictory statements has no objective to improve our knowledge of either genius or principles, but only to muddle them enough to make any situation fit. Set up this way, the two contradictory statements are scientifically insignificant; they are a trap for rationality, whereby any action or decision can be the product of genius or principle, because if it fails, we can blame lack of genius, and if it succeeds one can claim either principle, genius, or both. In all circumstances, we salvage the idea of principles, at the expense of the reputation of defeated generals. It does not resolve the problem: we are stuck asking ourselves if there can indeed be genius if that simply means following the rules. And an opposite problem also surfaces: is there such thing as a principle if genius can rise above it?

Clausewitz again borrowed from Kant for a logical solution to this intellectual impasse. To begin with, the fact that he employed the term Grundsatz rather than Prinzip with regard to best practices in the battlefield allowed him more flexibility with his use of the concept of "genius," because he was not seeking certainty, and that meant his theory could more easily accommodate situations that did not follow certain lessons of best practices that may have helped contribute to victory in another

27 Ibid. Citing Jomini, *Treatise of Grand Tactics*, 253–4.

context. By referring to Kant, Clausewitz found a way for both genius and "Grundsätze" to coexist logically in all situations, which is the opposite of how Jomini set himself up: whenever genius and principles were both logical, it was because the context had allowed them both to be right concurrently, which means on the victorious side of a war.

Clausewitz's analysis of genius is taken straight out of the *Critique of Judgement.*[28] He used it very early in his life in the anonymous article he published in *Neue Bellona,* while studying under Kiesewetter. Far from showing a "homeopathic" understanding of Kant, Clausewitz aptly used this concept of "genius" in refuting Bülow's geometric "rules" of war. Clausewitz objected to Bülow's conception of "art" on the grounds that it did not state a "goal," which is an important aspect of Kant's concept of art as "the use of given means to achieve a higher end."[29] Paret explains, "Clausewitz's teacher Kiesewetter chose familiar terminology when he defined genius as the union of imagination and reason, brought to life by spirit. Clausewitz adopted this definition, adding moral and physical courage to imagination and reason to characterize military genius."[30] Clausewitz had learned an idea written by Kant in the *Critique of Judgement*: that "genius is the talent (natural ability) that establishes rules for the arts. Since this talent, as an innate creative ability of the artist, is itself part of nature, we might also express ourselves in this manner: Genius is the innate psychological power (ingenium) through which nature establishes rules for the arts."[31]

As long as war theory avoided absolute principles and complete positive doctrines, it could entertain and accommodate the notion of "genius" in war. From maxims and examples of what succeeded in the past, the general could gauge the right course of action in battle. However, this relationship between "genius" and "principles" would become increasingly contradictory as theorists elaborated "perfect" principles of war, which by virtue of their formulation necessarily excluded the role of talent and art; yet, no theorist was actually willing to give up the role of genius and leadership altogether, creating an awkward relationship between the two, essentially downgrading "talent" to the ability to follow the principles well, or alternatively, the ability to "rise above" the principles. Either of these breaks the relation, since the former eliminates

28 Gat, *Origins of Military Thought,* 175.

29 Immanuel Kant, *Critique of Judgement,* trans. *James Meredith* (Oxford: Oxford University Press, 1961), 168. Cited in Gat, *Origins of Military Thought,* 175.

30 J.G.C. Kiesewetter, *Immanuel Kants Critik der Urtheilskraft für Uneingeweite* (Berlin: W. Oehmigke, 1804) and Clausewitz, *On War,* trans. Howard and Paret, 130–4, cited in Paret, *Clausewitz and the State,* 161.

31 Ibid. Citing Kant, *Critique of Judgement.*

genius in trying to save it, and the latter undermines the perfectibility of principles, which was the initial purpose.

Jomini's sophistry worked for him, because he had always considered them from the perspective of the victorious side. It should be noted that having fought alongside Napoleon up to Moscow, and turned his coat thereafter, Jomini was on the winning side throughout his entire military career. He knew tactical defeat on the battlefield, but had no experience with strategic or total political defeat. Clausewitz had the opportunity to start juggling with the problem of genius and absolute principles years before, because he was analyzing these ideas from the perspective of the other side, the losing side, which bore the brunt of the revolutionary fervour. As he aptly put it years later in a letter to Roeder in 1827: "The exceptional circumstances in which Bonaparte and France found themselves since the Wars of the Revolution, allowed him to achieve major victories on almost every occasion, and people began to assume that the plans and actions created by those circumstances were universal norms."[32]

It was simple in this context to assume, from the victor's perspective, that they were winning because the principles were right and the generals were geniuses, but the causality relation was more likely the absolute reverse of this: they thought their principles were right and that their generals were geniuses *because they happened to be winning*.

JOMINI IN HISTORY

While there are two different faces of Jomini, one before and one after Clausewitz, the man nonetheless occupies a single place in the history of war theory that is similar in many respects to Hume's place in Western philosophy. In both cases, they were the last of their breed: Hume the last Empiricist, and Jomini the last Enlightenment war theorist, both stuck at a paradoxical nexus where scepticism forces its way to the surface. The central reason for which they were the last of their kind is that they had in their careful methodology achieved an end point to their field, a set of contradictions that could not be resolved. While Hume celebrated this as his purpose and his contribution to philosophy, Jomini preferred to fight it off as best he could, making concessions and diluting his work into an old memory of itself, rather than admit the existence of certain categories and limits to knowledge. And so, Hume was the harbinger of scepticism to his field, whereas Jomini accepted only as much scepticism as he was forced to by counter-arguments and historical

32 Clausewitz, "Letter to Roeder, December 22, 1827," in *Two Letters on Strategy*.

incongruence in his former doctrines. Though Jomini changed in the process, he cannot be qualified as being "post-Enlightenment" for the simple reason that he did not theorize in the new fashion, but simply deleted those aspects of his works where the weaknesses of his reasoning were most damning as a result of the transition. Much like Hume, Jomini did not relinquish the methods of the Enlightenment, but would eventually come to face an impossible threshold of scepticism, which could not be escaped. Hume arrived at a similar place: keeping the method, but having to dilute the certainty of causality.

The arrival of dialectics represented a shift so powerful in war studies that it broke the very backbone of most of the theories of war that existed prior. Today, few are those who still quote Puységur, Maizeroy, and Guibert. Their geometrical and scientific theories became hopelessly dated. Among the Enlightenment thinkers, Jomini fared a bit better than the others and continues to have some minor uptake in the field. However, this is only true of his later work, the *Précis*. His earlier *Traité* is utterly forgotten. And none of the above authors comes close in numbers to the continued interest in Clausewitz.

A clear demonstration of this can be found by searching the various authors in Google Scholar (see Table 1). The number of Clausewitz citations outnumbers the total number for all the Enlightenment military theorists combined by a factor of twenty-four. Though Jomini comes second, were it not for his later work influenced by Clausewitz (it outnumbers his early work by a factor of ten to one), he too would have succumbed, like Puységur and Guibert, to quiet desuetude.

While Jomini may have had the last word on Clausewitz, it seems that history had the last word on Jomini. That being said, history has nonetheless failed to have the last word on positive doctrines. Perhaps it is their simplicity of use that makes them stick, because it is practical in the military arts to refer to maxims for making quick decisions. However, when we consider the difference between maxims and principles, it seems rather that the continuation of the latter may have more to do with personal egos, who are unsatisfied with only coining a good maxim ... they would prefer proclaiming it an immutable principle for all the ages. But to do this is to flirt with illogic as one tries to elevate "genius" and "principles" to a higher form of abstraction and contradiction in order to avoid having to come to terms with the impossibility of applying it concretely.

THE DESCENT OF PRINCIPLES INTO *REDUCTIO AD ABSURDUM* ILLOGIC

Despite the fact that Clausewitz's opus had been widely available for decades, the belief in positive doctrines did not subside but actually only

Table 1

Search item	*Number of citations*
Jomini Treatise on Grand Military Operations	12
Jomini Traité de grande tactique	5
Jomini The Art of War	128
Jomini Précis de l'art de la guerre	58
Puysegur Art of War	0
Puysegur Art de la guerre	23
Guibert A General Essay on Tactics	5
Guibert Essai général de tactique	54
Clausewitz *On War*	6,120
Clausewitz Vom Kriege	775

Source: Google Scholar (12 July 2011)

reached its culminating point by the mid-twentieth century.[33] Though it was a widespread and worldwide tendency, we can turn to the American example to provide its archetypal form. True to the philosophy of Jomini's later works, US Army field manuals did not proclaim perfect solutions to specific situations, but they nonetheless maintained an increasingly narrow set of fundamental principles, such as the "principle of concentration" and the "principle of economy of force."[34] The problem was that the greater the dilution of principles into such wide, vague, or unapplied categories, coupled with an even greater sense of certainty as a result of their higher scope, the more complete the full circle of the logic became. By the time circular motion reached its end, principles of war had come to a stagnant halt, where they had effectively done away with the role of genius altogether. Genius could no longer rise above the rule. Genius could no longer make the rule. Genius and its "*coup d'oeil*" could no longer serve as the go-to point for when principles failed. The fact was that genius had been replaced by its very opposite: common sense.

Bernard Brodie said it best, during a conference in 1952 in which he explained: "If by principles, we mean these maxims and axioms usually grouped in a list of seven to ten or more articles, considered immutable despite fantastic changes in everything else, then my sentiment is not that these are false or without utility, but that we have a tendency to accord them too much importance. And if this tendency becomes extreme and we elevate these principles to dogma, then they can become

33 Brodie, "Continuing Relevance of *On War*," 50.
34 Ibid.

positively dangerous. What needs to be said about so-called principles of war is that above all they are propositions of common sense."[35]

If "principles" are meant to represent something grand, but do not manage to raise themselves above the realm of common sense, or the most basic assumptions one might have on conducting a strategy, then in what sense is their proclamation useful? In *Principes de la guerre* (1903), Foch argued that were it not for such immutable principles existing, war could not be an art. Yet, at the same time, Foch's principles were "of variable application which follow circumstances,"[36] depending above all on his overarching idea that "no strategy can prevail against one which assures itself in, and aims for, victory in battle."[37] He essentially posited both the absoluteness of principles and their variable application at the hands of the strategist,[38] thereby reaching an almost complete emptiness of significance. If that which is absolute is also variable, then it is in effect nothing.

Thus, the full circle described by Coutau-Bégarie began with the realization that strategists needed some fundamentals and notions of a code of conduct. As the process reached its end, however, it had effectively created principles that were so immutable and certain that they depended on artful application by the strategist to be of any use to the outcome sought. The more strategy itself was elevated by theorists, the more its true meaning was relegated to the level of timely and smart leadership.

Granted, common sense is not something that is useless in battle, nor is that what is being implied here. Rather, if genius and principles are *nothing but* propositions of common sense then we should not claim that they form either a science or even an art, let alone represent something immutable for the ages. What generates uselessness is not the common sense itself, but the grand proclamations regarding tactics and strategy that have become so diluted as to mean altogether very little that is applicable or of use to one's common sense on the battlefield. In van Creveld's *Transformation of War* for example, we read: "Strategy derives its unique power from the fact that it is independent from the size of the conflict, the medium in which is takes place, the means by which it is fought, and even the amount of violence it involves. ... Strategy does not

35 Bernard Brodie, Conference held on 17 March 1952 at the Naval War College (USA). The passage is not perfectly quoted. While the meaning is maintained, the words may have been altered due to a process of double translation. Originally quoted in Poirier, *Les Voix de la stratégie*, 92.

36 Foch, *Des principes de la guerre*, 9.

37 Ibid., 41.

38 Cormier, "Reclaiming the Dialectic," 14.

give a hoot whether the conflict is fought with guided missiles, rifles, spears or coloured beans."[39] Another similar point of view is proposed in a section of Colin Gray's *Modern Strategy* entitled "Strategy Eternal": "The near paradox lies in the fact that, although the multi-layering of new concerns for the strategist has proceeded apace, with the air, the depths of the sea, outer space, the electro-magnetic spectrum (and cyberspace) – as well as nuclear weapons and irregular warfare – adding complication upon complication, nothing essential about war and strategy has changed."[40]

These statements are either false, or so diluted in their interpretation of the meaning of strategy that they are empty of meaning. The hoplite phalanx and the thermonuclear bomb are not merely tactically incomparable; they are so distant from one another strategically that it undermines the very notion of eternal strategy. The hoplite phalanx is a powerful weapon insofar as it is used. It pierces the battlefield. The thermonuclear weapon is only powerful insofar as no use is made of it. It negates, or obliterates, the very existence of a battlefield. Meanwhile the idea of "eternal strategy" also fails when applied to cybersecurity. The idea that the networks can possibly be compatible with strategic notions built on Euclidian geometry is altogether laughable. While it might be tempting, for its simplicity, to make the analogy whereby the internet connection between hacker and hacking victim is compared to a "line of operation" or a "supply line," and the bandwidth one's "base," it would be quite meaningless. To begin with, since the very multitude of nonlinear (i.e. web-like) attacks means that disrupting one such "line" would be offset immediately by increasing the use of another line, one cannot analyze or give strategic meaning to any one line. Secondly, while having a larger "base" of available bandwidth might appear to be useful in DDOS (Distributed Denial of Service) attacks (i.e. where a server is swamped with spam until it crashes), the decentralization of such attacks invalidates this analogy as well. Attempting to apply traditional notions of tactics and strategy actually muddles instead of clarifying our understanding of cyberattacks. The closer to formulating an absolutely "true" principle one gets, the further removed and abstract this principle must become. And reciprocally, the closer a principle is to any actual context, the less likely it is to be accurate as an overarching concept that can apply to other contexts. It is analogous to Heisenberg's uncertainty principle in quantum physics, and also a demonstration of what Brodie and

39 van Creveld, *Transformation of War*, 118–19.
40 Gray, *Modern Strategy*, 355–6.

Coutau-Bégarie meant when they first engaged with the circularity of the problem. Ultimately, by claiming to be everything, these principles become nothing at all.

Since the time of Jomini, those who have continued to advocate on side with positive doctrines have mostly done so through a process of dilution of the concepts of strategy and tactics, perhaps in the hope that the potency of these principles might have homeopathic properties. At best they were placebo for the taking. As principles of war are elevated, perfected, and simplified, so too do they become ever more abstract and irrelevant to everyday usage. Attempting to apply these to reality means tagging on so much content and so many conditions that it in effect represents more effort to validate these towards application, than to arrive at a similar or superior course of action through common sense. The illogical bases upon which "principles of war" are elevated are merely propped up by a fortuitous encounter with occasional rectitude, which does not necessarily mean that they are causing victory, since it could easily be true that they are rather the product of victory.

Clausewitz's use of Kantian dialectics and appreciation of Kant's notion of "genius," coupled with his understanding of the distinction between synthetic and analytic knowledge, contributed to the line of argument that certain Enlightenment thinkers had against the rising tide of positive doctrines: that they don't work. The Enlightenment theorists knew it from experience. That was why they kept disagreeing with one another – or burning their own volumes, like Jomini, when they couldn't even agree with themselves. In his refutation, Clausewitz demonstrated by opposing contradictions and extracting his limited theory of war that these disagreements were in fact inescapable, the product of the endemic lack of scepticism found in enlightenment thinking. Ever since then, every attempt to reclaim the lost glory days of positive doctrines is a reminder of this one truth, that they cannot climb out of the abyss into which Clausewitz threw them.

5

Real and Absolute War: The Second Dialectical Moment

NOW THAT WE HAVE SEEN what Clausewitz's dialectical war theory destroyed in its path, let us consider what it built. When it comes to the two practical levels of warfare, the tactical and the strategic, Clausewitz's answer to this plural question regarding how generals should carry out war in all its different facets (i.e. manoeuvres, logistics, combat, etc.) was a single, unitary solution: a theory of war must have a limited scope. This reply to the positive doctrines is the opposite of how Clausewitz analyzes the single, unitary question: "what is war?" Here, it is the answer rather than the question that takes on a plural form. Clausewitz argues that all wars contain two mutually exclusive and polarized concepts: real war and absolute war. Whereas his refutation of the positive doctrines involved many layers of dialectical reasoning to achieve its results, splitting the real from the absolute (or ideal) represents the culmination of the method, it is in fact the overarching dialectic in itself. By applying it to war in the way that Kant had applied it to philosophy, Clausewitz provided his overall war theory with a dialectical ontology, thus building something altogether new and original.

What was the meaning of these two mutually exclusive representations of war? Was it that absolute war should be understood as war's true form, and real war as simply the consequence of policies meant to hold back and limit war – as though war were a wild animal, and the government its cage? Or is it the other way around: there is real war – understood as limited war – and then Clausewitz, by positing the notion of an absolute war, unleashes a new and potent nightmare for governments to dream up? Or is it rather that both forms are equally political, where it is politics that push war to a standstill or to an all-out struggle?

Again, it is important to understand the Kantian element to this system in order to show how Clausewitz could use it to enhance and clarify ideas that he intuitively felt were right, even at a young age, but which he could not until then demonstrate objectively. In fact, the more we explore the depth of the Kantian influence in the absolute/real dichotomy, the less we shall be inclined to perceive it as a *subjective* concept based on Clausewitz's experiences, state of mind, prejudices, or change in perspective. Rather, the split between the ideal and real represented for Clausewitz an opportunity to develop, in his later life, the subjective theory of his youth into a more comprehensive and far more objective theory.

It comes down to a question of what came first, the chicken or the egg. Did Clausewitz, in his later years, reread history and stumble upon the concept of real or absolute wars, leading to the dialectic, or was his discovery of the dialectic what pushed him to discuss war as having both a real and an absolute side to it? While one could seek out with great effort proof that the former option is the valid option, intuitively the latter option appears more logical. Ockham's razor, if you will. That being said, intuition need not be where this argument ends. What happened right after the note of 1827 confirms it. Instead of getting right to work on the new objective, Clausewitz instead suddenly showed a renewed interest in writing military campaigns. Surprised by this unlikely tangent, Aron finds himself stating that he is truly uncertain ("une véritable incertitude"[1]) of its meaning. It is only surprising to Aron, however, because he is seeing it from the opposite viewpoint. If the method came first, and the content came next, then it makes perfect sense that Clausewitz would have returned to his books exactly when he did.

Far from reneging on his old ideas on extremes and standstills, he saw the two as fitting perfectly into a Kantian framework insofar as he could conceptualize war in a dialectic between the ideal form and the real form. Not only did the dichotomy coexist, in many ways it needed to coexist for war to be intelligible rationally. By integrating the dialectic, it became possible to better explain the contradictions and paradoxes that he had come across early in life: the fact that war can take on an all-out form or a standstill, as well as the relationship between politics and war. Far from changing his horse mid-course, Clausewitz understood that attaching his chariot to two horses would provide him twice the power. Clausewitz was far too well-read to fall accidentally upon the dialectical approach, and his clear understanding of the method excludes the possibility that he was stumbling about in self-contradictions and confusion. The paradoxes are planned and intellectually potent.

1 Aron, "Clausewitz et l'état," 1259.

CLARIFYING THE TERMS: "ABSOLUTE WAR" NOT "TOTAL WAR"

A central problem with recent interpretations of Clausewitz has its origins in a gross translation error committed by Howard/Paret, in which they attribute to Clausewitz the notion of "total war." This term and concept was not actually coined for another hundred years, in 1935, by the German general Erich Ludendorff who used it as the title of his book *Der Totale Krieg*. The problem with introducing total war in Clausewitz is that the term is usually understood as a very real thing, the mobilization of an entire country, its people, and its industrial production capacity towards the war effort, in which the objective is to completely annihilate the enemy's capacity to resist, whereas "absolute war" is purely conceptual. The two are "unrelated concepts."[2] By switching the two around, we undermine the value of absolute war as an idea: we are limiting it when in fact the very reason for its existence is to serve as an unlimited concept. Whereas total war may be the very worst type of war we can generate, absolute war is the very worst type of war we can dream up.

When the term total war appears in Clausewitz it generates a serious error by which interpreters refer to absolute war and total war as though they were equivalent and interchangeable. To be clear, the Howard/Paret translation did not actually make the mistake of confounding the two, but erroneously inserting it into the translation has led many others to, including van Creveld, who falls squarely into the trap.

Clausewitz never wrote the term total war, or *totale Krieg*. Yet, in Book VIII chapter 6B of the Howard/Paret translation of *On War*, we find these two problematic words: "Even if war were total war, the pure element of enmity unleashed, all factors that go to make up war and determine its salient features – the strength and allies of each antagonist, the character of the peoples, and their governments, and so forth."[3]

The original German passage starts this way: "*Diese Vorstellungsart würde selbst dann unentbehrlich sein, wenn der Krieg ganz Krieg.*" It actually reads much like the English expression "girly-girl" where the superlative is found in the repetition of the word *Krieg*, so in this case we are dealing with something like the phrase "war of all wars," with no reference to *totality* at all. Though the Graham translation also fails to present the term as a repetition, the advantage of having chosen the words "perfect war"[4] is that at least here, the term does not evoke the horrors of the two World

2 Bassford, *Clausewitz in English.*

3 Clausewitz, *On War*, bk VIII, ch. 6B, 675–6.

4 Ibid., 675.

Wars. The fact that the Graham translation was first published in 1873, several decades before the phrase "total war" became common parlance, might explain why it did not creep into the manuscript as it did in the late twentieth century.

Echevarria emphasizes the fact that "the term absolute war captures the idea of limitless escalation, but this idea is not associated with real war." Actually, the closest Clausewitz ever got to including the word total in his analysis of "absolute war" was not in regard to any totality of war, but in the exact opposite: to show that it was merely a concept, an idea. In an earlier draft of his manuscript, Echevarria notes, Clausewitz used the term "total-concept" – *Total-Begriff* – to clarify the uniquely conceptual significance of the term, which is "barely conceivable in the purely logical sense."[5]

It is useful to take a step back from the concept of absolute war. Though it has been the one term that has fuelled the most aggressive and systematic attacks on Clausewitz ever since, it should be noted that Clausewitz only used the term four times in his entire opus. If we also add the few other variants that he makes, such as war's "absolute character" and war's "absolute form," we find ourselves with a grand total of ten occurrences, or roughly twenty words out of 800 pages. Furthermore, where he does write "absolute war," on the first occasion he practically apologizes for it; on the second occasion he presents it as only a "concept"; on the third he talks about the "probability" of "approaching" it, as opposed to actually fighting with the ideal as one's objective; and on the fourth occasion Clausewitz writes that to "dwell" on it would be to condemn one's theory to falsehood. That is to say he takes this idea not just with a grain of salt, but perhaps more like a shovelful.

THE MISSING DIALECTICS I: DID CLAUSEWITZ SUDDENLY CHANGE HIS MIND?

The fact that Clausewitz was so uncomfortable with the concept of an absolute war, and that he was altogether reticent about using it or giving it much credence, explains why he would need to significantly counter it with an opposite, real war. It is often assumed that absolute war was something that the young Clausewitz thought up and that in his later life, a more mature and moderate man, he would reconsider his stance and integrate the limiting features embodied in the notion of real war. This assumption, however, breaks down with closer scrutiny. Real war is a term

5 Echevarria, *Clausewitz and Contemporary War*, 67.

he had been using for ages, whereas it was absolute war that suddenly appeared later in his writings and, in the process, also redefined his ideas on the meaning of real war. This was the challenge – and not the other way around – and it also explains at least in part why a complete re-edit of *On War* was required in order to make it coherent, or at least consistent, from cover to cover.

Van Creveld, for example, makes the case that Clausewitz integrated the idea of limited war as a last-minute change of mind, and as a result of his premature death, it was an idea that was never fully developed in *On War*.[6] There are many problems with this argument, the most obvious being the word choice: Clausewitz never actually talked about "limited war" at all. He discussed limited aims in war, standstills, and extremes, but the distinction was absolute war and real war, not the limited/total war dichotomy that van Creveld sets up, as though they are synonymous. The point he is trying to make is that real war came first, and absolute war came second, though he speaks of a limited war/total war dichotomy that does not in fact exist in the literature.

Let us recall that the original dichotomy is as follows: absolute war is the concept of what a war might be if it had no material or political restraints, if it was left entirely to the internal escalatory logic that violence generates when it is unleashed and begets a process of reciprocation towards extremes. Real war, on the other hand, is war as it exists materially, somewhere between a standstill and an all-out fight to the finish. Limited aims in war are simply one of many factors that will guide war into whichever form it takes materially.

The hidden problem with van Creveld's argument, however, is not language – it is history. He claims that the concept of real or limited war emerges in the works of Clausewitz at a later date, whereas absolute war was there from a much earlier time. The introduction of these two concepts happened in the opposite order, at this has an important impact on how we should be interpreting their meaning. To be certain of this, one need only search quickly where the two terms appear in *On War*: "Real war" can be found in Books I (ch. 2), III, V, VI, and VIII, whereas all three variants –"absolute war," the "absolute form," and the "absolute character" of war – are exclusively mentioned in Books VI and VIII. From this, knowing that Clausewitz wrote the books in sequence and had the time to review only the first parts of Book I to satisfaction, it is clear that given the many references to "real war" in practically every segment of the

6 van Creveld, *Art of War*, 114–18.

book, while "absolute war" is in fewer places and exclusively in later parts, that "real" came first and "absolute" second, not the other way around.

Paret also made the case – citing passages from Clausewitz's early books *Principles of War* and *Plan of Operations* – that absolute war was an early concept. But he bases his faulty assumption on the decision to accord to the words "utmost" and "absolute" complete interchangeability,[7] and by overlooking the fact that *Principles of War* and *On War* were written some twenty years apart. If we look at the passages Paret uses to suggest that young Clausewitz had absolute war on his mind, it becomes clear that Paret's argument is tenuous. While Clausewitz did in fact argue that in war, "the most decisive operations accord with the nature of war,"[8] and that one should use one's entire forces with the "utmost energy,"[9] he in no way mentions or develops anything immaterial, or totally conceptual, along the lines of absolute war. In fact, the phrase "absolute war" does not appear anywhere in his early works.

This is not surprising, given that Clausewitz did not come across the concept of absolute war for another five years.[10] Though we might observe a seed, which would explain why he adopted the idea once he came across it, the observations regarding the use of utmost energy are tactical, not ontological. Absolute war for Clausewitz is a hypothetical concept based on the rhetorical question, what if war had no material limits? The above items are contrary to this because they are only concerned with material manifestations of war. And so, while Clausewitz had begun years earlier to conceptualize war as having extremes, it was not until he started thinking in "absolute" terms that he chose to reframe the conceptual counterpoise to this. Thus the renewed interest, which suddenly appears in the late chapters of *On War*, in war's limited aims and the paradoxical relationship between waging wars of political extermination versus wars for bargaining a peace – a contradiction Clausewitz had been considering as early as 1804.[11] Until the dialectic kicked in Clausewitz understood war as merely real war; and eventually, when he discovered absolute war, he generated a system that countered the real against

7 Paret, "The Genesis of *On War*," 20.

8 Clausewitz, "Plan of Operations, 1804," 51–2. Cited in Paret, "The Genesis of *On War*," 20.

9 Clausewitz, *Principles of War*, 46.

10 The letter to Fichte was written in 1809. I will go deeper into the question in the coming section "Absolute War and Revolution."

11 Clausewitz, "Plan of Operations, 1804," 51. Cited in Paret, "The Genesis of *On War*," 21.

the absolute – with unlimited and limited political aims serving as the moderators and accelerators of the dynamics between the more and less extreme forms of war. This evolution shows Clausewitz become a more experienced and talented dialectician over time.

Interestingly, the way Clausewitz used the term "real war" in the early parts of *On War* (Books III–V, or even up to the mid-section of VI) is quite different from the meaning it takes on after absolute war is introduced (end of Books VI, VII, VII, and finally, in book I, ch 1, which was rewritten/edited last). In Book V, for example, "real war" is used in refutation of positive doctrines regarding base lines, and Clausewitz is saying that these theories don't apply in real war.[12] In this case, the word real has nothing conceptual to it, but is merely a rhetorical tool to undermine the *unrealness* of the other term. Otherwise, in Book III, Clausewitz writes that real war is the state of crisis on the battlefield, as opposed to the standstills.[13] Here the term is being used in a very static or unitary way, where the meaning of real war is something in particular – the actual fighting in war – as opposed to something paradoxical and fluid that actually encompasses all of the forms war can take, from the standstill at one end to the all-out struggle at the other. Indeed, once we push forward to the end of Book VI, where absolute war is finally introduced, then real war suddenly changes in scope. It becomes a concept in flux. Clausewitz spells this out: "Real war will generally be in a medium between the two different tendencies, sometimes approaching nearer to one, sometimes to the other."[14] Later, in Book VIII, Clausewitz adds that "real war is no such consistent effort tending to an extreme, as it should be according to the abstract idea, but a half and half thing, a contradiction in itself."[15]

The confusion is that when Clausewitz integrated the concept of absolute war, he realized that the relationship this conceptual thing had to real war was quite problematic. Can the absolute tend towards becoming materialized? If the political nature of war were to be proven through this dichotomy, then that also would give proper reason to go back and edit the early parts of the book. And so, what Clausewitz had was not a sudden turnaround – a change of heart that led him to appreciate the lighter side of war – but the opposite: a realization regarding war's potential for extremes and absolutes, which forced him to reconsider real war from the perspective of this conceptual duality. In effect, real war had

12 Clausewitz, *On War*, bk V, ch. 15, 339.
13 Ibid., bk III, ch. 18, 186.
14 Ibid., bk VI, ch. 30, 547.
15 Ibid., bk VIII, ch. 6B, 675.

suddenly become arguably *more* real – in opposition to the ideal form but also, paradoxically, less tangible too because it was no longer a fixed concept, but a fluid one with variants. The order in which Clausewitz developed the real war/absolute war dichotomy has been regularly misrepresented. Though it may not appear to mean much, turning around the order in which the two concepts appeared does in fact have an effect on what meaning we should be extracting from the terms.

Whereas the young Clausewitz knew that in war there were extremes and standstills, he could not make these fit together as belonging to a single logic until he had broken war into its actual and ideal forms, and it was this conception of war that allowed him to place existing contradictions in war into a higher level of analysis that made them logically connected despite their opposition. Clausewitz did not suddenly change his mind about war. He simply freed the dialectic, letting it encompass the real contradictions – such as wars tending towards both standstills and extremes – by allowing a higher level of conception to frame war.

THE MISSING DIALECTICS II: WAS CLAUSEWITZ IN DISAGREEMENT WITH HIMSELF?

Not everyone appreciates the art of thinking in paradoxes. We saw in the early pages of this book that reading Clausewitz without a dialectical lens has led to self-fulfilling prophecies and war doctrines that advocate preemptive extremes. It was simple in the case of Foch and Liddell Hart to demonstrate that they had grossly split apart the dialectic in order to focus on isolated poles, which were not conceived as standing alone. However, showing that a new generation of authors have more or less replicated the error of excluding the dialectic is more difficult, because they do in fact recognize that both poles exist, and they write with more care and erudition. But they nonetheless fall into the trap of making a superficial interpretation that undermines the role of dialectics in Clausewitz's thought.

Whereas interpreters at the turn of the century had seemingly forgotten the concept of real war altogether, today, some authors do not properly recognize the dichotomy as a thing in itself, a necessary relationship, and a demonstration of Clausewitz's talents as a dialectician – as opposed to a case of schizophrenic self-disagreements or an intellectual weakness that led him to contradict himself from cover to cover. It is rather the norm, and not the exception, to point out these contradictions disparagingly. This is so even among scholars who are not unsympathetic to Clausewitz, as we saw in Gallie above or in Heuser's *Reading Clausewitz*, where she writes, "*even* in his contradictions, Clausewitz shows great wisdom."[16] This begs the question, though: was not Clausewitz's wisdom, rather, that he could conceptualize war within the context of such inherent contradictions? In fact, the way Clausewitz plans and executes contradictions – the source of his real/absolute dichotomy as well as various other examples in *On War* where paradoxes are drawn out – is a trick he learned from Kant. In fact, not only are they to be contradictory, they are meant to be *as contradictory as possible*, fully mutually exclusive conceptual pairs that showcase the effects of the antinomies of reason. When Clausewitz describes one thing, then its opposite, he replicates a technique that Kant uses, and which Gallie describes particularly well in *Philosophers of War*: "The principle of division should be stated in the sharpest, most extreme possible form ... once our principle of division has been established in this extreme, unmistakable form, then we can safely consider any factors which may seem to modify it in particular cases. Clausewitz uses this methodological principle at every stage of his thought, up to his final revision of Book I, chapter 1 in order to distinguish war from other forms of organized social action; and the result is his idea of absolute war."[17]

However, what is more interesting still in this method is that within these paradoxes, Clausewitz is able to show that both opposite propositions can in fact be simultaneously true. Kant explained in the *Critique of Pure Reason* that conflicts in the laws of pure reason (antinomies) produce such two-way splits – (*Zwiespalt*)[18] – and Clausewitz did in fact integrate this observation, even making use of the word "*Zwiespalt*" itself to clarify his exposition of the real/absolute dichotomy: "Having made the requisite examination on both sides of that state of antagonism (*Zwiespalt*) in which the nature of war stands with relation to other interests of men individually and of the bond of society, in order not to neglect any of the opposing elements ... an antagonism (*Zwiespalt*) which is founded in our own nature, and which, therefore, no philosophy (*philosophische Verstand*) can unravel."[19]

The division between the ideal and the real is, Hutchings explains, "fraught with paradox, as Kant himself recognizes, and none of the ways in which Kant grounds a connection ... is genuinely secure."[20] Indeed, this is alluded to by the fact that Clausewitz is saying that no philosophy can unravel it. That being said, what is lost in translation is that

16 Heuser, *Reading Clausewitz*, 42, emphasis added.
17 Gallie, *Philosophers of War and Peace*, 52.
18 Kant, *Kritik der Reinen Vernunft*, ebook location 3978.
19 Clausewitz, *On War*, bk VIII, ch. 6B, 674.
20 Hutchings, *Kant, Critique and Politics*, 55.

Clausewitz does in fact take the time to qualify *which type* of philosophy (*Verstand*) cannot unravel this division between the ideal and the real, which suggests that he has plans down the line to propose an alternative philosophy to do the job. This is quite a complex item to deal with, and we shall soon return to it. What is clear, though, is that while these paradoxical tensions are planned and purposeful, they nonetheless represent a difficulty not only for the reader, but also in fact for Clausewitz himself. In writing about the impasse, Clausewitz found it quite difficult to cope with distinguishing the ideal from the real, especially in the context of Napoleon, who seemed to push war so far toward its absolute form that the paradox was all the more frustrating and fragile.

Clausewitz's goal in bringing up the contradiction between absolute and real war was to try to make sense of another underlying contradiction he had experienced in his own life: how the single concept – war – has on the one hand a tendency towards a "struggle for life and death," while also being capable of provoking a mere "state of observation," or a standstill, between the two opposing forces.[21] And more confusing still: how is it possible that each singular and particular war is equally infused with this paradox? Clausewitz had no intention of somehow bypassing or avoiding it, but exposing these contradictions meant he risked sounding contradictory himself.

In *Reading Clausewitz* Heuser asks the rhetorical question, "How could Clausewitz state dogmatically that 'The shattering of the enemy is the aim of war,' requiring the 'annihilation of the inimical armed forces,' if two lines later he realized that the objective could be anything on a wide scale of political objectives? If only an insignificant patch of territory is to be conquered in time for political negotiations, surely it is not necessary to destroy the enemy's entire fighting forces to do so. This passage thus shows the continued coexistence of his two different mind-frames."[22] Heuser goes so far as to entitle her chapter "Clausewitz the Realist vs Clausewitz the Idealist," as though the conflicting mind-frames were somehow a personal disposition, rather than an intellectual system of analysis. Though framing Clausewitz in such twentieth-century academic terms has an anachronistic feel to it, it is not without merit since there is a highly heuristic value, insofar as it helps us understand Clausewitz from a crisp perspective with which we are familiar. It establishes compartments to how we should understand the lessons one can take from Clausewitz. However, this perspective on Clausewitz is not unproblematic

21 Clausewitz, *On War*, bk VI, ch. 28, 530.

22 Heuser, *Reading Clausewitz*, 33.

either, since it frames his work by attaching it to an external set of concepts. The danger is that we wind up bypassing *On War*'s planned complexities by extracting the contradictions as they appear from our external framework. Clausewitz is not necessarily contradicting himself if he is in fact exposing self-contradictions in war itself. In a segment that precedes the quote Heuser used, Clausewitz explains that war has "inner laws"[23] so that even though a nation may not have to annihilate another in order to take over a small territory, this does not eliminate the propensity of war to rise to extremes. In fact, is it not fair to say that a many great wars started with a minor dispute? Within this reality, the political element is *both* the driver and the moderator of this propensity toward extremes. Once we realize this, the contradiction of which Heuser speaks dissipates. War's absolute and real natures are both accounted for in how Clausewitz describes war. They are interconnected. This does not mean that a limited war does not have something intrinsically absolute to it, nor does it mean that the closest one might get to waging an absolute war would not equally contain elements that would limit it from ever reaching this conceptual end point, which is stated as an unlimited ideal, and not a fixed and attainable point. To use a mathematical analogy, real war is imbued with both an absolute element and a limited element, which are like asymptotic lines on a chart that never reach the point towards which they tend – in this case because they are opposite forces exerting a constant pull against either.

The problem in Heuser's reading of "twos" in Clausewitz is that her text does not properly distinguish dialectics from dualism.

> Clausewitz almost falls into a new trap, that of thinking of war dualistically, as one of merely two possible forms: limited or unlimited … back in 1804, Clausewitz had not yet believed that the conduct of war might vary as a function of its political aims. In a note of 1827, however, … he again invoked the "dual nature of war." This curiously dualistic notion … almost led Clausewitz to the logical dead end of thinking of war as one of two possible manifestations. His own logic, however, led him to acknowledge elsewhere that wars have to be classified along a sliding scale, from defensive but unlimited … via very limited … to an all-out unlimited … war of conquest.[24]

Heuser is right to point out that Clausewitz describes war as a dual concept as well as a sliding scale of manifestations. It is not, however, a

23 Clausewitz, *On War*, bk I, ch. 1, 4–5.
24 Heuser, *Reading Clausewitz*, 34.

contradiction in terms. To use an analogy, when a couple engages in a love-hate relationship, this does not exclude the existence of all the other feelings involved in their affair: passion, romance, frustration, etc. A love-hate dichotomy is used to describe the unlikely existence of mutually exclusive poles in one and the same thing, not to suggest that in this couple there is nothing but love and hate, one minute the former, one minute the latter. The novelty of such a relationship, were it to exist, would probably require a name of it own, given that a love-hate relationship implies something far less categorical and dramatic. Clausewitz's dual concept of war, or it might be better yet to refer to it in the plural – dual concepts of war – is not a quest to define all of war as belonging to two poles, but rather a quest to understand why these two mutually exclusive conceptual extremes seem to exist in reciprocation in all wars.

Further from the mark is the idea that a love-hate relationship automatically means that the hate part of the equation would be all the more hateful. This is the kind of reasoning that allows van Creveld, like Liddell Hart before him, to argue that because Clausewitz explored the real war/absolute war dichotomy, he was to blame for creating a "brutally realistic doctrine."[25] The reason these authors arrive at this point is that they isolate both poles and fail to consider them as a pair. This is well demonstrated by the fact that when van Creveld decides to take on the concept of absolute war and attack it from all sides, he does so without considering it alongside or in parallel to real war. He only introduces real war after the fact, once the rhetorical process of describing absolute war as something altogether morally abhorrent is complete.

Van Creveld brings up the partially correct point that the absolute concept is borrowed from Kant,[26] but in reality – as we shall see below – it was in fact a student of Kant's, Johann Gottlieb Fichte, who coined "absolute war." What is most Kantian about it is not the term itself, but the fact that it is counterbalanced with the real. In van Creveld's defence, however, it is possible to blame a part of this failure to appreciate the Kantian connection properly in *On War* on the grounds that he was citing the Howard/Paret translation of *On War*, which systematically omits or misinterprets the philosophical terminologies at the heart of Clausewitz's project. Indeed, the Howard/Paret translation of Clausewitz, which van Creveld uses as his source in *The Art of War*, makes a right proper mess of the "real" part of the real/absolute dichotomy. For example, the word *wirklich* – a term Clausewitz used to distinguish that

25 van Creveld, *The Art of War*, 117.
26 Ibid., 114–18.

which is real from what is ideal or abstract – is at times omitted entirely from the translation, thus "real war" is translated as simply "war." Moreover, the translators are not consistent in their word choice – interchanging, for example, the words "actual" and "real" from one occurrence of *wirklich* to another.[27]

As we explore the true nature of his paradoxical observations, we find Clausewitz was not "in contradiction" with himself at all, but rather that his system of thought made use of contradiction in a planned, clear, and necessary way. Failing to see the dichotomy as a thing in itself, a paradox that needs to be understood as such, has caused serious misinterpretations over the years. And yet, the far more interesting question to ask is rather: how fragile is this form of paradoxical thinking on the subject of war? In trying to make war more intelligible, how close can it get to making itself unintelligible?

ABSOLUTE WAR AND REVOLUTION

Fichte is the one who first coined the term *absoluter Krieg* (absolute war) and introduced it to Clausewitz. We know this because in 1809 Clausewitz read Fichte's *On Machiavelli* (six years before he began to write *On War*)[28] in which the term appears, and he actually took the time to write a reply, which he sent to the philosopher. Prior to this, Clausewitz had not made use of the term. In fact, it seems that amongst the texts that have been translated to English, Clausewitz did not actually introduce the concept of absolute war until very late in his life.

Fichte used absolute war to describe revolutionary conflict, or a war between the people and their prince. Specifically, he was describing his agreement with what he considered to be the "fundamental principle of Machiavellian politics," which is that in order to be stable, whoever founds a republic or state and gives it laws must presuppose that all men are evil, and that given the occasion they will make use of this evilness for their own gain. Fichte is not commenting on whether that is a right or wrong presumption, but rather that it serves as a premise in order for the state to act as a constraining or coercive institution (*Zwangsanstalt*). The problem is as follows, however: if the people refuse to recognize the laws

27 Compare, for example, the Paret/Howard translation on pages 90 and 119 using the word "real" with page 580 where it is omitted, or the Graham translation's "actual" on page 542 with "real" on pages 642 and 643. Both translations use "real war" to render "*eigentliche Krieg*," which would be clarified in this particular case by using the word "actual" instead (Graham 186; Paret/Howard 222).

28 Paret, "The Genesis of *On War*," 3.

and the authority of the prince and rather choose to fight and reclaim their original independence and collective sovereignty, they merely confirm (from the ruler's perspective) what was always already assumed – i.e., that they are evil. And this is what justifies the prince in his perceived right to defend himself from the villainy of others. Hence, revolutionary conflicts exist at the utmost threshold of the political relations between war and peace, because the prince wants peace, by which he implies that he wants to maintain his right to make laws and maintain his sovereignty, and the people in arms cannot be satisfied until both this sovereignty and lawmaking are fully annihilated. A half victory would be no victory at all. This is what makes war absolute, since the objectives are themselves absolute and fundamentally irreconcilable.[29] In Fichte's version of it, absolute war contains a political idea; it does not imply a judgment or analysis of the form the violence takes, or of its strategic or tactical implications. Instead absolute war is nothing more than the armed-conflict aspect of a political revolution.

Clausewitz borrowed Fichte's concept and enhanced it intellectually. His version retains something deeply political to it, but brings forward much more depth with regard to the nature of pure political violence. When Clausewitz borrowed the concept of absolute war from Fichte, his primary goal was visibly to clarify the role of violence unleashed in war, to isolate the idea in its most extreme form so that he could distinguish the political aspects that generate the central features of his theory – such as escalation, reciprocation, all-out war, and standstills – from the self-fulfilling nature of violence, which also inherently produces these very same effects. So, while the violence of war is naturally or inherently escalatory, different policies can have the effect of restraining this tendency, or the opposite, of releasing and even enhancing it. Absolute war is a concept that is at the very threshold between the natural tendency of war and the political will to bring this tendency out to its extreme. And for Clausewitz, as for Fichte, this had a revolutionary connotation.

Clausewitz himself recognized that the closest anyone had gotten to absolute war was the revolutionary French under Napoleon. Even though he often described Napoleon as having an unlimited approach to war, Clausewitz nonetheless reiterated the fact that absolute war remained a conceptual thing, an abstraction, "which has never in fact been achieved."[30] A few paragraphs below, he adds that the campaigns of

29 Fichte, *Machiavel et autres écrits*, 56–7.

30 Clausewitz, *On War*, bk VIII, ch. 3, ed. and trans. Howard and Paret, 582. In this case, the Graham translation is literally closer to the original, but lacks the clarity of meaning offered by Howard/Paret.

1805, 1806, and 1809 make it "easier for us to grasp the concept of modern, absolute war in all its devastating power."[31] He is in fact walking the tightrope of a paradox where absolute war does not exist per se but there are ways in which campaigns approach it. The first way in which it approaches it is the attempt and fulfilment of annihilating a political unit's ability to resist and to exert its will, and secondly, the attempt and fulfilment of dethroning, replacing, and dismantling the very political structures and their functioning. The latter is evidently all the more extreme and represents the backdrop of the French Revolution. Trying to find equilibrium between his theoretical concept of absolute war and Napoleon's constant approaching of it, Clausewitz grapples with his concept, eventually writing candidly that: "we shall have to grasp the idea that War, and the form which we give it, proceeds from ideas, feelings, and circumstances which dominate for the moment; indeed, if we would be perfectly candid we must admit that this has even been the case where it has taken its absolute character, that is, under Buonaparte."[32]

The tension is extreme in this paragraph, which might encourage some to argue that Clausewitz's concept of absolute war was not merely an idea, but something concrete that could in fact be enacted. Yet, the words on the page clearly state that the concept belongs to the realm of "ideas, feelings, and circumstances," which means that while Bonaparte may be bringing war closer to its absolute character, this absolute exists in the idea rather than the physical aspect of war. This does not mean that Bonaparte succeeded in achieving *the* absolute, but rather that he pushed his forces in this direction in ways that had arguably never been seen in the history of mankind. "Candidly," says Clausewitz – because he hates having to say it. It is troubling to him because in the same paragraph, right above this quote, Clausewitz reminds the reader to avoid a "pure conception" and to "allow room for everything foreign in nature which mixes up with it and fastens itself upon it – all the natural inertia and friction of its parts, the whole of the inconsistency, the vagueness and hesitation (or timidity) of the human mind."[33] And so revolutionary war contains within it an absolute nature and propensity for extremes like no other war, but it remains subdued to limiting features nonetheless, even though it aspires to no limit other than political overthrow and annihilation.

31 Ibid., 584. Here I continue to use the Howard and Paret translation for consistency. This passage is also more clearly translated than the Graham alternative.

32 Clausewitz, *On War*, bk VIII, ch. 2, 644.

33 Ibid.

Napoleon was in fact "exporting" the revolution, bringing to life a political conception of war that had as its only limit the non-limit implied by completely destroying the political structures of the other. It was not merely that Napoleon was conquering Europe, but that in doing so he brought forth significant political reforms – proclaiming, for example, new laws, rights, and constitutions for the peoples of Prussia, Poland, and the Rhineland. This, however, did not mean that war itself had become unlimited, or had achieved the full abstraction of the absolute. The full abstraction was the aim and the political nature or rather revolutionary aspect of the war. The physical conditions of battle remain unchanged. The limiting features of fog and friction, for example, still haunted the commander, as for the most part technologies and tactics had not particularly changed since the Seven Years' War.

Politics had changed. This could be felt both in the size of the engagements, because of the *levées en masse*, and in the fervour and moral force of the revolutionary citizen-soldiers. Or as Clausewitz explained:

> War had suddenly become again an affair of the people, and that of a people numbering thirty millions, every one of whom regarded himself as a citizen of the State ... By this participation of the people in the war instead of a cabinet and an army, a whole nation with its natural weight came into the scale. Henceforward, the means available – the efforts which might be called forth – had no longer any definite limits; the energy with which the war itself might be conducted had no longer any counterpoise, and consequently the danger for the adversary had risen to the extreme.[34]

What made war absolute was not Napoleon himself, and surely not his tactics and strategies, but rather the politics of revolution, which led hundreds of thousands of invigorated citizen-soldiers with ambitions to do away with the Ancien Régime, at home and abroad. "Since the time of Buonaparte, war, through being first on one side, then again on the other, an affair of the whole nation, has assumed quite a new nature, or rather it has approached much nearer to its real nature, to its absolute perfection. The means then called forth had no visible limit, the limit losing itself in the energy and enthusiasm of the Government and its subjects."[35]

Clausewitz reaffirms that what leads war towards an absolute form is its political nature – in effect the revolutionary fervour, the will to transform the ambitions of policy into the ambitions of warfare. Only absolute

34 Ibid., ch. 3B, 658.
35 Ibid., 658–9.

politics can lead to absolute war. And the only true absolute policy is revolution. This realization will serve us in the later chapters when we discuss the role of freedom and emancipation in shaping the modern ethos of warfare.

That being said, what is important for the time being is to recognize that Clausewitz did not present absolute war as an apolitical concept and real war as the outcome of some external source of politics that restrains absolute war. His analysis was far too complex to be satisfied with such reductive formulations. For Clausewitz, war contains this absolute at the very centre of its concept. The reciprocation of violence leads to extremes, independently of politics. However, what is essential to add is that Clausewitz recognizes that this internal logic is understood by the state, when it applies reason to making use of war as a tool. It can restrain war, or at least try – though not always successfully – to restrain war, when objectives demand this. But in other cases, the policy may be to unleash war, enhance war, to provide it with more force, with more destructive technology, with more soldiers, etc.

This is precisely what Clausewitz was trying to explain in the passage cited above, in which he is speaking of *Krieg ganz Krieg*. Now we can appreciate the second part of his statement: "This kind of idea would be indispensable even if war was perfect war (*Krieg ganz Krieg*), the perfectly unbridled element of hostility, for all the circumstances on which it rests, and which determine its leading features, viz., our own power, the enemy's power, allies on both sides, the characteristics of the people and their Governments respectively, etc., as enumerated in the first chapter of the first book, are they not of a political nature, and are they not so intimately connected with the whole political intercourse that it is impossible to separate them."[36]

In the world of ideas, war is absolute. It is the pure reciprocation of extremes that produce ever-greater extremes. In real war, between the standstill and the all-out war, whether the beast is restrained or unleashed is equally the product of politics. That is in fact their fundamental unity. To suggest that politics only apply to the restraint side of the equation is to miss Clausewitz's argument altogether. The failure to recognize this unity in the dialectic is precisely what leads certain interpreters to conceptualize Clausewitz as being dualistic, in contradiction with himself, and having changed his mind over time, rather than having deepened what he had started with, uncovering the paradox and building his concept of war upon it.

36 Ibid., 675.

To make the point that the absolute war/real war dichotomy is an objective ontological system in which to understand the nature of war, it is best to reach it by demonstrating the opposite: that it is *not subjective.* Had Clausewitz indeed suddenly changed his mind on the question then it would have been subjective – but we have seen that this is not the case. The dichotomy emerged logically both as an internally coherent system and as one that did not appear, but developed over time through deepening itself. Secondly, if the dichotomy was haphazardly posited and contained clear signs of Clausewitz caught in hopeless self-contradiction, then again, it would appear to be subjective – but in fact the paradoxes that he exposes are not self-contradictory. Rather, they provide an external glance into the contradictions inherent in war. Hence, the two most likely sources of subjectivity having been excluded, and Clausewitz's method appears to be rather objective: it allows the internal logic of violence and reciprocation on one end, and risk aversion on the other, to coexist as two forces of policy that generate war's sliding scale of manifestation.

That being said, however, Clausewitz offers some critical assessment of what he himself is writing when he considers the problem with speaking of absolute and real war as separate concepts in the context of revolution. He recognizes that revolution represents in some sense the breaking point or the logical limit of the real war/absolute war dichotomy, because it brings out the logic of the absolute in its manifestation of the real, because the policy of a revolution is itself absolute, a willingness to risk it all. The difference between the two separate concepts becomes terribly blurred in revolution. That is to say, the policy of revolution being absolute, the form of revolutionary war follows, as is the reverse case when policy has limited aims.

The discovery that both real war and absolute war were equally the products of policy gave Clausewitz a glimpse into war's political nature. But to complete this dialectical reconciliation of the real and the absolute, he could not simply state it as the continuation of policy by other means, simply because jumping from the former part of this equation to the latter actually makes very little sense unless it is grounded in some logic or method. Why should war's dual concepts serve as a demonstration of its political nature? Could it not just as well show an infinite set of other properties or conclusion regarding war? Somehow the two need to be logically connected. Had Clausewitz been influenced only by Kant, he would not have been able to tie the impasse between real war and absolute war directly to the political. He would have been forced to generate the real and the absolute alone as objective observations, a static impasse in itself, to which he could supplement a fully subjective and external corollary regarding war's political element. However, this was not satisfactory. Clausewitz wanted to show objectively as well that war was the continuation of policy by other means, and to do this, he had to show that it was a dynamic solution to the impasse he had uncovered. For this, however, he would need to find a metaphysical solution to Kant, a way to overcome that which philosophy of "Verstand" *could not unravel.*

6

Transitioning from Kantianism to Hegelianism

IN THE FIRST FIVE CHAPTERS, we set out to demonstrate that Clausewitz's method converged with Kant's philosophy and that this shaped the first two moments in his dialectical war theory, the refutation of the positive doctrines, and the development of war's dual nature as real and absolute. We were thereby able to demonstrate that the effect of Kant's critical method on metaphysics resulted in parallel impacts on war theory when Clausewitz made use of it in his writings. Instead of seeking out truth regarding war in forms that were immutable, natural, and external to the thing, best exemplified by the quest for "principles of war," Clausewitz pursued an opposite direction: where the object of study is the thing in itself, and the prescriptions are not fixed, eternal, and perfect, like god, but in flux, mortal, and imperfect, like man. On the one hand, fundamental principles and positive doctrines fail because war is so human; it is an element of "social life,"[1] the fact that it is in constant mutual reciprocation between human actors makes it a game (*Spiel*)[2] in which players act and react, and this is what undermines the absoluteness of doctrine. On the other hand Clausewitz's ontological exploration of war's dual concepts again breaks war away from naturalistic and mystical explanations for war because it shows that the forms war takes are not predestined externally but the product of human, political agency. In either case, the need for systematizing causality from some divine origin is eliminated; there is no need for a *causa prima,* because even if we exclude it from the analysis the theory of war remains intact logically – even in a universe where there is no god and where causality itself offers no

1 Clausewitz, *On War,* bk II, ch. 3, 92.

2 Clausewitz makes numerous references to this, including when he compares war to a card game in bk I, ch. 1, and to a game of chess in bk VII, ch. 13.

certainty, war can function within an internal logic that straddles game theory and politics.

The two moments, methodological and ontological, are distinct in that the first is a negative task, and the second is a positive one. They are however both analytical, rather than synthetical in scope. In both cases, Clausewitz transposed the Kantian lessons regarding the Enlightenment metaphysical debates into the field of war theory. A pragmatist, no doubt, he most certainly did not do this for the sake of high scholasticism, but simply because it did the job so well. He had perceived the fact that there were similarities in the weaknesses he saw in the scientific theories of war and the solutions Kant had provided in his theories on human understanding and aesthetics. The process of positing and refuting the scientific demonstration of the divine generated an intellectual history that was incredibly informative to the study of war. And Clausewitz happened to be at the right place, at the right time, to be the first to make this transposition.

Clausewitz did not merely refute one positive doctrine or another, but the very principle of codifying principles of war to begin with. Clausewitz's scepticism revoked the claims war theorists had to "certainty" regarding their observation and proclamation of causal relationships in the battlefield. Therefore, he replaced these doctrines with a far less ambitious idea of what war theory should and could afford generals and heads of state. His was a limited theory built not on mere scepticism but on a sceptical method that made use of dialectics to uncover both the antinomian nature of opposing positive doctrines, and the critique to extract a moderate or relative scope of knowledge from experience and history. As a result of this, faith in positive doctrines began to waver. Jomini had to rewrite his entire opus just to keep afloat. And the more people explored new ways of generating positive doctrines, the more pronounced became their descent into circular logic, until the very glue that was keeping it altogether, the concept of genius was in effect replaced by its opposite: common sense. As of the moment Clausewitz exposed the problems of positive doctrines, clarified the role of the Kritik, and then developed his limited theory of war, the field was forever changed. From that point on, all theories would be forced to measure up to the same standards of proof. And since principles could not be proven any more than their metaphysical counterpart in philosophy, these principles ballooned up into vagaries that were condemned to either pop or deflate whenever one made use of them in concrete ways.

Meanwhile importing Kantian metaphysics into war theory had positive ontological implications as well. By conceiving war *in twos* as a reciprocation between opposite tendencies, towards extremes and towards standstills, Clausewitz was able to posit a theory of war, which unlike his stance on positive doctrines was not a limited theory but the opposite: an absolute theory of war, built on a paradox, which established two mutually exclusive concepts of war: the real and the absolute, in reciprocation. To the single question "what is war?" Clausewitz provided a plural answer. His dual answer would generate the political element in war, but to understand fully how this was achieved, and by what method, the previous chapter can only serve as a first step in that direction. The connection to Fichte and Kant provides only part of the answer. To understand how it was possible for Clausewitz to jump from the ontological realm to the ethical realm – that is, from positing the opposition between absolute war and real war to extracting or synthesizing from this the conclusion "war is the continuation of policy by other means" – we must enter into a discussion of how Hegel and Clausewitz converged on method, and what this meant for both their dialectical theories of war. At this point, we enter the third dialectical moment of war theory, where the political and ethical aspects of war are uncovered.

In chapters 3 and 5, we explored the origin and scope of Kant's role in shaping the dialectics that Clausewitz made use of in his war theory. What started as an argumentative technique regarding methods in war (tactics and strategy) grew into an ontological framework based on war's dual concepts as real and absolute. The next phase of this exploration leads into the question of ethics. However, before taking on such a distinct task, it would be useful to ask first, how do these three layers of analysis link up? The transition from the first, to the second, to the third moment is possible because these three levels of analysis are fully integrated, and mutually necessary to one another. The development of Clausewitz's dialectics in *On War* is not only a matter of him learning, testing, and developing the method over time and further integrating it into his book, it was also in some ways a calculated plan to guide the reader into a deeper and deeper understanding of the dialectical method and its conclusions. *On War* moves the reader through these three *moments* in a logical order, from the simple to the complex, which is akin to how Hegel generally developed his thoughts. What is more, he also accomplishes, as Hegel does, a developmental process in knowledge whereby each subsequent moment is of a higher order, where that which precedes it is encompassed in the logic of that which follows, and that which follows grows out of the logic of what preceded it.

The first layer dealt with the single and isolated problem of violence, or the use of force in defeating one's enemy. The interrogation was happening at a methodological level, or at the level of the question "How to?" Clausewitz's refutation of positive doctrines was universal in character, it provided an argument that invalidated all principles of war, rather than attempting to refute them one by one. This required that he demonstrate the faulty logic that united them all. To do this Clausewitz needed to rely on a system of dialectics that could showcase the antinomies of reason, which gave the false impression that these principles were synthetical when in fact they were not. Since context could always invalidate an absolute theory of strategy or tactics, only a limited theory was tenable.

Having introduced dialectics at this first level, a second level of theory automatically emerged regarding the structural question "what is war?" because the conclusion of the first level was, in fact, that context itself determined strategy and tactics. So then, what was this context? What unchanging nature of war was providing a frame to all the elements in war that were in fact forever changing? Clausewitz went from a negative theory, a refutation of positive doctrines, to a positive, speculative theory about the nature of war as having an absolute dimension and a real dimension. Somewhere in a bipolar realm that is defined by standstills at one end, and all-out war at the other, politics would determine the equilibrium point. Here Clausewitz was not proposing a limited theory at all but quite the opposite: an absolute theory based on there being two poles which by definition include all wars spanning from that which can be imagined to that which can be carried out. And out of this emerges his conclusion that war is political, which is to say it is the product of a state's "intelligence," or the activity of political deliberation and the consequent application of policy by the executive powers of the state. If the first level of dialectics represented the question "how" and the second the question "what," we find that the how results in the necessity of context for its validation and the what emerges from asking what defines this context.

Eventually, though, Clausewitz arrives at a third moment, or plane of analysis, because the question "what" begs a set of questions of its own. If war is a political thing, then why does it take the forms it takes – and what is the nature of the relationship that binds war to politics? The very attempt to answer this question elevates the discussion from the ontological to the ethical realm. And this transition actually serves as the validation of the ontological system. That is to say that politics *take possession* of war, becomes responsible for its objectives and the form it takes. As a result of this subjugation, the political becomes the agency, the focal point of war's ethics, and can therefore be blamed if its actions are deemed unjustified and evil, or honoured if they are deemed just and good.

As of the moment Clausewitz began applying dialectics to his refutation he became ensnared in a system of logic that eventually fulfills itself in the process of being applied. Clausewitz could not expect to break down the arguments of the Enlightenment including their methods using Kant's tools (i.e. critique, categories of human understanding, antinomies) without arriving, as Kant did, at a distinction between the real and the ideal, since the method only succeeds in its refutation as a process of constructing this dichotomy between the material and the ideal. And in the end, the only way to make the chasm intelligible and rational was to uncover what was creating it in the first place, the hierarchical relationship between politics and war, which is in itself the first step in proclaiming a modern and secular ethical proposition.

Clausewitz's dialectical reasoning contains a dynamic element to it, where each moment appears to be the continuation of what began in the previous moment. It is a boulder that accelerates once it has been nudged off the hill. Yet this movement in the dialectic has something distinctly non-Kantian to it insofar as Kant's philosophy was static. And it is here that we must begin to consider what, then, is being observed. In chapters 7–11, we shall go through the entire process of uncovering the Hegelian effect in Clausewitz. But for now, let us present a preliminary clue regarding the impasse and distinction that separates this later part of the book from the exploration of Kant and Clausewitz in the first half. What is this jump from Kantianism to Hegelianism?

In Book VIII Clausewitz presented both the absolute and the real concepts of war, and eventually these led to chapter 6B, entitled *War as an Instrument of Policy*, where he offered to "look for that unity into which, in practical life (*im praktischen Leben*), these antagonistic elements combine themselves by partly neutralizing each other."[3] Each word in the first paragraph of chapter 6B must be taken at its full worth, because they were chosen and arranged in a way that shows a deep understanding of Kant that, if ignored, leaves an incomplete impression. Let us therefore consider the whole paragraph, while paying special attention to certain words for which I have provided the German original and also the Howard/Paret translation when different from the Graham translation:

HAVING made the requisite examination on both sides of that state of antagonism (*Zwiespalt*) in which the nature of war stands with relation to other interests of men individually and of the bond of society, in order not to neglect any of the opposing elements ... an antagonism (H/P tr. incompatibility) (*Zwiespalt*) which is founded in our own nature, and which, therefore, no philosophy (*philosophische Verstand*) can unravel ... we shall now look for that unity into which, in practical life (H/P trans. real life) (*praktischen Leben*), these

3 Clausewitz, *On War*, bk VIII, ch. 2B, 674.

antagonistic elements combine themselves by partly neutralising each other. We should have brought forward this unity at the very commencement, if it had not been necessary to bring out this contradiction very plainly, and also to look at the different elements separately. Now, this unity is the conception that war is only a part of political intercourse, therefore by no means an independent thing in itself.[4]

Some depth to the passage is missing in either translation with regard to the omission of the word "Verstand," which was mentioned earlier, but with regard to the second translation issue, Howard/Paret's use of the word "real" – as opposed to "practical" – robs the reader of in important aspect of the text. With regard to the second element, practical life is not interchangeable with "real life" or simply "life" itself because in German philosophy "practicality" is a reference to moral philosophy – as is the case in the subject matter of the *Critique of Practical Reason*, which is essentially an essay on morality and ethics. Practicality is how one renders philosophy into everyday use, that is to demonstrate how it applies to decision-making on ethical questions or *how* one is to *act* in the world: "Practical reason is the general human capacity for resolving, through reflection, the question of what one is to do. Deliberation of this kind is practical in at least two senses. First, it is practical in its subject matter, insofar as it is concerned with action. But it is also practical in its consequences or its issue, insofar as reflection about action itself directly moves people to act."[5]

The fact that the ontological concepts of absolute and real war are coming together in a concept that applies to ethics and morality, as opposed to a further ontological exploration, marks an important transition. We are exiting one level of analysis in order to construct a higher one atop it. This dialectical upward construction, we will see in the upcoming section is distinctly a Hegelian use of dialectics. If we recall, Kant stopped short of reconciliation and understood paradoxes as sterile and fixed, rather than fertile and dynamic.

To appreciate this, we must return to the term to our previous discussion of Kant's two-way splits (Zwiespalt). Clausewitz is not making the argument that philosophy, generally, cannot resolve the dichotomy he has uncovered in the absolute and real forms of war; he is actually arguing that a specific branch of philosophy – philosophische Verstand – is unable to resolve the antagonisms (Zwiespalt) that emerge from the

4 Ibid.
5 Wallace, "Practical Reason."

antinomies of pure reason.[6] The difficulty for English readers is that the word "reason" can be translated to either *Vernunft* or *Verstand*, each of which has distinct connotations. Hannah Arendt explains that for Kant, the latter is closer to the concept of intellect. Vernunft is associated with the meaning of things whereas Verstand is associated with knowledge of things.[7] Another way to consider it is to see Verstand as the type of knowing that is spontaneous in the mind and can exist outside of sensorial certainty,[8] but which is not in and of itself intuitive, like sense-certainty. Vernunft, on the other hand, represents the intuitive, the type of reason that makes sense or appears to be intuitive, through experience for example. Vernunft is therefore the reasoning that attempts, in the case of conditioned knowing, to encompass the "totality of conditions, which is to say, unconditionality."[9] And so Clausewitz recognized that although the impasse he had uncovered belonged to the area of Verstand, its solution lay elsewhere. He thereafter sets himself up to discuss the higher meaning of this impasse and its reconciliation. But this reconciliation does not undo, it cannot undo, the contradiction; it merely makes sense of it or gives it *meaning*.

Finding an equilibrium between the two is in fact the central problem that Hegel has with Kant's works: that his philosophy had in fact churned Vernunft into a Verstand, a discourse on meaning and pure reason that does not elevate itself beyond intellectualizing it, splicing it, categorizing it. In his own view, Vernunft's very function is to suppress and consume the oppositions in Verstand.[10] Keeping this in mind, it becomes clear that the paragraph introduces something new and "post-Kantian" in Clausewitz's thinking. Using the terms in a very precise way Clausewitz brings forward the possibility that within the paradox that divides the real from the absolute there exists a possible "unity" with or consumption of the opposition, upon which emerges a new, higher concept (*Begriff*). Was he in fact flirting with Hegelianism? Before we can answer this question it is essential that we start by exploring Hegel's philosophy and method, and this is where the next few chapters are about to take us: away from strategic and tactical questions, away from ontological questions, and into the sphere of practical life, ethics.

6 Kant, *Kritik der Reinen Vernunft*, ebook locations 6342 and 3978.
7 Arendt, *La vie de l'esprit*, 29.
8 Vaysse, *Le vocabulaire de Kant*, 36.
9 Ibid., 85.
10 Benoit Garceau, "Les travaux de jeunesse," 31–2.

7

The Unresolved Ethical Impasse in Dialectical War Theory

BY UNDERSTANDING THE DIALECTICAL SYSTEM of thought as meaning not only a process of thinking in twos, but also of thinking in terms of how larger paradoxes can emerge from our attempts to resolve smaller paradoxes, we begin to grasp the method as a continuum and something in motion. As a result, if we wish to give ourselves a full view of the paradox that splits apart the political ethics of Clausewitz and Hegel, it is not enough to consider it in isolation. In order to clarify the significance of the modern political ethos born of the bourgeois revolutions and the republic, it is useful to compare it to the morality that proceeded it and from which it emerges in its contradiction to what preceded it. It will appear as its own dialectical process that arrives as a reply to the moral premises of master and slave moralities, as an intellectual basis for the disintegration not only of social bonds built upon the right to life and ownership of people, but the systems of justifications upon which these social bonds are sustained.

I must start by apologizing to the reader for what this means to the flow of this book and its argument. In the coming pages, we are going to divert our attention from the core subject and take a detour – a scenic route, perhaps – in order to return to our subject in chapter 8 and onwards with an additional building block that will anchor some of the conclusions that can be made regarding the ethical concepts found in Clausewitz and Hegel. The object of chapter 7 is to briefly consider the evolution of political and religious ethics and to distinguish pre-modern from modern constructs regarding justification and morality in the context of war.

The commonality between Hegel's and Clausewitz's ethical systems is that they introduced a secular, political ethos to our concept of war, which replaced the ethical context that framed warfare prior to modern times: a naturalist, theistic ethos, where war could be understood as a fact of nature, the wrath of god or the fulfillment of scripture, where war could be legitimized insofar as it pleased the gods. The modern secular ethos developed by Hegel and Clausewitz was not immaculately conceived, but can be understood as the logical unravelling and effective replacement of the paradox that was inherent to the previous theistic ethos of war. To fully appreciate the significance of the new ethical system, it is necessary that we should go back briefly in time, consider what preceded it, in order to perceive its birthplace and the momentum of contradiction in history which brought forward its necessary and logical fruition.

That war is a political thing may appear to be simple and not very contentious a proposition to our modern ears. And with regard to Clausewitz's famed formula, "war is the continuation of policy by other means" some twentieth century authors have indeed played around with arguments along the line of "so what?" It is indeed tempting, because it is easy, but it ignores just how complex and original this idea would be from the perspective of those who had never reflected upon it. Foucault stands out for having best phrased this easy retort in his critical analysis regarding whether one should ever separate politics from war, asking: "Should we turn the expression around, then, and say that politics is war pursued by other means?"[1]

While there is good reason to agree with the counter-strategic tradition in war theory in which war and politics are understood as a historical and "mutually generative relationship,"[2] Foucault's counter-formula is far from being problem-free. In trying to play on the reciprocity or interdependency that shapes war and politics, Foucault doesn't consider that while policy may depend on force and force on policy, war itself – as Clausewitz argues – does not and cannot exist *independently* of policy.[3] Foucault's observation suggests that war can come first, and policy second, but this could very well be an indemonstrable proposition. The inverse, however, can be shown to be true in most instances, even those where one would least expect it. Even in a timarchy, where the whole apparatus of society is based on military governance, and where one might expect that war is most likely to emerge immaculately conceived as a cultural or social phenomenon that exists independently of policy, this is not the case. War remains a decision, and therefore an act of policy. Plans are drawn up. Directives are given from the generals to the foot soldiers. There might be a propensity toward choosing to engage in war

1 Foucault, *History of Sexuality*, 93.

2 Reid, "Re-appropriating Clausewitz," 277.

3 Clausewitz, *On War*, bk VIII, ch. 2B, 674.

in such society, but there is no war until a decision has been taken to make war, regardless of how this decision-making process takes form. If that is the case in even the most purified form of war-related government, then it must necessarily be even truer of all non-military governments. Foucault's inversion of the formula, though it is an aesthetically pleasing approach to refutation, ultimately has very little scientific weight: even if one had irrefutable data that demonstrated a credible set of wars that were conceived independently of policy and thereafter shaping policy, the argument would nonetheless remain rather meaningless, because, as Raymond Aron pithily explains: "These formulas are, formally, equivalent. They both express the continuity of competition and the use of alternately violent and non-violent means towards ends which do not differ in essence."[4]

Once war is conceived as inherently tied to the political in one way or the other, it is freed from all other conceptions, of which the most historically important would be the idea of war as an act of god or the fulfillment of scripture. Understanding war as policy is part and parcel with the secularization of warfare and its demystification. From this perspective, for example, we can even look at holy wars from an external standpoint and perceive them as having nothing holy to them at all, being merely policy orientations that happen to be dictated by clerical authorities. It is a significant breakthrough, first, because once observed objectively as policy, war's nature can never *un-secularize* itself (as the above example shows), and second, because the ethical consequences of excluding the divine are extreme: it implies that responsibility in war is located at the human level. Here, the greater good is constructed as an intelligible object, not as the subjective whims of deities.

The difficulty with studying the ethics of modern secular war is that the notions of good and evil are not as clearly demarcated as in religious ethics, where they are not only categorical but also explicitly stated in scripture. Breaking war away from mythology does not necessarily lead to more benign or more malign forms of warfare, however – but it does pose a major conundrum for the justification for warfare. If, on the one hand, the secular frame allows a more logical understanding of the motivations in war and generates the bases for a sociology of war, rooted in the human condition and its social organization, thereby lending itself to a more systematic and scientific study, the difficulty that haunts it is whether or not there is such a thing as a *secular conscience*, a voice within the human – as opposed to divine – world, which

4 Aron, *Peace and War*, 162.

can serve as the ethical focal point where decisions regarding greater goods and lesser evils take form.

Defining war as a purely political thing, thereby excluding the divine, is precisely where the dialectics of Hegel and Clausewitz converged. Clausewitz's perspective on this was presented in chapter 5, and now, in chapter 7, we shall go over the way in which Hegel understood this political nature. Their convergence reaches an impasse as both authors draw conclusions with regard to the ethical form the demystification of war should take. While they both agree on the questions "who?" and "what?," when it comes to war's relation to politics, they disagree on the questions "how?" and "why?" – that is to say, war is political, and it belongs to the state or the political will, but the ethical implications are distinct because they disagree on how the state takes ownership or is in possession of it.

Hegel will find the ethical element of war residing in the thing itself, a self-justifying right of the state or institutionalized political will, whereas Clausewitz makes a neutral conclusion, where war is an instrument of the state, and therefore deprived of any self-contained ethical rationale. Thus, while the political element is raised to the centre, the ethical element remains unresolved, because even within this common political frame, the locus of responsibility for good and evil in war can be distinct.

Addressing this subject of good and evil in war is a delicate task in that, regardless of the angle one takes, there is an almost oxymoronic element to the term "war ethics" that leads to the criticism that those who make the attempt are merely trying to cover war's dirty, ugly face with a glossy mask. How can anyone distinguish good and evil, in the context of war, if all sides claim to be fighting for the greater good and all sides are committing evil acts? Studying ethics in war cannot undo this greater problem altogether, but it can contribute to improving our discernment and understanding. And there are lasting and measurable positive effects, such as laws of war, the creation of an international criminal court to punish crimes against humanity, heightened care for avoiding attacks on civilians, and most importantly – as the next few chapters will explore – a narrowing the set of reasons for going to war in the first place. Finally there is only one logically inescapable reason, as opposed to the wide array of reasons that could be claimed in previous eras of human history: evangelization, manifest destiny, glory, plunder, debt collection, monarchical successions, formal colonization, and capturing slaves – though the list may go on.

To codify war ethics, it is useful to avoid categorizing all of evil on one side of the conflict and all of good on the other. Rather, the problem of war ethics resides in the fact that the categories are usually intertwined and relative: first, war may be conceived as a particular evil that is justified by the idea that it is being fought towards the greater good or in reply to an immediate wrong or aggression, and secondly, within the context of war's evils, there can be ways in which this evil can be mitigated by good actions in war. The latter of the two is generally referred to as *jus in bello*, justice in war, an approach to finding "good" practices in war – including, for example, prohibitions on certain types of weapons (e.g. landmines, mustard gas, etc.), the discrimination between civilian and military targets, proportionality in the application of force. This subset is not the principle subject of the coming pages, however, though some themes might indirectly cross over from time to time. The subject at hand is rather the former of the two, generally referred to as *jus ad bellum*, the reasons for going to war in the first place. Within this category, there are highly tangible reasons for war, or *just cause* for war, such as fighting back an invasion or punishing a grave wrong, but there has always been some wiggle room for much less tangible justifications for warfare where it is the promise of a greater good, a dream to spread by war something that would justify the evils of war – and here one should be cautious and critical regarding what such justifications entail.

It is typical in the field to speak of the wars justified in this manner using the term crusade, be it religious, liberal, or revolutionary. However, this term is as overused as it is imprecise, since it assumes the intangible reasons for war lead to intangible or unlimited aims in warfare. A war justified by scripture or by gods may have ambitions that are in fact quite limited, and unmotivated by grand schemes for converting new adepts or reclaiming all lands holy. Rebels fighting to topple a prince or a tyrant may be grounded in some ideology without necessarily having any intention to embark on a campaign to spread the revolution. And so the question at hand is not so much where and how far an idea can take war, but rather which ideas have this power to justify war in intangible ways – why and how they generate such a powerful sense of greater good that they can justify not any singular evil, but forms of evil that shift and evolve over time for reasons of policy, strategy, and tactics.

Even within a secular notion of war ethics, the concepts of good and evil imply metaphysical properties. The dyad of good and evil is unavoidably imbued with theistic vestiges, its connotation and etymology being spiritual to begin with. As Nietzsche explores in his *Genealogy of Morals*, goodness – even as a collective concept – is by no means an objective and immutable thing, but one that has varied dramatically in time and space according to the subjective values of different peoples. In fact, Nietzsche argues that completely opposite notions of goodness can exist concurrently, depending on context or experiences of social life, as is the case with populations in positions of slavery or mastery. "The real homestead of the concept 'good' is sought and located in the wrong place. the judgment 'good' did not originate among those to whom goodness was shown. Much rather has it been the good themselves, that is, the aristocratic, the powerful, the high-stationed, the high-minded, who have felt that they themselves were good."[5]

The English word "good" itself is derived from "god," a fact equally true of the Latin languages, where "bene" ("bien" in French, "bueno" in Spanish, etc.) is derived from the Indo-European root for the "word of god." Given this, it is best to understand goodness as it pertains to being godlike or at the very least, in concordance with godliness. It should be assumed, then, that if the gods to which peoples pray change over time there will likewise be serious shifts in the motives for war – or more precisely, in how it is justified by scripture and without heresy.

Without wanting to go too far into what form a theistic concept of good and evil takes when it is applied to war, it is worth taking a quick look, which will clarify the distinction of modern ethics to pre-modern ethics. In the ancient Greco-Roman world, justifying war as "godlike" would have been a very simple thing, for the gods were vengeful, vain, and cruel. There had been war among the gods and the Titans. There were fierce episodes of violence and viciousness. Cronus ate his own children. Zeus sliced Cronus open to free his brothers Poseidon and Hades. In this world, savage and eternal punishments abound and were imposed by powerful gods onto lower gods, or by any god onto humans. The god Prometheus was tied to a boulder and suffered the pain of having his liver eaten out by an eagle daily, only to regenerate by night. Sisyphus, a man, suffered another such eternal fate, carrying a boulder uphill only to let it roll down in order to carry it uphill, again and again, forever. To act godlike in this context is to act as the master acts towards the slave, with no recognition of any right – not life, not dignity, nothing. In such a context, even the idea that war should be "justified" could be questioned in the first place. Why would it need justification at all, if the universe is understood as an essentially brutal place, governed naturally by force and cruelty? Man was not responsible for war, because war was a fact of nature, and to fight was merely to survive, to live. In this context, Thucydides's famous maxim takes its fullest meaning: "The strong do what they can and the weak suffer what they must."[6]

In complete opposition to this, in the Christian tradition, derived from the Judaic experience of exodus and slavery, the difficulty in reconciling

5 Nietzsche, *Genealogy of Morals*, 634.

6 Strassler, *Landmark Thucydides*, 352, #5.89.

Jesus's pacifism and meekness with warfare was a more difficult task – but it was a difficulty that nonetheless could be overcome. If a legitimate authority amongst Christians could identify a just cause, then war could be just in the eyes of god insofar as his meek warriors intended the advancement of good, or the avoidance of evil, which essentially means working towards advancing god's justice in the world.[7] This was the required rhetoric, which could smooth out the coexistence between the teachings of Christ and the realpolitik of sustaining his Church. It was achieved by separating the idea of good and evil as it relates to the personal and to the universal and spiritual, making it thereby possible to be a warring Christian, meek and pacifist at heart, while also projecting a violence thoroughly external to the self, the will of god fought for the glory of god, as opposed to an individual act for gain and glory. *Non nobis Domine, non nobis, sed nomini tuo da gloriam* was the motto of the Knights Templar: "Not to us, Lord, but to Your Name give the glory."[8] Whereas Greco-Roman goodness could be achieved directly in imitation of the cruel gods, the Christians needed to remove themselves from the act, thereby *incarnating the divine* (a concept that is central to Christian faith) through meekness and self-sacrifice, in imitation of the form of goodness expressed in the teachings and the life and death of their "Son of God."

Religious coherence was achieved with regard to war in both cases, though for very distinct reasons. The common element was that both forms of religious justification implied the non-accountability or non-responsibility of the human element in the inhumanity of war. The actions of war were pre-ordained in mysticism, because war had yet been conceived as a social construction, but assumed to belong to the natural order of things or to the fulfillment of god's will. The externalization of responsibility in the dehumanization found in warfare is analogous and therefore the logical outcome of religions based on the slave/master duality, since the basis for godliness in both cases is the outcome of this dehumanizing pair. The spiritual element is conceived as either cruel and warlike and causing war, or meek and redeeming and repairing the harms of war.

If Nietzsche judged it better to assume a master morality than a slave morality what he missed in the process was the possibility that the master/slave relationship had in fact been transcended, finished conceptually by the ideals of the bourgeois revolutions. The modern political realm was no longer dependent on either of the two moral systems that Nietzsche placed

7 Aquinas, *Summa Theologica.*

8 Psalms 115:1, *King James Bible Online,* accessed 27 April 2016, http://www.kingjamesbibleonline.org/Psalms-Chapter-115.

in opposition but could instead be grounded in new precepts, where mutual recognition of rights and equality in the brotherhood of man would exclude the role of gods as either the justification for a brutal state of nature, or alternatively, a redeemer or payer of debts. The synthesis of a new war ethic from the vestiges of two previously opposed ethics was only possible because the new social relations of man excluded the dehumanization of mastery and slavery. Mutual recognition of rights raised the human element upwards, and rendered the divine element unnecessary to social relations – not only within borders, but also beyond borders.

It was the French who best constructed or verbalized the ethical doctrine of the modern republic in their *dévise*: "Liberté. Égalité. Fraternité." The triad is not a mere slogan, but a system of internal necessity that generates political universality. There can be no liberty and equality for all unless there is universal mutual recognition of these: fraternity. There can be no universal liberty unless all are equal and recognized as such. And there can be no universal equality unless all men are free and recognized as such. The emergence of this triadic concept was the ultimate demise of the master/slave relationship and its derivatives in serfdom, monarchy, etc., because it eliminated the very essence of these relationships. Thus liberty, equality, and fraternity were at the very heart of a secularization process in politics in that their logic was self-contained, self-ordained, and independent of an external or metaphysical force to qualify or define good and evil. Together, the three represented a new worldly concept of goodness that occurred without any imitation of the divine.

The process of arriving at a political rather than theistic ethical framework for war was a long historical process involving the development of ideas about community, about the divine, and about the intersection of the two. While we can notice in the bourgeois revolutions a beginning of this transition, it was not written into war theory in an exhaustive and systematic way until Hegel and Clausewitz. Could their political ethos change the shape and form that wars could take, not only in why a nation might choose to fight, and who it would fight, but also how its fighting doctrines would themselves evolve? If there is indeed a secular conscience, which resides outside of the divine world and in the human spirit, what form would it give to war? War is an exercise at the very cusp of good and evil, where lesser evils are meant to be tolerated for greater goods, and where we often attempt to add minor illusions of good onto a canvas of much greater evil. The advantage with a divine ethical concept is its absoluteness. It makes decisions easy. But in a system that relativizes and places mankind at the centre of responsibility for its actions in the world, what guidance will a secular conscience provide?

8

Framing War as a Right: The "Actualization" of Freedom

IN ORDER TO UNDERSTAND Hegel's perspective on war and why he sees war as having an "ethical element," one must step back and analyze what Hegel perceived as the greater good worth defending in society. The term he uses, "actualized freedom," is far more complex than what we might assume when looking at these two familiar words in juxtaposition. And as I will discuss in the final chapter and epilogue, improperly understanding the concept of freedom in one's attempt to use it in justifying war can lead to types of war that are all the more brutal and unjustifiable. Again, we must be patient in breaking down complex ideas before attempting to draw meaning from words. In this case, Hegel's theory of war is a sub-product of his political theory, which is itself only one of many building blocks that – together with his theory of reason and history – form a larger metaphysical theory that stretches from the human experiment, our perception and thought, to the cosmic and divine.

Before we dive into this overarching philosophical system, it is worth noting, in keeping with the subject of the previous chapter, that Hegel's ideas on the relationship between master and slave are the backbone of his political theorizing. The idea that a slave's fear of death and the master's power to kill can lead the former to submit to the latter's will is not difficult to grasp – it comes intuitively, but there is nonetheless an intellectual process that underlines this intuitive conclusion. Understanding this process is all the more essential in our attempt to understand the less intuitive continuation of this relationship into the future: why does one remain a slave years after being captured, or why is slavery perpetuated intergenerationally sometimes? The explanation is not as evident as the one underlying the original moment of submission.

"Hegel's account of slavery is unique," explains Smith, in that it is derived "neither from nature, nor providence, nor chance, but from the very structure of self-consciousness."[1] Indeed if two individuals clash they are both self-aware of their own individuality, but to recognize this in the other is to confer equality, which is neither's desire – to fight is the assertion of oneself and one's will. "The fight ends in the first instance as a one-sided negation with inequality. While the one combatant prefers life, retains his single self-consciousness, but surrenders his claim for recognition, the other holds fast to his self-assertion and is recognized by the former as his superior. Thus arises the status of master and slave."[2]

The same approach that allows Hegel to see this backdrop of the master/slave relationship also helps us understand what underlies it, from the perspective of the slave: the impetus for emancipation, the idea of freedom as a reason to live. The work of slavery, Hegel explains, is a "formative activity"[3] because it objectifies the slave's concept of freedom, gives him a purpose and a future, and though he may fear the master, the slave nonetheless achieves an idea of permanence – a future – that contributes to overcoming this fear. Meanwhile, the master may have superiority in the present moment, but he has no future. He is dependent on the slave in order to maintain the status he enjoys in the relationship. His existence is in the past and the present, while the slave owns the future and lives for it. This is why it can be said that "the history of the world is none other than the progress of the consciousness of freedom."[4]

This idea of history, its objective, and justification along the way is a key component of how he understands the ethical element in war, but to appreciate how this idea is grounded in reason, rather than opinion, one must go back to the very root of the method. It departs considerably from the means by which dialectics found their initial point of entry in Clausewitz's theory of war, but it nonetheless has a common ancestor in Kant.

While Clausewitz was adapting Kantian methodologies to war theory directly, Hegel was exploring the consequences of Kant's ideas philosophically, trying to move beyond the metaphysical impasse between the real and the ideal that Kant had bequeathed to philosophical posterity. As a result the dialectics of war were split methodologically from their very onset: Clausewitz was developing an isolated dialectical theory of war, and Hegel was developing a dialectical universe that would eventually encapsulate the question of war as well, not as a distinct study, but rather as a sub-section in his chapter on the state. This gap would eventually

1 Smith, "Hegel on Slavery and Domination," 100.
2 Hegel, *Encyclopedia*, vol. 3, par. 426, 167–8; *Werke*, vol. 10, 215–16. Cited in ibid., 101.
3 Hegel, *Phenomenology of Spirit*, #196, 119.
4 Hegel, *Philosophy of History*, 18, 19; *Werke*, vol. 12, 32. Cited in Smith, "Hegel," 108.

converge as Clausewitz began experimenting with Hegelian dialectics and increasingly integrated them into his works. That being said, before we can start exploring this convergence, we must first ask what Hegelian dialectics actually are, and how Hegel himself applied them to war.

This chapter is devoted exclusively to the study of Hegelian method and Hegel's own understanding of the ethical underpinnings of state and war. This is no easy task since it is impossible to appreciate the depth of Hegel's ideas on war and state simply by extracting certain ideas and quotes; one must analyze his conclusions in the context of his system as a whole, or else they either come off as wry or altogether unintelligible. Therefore, we shall go through the steps of framing Hegel's philosophy as a reply to Kant's *Critique of Pure Reason*, and thereafter explore Hegel's method in its simplest form, followed by its more complex application to the realm of politics and society. This step-by-step process will clarify Hegel and provide the whole picture, which allows us to develop a better than average, and more balanced, appreciation of Hegel's most controversial conclusions on war. The oft-cited and generally loathed passage, "*War is the moral health of peoples in their struggle against petrifaction*,"[5] will be shown to have a legitimate underlying logic – because the state is in itself an ethical system meant to generate, develop, and protect individual freedom. The strength or decay of the nation is for Hegel deeply linked to the notion of freedom, because freedom represents both the central raison d'être and the modus operandi of the state or modern republic. Freedom is presented as a self-fulfilling loop that vitalizes both the state and its citizens. And insofar as war is fought for this freedom it is, by Hegelian standards, justified in itself as a right of the state.

HEGELIAN DIALECTICS: AN OVERVIEW

Hegel's phenomenological system is organized from the simple to the complex. In keeping with this approach, I will start off by presenting the first building blocks of the method – understanding how we become certain of what we perceive with our senses – so that we may quickly get a modest but practical grasp of how it works, and thereupon begin a deeper exploration of how to use it in the context of war and politics.

In the first pages of the *Phenomenology*, which is one of Hegel's earlier works and also serves as an introduction to his philosophical system, Hegel explains his approach in the very first pages by discussing a paradox, or

5 Hegel, *Phenomenology of Mind*, 432. Note: exceptionally I am referring here to the Baillie translation, since it is the formula for this phrase that has caused the most controversy.

what he refers to as an "uneasiness":[6] the fact that one can regard cognition as either an instrument for constructing the world in a way that makes it intelligible, or else as a medium, a lens through which the world makes itself known to us. The problem being that in either case, the truth is not arriving at us in its pure form, but either as one that is distorted by the medium or shaped by the instrument.[7] Hegel is in fact attempting to create a philosophy that falls into neither category and recognizes the limits of attempting to understand the idea of knowledge from either of these perspectives. He rejects the duality that gives rise to the problem in the first place, and replaces it with the method itself: objectivity is the overcoming of subjectivity in becoming self-aware of it. The very same way in which Hegel describes his system, is in fact his system itself, and this becomes clear when we consider how he applies it to man's first level and simplest form of understanding, which is perception, or how we achieve sense-certainty in space and time, through such a process overcoming oppositions.

To situate where this is coming from, it is necessary first to return to the legacy of Kant's *Critique of Pure Reason.* Having spliced human understanding along the lines of mutually exclusive categories, where theology and the sciences no longer coexisted, Kant had created a chasm between the real and the ideal. In answer to this impasse, Hegel questioned its very premise on the grounds that it was impossible for an idea to be beyond or outside the scope of the real world, since the very act of conceiving an idea happens in the real world. Hegel thereby exposed a major contradiction at the very heart of Kantian thought, in that this abstract world of ideas, which is supposedly external to actual thought, is in fact posited by thought in the first place.[8] To break down the divide between the real and the ideal, Hegel proposed rather that, "what is rational is actual and what is actual is rational"[9] – in effect transitioning from Kant's dichotomous chasm between noumena and phenomena to a higher order of understanding meant to encompass both the real and the ideal realms.

To do this Hegel returned to the original problem, formulated by Hume, questioning the possibility of "necessary connection," which had been the central impetus for Kant's work – and then he turned it on its head. Hume had argued that "we are never able, in a single instance, to discover any power or necessary connection";[10] and now Hegel, instead

6 Hegel, *Phenomenology of Spirit,* #73, 46.

7 Ibid.

8 Taylor, *Hegel,* 117.

9 Hegel, preface to *Philosophy of Right,* 10.

10 Hume, *Enquiries,* 63.

of accepting that necessary connection was not in the purview of human understanding, would reverse the question and generate instead a "system of necessary connection,"[11] in which necessary connection is no longer the unattainable conceptual end that Hume had uncovered, nor must it lead to Kant's strict categorization, but is in fact the universe's underlying logic itself, a dialectical process by which the ideal becomes manifest in the real world, or what Hegel referred to as the "Spirit of the world" or Geist.

The implications of this are significant, because if "what is actual is rational" and "what is rational is actual," then the logic behind this universe depends on the fact that the rational can be actualized and the actual can just as well be rationalized. This is the major objective of Hegelian thought. He was trying to show us how these processes take place. In the first pages of the *Phenomenology*, Hegel demonstrates how reason works using the simplest form, where the individual perceives his world and becomes self-conscious. However as we read onwards, we realize that reason builds upon these first steps and raises itself to the more complex – it is like how a child learns over time, from seeing and touching to eventually building on these experiences an idea of the world – synthesizing a more complete picture based on the accumulation and development of knowledge. Yet, no matter how complex knowledge happens to be, Hegel presents it as developing according to the same logic unfolding at each new and higher layer, where negation plays the central role in the formation of knowledge.

In Hegel's initial section on sense certainty – which opens the *Phenomenology* – this process becomes evident. We find that one understands "seeing" only insofar as one has seen, and then not seen, the same object. This ability to discern between something one sees and something one doesn't see is precisely the basis upon which negation generates knowledge. This process of negation is what one could call a negation upwards, where the simple is transformed into the more complex, where two acts of perception (positive and negative) come together as one process of understanding. But the higher understanding that emerges depends on transcending the contradiction in a way by which the "lower stage is both annulled and preserved in a higher one."[12]

For seeing to occur, Hegel explains, the observer and the object observed must be in relation to one another in time and place. Yet, there are a variety of mutually exclusive possibilities within this occurrence of a relation, given the questions of how we define the here and the now.

11 Taylor, *Hegel*, 128.
12 Ibid., 119.

For example, Hegel proposes that one can be looking here and see a tree or looking at another here and see its opposite, not-a-tree. Also, the act of seeing is happening now but this could be, for example, day or night.[13] How can any of the posited ideas be true if it is possible that the very opposite is just as valid, depending on context? These are not absolute, but rather fleeting notions of truth: "Both truths have the same authentification, viz. the immediacy of seeing, and the certainty and assurance that both have about their knowing; but the one truth vanishes in the other."[14]

So we reach a first impasse. Now I see a tree, then I turn 180° and, in the new now, I no longer see a tree. Yet there remains one universally valid reality within these opposites: the "I" in either time or space is nonetheless seeing. Recognizing that one can "see" is a higher form of knowledge than just the act of seeing itself: if I saw something then, and now I don't see it, then there must be a relation between these two facets of seeing. The fact that I can distinguish having seen from not seeing is precisely the source of seeing's universality as a concept. It exists outside of me; it is objective, because I can conceptualize both its posited reality and its negated reality. Despite the demonstration of opposites, the "'Here' itself does not vanish," pointing it out as "'This' shows it to be a universality."[15] This is the second moment in the process of cognition: where the negation subdues what has been posited. Yet, something greater has emerged in our understanding.

When we try to conceptualize the now, we go through the same impossibility of seizing it – since as soon as one has pointed it out, it has ceased to be. To understand time, we must conceptualize how the now is no longer now once it has been identified as now. The truth about the now is that, when it is shown to us, it is already a "has-been."[16] In this case, the act of "pointing out" is an act of negating. Yet it is in this very "movement" that we uncover its truth: when one acknowledges the "has-been" as "having-been," then the negation is itself negated and the idea is elevated or superseded. Hegel describes our knowledge of the here and the now as "self-reflected movements," where to achieve knowledge of them, we must have gone through three phases, or what Hegel refers to as "moments": positing, negating, and negating the negation. Unlike the philosophers of the Enlightenment who saw knowledge as a static object for us subjects to grasp, Hegel is making the argument for a concept of

13 Hegel, *Phenomenology of Spirit*, #96, 60.
14 Ibid., #101, 61.
15 Ibid., #98, 61.
16 Ibid., #106, 63.

knowledge that is in constant flux, a process that advances in time and builds up its own certainty and self-awareness. "It is clear that the dialectic of sense-certainty is nothing else but the simple history of its movement or of its experience, and sense-certainty itself is nothing else but just this history."[17] Even the simplest form of Hegel's system – knowing that we can see – is a "historical" process. So we can imagine how interesting things will get when this approach is used to study… human history itself.

The process of overcoming dichotomous pairs and achieving new levels of knowledge is what Hegel calls the "*Aufhebung*," which translates roughly in English to "sublation." It is the coming together of opposites towards achieving a higher conceptual plateau. While on occasion one might come across this word translated directly as "negation" or "invalidation," these undermine an important aspect of the process: what is sublated is neither lost and vanished nor is it made false, but rather incorporated. Through Aufhebung, "the higher unity integrates the principles found at the lower level and supplies new content on its own. The principles at the lower level acquire new patterns of meaning by being integrated into the higher conception."[18] This is how knowledge develops and materializes in time, as we gain better insight into its building blocks, its scope, its depth, and its richness. And this is enhanced through each opposition and overcoming of opposition.[19] Thus, Hegel sees understanding knowledge as a dynamic process in time, and he explains that truth is history developing itself over time: "The truth is the whole. But the whole is nothing other than the essence consummating itself through its development. Of the Absolute, it must be said that it is essentially a result, that only in the end is it what it truly is."[20]

If we saw in the question of sense-certainty Hegel's micro-level of analysis, we are now catching a glimpse of the other extreme, the macro-level, which is useful here because it gives us a sense of where the individual and the state exist: somewhere between these two poles. Given that he was answering Kant's discussion of the universe and its breakdown into the real and the ideal, Hegel had to conceptualize the whole as well. If reason is indeed making its way through time, materializing and deepening itself as a process of encountering and overcoming dichotomies, one might expect that there should be an end point to this progress of knowledge. If there were, it could only be one thing, the whole of knowledge

17 Ibid., #109, 64.

18 Pinkard, "Freedom and Social Categories," 232.

19 Plant, *Hegel*, 139.

20 Hegel, *Phenomenology of Spirit*, #20, 11.

reflected onto itself and recognizing itself objectively as this whole. There is a godly aura to this, as though the universe is somehow the spirit making itself manifest in the universe. Hegel considers that reason materialized is a real whole: it is imbued with a certain substantive life of its own, a power of sorts, but only insofar as it has become objective, or self-aware of its totality. Hegel refers to this self-awareness of reason as a whole, negated and transcended into objectiveness as "Geist." Hence, Geist is the idea that synthesizes the "concept" with the "actual."

Existing within it, or rather "for it," individuals and states give this "spirit" its shape and substantive life: they are the "vehicles" by which Geist exists in the world. "In this process," Taylor explains, "men come to a new understanding of self: they see themselves not just as individual fragments of the universe, but rather as vehicles of cosmic spirit. And hence, men can achieve at once the greatest unity with nature, i.e. with the spirit which unfolds itself in nature."[21] That is to say, in a world of inherent oppositions and contradiction, the arrival at certainty and unity in the world is achieved as a process, a method that consists of becoming aware of paradoxes and learning to integrate them into our understanding onwards to larger and more complex paradoxes.

In order to transition into a discussion about politics then, we must keep in mind that human affairs occur somewhere in the mid-section between Hegel's most basic form of material history, sensory knowledge, and the other extreme, which has cosmic proportions. The logic that generates this mid-section is no different for Hegel, and it also advances and develops itself as the progression of rationality making itself evermore manifest.

When applied to human affairs, this method of reasoning provides a new depth of analysis because it describes how self-awareness is a process of reciprocation as well. Achieving universality is a process of negation, and this is equally true in human affairs. In the case of the master and slave relationship that we considered briefly above, there was something incomplete to it. There is no mutual recognition yet, but we can conceive its eventuality. When mutual recognition is achieved, the moral guidance of a nation is no longer a mere vow of obedience of one person to another, but obedience to the law and the legal arrangement of the state.[22] The space in which this arrangement can exist is the modern state, which establishes the equality of its inhabitants and their social interactions as such. The state is a historical advancement, and though we can easily conceive of it from our vantage point – living within political

21 Taylor, *Hegel*, 128.

22 Hegel, *Encyclopedia*, vol. 3, par. 552, 286; *Werke*, vol. 10, 358–9. Cited in Smith, "Hegel on Slavery and Domination," 115.

systems that have been in place for over 200 years – we may forget to notice the complex paradoxes upon which it rests. These are the very same paradoxes that we find at the heart of the master-slave relationship: achieving self-consciousness as an individual nation or state, manifesting its will for its people and institutions to exist, but also confronted with the encounter of other nations, states, institutions, and peoples.

STATE INTEREST AND CONTINGENCY IN INTERNATIONAL LAW

A good place to start in our quest to understand the basic form of Hegel's concept of state is to contrast his point of view with Kant's famous essay *Perpetual Peace*. Published in 1795, the short manifesto stands out not only as one of Kant's last articles, but also as one of his rare political pieces. Kant and Hegel had opposite views on the questions of state and peace. Deconstructing the parts of the argument will help us build up a better understanding of how Hegel's opposite conclusion stems from its basis in a distinct philosophical system from which the modern state is not assumed as a thing in itself so much as an idea that emerges in history and asserts itself materially as a right of constituted free men.

Timing explains part of the disagreement. Kant was writing at the height of the French Revolution, and was therefore fuelled by a certain optimism regarding the possibilities for peace among the emerging republics. Europe at the time was still scarred by the memory of the Seven Years' War, which had been fought on an unprecedented scale: the size of the engagements as well as the global reach of the conflict, beyond oceans. The war had been so expensive that it would alter the geopolitics of Europe, kings were bankrupted, heavily indebted, and on the decline, while the bourgeois class rose in wealth, power, and prestige. Many still viewed the Seven Years' War as completely unjustified because of the relative imbalance between the level of violence and the futility of its objectives. Voltaire's description was particularly pithy: "It is another kind of folly. You know that these two countries are at war for a few acres of snow in Canada, and they spend over this beautiful war much more than Canada is worth."[23] The arrival of the modern republic provided a hope that war, these violent whims of a disconnected and irresponsible nobility, belonged to less advanced, less perfected forms of government.

Hegel, on the other hand, was writing after the Napoleonic Wars, and consequently perhaps was less optimistic about the reasonableness of republics. He had seen the power of counter-revolution, the massive effect

23 Voltaire, *Candide*, 67.

of France's *levées en masse*, and the passions and power of its citizen-army as they brought war from one end of Europe to another. In this context, he could not think of war as merely an unjustified game played by kings for the control of populations to tax and colonies to exploit. He had to ask himself if free citizens of France had the right to wage war against counter-revolutionary movements coming from Austria, England, or Russia, and to spread the new constitutions and liberties of the revolution abroad. If war could be justified for reasons of independence from foreign occupiers or to safeguard the institution of a government for and by the people, what exactly was the source of this right, how was it ethically constructed? This was the end goal of Hegel's *Philosophy of Right*, which begins with a discussion of the formation of individual rights and moves towards the question of the rights of states.

Historical context explains in part why Kant could easily understand war as a defect of the political system, attributable to royal discretion, moral decadence, and the failure of reason to prevail. But more importantly, the Enlightenment's optimism and ideal of perfectibility was still present in Kant's writing. "The principle of the moral politician will be that if defects have slipped either into the constitution of the state or into the relations of states with one another, it is principally the duty of the chiefs to make instantly such amendments as are conformable to the natural right founded on reason."[24]

According to Kant, providence, destiny, and nature have the "aim to produce a harmony among men, against their will and indeed through their discord."[25] Hence, while Kant's sympathies in the matter of revolution were on the side of the French Revolution, his sympathies in the matter of war were squarely with peace.[26] Republicanism, Kant argued, allowed reason to reign – not only internally, but also in interstate relations. War represented a threat to these structures of rationality, which explains why Kant wrote that "reason, from its throne of supreme moral legislating authority, absolutely condemns war as a legal recourse and makes a state of peace a direct duty, even though peace cannot be established or secured except by a compact of nations."[27] Kant sought a "judiciary order" for the world, and only the federative model could achieve this while respecting the freedoms of states.[28] Through federation, states would establish a world sphere governed by reason, where laws and

24 Kant, *Perpetual Peace*, 50.
25 Kant, *Project for a Perpetual Peace*. Cited in Arendt, *Lectures*, 52.
26 Arendt, *Lectures*, 52.
27 Kant, *Project for a Perpetual Peace*. Cited in ibid.
28 Kant, *Perpetual Peace*, 72.

reciprocity among state would lead to morality on an international scale. Kant's *Preliminary Articles* enumerated a set of such laws to reduce and limit the causes of war among states, which included the signing of secret treaties, the purchase or exchange of states amongst powers, the way in which foreign debt was contracted, and the abolition of standing armies.[29]

Hegel's reaction to this proposal could be understood as a pragmatist's take, but there is much more to it. Without a higher power to impose international law, Hegel argued that these best intentions would crumble whenever states failed to achieve consensus or harmonization of policy. By resting a world order atop the sovereignty of states, international law would be doomed to existing only as mere contingency, rules that "ought to be kept" but can never "go beyond an ought-to-be,"[30] because:

> There is no Praetor to judge between states; at best there may be an arbitrator or mediator, and even he exercises his functions contingently only, i.e. in dependence on the particular wills of the disputants. Kant had an idea for securing "perpetual peace" by a League of Nations to adjust every dispute. It was to be a power recognized by each individual state, and was to arbitrate all cases of dissension in order to make it impossible for disputants to resort to war in order to settle them. This idea presupposes an accord between states; this would rest on moral or religious grounds and considerations, but in any cases would always depend ultimately on particular sovereigns will and for that reason would remain infected with contingency.
>
> It follows that if states disagree and their particular wills cannot be harmonized, the matter can only be settled by war.[31]

A simplistic reading of these passages can lead one to describe Hegel as an early equivalent of the twentieth-century realists, who see states and their agents moralistically as bad or as unable to operate within the framework of international norms and laws. However, Hegel's view is quite contrary to this, for he saw in the state a higher order of reason, an instrument for materializing the "ethical life" within it, where the common good constitutes a higher sphere that integrates but does not submerge the claims of individuality.[32] Actually, the reason why Hegel considers that the state need not fully submit to an external international order, beyond contingency and national interest, is not that it is

29 Kant, *Project for a Perpetual Peace*, ed. Vincent Ferraro, Mount Holyoke College, accessed 29 April 2016, http://www.mtholyoke.edu/acad/intrel/kant/kant1.htm.

30 Hegel, *Philosophy of Right*, #333, 213.

31 Ibid., 213–14.

32 Pinkard, "Hegel's Ethics," 221.

subjectively bad in its external dealings but the opposite: because it is objectively good in its internal purpose, which is to protect its citizens' freedoms and interests.

Where Hegel and Kant agreed with regard to war was that it is an act of discretion. And while Kant saw that as a bad thing, Hegel rather thought that as long as it is an act of discretion that belongs to freely constituted citizens, it is imbued with the ethics inherent to the state. Hegel understood the state as having a universal character, for when citizens constitute the state, they are creating an absolute power under which all are governed equally, an ethical realm in which laws can be legitimately written, and legitimately enforced: the "substance of the state is that it has an absolute power against everything individual and particular, against life, property, and their rights, even against societies and associations."[33] In order for the state to be everything that it pertains to be internally – universal and absolute – it must equally embody this "universal" character in its exterior dealings. It does not need to impose its laws on other states, but the very process of encountering other states confirms its own universality, in reciprocation. By recognizing the existence of states and their own universality, it reaffirms its own concept of self: "The negative relation of the state to itself is embodied in the world as the relation of one state to another and as if the negative were something external ... This negative relation is that moment in the state which is most supremely its own, the state's actual infinity as the ideality of everything finite within it ... become an accomplished fact bringing it home to consciousness."[34]

We can now see more clearly why treaties and international systems find themselves always subject to contingency and state interest. The very process of interacting with other states creates within the state a higher appreciation of its own universal role towards its constituents. The rise of self-consciousness within the state is reciprocal amongst states and thus reinforces contingency at every step that is taken towards harmonization and cooperation. The contradiction becomes truly evident when we consider treaties like the Kyoto Protocol or the Convention on Biodiversity, where numerous signatories are actively, consciously, strategically, and systematically undermining their own commitments despite having ratified certain obligations into national law. Contingency is inherent to treaty making, and to blame treaty failures on morality is to pass the

33 Hegel, *Philosophy of Right*, #323, 209.
34 Ibid.

buck: vilifying individuals and political parties, instead of seeing in their actions a systemic weakness in the concept of international law in the first place.

This leaves us with a question: is there legitimacy to the state's subjectivity? If Hegel relegates war to the ethical legitimacy of statehood, what is this ethical ground upon which the state is elevated? What gives the state the right to view all other forms of law making, including international treaties, as mere contingency? For Hegel, this special status of the state depends on its ability to provide freedom to its citizens. That is the moral basis for the state's right to act upon the world. And this, at times, can be taken to mean war.

That being said, Hegel was by no means an advocate of war, nor did he believe society should be organized in a Spartan or militaristic tradition. Rather, he hoped wars would be rare and only fought for vital interests of the state, such as the redress of injustices or the protection of national independence. Plamenatz notes that: "The Prussians had fought a hard war against Napoleon which had led to domestic reforms and to a burst of patriotism which had other good effects. It is not surprising that a German who had lived through the war of liberation should have believed that war was good for the moral health of the people ... Hegel does not advocate frequent or continuous wars or suggest that war is the noblest activity of man."[35] Many passages from Hegel's works show him "to have been acutely aware of its evils, even though he held that there were times when it was both necessary and right ... nothing in his words justifies the charge that he 'glorified' war, and to maintain that he did is to give an extravagant and misleading description of his ideas."[36]

To illustrate this, we can turn to Hegel's *Lectures on Aesthetics*, in which he wrote: "Now in Europe each nation is limited by another one and it should not, arbitrarily, start a war against another. When we traverse the realm of morality up to its highest stage, the life of the state, and watch whether its purposes are fulfilled or not, we certainly will experience that many are, but more, even the greatest and noblest of them, are spoiled and frustrated through the passions and viciousness of man."[37]

Someone may disagree with the premises of international perpetual peace, but there is a clear distinction between that and being a warmonger. It rather comes down to a question of ethics, rather than a question of war and peace. One should be asking what kind of peace shall we

35 Plamenatz, *Man and Society*, 142–3.
36 Smith, "Hegel on War," 282–5.
37 In ibid.

have, and will it be a good peace? Or shall this peace be the undoing of what we hold as the central purpose of modern citizenship: individual freedom? Where is the greater good? It is this notion of a greater good versus a lesser evil that frames the overarching question: what constitutes an *ethically justifiable* war?

From these questions, we can begin framing the disagreement between the two philosophers based on their distinct definitions of freedom, especially with regard to how this idea exists in the relationship between state and citizen. To begin with, Pinkard explains:

> The basic concept for Hegel's ethics – like that of Kant – is freedom. The Philosophy of Right is an articulation via dialectical argumentation of what the ontological and institutional conditions for freedom would be. Both Hegel and Kant are concerned with explaining the possibility of freedom. However, whereas Kant's explanation rests on the idea of the will's legislating for itself, Hegel ... would argue that only when our straightforward desires (the particulars) coincide with our evaluations of what would be good and right to desire (the universal), is our will truly free.[38]

Thus both authors agree that freedom is rational – but whereas Kant's freedom stands alone, Hegel's freedom is contingent on there being consistency between what one might call the immediate good and the greater good. When applied to the state, this consistency takes the form of there being a mutually constitutive freedom that arises jointly from the state and the citizen. The coinciding of universal and particular desires is pursued in time by the state contributing to the enhancement and development of the individual's empowerment and freedom to act out his or her desires. The state doesn't simply grant freedom to its citizens, it is the act of becoming a state, the mutual recognition of citizens that *constitutes the individual as free*, and this Hegel understands as an enhancement of individual freedom, making the individual more free, more complete than he could be outside the state or in the natural world. Ultimately, the state's existential justification exists in its effect on human development (and here the UNDP, with its Human Development Index, would likely agree). The state is this freedom itself. And while it can appear instrumental, in a sense, that is, the citizen empowers him or herself through and by the state, the state is not for this reason a mere tool of freedom, but the embodiment of freedom in which the individual is elevated to freedom and takes possession of their actions in the world.

38 Pinkard, "Hegel's Ethics," 210–11.

THE STATE AS AN ETHICAL REALM

Before taking on any concrete form, whether a border crossing, barracks, a parliament, a president, or a passport, the ideal Hegelian state is first and foremost a state of mind, an idea that binds people within a single political community, and makes itself manifest through the creation and upkeep of various institutions, founding documents, laws, etc. The idea of state also includes mutual recognition of legal and political rights amongst citizens, which can, for example, take the form of abiding by the outcome of election – even if one is on the losing side of it. These consensual relationships are paradoxical in that they are at any time being coerced onto the people by the state structures, while also being willed by the people themselves. The state structures are composed of people: judges, police, public servants, politicians, all of whom are making decisions and taking actions within a code of conduct that frames their duties and obligations within the state apparatus. That is to say, that whether one is *willing* the form of the laws and institutions of the state, or one is *forming* the will of the laws and institutions of the state, all are acting within a frame of mind with regard to what they perceive as the greater good, in abstraction of personal gain, but in concordance with personal goodness in the conduct of the affairs of the state. Thus, it can indeed be claimed that beyond its material features, the state is beyond these, an ethical frame of analysis, within which people are making decisions and taking action when embodying the state.

As we saw while discussing perpetual peace and the relation of freedom between state and citizen, when reading Hegel it is possible and perhaps even beneficial to move away from the metaphysical implications of materialized reason as a cosmic or higher power as we saw above, and instead view individuals and states as "vehicles" of reason for its own sake, for the immediate benefits of applied rationality, as opposed to the continuing quest to make sense of the divine, by further rationalizing its existence. Frost proposes that by excluding the higher-end metaphysical aspects of Hegel's system, we can focus in on how Hegel established "a constitutive theory of the individual"[39] where the state exists conceptually as the Aufhebung of individuals acceding to higher levels of reason by transcending or surpassing simpler forms of social unity to more abstract or more "reasoned" or intellectually constructed forms, from family life, to civil society, to citizenship within the state. These moments in the development or actualization of the self represent three distinct

39 Frost, *Towards a Normative Theory*, 161–84.

ethical realities, which exist, develop, and come to fruition as the state (which is both an idea in its citizens as well as a material expression of this idea in the world).

Hegel's dialectics are central to his understanding of politics, because the state and the individuals exist in history and are part of its progression. The individual at birth is not the same as the emancipated and empowered adult citizen. But the process that leads individuals from their birth and family life, to existence in a society of others, to becoming part of the actual governance of this society represents three distinct conceptual plateaus which are linked in that each one emerges from the Aufhebung of the preceding one. They are tied dialectically to one another. And while the individual develops in time by further constituting himself as a full participant of the state, a dialectical reverse to this can also be perceived. The stronger the idea of state is among the population, and the more its individuals incarnate this idea in their interactions among themselves and externally, the more the state lives out its materiality. The state is a tool that contributes to constituting and developing the individual, while the process of individual constitution is the state itself. A state without citizens is no state. It is a mutually binding and mutually building relationship.

Hegel built this constitutive theory in reaction to the contractarian tradition we find in Hobbes, Locke, and Rousseau. The difference between the two approaches is how they reconcile individual rights with state sovereignty. In contract theory, the autonomous rights holder agrees to subject himself to the state out of self-interest, to secure his rights.[40] Thus, the individual is the true sovereign, and the state is an institution serving this fundamental sovereignty. The state comes into being because the individual has willed it and accepted self-imposed constraints. On the other hand, "for constitutive theory, to be a rights holder at all already presupposes a constraining relationship with other people."[41]

One of the reasons why Hegel is often cited alongside examples of totalitarianism is that he was in fact deeply against the idea of humans being endowed with "natural rights." "Hegel was better known as a critic of rights than as a defender. In the first place, he attacked natural rights theories for proposing an 'atomistic' conception of the self as denuded of all cultural traits and characteristics."[42] In the Hegelian tradition, rights are not considered to be a priori conditions of human existence, but rather posited within the social context. These emerge and grow in

40 Ibid., 164.
41 Ibid.
42 Smith, "What Is 'Right'?," 3–18.

scope and depth as the individual transitions into increasingly complex relationships from those within the family, to interactions in civil society, and finally at the state and citizen level. Hegel's central criticism of the contractarian methodology, as Seyla Benhabib explains, was that "It ignores the condition of men in the human community and begins with an arbitrary abstraction called the 'state of nature.' The modern tradition falsely considers human nature or rationality to be given, argued Hegel. As long as individuals are seen as complete and mature outside the bounds of ethical life, as long as their fundamental nature is juxtaposed to their life in civil society, the relation of the individual to the ethical community is perceived as accidental."[43]

Instead of making judgments regarding man's rights in nature, Hegel is analyzing man within his social system, arguing that his rights are built up and strengthened by the increased rationalization of social relations that we find in the state, and that these are protected or guaranteed by sovereignty. The constitutive theory of the state tries to understand the individual processes that lead to the state, and the effect of the state on the individual, arguing that this process of rationalization, or Geist, allows individuals to form something greater than themselves, and, through this process, achieve a final and higher state of personal development as well.

Starting at the family level, Hegel recognizes that certain forms of family life are unethical. For example, in Roman law, the father was granted the right to the life or death of his own children, or the right to sell them off into slavery. This, Hegel argued, was inadmissible, since the ethical basis for an ideal family is that the child must be considered a nascent autonomous or free person in becoming.[44] Love alone can bind such a family, for there is no gain or proprietorship in the family relationship. However this very strength is also the family's greatest shortcoming, from the perspective of individual development, because basing one's rights on mere feelings is not enough. Feelings cannot be demanded as a right since they are inherently changeable, and therefore they are not as secure a basis for ethical life as laws, which are consciously recognized – instead of being merely felt. The family's second shortcoming stems from the individual not being fully capable of expressing their personality, since they are forever a part of the family unit, a member.[45] In order to pursue their development, the individual must eventually break the bonds of the family and engage with the world outside, to seek "the

43 Benhabib, "Obligation, Contract and Exchange," 170.
44 Frost, *International Relations,* 168–9.
45 Ibid., 169–70.

development and realization of his particular needs, interests and purposes."[46] Far from destroying the family, when one leaves the family and goes out into the world, they bring with them what they have learned to be as part of the family, and they also bring back to the family whatever recognition they might gain in the next level of ethical life, civil society. The family has been negated, but integrated into the next plateau of development: civil society.

Hegel was the first to distinguish civil society from the state. He used the term to "describe the particular dimension of the modern state as a political community – the 'civil' sphere in which individuals seek to satisfy each others' needs through work, production and exchange; in which there is a thorough-going division of labour and a system of social classes; and in which law courts, corporate bodies and public regulatory and welfare authorities ('the police') promote security and property, livelihood and other rights."[47] In his own words, Hegel described "civil society" as "the battlefield where everyone's individual private interest meets everyone else's."[48] While property might exist within the family as a whole, it did not feature within the family's internal ethics; however, in civil society, property becomes the definitive aspect of relations on this level, where people who are born free and equal can now test this equality and freedom by engaging in private interactions in the public space generated by the state for that purpose. In this sense, Hegel was not at all a friend of aristocracy, though his detractors have attempted to brand him this way – he recognized that the way private interest and public authority attract and repel each other makes aristocracies verge on tyranny and anarchy.[49]

Civil society is also an ethical realm, albeit on a different intellectual level from the one that develops within the family. Its laws and norms, its expectations regarding trustworthiness, fairness, virtue – in fact every process of operating material exchanges within civil society – are constituted by a process of rationalizing interactions between individuals. This rationalization, which is shaped in law, provides increased efficiencies because it creates predictability, regularity, and coercive guarantees. "The regulation of social life through general norms," explains Benhabib, "guarantee[s] uniformity of treatment and render[s] the behavior of the central authority predictable, from the standpoint of modern economic and legal actors."[50] Unlike the family, transactions in civil society cannot

46 Charvet, *Critique of Freedom*, 177.
47 Pelczynski, *State and Civil Society*, 61.
48 Hegel, *Philosophy of Right*, #289, 189.
49 Black, "Hegel on War," 580.
50 Benhabib, "Obligation, Contract and Exchange," 167.

be (or rather could not rationally be) bound in love towards everyone else in society. Therefore, they depend on a different set of values, a different ethical realm involving contracts for the exchange of property and services. If love is what allowed the individual to be recognized as a nascent free individual within the family, it also places a limit to what freedom can be enjoyed within it. Love is a subjective feeling within the family that is there but cannot be earned; it is unsatisfactory to the individual's development. Once children have been "educated to freedom of personality and have come of age within the family, they become recognized as person in the eyes of the law;"[51] they go forth into society and found their own families. Yet, within the family, one could only experience freedom as a particular rather than universal concept, always inward-facing rather than all-encompassing. This is what causes the dissolution of the family and the emergence of civil society, the need for the individual to transition and develop their freedom relative to others, through mutual recognition of such a principle in the external world.[52] Only in civil society will the individual discover all others, and by recognizing their rights, and perceiving their recognition of his rights, at last confirm or take possession of his status as an objective rights holder, rather than someone merely born into rights.

Hegel's system distinguishes itself strongly from Rousseau's social contract. With Hegel, the idea of contracts exists only in the realm of civil society, that is, at neither the family level nor the state level, which are the other two moments in this constitutive process. He disagrees with Rousseau's social contract on the grounds that it implies a mere amalgamation of sovereign individuals in contract.[53] For Hegel, the individual is neither born sovereign, nor does the state grant individuals sovereignty. The existence of the state as sovereignty actually renders personal sovereignty impossible: the individual has no right to make and apply his own, subjective laws and attempt to impose them on others. In the state, men are no longer in the same state of freedom that they were prior to being citizens. Freedom has either been restricted or transformed, and the new freedom that the state provides is a higher freedom allowing citizens to act at a universal level. In contrast, social contract theory falls short, as Pelczynski explains: "Rousseau's general will remains an artificial construct, the will of all or majority will, instead of becoming the living ethos of a political community."[54]

51 Hegel, *Philosophy of Right*, #177, 118.
52 Ibid., #181, 122.
53 Ibid., #258, 155–9.
54 Pelczynski, *State and Civil Society*, 63.

Unlike Rousseau, Hegel did not see the state as an amalgam of sovereign people who are born free, but rather understands citizenship as the socialization and development of individuals into freedom. Hegel saw the state as the process by which and through which the individual can succeed in his quest for freedom: born predisposed to freedom, but not yet in full possession of this freedom, the individual progresses in society from the family, to civil society, to active citizenship. Through these structures and institutions, the individual transcends the natural potential for freedom and achieves a higher form of freedom, mutually recognized, and materialized by institutions that the citizen ultimately takes possession of as well. It is not mere freedom as an endowment, it is freedom that is built up, surpassed, and taken as one's own to further develop as one sees fit. It is the ultimate, perfected freedom in that it provides the empowerment, the tool, and the personal space required for a free person to define what his or her freedom shall resemble.

This type of freedom is not construed as something one has but something that takes shape through an evolving process of self-constitution, through moments in one's social development. Hegel was positing the existence of three social categories, or as Pinkard explains, "expressions of a basic form of unity among people – a structure of mutual acknowledgement – in which various moral principles (rights, duties and virtues) are embodied and which explains their possibility, which Hegel refers to as 'ethical substance.'"[55] Within these categories, "ethical life, as Hegel understands it … is the 'concept of freedom developed into the existing world.' As such it comprises certain specific structures and institutions that are required for, and promote, freedom."[56] Freedom and, equally important, the recognition of freedom in the political community both remain contingent on the presence of a higher power, as Frost explains: "In civil society, the individual gains recognition as a free person able to own property and enter into transactions with other people who are free in the same way. The importance of these rights is recognized in a system of law which is impartially administered and enforced."[57]

Without an impartial guarantor, administrator, and enforcer upon which civil society can depend, these interactions and transactions could not take on a universal form. As was the case with the family, an inherent weakness emerges from the very strength of civil society's ethical realm as well. Freedom demands mutual recognition and virtuous dealings among individuals, but these relations – which can only exist if guided by

55 Pinkard, "Hegel's Ethics," 225.
56 Houlgate, introduction to Hegel's *Philosophy of Right*, xxvii.
57 Frost, *International Relations*, 172.

a certain degree of self-interest – cannot guarantee themselves as fair, since each side is subjective. There must be an objective arbiter in order for various self-interests in competition to be beneficial and rational in a systematized way. Only a mutually recognized higher authority can act in such a role. Even mediation and arbitration depends on the existence of a higher power that generates contract laws in the first place. The idea of state emerges as necessity from the tensions and conflicts located in the realms of civil society, since this very civil society cannot properly operate or even exist as a functional realm of human interaction without some way of making and enforcing rules.

If civil society was a "battlefield" where private interests meet, at the state level, "we have the struggle (a) of private interests against particular matters of common concern and (b) of both of these together against the organization of the state and its higher outlook."[58] This concept of a "higher outlook" is essential to the state because it implies the ethical frame of mind which an individual must be in, when thinking as a citizen, a statesman, or an administrator of the state. The "higher outlook" is the source of the state's objectivity towards what is internal to it: its police, its judges, and its laws; yet it is equally the source of its subjectivity towards what is external to it. To act as the guarantor of its people's freedoms, the state is infused with structures that protect individuals from individuals whether at the family or civil society level, and equally protect this sovereignty from outside threats to this freedom and independence. "As such, Hegel says, the state must be a 'union' organized for the sake of common defence, and war, or at least the willingness to wage war is a major component of statehood."[59]

To understand the state as "the actuality of concrete freedom" is to see it as the materialized fulfillment of individual freedoms within its borders, infused with the external freedom to act and guarantee this internal freedom. Most importantly, to become fully actualized, this notion of freedom as embodied by the state must become aware of itself, recognizing its role and purpose in the minds of those who incarnate the state: judges, police, military, civil servants, politicians, etc. In their minds specifically, and in the minds of all citizens more generally, the state becomes self-aware and empowered *to actualize freedom*. Hegel writes: "The state is the actuality of concrete freedom. But concrete freedom consists in this, that personal individuality and its particular interests not only achieve their complete development and gain explicit recognition for

58 Hegel, *Philosophy of Right*, #289, 189.
59 Smith, "Hegel's Views on War," 628.

their right (as they do in the sphere of the family and of civil society) but, for one thing, they also pass over of their own accord into the interest of the universal, and, for another thing, they know and will the universal; they even recognize it as their own substantive mind; they take it as their end and aim and are active in its pursuit."[60]

The "actuality of concrete freedom" emerges from the same methodology that Hegel used to discover the truth of sense-certainty as a dialectical process in time, but this time applied to the social realm. Freedom is almost construed as a self-fulfilling loop, whereby the individual seeks individual freedom and thus wills himself a state to act as the guarantor of this freedom, but the only way by which it can act as guarantor is for it to be free as well: universal, subjective, and potent. When freedom is the ethical grounds upon which society is built, every aspect of society must in the end embody that ethic, and this is achieved by maintaining this dialectical tension between the collective and the individual: where each is the source of the other's greater freedom. And this realization is the third and final moment of the constitutive process: I recognize the state as my own, because through its freedom, my freedom is enhanced and universalized.

The state exists to embody the citizens' collective best interest in the world, and reciprocally, when the citizen recognizes this purpose of the state, he takes ownership of it: *the state works by me and for me.* This very appropriation completes itself as a moment of the individual's development when the individual comes to terms with the negation of his potential individual sovereignty in exchange for a role or space in the universal. This recognition of ownership, which Hegel calls patriotism, binds the citizens of a state into an ethical whole in a way not entirely different from the way love binds the family or laws bind civil society. Hence, for Hegel, "what is common in love and patriotism is that the other is perceived as not being other."[61] However, the process of sublating the other leads also to a new concept of "others." If patriotism binds the state, and eliminates other individuals as others, it nonetheless generates, perhaps inadvertently, the concept of "other peoples," "other states" to recognize and be recognized by.

The state emerges as a "substantive life" because it is infused with a "spirit" that resides in its institutions and citizens, who are called upon to incarnate them. The choice of the word "life" is not by any means haphazard. In fact, Hegel was influenced by botany from very early on in his

60 Hegel, *Philosophy of Right*, #260, 160.
61 Westphal, *Hegel, Freedom and Modernity*, 51.

career and perceived contradiction as a source of vitality in nature as well as in concepts.[62] The explanation for this stems from Hegel's observation that the principle of non-contradiction – the idea that something cannot be itself and its negation at the same time – is an intellectualized proposition of Verstand, but in the real world, things are constantly changing and in flux. What gives life to the rose is the fact that it contains in its very nature the fact of being in bloom, of not being in bloom, and the stages of development that make this contraction a single whole.[63] It is therefore not surprising that Hegel would claim that "There is no proposition of Heraclitus which I have not adopted in my Logic."[64] Flux is the essence.

It is in the state's substantive life, in its ability to enact itself in time, that we find its somewhat mystical "personality" or "intelligence," where the state's "essential being is the union of the subjective with the rational will."[65] By embodying a will that is endowed with rationality, the idea of the state achieves its actualized freedom, its ability to use its capacity to reason in order to shape the material world. When the state enacts or applies laws, for example, these are real, objective, and universal in the eyes of the citizens – despite the fact that they arise subjectively, from the self-consciousness of the state. As Hegel explains, "The state, therefore, knows what it wills and knows it in its universality, i.e. as something thought. Hence it works and acts by reference to consciously adopted ends, known principles, and laws which are not merely implicit but are actually present to consciousness."[66]

If the state emerges as a substantive life, in the process of constitution, and the transcendental process of individuals transforming themselves into citizens, it owes its self-awareness and self-consciousness to a process of reciprocation with other states. The state is confronted with the idea that it is not alone in the world: there are other peoples, other states, interactions, and potential conflicts. That is why Hegel recognizes statehood as being intimately related to war. The independence, sovereignty, and territory of the state are not merely founded on its armed forces but built in conceptually, as a necessity. The ethical element in war, Hegel explained, is implied by the final end of the state to provide freedom,

62 Songsuk Susan Hahn, *Contradiction in Motion* (Ithaca: Cornell University Press, 2007), 1–3.

63 Bruce Gilbert, *The Vitality of Contradiction* (Montreal and Kingston: McGill-Queen's University Press, 2013), 58–60.

64 Hegel, *History of Philosophy*, 279/320. In Gilbert, *Vitality of Contradiction*, 3.

65 Westphal, *Hegel, Freedom and Modernity*, 51.

66 Hegel, *Philosophy of Right*, #270, 165.

individual life, security, and property to its people.[67] Thus, "war is not to be regarded as an absolute evil and as a purely external accident."[68] It can be an essential part of a state's rational necessity.[69] The state makes a *conscious* decision to apply force, grounded ethically on the idea that its actions are conducted in the interest of justice or self-preservation and on behalf of a free and constituted people.

Reciprocally, the psychological internal reality of the state is in many ways tied to war as well. The model citizen of the modern state would retain certain vestiges of ancient Athens: a freeman, democrat, merchant, and militiaman. This would be the foremost expression of the individual cum citizen, transcended and elevated by the state. In this context, we can appreciate in what sense the state cannot merely be an amalgam of individual sovereigns as in the contractarian tradition. The citizens in a constitutive system generate sovereignty; they aggrandize the state in the very process of aggrandizing themselves within this ethical realm that they have created for themselves. Thus, while in the contractarian tradition, the citizen is assumed to be constraining his natural rights for the sake of the social contract, in the constitutive sense, the citizen and the state converge in their mutual freedom: where the state is the source and guarantor of the individual's particular freedom, and the citizen is the source and guarantor of the state's universal freedom. And this coexistence is the aggrandizement of the individual, which at its utmost embodiment – self-sacrifice in the name of collective freedom – is the epitome of courage. "The intrinsic worth of courage as a disposition of mind is to be found in the genuine, absolute, final end, the sovereignty of the state. The work of courage is to actualize this final end, and the means to this end is the sacrifice of personal actuality … a self-sacrifice which yet is the real existence of one's freedom."[70]

Hegel is suggesting that in war, the citizen/state relationship takes on its purest form. The citizen-soldier lives out the state's ethical concept to its absolute depth, where he is willing to die in the application of the state's "higher outlook" and sovereignty. In this sense, the citizen-soldier is even better positioned than a king to pronounce the words "L'État, c'est moi," because when he fights, the state belongs to the citizen-soldier to the extreme, and the citizen-soldier reciprocally belongs mind and body to the state. Should he choose not to fight, the state would be powerless and dead. Should he turn around in mutiny and dethrone the

67 Ibid., #324, 209.
68 Ibid.
69 Ibid., 209–10.
70 Ibid., #328, 211.

king, the king would be nothing. The state is the sum of its ethical premise plus its material exertion of authority in pronouncing and enforcing laws, and sustaining independence from outside forces. And while all of these represent an aspect of the state's ideal/material reality, none is more powerfully attached to this concept of statehood than citizen-soldiers, because in their bravery and sacrifice, they *are* the state – an ethical concept backed by individuals in arms and who are willing to kill or die to ensure its collective survival. It is only because the state is constructed as an ethical realm worth fighting for that Hegel could logically uphold the idea that "War is the moral health of peoples in their struggle against petrifaction,"[71] because if a state is not worth fighting for, or incapable of fighting, it would be reaffirming its mortality and transience, disappearing in history.

Between states or between peoples, we can again see the vestiges of master/slave relationship – strong nations versus weak nations. The nations that do what they will and nations that suffer what they must, to use Thucydides's famous words. To struggle is to affirm a nation's individuality and its self-perception as a right holder relative to other nations. Since states exist relative to one another in an anarchical situation, they cannot expect their rights to come from outside or from above: they are engaged in continual competition, whether this is military, economic, or social in its manifestation. Tyrannies and democracies equally struggle for internal safety from outside forces. There is no difference at all with regard to how they would seek to exclude invading forces. The main difference with regard to their internal situation has no bearing either, because whereas the tyrant may seek to protect themself from the population and its external allies, democracies rest their internal power on the exclusion of would-be tyrants and their allies abroad. It is reciprocal, but identical in its manifestation. The only true difference is legitimacy as a source of vitality. Like any master, the secure tyrant has no vitality – but his people do. Meanwhile, any state or proto-state that takes on the objective to actualize freedom for peoples holds this vitality, like a slave seeking emancipation. The danger, as we shall consider later, is that this very vitality of liberation itself can in fact be usurped by ideology.

The complete actualization of freedom, however, cannot be understood as something that can be fully achieved or institutionalized. The state is not a resolution of all the paradoxes that exist within it. It is in fact a tense and vulnerable equilibrium of these paradoxes. A society

71 Hegel, *Phenomenology of Mind*, 432. Note: exceptionally I am referring here to the Baillie translation, since it is the formula for this phrase that has caused the most controversy.

that aims for Absolute Freedom – like the French Revolution, which Hegel uses as an example – will come face to face with the "dangers of particularity and the threat of domineering universality."[72] And even the foundational building blocks of statehood, the family and civil society, are continuously at odds with the state by virtue of having interests that can at times be in sync, but perhaps more often than not are fully opposite, whether it is taxation, or having to send one's child to fight a war, or laws against nepotism in political affairs. And yet, this tension is the source of the very vitality in interaction upon which our freedoms can be elevated.

It is a path in history. We can generate for ourselves the greatest material freedom we can dream up at any given time, but the primordial demonstration of freedom is the ability to project one's freedom to new meanings and reiterations of itself over time. The perfect state of freedom is not what freedom one has at any given time, nor any future concept of freedom, but the knowledge that the freedom one currently enjoys is sufficient to imagine, pursue, and reach new improvements in one's dignity, empowerment, and ability to be "more free" as a result. This quest is an active one, and is equally true for the individual and the collective. A nation at rest is a nation dead – as dead as any tyranny that exists only in a useless quest towards sustaining its power over others. Meanwhile, a nation seeking to actualize freedom, at home and abroad, is never at rest.

CRITIQUE: THE REVERSIBILITY OF WAR'S RELATION TO THE MORAL HEALTH OF PEOPLES

The ethical aspect of war in Hegel resides in the fact that the state is the locus, origin, and purveyor of right, and it exists only insofar as it is upheld by a pact of mutual defence among citizens. This is why the idea of courage and sacrifice epitomizes the ethical bond of statehood. Dying bravely for your country is the ultimate demonstration that the very notion of this country does in fact exist in your mind and in the physical space in which this state of mind manifests itself. Hence, for Hegel, war and sacrifice not only invigorate the state externally, they enhance the state in the minds of those who belong to it, which is the most central part of statehood to begin with. This, however, suggests that not all forms of warfare necessarily "reinforce" the idea of statehood equally or in the same way. A small professional army will effectively protect the borders

72 Gilbert, *Vitality of Contradiction*, 130.

and manifest the physicality of a state, but it may not be as effective as mass conscription in enhancing the ethical idea of statehood among the population. That being said, if "bravery" is the vehicle by which this enhancement is achieved, then another question arises: do all forms of warfare equally lead to bravery and sacrifice in the minds of men? Any variance in these features of war should have proportional impacts on war's relation to the moral health of nations. If ever a war should exist that involved no citizens, no patriotism, and no bravery, then what might this mean for the pact of mutual defence that holds the state and the bond of its citizenship together?

The first place to look for this phenomenon is not new to our era, but as old as civilization: in the context of usurpation of state power, where a tyrant or oligopoly appropriates for itself political power and force, whether by turning the army against the population, or else hiring mercenary forces to exert the power of the state as opposed to harvesting this power from the citizen base. This is a clear example of where we would not be dealing with anything near an ideal incarnation of the state. As Machiavelli explained, relying on mercenary forces is a sure way to weaken the prince,[73] since even though the sovereign increases his physical power, the ethical whole collapses because the bonds of mutual defence, upon which his authority and legitimacy rest, begin to rot from within. How a state embodies its wars has a direct bearing on whether or not war contributes to the moral health of its people, for in the hands of mercenaries, war can be detrimental to the ethical bonds that make up the body politic in the very act of carrying out policy, because it excludes the citizen from participating as the active element of the state's materialization of policy. However, the fact that mercenary warfare is contrary to the moral health of peoples does not necessarily undermine Hegel's analysis. He understood states as being fraught with tense relationships between factions and their attempts to embody the state's power. The problem of mercenaries is that they straddle the realms of civil society and the state. They are contracted in civil society and thus obey the laws of the market, but they cannot embody patriotism and the ethical dimension of embodying the state's "higher outlook." If they happen to be hired towards usurping state power internally, the particularity of their power, the fact that it is a private actor, cannot achieve state universality – it undoes the state in the very process of claiming it. It is not a different kind of tension than what Hegel perceives within the state as particular forces (i.e. estates, political parties, factions) vie for embodying the

73 Machiavelli, *The Prince*, 54–9.

universal, but it is nonetheless its most extreme form – a form that brings into question the state's legitimacy and individuality.

Among the many inherent such tensions that can make up the state, one particular contradiction is worth exploring further. At any given time two opposite tendencies form in the state: political apathy, immobility, and pusillanimous comfort within the state at one extreme, and at the other revolutionary, criminal, or violently anti-state sentiments. Both are equally damaging, even though the latter may have more noticeable impacts and cause stronger reactions. Furthermore, as we explained above in chapter 1, elements of society that tend towards the latter can, in certain situations, be more state-like in their manifestation than the state itself, and infinitely more so than the politically apathetic. It is precisely at the intersection of these two conflicting phenomena that we can perceive an inescapable risk: the process of statehood is a quest to enhance and manifest freedom in the world, but the more it achieves this goal, the more complete its materialization, the greater the two above internal threats become. The state cannot, on the one hand, provide freedom from the state to those who seek to abolish it, and on the other hand, it cannot undermine the provision of freedom that was its goal in order to vitalize those who have found comfort and apathy within it. Thus, the tension is inherent to the state, and becomes tenser as the state develops and empowers itself. No state, not even an ideal concept of state, is totally free from the truest form of internal social decay: an interaction that opposes a fledging defence of the state against a powerful dissension. In both cases, there is a process of exclusion at play: an exclusion that is passive in the case of the apathetic, an exclusion that is active in the case of the rebels.

Hegel recognized the problem of exclusion in his analysis, but from a perspective that is slightly different from what I have in mind here. Hegel's concept of exclusion in the *Philosophy of Right* is understood as a feeling that certain citizens might have depending on their situation in society. The example he provides is that the poor feel a "division of emotion" between themselves and society. This can give rise to an "inner indignation," continues Hegel, and within this frame of mind, the individual, feeling as though he has no freedom, may cease to recognize the existence of a universal freedom. This generates "rabble," which Hegel describes as "when there is joined to poverty a disposition of mind, an inner indignation against the rich, against society, against the government, etc."[74] Allen Wood explains: "Hegel refuses to blame either the

74 Hegel, *Philosophy of Right*, #244, 150.

wealthy or the poor, as individuals, for the fact of poverty. But he does regard poverty as a cause of moral degradation, turning those subjects to it into a 'rabble.' Since Hegel thinks that every member of civil society has a right to earn an adequate living as a member of a recognized estate, he regards the poor as victims of a wrong at society's hands. The basis of the 'rabble mentality' is the outrage of the poor against the rich, civil society and the state at the wrong they suffer."[75]

To be clear, Hegel does identify wealth as a source of rabble and moral degradation as well, pointing to "luxury" and "passion for extravagance"[76] as part of this problem. But from the perspective of revolt it is more of interest for us to focus on the "rabble of paupers."[77] The moral degradation that results from it is a product of the "civil society" realm of the state, but it nonetheless has a bearing on the identification of the poor to the state's higher outlook or the concept of citizenship. As we shall explore in a later chapter, this very problem becomes the source of Marx's great disagreement with Hegel, because he perceived the state as a subjective bourgeois institution rather than an objective universal product of citizenship. This may be taking the analysis far into the realm of speculation, but it nonetheless unveils the existence of possible scenarios where there is a rationale for introducing reversibility to certain concepts in Hegel. More specifically, in this case, if there is such thing as a particular form of moral decay that can exist within the realm of civil society, can the same process of exclusion – if it is understood as taking form at the higher, state level – introduce a universal form of moral decay? With the case of poverty, the mere "feeling" of exclusion at the level of civil society can nonetheless cause such a potent form of tension within the state that it causes revolutionary factions to emerge. What then are we to expect if actual physical and technological exclusion – rather than feelings of exclusion – appear in society, not at the family level or civil-society level but at the pinnacle that unites citizens and the state: the bonds of mutual defence and the embodiment of patriotism and bravery?

One can interpret from Hegel that war is to be understood as the moral health of peoples because it is the moment, the process whereby the citizen takes full possession of the state and the state takes full possession of the citizen. One should not understand this as meaning that Hegel was necessarily an advocate of participatory democracy or that he was suggesting that the consent of the citizens is necessary to the

75 Allen W. Wood, introduction to Hegel's *Philosophy of Right* (Cambridge: Cambridge University Press, 1991), xxi.

76 Hegel, *Philosophy of Right*, #253, 153.

77 Ibid., #244, 150, and #253, 153.

creation of authoritative and legitimate policy; but the reverse of this perspective is important: the enactment of policy can be modified or stunted in its potency by the unwillingness of citizens to comply. Though a state's legitimacy is not necessarily tied to universal citizen consent, as in the Rousseauist tradition, this should not be taken to mean that no consent, not even tacit consent, is necessary when it comes to carrying out policy. In the contractarian viewpoint, the citizen is understood to have a permanent and natural right to refuse to comply with and act out the policy of state, because the premise of this philosophy is that individuals are sovereign, they are the focal point of legitimacy and authority and merely in a contractual relation with the state at any given time. From a constitutive perspective, however, individuals are not sovereign. They are not endowed with any such right. And to claim it is to revolt, to de-constitute oneself. It is not an affirmation of the natural self, but the opposite – the de-affirmation of the constituted self. Though this de-constitution is an act that poses a challenge to the idea of legitimacy, what revolt and mutiny actually do is weaken authority in very real, concrete ways, the objection of conscience stops authority from manifesting itself materially. It is also the seed of revolt, the process of constituting and materializing a rebellion.

This is particularly true in the battlefield. For a recent example of this we can turn to Libya during the Arab Spring in 2011, when anti-Gaddafi rebels fought on land, and one fighter pilot crashed his own jet so as not to attack them. Had this been a drone and not a fighter, the situation would have been different: the pilot would have been arrested on base and court-martialled, and another drone pilot would have stepped in to finish the job. In this case, however, the Libyan pilot was able to eject and land safely with the rebels. One might say the drone is the modern mercenary, because it does not have the ethical bonds of statehood infused in the way it carries out its mission, not when it is remotely controlled, and far less so if it is fully automated. The difference is the ability to enact individual conscience on the battlefield: this is where peaceful mutiny lies. However, without this pressure valve, represented by the individual soldier and his moral choices, tyrants would be far more difficult to depose once they had risen. This relationship between tyranny and revolt is the key to uncovering where the state's "right" to wage war reaches its limit. If the individual refuses to wage war on behalf of the state, this non-compliance is a passive form of the limit: the inaction of the state. In the active form, we see the emergence of either a revolt or a revolutionary war against the state itself, which becomes a counterpoise to the state's right to wage war, a fight to eliminate the sovereign's hold on power, to reclaim and reaffirm the constitution of the people.

When fighting to dismantle a tyrannical regime, the revolt itself forges the true ethical community, the citizens united in a pact of mutual defence against their perceived threat within the state's institutions. Here, it is the revolt that represents moral health in action, and the tyranny is the rotten and petrified element of statehood. There is a split whereby the perceived universal has succumbed to particularity, and the particulars vie for universality. Drones and mercenaries in the hands of tyrants, however, are a particularly grave endangerment to the rights of man, because they not only empower tyranny, they effectively exclude citizenship from a most important power: the power not to comply. One who has this power is more free than one who does not, and is better poised to become a vehicle for the materialization of freedom in their subjugated community.

Exclusion is the Achilles heel of the constitutive approach to understanding the state, because regardless of whether it comes from de-constitution at the level of the individual, policy, or even technology, it deteriorates the concept of state as mutual ownership between citizen and state. The difference between the constitutive and contractarian traditions is precisely this, that the latter is contingent – an amalgam of sovereigns – while the former is bound in necessity, where the freedom of the person depends on the state and vice versa (i.e. freedom is not asserted as a natural given). The problem, therefore, with exclusion is that even if the state continues to preserve and enhance freedom for its people relatively and internally, the exclusion of the citizen base from the collective security of the nation renders the citizen less free in one very important way: they lose their most important power within the state, which is to embody, to be the state's freedom. In the context of usurpation, this is what salvages the moral health of peoples, since when the authority has broken with the citizens, then the unwillingness to comply, the objection of conscience, the decision to reverse the policy of the state by refusing to act, all these become acts of de-constitution. Mutiny and revolt are the last resorts of citizens: to act as a pendulum, constant and balanced in good times, but capable of swinging back when pushed to unethical extremes or when the bonds of statehood have been destroyed.

If the exclusion of the citizen from the state's enactment of political violence is the natural limit to the notion that war necessarily serves the moral health of a state, should this be understood as meaning a categorical limit to the idea that war is a right of the state? It is important to step back and distinguish the two. Hegel's notion of the state is not in contradiction to the idea that certain groups within the state may be more empowered and others less, nor even the possibility that certain groups might be excluded in the process. These are all within the realm of possibility in a state that fraught with natural tensions and paradoxes by virtue of being both a universal idea that is nonetheless composed of so many parts, whether individual people or groups of people within the whole. The very process by which a state becomes a notion in and for itself, an "individual" in its own right, is by overcoming, recognizing this very internal tension that constitutes it. The modern state is able to assert itself beyond these tensions and find unity precisely because it will have established laws and norms that facilitate and encourage this healthy and dynamic plurality.

Usurpation, however, is an unavoidable threat to any such society, because it is not impossible for a faction within the state to aspire to dismantle this very universality. It is also a threat that cannot go away because plurality allows for this phenomenon to exist as a latent force within society, while the relationship between apathy and revolt represents an inherent and constant pressure against sustaining and striving for the ideal: those who would defend it weaken as those who would destroy it gain in strength.

Furthermore, as it specifically relates to warfare, whereas war empowered those citizens who would embody the state's will and exertion of strength, at the expense of those set to undermine the state, this has perhaps become at least in part dated due to technological development. As technology increasingly distances warfare from hand-to-hand combat and individual acts of bravery, there is no going back to the heyday of warfare. The exclusion of the citizen from the application of foreign policy is irreversible; state power is transferred from the citizen to the machinery of state. The machinery of the state, however loyal it may be to those who hold it, is nonetheless ill-equipped to "invigorate" the citizenry or reaffirm their social bonds, cemented in mutual defence and recognition of their "unity," despite the tensions of their own particularity within the universal.

Exclusion within the state is not in itself problematic, especially if it occurs at the family or civil society level, but exclusion from embodying this pact of mutual defence may well be, because it is so central to the bond that holds the ethical community, its unity, together. As wars between nations peter off in history and world security increasingly resembles highly armed policing intervention with very sophisticated machinery and fewer and fewer citizens in arms, is it possible that the very purpose of the state is at stake? Is this making the citizen *less* free, in contradiction to the very purpose of statehood in the first place? To be clear, I do not mean by this that everyone has the calling to be a soldier or that this should somehow be elevated as a good thing, but rather that this calling is always open to the citizen who would choose it as a calling, which is no different in fact than those who may one day choose to embody the state by accepting the position of police officer, judge, or statesman. What matters is that this access remains.

If the purpose of the state is to provide the maximum freedom to its citizens by creating a set space where their self-chosen laws are valid, then it needs war – or rather the idea or the possibility of waging war – not only as a guarantee with regard to this space from external threats, but also as a means to resting its authority and ethical claim to that space internally as well, as the possessor of the monopoly of force. In this context, the use of force is not accidental, but a matter of right, under a tradition or better yet a constitution that proclaims it as such. But regardless of how ideal this constitution is, it is never completely free from the risks of revolt, because revolt lies dormant at all times in the state, and sometimes the very act of repressing it is precisely what awakens it.

War in the hands of the state, or more precisely in the hands of constituted free citizens, is the only basis upon which war can ever be proclaimed as something objectively ethical. This theoretically excludes non-state actors, rebels, tyrants, or usurpers of state power, because their violence cannot achieve the same objectivity. It is necessarily subjective. Of course when critically assessing this point we must question whether or not the state apparatuses as we know them today actually have achieved the model set out for the modern state – whether this constituted, objective whole actually does take form, or if its wars remain subject to any biases, foundational predispositions, or procedural factors that render wars of the state no more objective than those of stateless powers. The relationship between war and state is forever befuddled in its quest for objectivity or actualized freedom, because even in the epitome of the idea, which brings together its universality and potency, there is a root of scepticism that can emerge. The question regarding "whose universality?," as it was elaborated by Marx, represents a real contention that forces us to further our exploration of the Hegelian state. And as we shall see, the question regarding "which type of potency?," as articulated by Hannah Arendt, is also a challenging one to consider. The Hegelian state is a powerful device for understanding war and human affairs, but it is not sacrosanct, despite Hegel's attempt to elevate it to such holiness. The subjects of technology and social classes do not undermine the Hegelian perspective, but they force us to question its scope and consequently to better understand and appreciate the Hegelian contribution to political philosophy in general, and war theory in particular.

If the ethical aspect of war expressed as a right is indeed a limited concept, then the logical place to look for the threshold representing this limit would be at the superposition of both social class revolution and modern technological progress, where the universality of the state and the type of potency that makes it manifest can be challenged. In the final chapter, we will explore the Hegelian war ethic as it relates to the context of the great revolutionary doctrines that defined twentieth century war. But first, in the next two chapters, we will consider a parallel and opposite limitation found in Clausewitz's notion of war as an instrument of the state. From these two perspectives, it will be possible, in the end, to consider what conclusions can be reached when the two limits are superimposed – is there in fact a conceptual limit for dialectical war theory's dual ethical system?

9

Clausewitz and Hegel: Where the Convergence on Method Begins[1]

WHILE HEGEL'S ETHICAL CONCEPT OF WAR becomes problematic as it arrives at the threshold of revolution, Clausewitz actually began with the problem of revolution in his exploration of war's political and ethical nature. As we saw above, by borrowing Fichte's absolute war Clausewitz was able to develop war's dual concepts in a way that allowed the coexistence of revolution at one extreme, and at the other, the limited scuffles and standstills that war can also become. Clausewitz was able to rely on his own experiences and the theories of Fichte and Kant in order to arrive at this apparently static chasm between the real and the absolute. But what this chapter attempts to show is that in the final years Clausewitz's work came increasingly in line with the approach Hegel developed: it broke impasses and generated dynamic contradictions. It was this new approach that informed and shaped his attempt to reconcile the two poles into the synthetic formula "war is the continuation of policy by other means."

Azar Gat has provided a good first step with regard to the framework and larger picture of how we can effectively gauge the link between Hegelian and Clausewitzian ideas, and the goal of this chapter is in fact to further legitimize some of Gat's conclusions with additional arguments, examples, and analysis that will move us away from the similarities themselves, and towards the underlying unity shaping these similarities. Though I will address one particular error that comes up in Gat's argument – the repetition of an older, faulty argument made by Camon – Gat's point of view remains altogether on much safer grounds than that of Bernard Brodie who went so far as to argue that the Hegelian

1 An earlier version of this chapter, which also integrated parts of chapter 10, was previously published as Y. Cormier, "Clausewitz & Hegel: Convergence on Method, Divergence on Ethics," *International History Review* 36, no. 1 (2014): 419–42.

influence was in fact more secure and clearer than the Kantian influence.[2] This second claim is quite a stretch, given the many conspicuous and demonstrated references to and near-perfect citations of Kant that we discussed in chapters 3 and 5 above. Furthermore, any possible link to Hegel would automatically reinforce any link to the Kantian system in some way or other since the Hegelian project was a direct reply to Kant. Most importantly, though, the convergence of ideas with Hegel is more obscure, since the similarities are not the result of such direct transparency. The trick to uncover it is to provide additional examples to those already offered by Gat – and more significantly, to delve deeper into the underlying logic that united the three Prussian thinkers instead of sticking to the surface.

Unlike Gat's contribution to the subject, which includes a few good comparisons of the later works of Clausewitz and Hegel's *Philosophy of Right*, encompassing some ethical and political ideas (i.e. the two men have similar analyses on international law and perpetual peace),[3] this text goes further and seeks out distinctions in the proximity as it evolves over time. Gat mentions this important distinction between the young and the older Clausewitz, in his counterargument against what he describes as Raymond Aron's "myth of 'Clausewitz's lifelong method,'" to which Gat replies that the twentieth-century French philosopher, "instead of clarifying Clausewitz's late ideas, ... obscured earlier ones."[4] In my humble opinion, however, it would be useful to develop this line of inquiry further, by providing a set of examples that distinguishes specific ideas that evolve from being considered in non-dialectical terms early on in Clausewitz's life, to highly dialectical ones later in life – and not just any dialectical reasoning, but specifically the form we associate to Hegel. By comparing concepts from Clausewitz's early life and those found in his mature works, it becomes possible not only to pull out increments of convergence, but also to propose a cut-off point, in the single term "Aufhebung," where a proper Hegelian idea seems to appear first as a one-off, unsystematic reference, before the method implied by this term is systematized in the following chapters of *On War*.

This approach, however, causes a special kind of difficulty for the reader to keep in mind: some words seem to evolve in their meaning over time and incidentally this means they also vary from one section to the next within the single work that is *On War*. It is worth adding that the converging ideas occur in very precise and particular ways that did not

2 Brodie, "Review of *Clausewitz: A Biography*," 290.
3 Gat, *Origins of Military Thought*, 241–2, 243.
4 Gat, *History of Military Thought*, 231.

touch every aspect of *On War*, only sections of it and particular arguments. While this might frustrate certain scholars who are adamant about showcasing a clearcut influence, it is the opposite effect that I seek in this chapter: I perceive this segmentation as a positive thing, since it allows us to delineate and clarify similarities by exposing them in opposition to where there are none.

These similarities seem to indicate a learning curve in how Clausewitz made use of Hegelian ideas, and such an idea would fit particularly well with the suggestion that when Clausewitz died in 1831, he had not yet completed the process; that while he appreciated the Hegelian system and tried to make use of it, his attempt was partial and not entirely successful. That being said, I cannot substantiate this claim, it is once again one of those impressions that comes up, and I must leave it to the discretion of the reader to determine whether or not this idea of a "learning curve" is probable. Perhaps further research into the question will lead this proposition from being a mere impression to demonstrable conclusion one day, but this will not be done in the following lines. More importantly still, what we should try to do as scholars is to provide more depth to what Aron, Gat, and many others have alluded to in their writings: in the last four years of his life, Clausewitz's writing underwent a rupture, a crisis, a sudden bolt in creativity, a turnaround in methodology, and a quest to reconsider the entire project all over again from page one. What would lead Clausewitz to such a dramatic turnaround? The closer we get to answering this question, the clearer the perspective into what made Clausewitz both converge with and diverge from Hegel.

If we consider the divergence, the major element of discrepancy that comes up regarding ethics happens not in those regions of *On War* that are devoid of any Hegel-like ideas, as we might expect, but the opposite: it happens in the very middle of those sections that are the most similar. It is not so much that we begin, when analyzing Hegel and Clausewitz in tandem and over time, with a divergence and end in convergence. Such a trajectory could be understood as a form of natural progression – but instead the methodological convergence coincides with the ethical divergence. It is a conundrum, indeed, but one which has a logical explanation.

This chapter will argue that whereas war is an intrinsic right of the state in Hegel, Clausewitz sees it rather as an instrument and therefore devoid of any self-justification. This implies that the state inherits moral agency by carrying out war and deciding to pursue it as policy. It focalizes the moral element, separating agency from the thing itself. To put this as an analogy, whereas Clausewitz's notion of war's relation to the state is like that of a hammer to a carpenter, Hegel's war is the nail, and the state its hammer; its existence and form are predetermined by its purpose. Hegel, who understood the state as "the actuality of concrete freedom"[5] and as a "vehicle of spirit"[6] that materializes the idea of freedom in the real world, could from this perspective understand the state as having a substantive life of its own, an ethical dimension emerging from the greater good that it provides simply by existing and embodying the greater good that is freedom. As such, its wars were not *purely accidental*,[7] but in some ways necessary to the fulfillment of its existence. In Clausewitz, on the other hand, since war is not defined as an inherent right but as an instrument, the justification for it resides in the handler – not in the thing itself. The two visions are diametrical and mutually exclusive by definition: the hammer is what it is, whereas the carpenter has a choice.

This chapter is divided into four sections that explore the distinctions and convergences between both authors. The first looks for general hints into the question of a connection, especially in historical information and one particular note that Clausewitz wrote during his final edits. The second, third, and fourth sections are concerned with a historical comparison of various Clausewitzian concepts and word choices that evolved over time. They focus, respectively, on the subjects of "Aufhebung," "intelligence of the personified state," and the coming together of real war and absolute war into the "continuation of policy by other means." Having discussed how the two authors converged in the previous sections, we will then transition to chapter 10 in order to study how the convergence peaks right when the divergence on ethics sharpens. The argument will then be made that a distinct understanding of the meanings of subjectivity and objectivity could explain why this unlikely scenario takes place.

Azar Gat has described Clausewitz's later works as having "highly distinctive, new intellectual patterns" that support the thesis of a Hegelian influence,[8] but much remains unsaid with regard to what these patterns are or in what sense they are Hegelian. Gat names a few of these, for example the dialectical reasoning behind the concept of "attack-defence," referring to it (as Camon had before him) as an example of dialectical reconciliation à la Hegel.[9] But this example was effectively dismissed in Raymond Aron's analysis of the question – and also in fact, and more interestingly, in Clausewitz's own apparent discernment of different types

5 Hegel, *Philosophy of Right*, #260, 160–1.
6 Taylor, *Hegel*, 128.
7 Hegel, *Philosophy of Right*, #324, 209–10.
8 Gat, *Origins of Military Thought*, 234.
9 Ibid.

of dialectical methods including the one most clearly associated to Hegel (see the section below on "Aufhebung"). Another example Gat provides muddles rather than clarifies the question. He suggests that Clausewitz was using a Hegelian approach when he wrote that two "true logical contrasts" in reciprocation can help shed light on each other.[10] To be certain this is indeed a dialectical formula – but it is by no means distinctly Hegelian. Many authors of his time wrote in such a fashion, including those we know with certainty that Clausewitz had read, including Kant and Fichte.

Where we can begin seeing a more complex similarity in thinking between Hegel and Clausewitz has much to do with Gat's argument that Clausewitz did not believe in any "world of ideas."[11] Gat wonders why Clausewitz would have needed an abstract model to begin with. It is worth developing this line of inquiry, because indeed it is no small question: it is essentially the root and underlying question of Hegel's entire philosophy. The distinction between Hegel and Kant was that the latter was an idealist who believed this abstract realm existed, whereas Hegel, a phenomenologist, perceived existence as part and parcel with essence. As was mentioned above, Hegel exposed a major flaw at the very heart of Kantian thought – in that his abstract world of ideas, supposedly external to real, actual thought, is in fact posited by thought in the first place.[12] Hegel argued instead that "what is rational is actual and what is actual is rational,"[13] in effect transitioning from the dichotomous chasm left by Kant, to a higher order of understanding meant to encompass both the real and the ideal realms. This answers Gat's question in part, in that a Hegelian take on the universe allows one to analyze abstractions in the ideal realm as well as the real realm. But what it doesn't allow is the assertion that these are distinct or mutually exclusive. In Clausewitz, all war is real war, but all wars contain a varying degree of the absolute or ideal essence of war, this concept that pushes back its limits on objectives and the application of violence. For Clausewitz, war is not a fixed concept, but one in perpetual flux that goes from standstills to all-out wars, between its absolute limitless concept and those factors that place limits on it, like friction, the fog of war, limited aims, etc. Clausewitz spells out this fluidity in his concept of "real war" quite clearly when he explains that "Real war will generally be in a medium between the two different tendencies,

10 Ibid., 235.
11 Ibid., 228, 236.
12 Taylor, *Hegel*, 117.
13 Hegel, preface to *Phenomenology of Spirit*, 10.

sometimes approaching nearer to one, sometimes to the other."[14] Later, in Book VIII, Clausewitz adds: "real war is no such consistent effort tending to an extreme, as it should be according to the abstract idea, but a half and half thing, a contradiction in itself."[15]

Arguing that the ideas of Hegel and Clausewitz converge means going up against many credible scholars who have argued the opposite. Peter Paret, for example, made the case that the question of a Hegelian influence is altogether irrelevant on the grounds that the dialectic was "standard equipment in German idealistic and romantic philosophy."[16] This, however, robs his readers of the subtleties of the philosophical aspects of *On War*. Hegelian dialectics are quite distinct from those of Hume, Kant, Fichte, or others, and passing over them as though they were all the same muddles our capacity to appreciate both the depth and particularities of Clausewitz's technique, as well as his erudition. In the case of Paret, this lack of discernment should not come as a surprise, given that his knowledge of Hegel appears superficial at best: he makes the popular error to sum up Hegelianism as a system of "thesis" and "antithesis,"[17] an oversimplification that not only pays little justice to the philosopher's work, but is also altogether the wrong starting point for understanding Hegel. Furthermore, there are many examples to be found in the Howard/Paret translation that show how the philosophical terms used by Clausewitz were either misrepresented or altogether omitted from this particular translation, such as the distinction between the words Grundsatz and Prinzip, the use and omission of the word wirklich in the context of real war, as well as various philosophical terms such as Aufhebung and Wechselwirkung (reciprocity of action).[18]

At the other extreme, there have been cases of grossly overstating Hegelian influence. As Gat points out, this happened in the works of Paul Creuzinger, who argued in *Hegel's Influence on Clausewitz* (1911) that practically every inch of *On War* could be traced back to Hegel. This of course is not only far-fetched, it is thoroughly impossible, since Hegel was relatively unknown before 1820, let alone at the turn of the century,

14 Clausewitz, *On War*, bk VI, ch. 30, 547. This line occurs in the context of Clausewitz speaking about the advantages of the "state of expectation" on the defensive side, the difficulties in executing the attack, and the concepts of "mutual destruction" and war's "absolute form."

15 Ibid., bk VIII, ch 6B, 675.

16 Paret, *Clausewitz and the State*, 84.

17 Ibid.

18 See also Jan Honig's chapter "Clausewitz's *On War*: Problems of Text and Translation," which provides a good look at the difficulties involved in translating Clausewitz into English, and examples of where this poses problems in the Howard/Paret transation.

when many of Clausewitz's ideas were taking shape.[19] Furthermore, *On War* is scattered with references to so many other influences, such as Scharnhorst, Machiavelli, Kant, and Montesquieu, that it seems foolish to claim only one with such vigour. Clausewitz was quite transparent with regard to his appreciation for such figures: he referred to Scharnhorst as the "father and friend of my spirit" in a letter to his fiancée[20]; in the case of Machiavelli, not only did he write on the subject directly in a letter to Fichte, he also shared various similarities in his outlook on the question of people's wars (guerrilla),[21] and had shown interest in both Machiavelli's *Prince* and his *Politics* in many regards.[22] Regarding Montesquieu Clausewitz wrote in an editing note that "Montesquieu was vaguely on my mind,"[23] though the similarity in the argumentative form reveals a "much deeper affinity."[24]

Unfortunately, for those who seek to reclaim the case for a convergence of ideas between Clausewitz and Hegel, the difficult lies in the fact that are no clear-cut references or mentions of Hegel available in the letters or essays by Clausewitz.[25] Gat notes that this might be expected since during the time when both figures were living in Berlin, the correspondence between Clausewitz and his wife, which provide us a good record of other times in their lives come to a normal cessation since the two were living together and had no reason therefore to write.[26] At best, we have circumstantial evidence, regarding the fact that Hegel and Clausewitz were regularly invited to the home of a common friend, Meusebach,[27] and had been acquainted in the salons of Berlin,[28] given their special parallel status: Hegel was the president of the University of Berlin, while Clausewitz commanded the War College in Berlin.[29]

For lack of a clear historical link or record, Aron wondered whether or not Clausewitz even read Hegel.[30] But this is no reason to stop everything

19 Gat, *Origins of Military Thought*, 232–3.

20 Clausewitz, letter to his fiancée, 28 January 1807, in "Carl und Marie von Clausewitz, Ein Lebensbild," 85.

21 Gat, *Origins of Military Thought*, 203–4.

22 Paret, *Clausewitz and the State*, 169–79.

23 Clausewitz, *On War*, bk I, ch. 1,63.

24 Gat, *Origins of Military Thought*, 194.

25 Aron, *Penser la guerre*, vol. I, 362.

26 Gat, *Origins of Military Thought*, 233.

27 Ibid. Citing A.H. Hoffmann von Fallersleben, *Mein Leben* vol. 1 (Hannover: Rümpler, 1868), 311–12. Cited in Paret, *Clausewitz and the State*, 316.

28 Ibid.

29 Gat, *Origins of Military Thought*, 233.

30 Aron, *Penser la guerre*, 361.

and call the case closed. Indeed, while direct terms, ideas, and methods are borrowed from Kant word for word throughout *On War*, Clausewitz never mentions Kant by name, nor did he ever quote Montesquieu directly. This, of course, did not stop Aron from claiming Montesquieu's influence left, right, and centre,[31] which shows that he was not applying the same academic standards to his argument in favour of one influence in his dismissal of others.

Aron's position on the Hegelian link is similar in spirit to his stance on the Kantian link. Aron agreed with the overall idea that something changed dramatically in Clausewitz's writing in the late 1820s, and actually went so far as to describe these years as a "rupture in the evolution of Clausewitz's thought,"[32] though he did not attribute it to a recent discovery of Hegel's methods of dialectical reconciliation. At the time, Clausewitz explained in editorial notes (which we shall look over below) that one of his objectives in taking on such an ambitious re-edit of his works was to centre and enhance the importance of the political nature of war elsewhere in the book, and to expand on the question of the real and the absolute. Though Aron recognized that Clausewitz "went to great pains to reconcile these two principles of absolute and real war into a final synthesis,"[33] he avoided the question of whether there was a Hegelian influence to this sudden breakthrough in the synthetic reconciliation of a dichotomy. Perhaps he felt that having already settled the question elsewhere in *On War*, where there was no Hegelian influence, it did not strike him as useful to test his hypothesis again in later sections, against a different dialectic: absolute war and real war. This dialectic can in fact be shown to pass the very same test used by Aron to deny the link.

WHAT HAPPENED TO CLAUSEWITZ IN THE LATE 1820S?

Aron never provided an adequate explanation for the "rupture" he identified in Clausewitz's final round of edits. Instead Aron attributed the whole of Clausewitz's understanding of politics to Montesquieu.[34] However, this focus on Montesquieu could not fit the timing of the re-edit. Clausewitz had already read Montesquieu by 1805,[35] and had mentioned him in the early phases of writing *On War*, in an editorial to the

31 For example ibid., 23–4, 107, 350–70.
32 Ibid., 355.
33 Aron, *Sur Clausewitz*, 103.
34 Aron, *Penser la guerre*, 173.
35 Paret, *Clausewitz and the State*, 171n.

manuscript dated circa 1818.[36] Would he have required nine more years to integrate this perspective into his work? It seems untenable. It is far more likely that recent discoveries and readings were influencing his thoughts, or else one would not describe the sudden changes with as dramatic a term as "rupture."

The first hint that we should consider is another undated editorial note attached to the manuscript. Azar Gat provides a convincing case that it was not written in 1830, as many have assumed (including Howard/Paret[37]), but rather in 1827, perhaps even slightly before another editorial note dated July 1827.[38] This places it right at the threshold of when the "rupture" is assumed to have begun, and many years after the one-off reference to Montesquieu in 1818.

In this second note, three concepts are brought together into a single whole that carries a Hegelian message that can be clearly distinguished from Clausewitz's Kantian influence. He writes: "Die klaren Vorstellungen in diesen Dingen sind also nicht unnütz, außerdem hat der menschliche Geist nun einmal ganz allgemein die Richtung auf Klarheit und das Bedürfnis, überall in einem notwendigen Zusammenhang zu stehen."[39] Peter Paret came across the above words and was so struck by them that he decided to use a truncated version of this exact sentence as the opening quote for his book *Understanding War: Essays on Clausewitz and the History of Military Power*. He did not, however, notice that he had one of the best examples of a convergence between Clausewitzian and Hegelian thought right under his nose. Paret's translation of the original misses the mark, as does Graham's, which may explain why the passage's relation to Hegel has gone unnoticed.

Graham translated the above passage as follows: "Clear ideas on these matters do, therefore, have some practical value. The human mind, moreover, has a universal thirst for clarity, and longs to feel itself part of an orderly scheme of things." As for Howard/Paret, they chose: "Clear ideas on these matters are therefore not wholly useless; besides, the human mind has a general tendency to clearness, and always wants to be consistent with the necessary order of things." In both cases, we miss a trio of ideas, which when brought together and contextualized in larger debates of the time actually show a greater philosophical depth. The first is a philosophical term, "notwendigen Zusammenhang," which translates

36 Clausewitz, *On War*, bk I, ch. 1, 63.

37 Clausewitz, "Two Notes by the Author," *On War*, ed. and trans. Howard and Paret, 70–1.

38 Gat, *Origins of Military Thought*, 255–63, appendix.

39 Clausewitz, Nachricht, *Vom Kriege*.

to "necessary connection," and for which the claim to fame is having been the centre of the discussion on causality that pitted Hume against earlier rationalists, and thereafter Kant against Hume. The two next terms, "allgemein die Richtung," which means universal direction, and "menschliche Geist," the human spirit, are more innocuous. But when all three are placed together in a single phrase, they take on a very rich and philosophically significant tone. A translation closer to the mark should therefore read: "Clear ideas on these matters are therefore not wholly useless; the human spirit, moreover, is endowed with a universal direction to clarity, and with a need to stand at every point in a necessary connection."

Clausewitz's appreciation for the concept of "notwendigen Zusammenhang" in this paragraph shows a clear evolution, from when he first used it in an earlier chapter. In the "Kritik" chapter of Book II, Clausewitz wrote that "kein menschlicher Blick imstande ist, den Faden des notwendigen Zusammenhanges der Dinge bis zu dem Entschluß der besiegten Fürsten zu verfolgen,"[40] meaning that: "no human eye is able to follow the thread of the necessary connection of events, which led to the decisions of a defeated prince."[41] Here, we find that "necessary connection" is used conceptually in the way that Kant and Hume understood it: as a static concept of causality itself. The scepticism to the phrase is quite reminiscent of Hume, though in the context of this chapter, which is on the whole Kantian, it follows that this scepticism is the starting point, for which critical analysis provides the necessary testing to properly ground theory in historical fact.

When we move to the 1827 quote, we find that something has changed dramatically in Clausewitz's understanding of necessary connection. Unlike Hume and Kant, Hegel's idea of necessary connection is not static, but is in fact the underlying logic of the universe in which spirit and history materialize. The Hegelian link comes from the fact that prior to his philosophical works, whether in Kant or in Hume, necessary connection was not something one could "stand in" for the simple reason that causality was construed in the Enlightenment tradition of an external phenomenon that one studies as an object. For Hume, there was no possibility of causal demonstration at all,[42] while in Kant, necessary connection was demonstrable, but only insofar is it is locked up into certain categories of human understanding.[43] However, the passage it is perfectly in line with the Hegelian interpretation, because only in Hegel's

40 Clausewitz, *Vom Kriege*, Buch II, Kapitel 5.
41 Clausewitz, *On War*, bk II, ch. 5, 114.
42 Hume, *Enquiries*, 63.
43 Kant, *Critique of Pure Reason*, 212–26.

work does necessary connection exist in Geist, or Spirit, and represent the logic of the universe as a process unfolding towards greater clarity. Something one can be part of, and stand in. Of the three versions of what necessary connection can be, what Clausewitz is trying to express is only intelligible in the context of the third, where necessary connection not only exists, it is also a fluid rather than static concept. From a Hegelian perspective, we are always standing within this realm of necessary connection because, as we noted in the previous chapter, "The truth is the whole. But the whole is nothing other than the essence consummating itself through its development. Of the Absolute, it must be said that it is essentially a result."[44] In this context, the subject is the very embodiment of "necessary connection" as it makes itself real and objective in the world: the subject is the "vehicle"[45] by which spirit or rationality is materialized in the world.

This transition from a first to a second interpretation of necessary connection suggests a clear understanding of Hegel. However, once we couple this one concept with the rest of the sentence, the case for a convergence with Hegelian ideas becomes much harder to counter. Adding "human spirit" and "universal direction" to the idea of "standing in necessary connection" completes the picture. Human spirit exists in the universal only insofar as it stands "in" necessary connection; and necessary connection in Hegel is conceived precisely as this relation by which universal spirit is materialized through its particular embodiments or vehicles. When considered in light of the timing of the rupture in Clausewitz's thought, we are led to the conclusion that some way or another, his reasoning was becoming more in line with that of Hegel, and that having perhaps discovered something useful in thinking this way, it forced him into an ambitious set of revisions. Clausewitz's mention of "clarity" is telling given his lifelong struggle with the problem of the political nature of war and its lack of clarity; the note seems to express a sudden "Eureka!" moment in Clausewitz's later life, one that coincides with a way of thinking similar to Hegel's in a variety of ways.

As we shall see in the coming lines, the convergence between the two does not appear all at once, but in increments over time, and while this should not be considered as proof that Clausewitz had a motivation or desire to write more like Hegel, he did in fact wind up attempting more ambitious arguments that replicate and build upon systems that were distinctly Hegelian. What is most interesting, when we consider the

44 Hegel, *Phenomenology of Spirit*, #20, 11.
45 Taylor, *Hegel*, 128.

increments rather than the whole, is that it is a progressive initiative that increases in depth and scope as time advances, but in the ends stops short. There appears to be an incompletion in the rapprochement with Hegel that fits well with that possibility that, just like *On War*, this lesson was also a work in progress, unfinished when Clausewitz died.

AUFHEBUNG: FROM DISCERNMENT TO APPLICATION

What is practical about the test Aron used in his dismissal of the Hegelian links is that, in doing so, he established a set of criteria upon which to judge whether or not the ideas of Clausewitz had a Hegelian form, without realizing that his argument provided the seed of its own undoing. He proposed that it was unnecessary to limit himself to a historical demonstration of the lack of influence (there being no record of influence) since, through reasoning alone, he could show that the work was simply not Hegelian. Focusing in on the concept of "defence-attack" found in *On War*, Aron makes mincemeat of Camon's weak argument (and, as it were, of Gat who repeats it[46]) in which it was suggested that Clausewitz was being Hegelian here, using a thesis, attack, an antithesis, defence, and a synthesis, defence-attack. Aron countered that the term had nothing Hegelian to it, since the second term was not in any way a proper negation of the first term, and the third term did not represent a superior conceptual or historical plateau that negated the previous two and built atop them a higher level or a new triad.[47] He was absolutely right.

However, much like Paret, who found the right quote but failed to fully grasp its implications, Aron brings our attention to a very important passage in *On War*, regarding defence-attack, which counters his own overall dismissal of the Hegelian similarities. The passage reads: "Eine Verteidigung des Landes also wartet nur den Angriff des Landes, eine Verteidigung des Kriegestheaters den Angriff des Kriegestheaters, eine Verteidigung der Stellung den Angriff der Stellung ab. Jede positive und folglich mehr oder weniger angriffsartige Tätigkeit, welche sie nach diesem Augenblick übt, wird den Begriff der Verteidigung *nicht aufheben* emphasis added, denn das Hauptmerkmal derselben und ihr Hauptvorteil, das Abwarten, hat stattgefunden."[48] This is translated by Howard/Paret as: "Once the enemy has attacked, any active and therefore more or less offensive move made by the defender does not *invalidate* the concept of defence, for its salient feature and chief advantage, waiting, has

46 Gat, *Origins of Military Thought*, 234–5.
47 Aron, *Penser la guerre*, 363–4.
48 Clausewitz, *Vom Kriege*, Buch VI, Kapitel 8.

been established."[49] The other translation, by Col. J.J. Graham, proposes: "A defence of the country, therefore, only waits for attack on the country; a defence of a theatre of war an attack on the theatre of war; and the defence of a position the attack of that position. Every positive, and consequently more or less offensive, kind of action which the defensive uses after the above period of waiting for, does not *negate* the idea of the continuance of the defensive; for the state of expectation, which is the chief sign of the same, and its chief advantage, has been realised."[50]

Having taken the time to explain Hegel's philosophy and the concept of Aufhebung, in the previous chapter, it is plain to see that no translation to English is quite adequate to savour the complexities implied in the word choice. The translations provided by either Graham or Howard/ Paret do not pay justice to the concept by which a system of opposition sublates itself, generating a new level of knowledge that incorporates the lower level into the new. Clausewitz did not use the term "ungültig machen," meaning to "make invalid," which would have proven the Howard/ Paret version correct. Nor did he use the term "verneinen," meaning to "negate," as Graham has it. While there were many word options available to Clausewitz in order to make his point, he chose the specific term "aufheben," which, if we recall, is the "self-dissolution of extremes" as they come together. And as Hegel wrote in the *Phenomenology* regarding abstract negation, this "supersedes in such a way as to preserve and maintain what is superseded, and consequently survives its own supersession."[51]

What Aron described as the criterion he was using to demonstrate that defence-attack was not a Hegelian concept was in effect a simplified interpretation of Hegel's Aufhebung, whereby the parts of a dialectical structure are sublated, surpassed, and integrated into a new conceptual plateau. In the above paragraph from *On War*, Clausewitz actually spelled out the criterion himself by describing the relationship between attack and defence, and immediately the dialectical construct did not achieve a new conceptual plateau – it was not an Aufhebung. Here he was indeed using, as Paret argued, a simplified dialectical construct common to German Idealism, but the fact that he could identify it as such demonstrates that he could differentiate Hegelian dialectics from other dialectical systems. Hence, he knew of Aufhebung, which strongly suggests that he knew of Hegel's method, though he had not yet reached the point of actually experimenting further with this methodology. The discernment

49 Clausewitz, *On War*, ed. and trans. Howard and Paret, bk VI, ch. 8, 379, emphasis added.

50 Ibid., 385, emphasis added.

51 Hegel, *Phenomenology of Spirit*, #188, 114–15.

is nevertheless extremely important since it marks the apparent beginning of Clausewitz's transition, and arguably took place precisely as he was entering the supposed moment of "rupture" in his thought. The timing does not seem very coincidental, but actually determinant.

What is most striking with this quick one-off reference to Hegel in Book VI is that it would have been written before Book VIII and the Book I ch. I edits, which are commonly accepted to have been the last parts of *On War* that Clausewitz wrote. This might suggest an earlier acquaintance to the Hegelian method, albeit an incomplete one – a preliminary discernment, which had not yet evolved into its systematized application. If we consider the timing as an introduction, leading into a learning curve, then it explains in what sense a slightly later period, such as the years 1827–30, could have corresponded with a more mature appreciation for dialectical reconciliation.

However, there is more detail to add. We know that Clausewitz was interested in the concept of "active defence"[52] in his early years, and he had developed the seed of his "attack-defence" concept most probably while studying under Scharnhorst. "Defensive warfare," Clausewitz wrote in his textbook for the crown prince decades before writing *On War*, "therefore, does not consist of waiting idly for things to happen."[53] The idea was already in his possession, but he did not develop it as a dyadic relationship between offence and defence, where aspects of the former are contained in the latter. In these early writings, Clausewitz also made the case for transitioning from the defence to the offence, which is something he believed in throughout his life. "We must begin, therefore, using the defensive, so as to end more successfully by the offensive";[54] yet, at this early stage, he presented it as sequence of events, or a relationship that is subsequent, rather than inherently paradoxical. Years later, when he wrote Book VI of *On War*, Clausewitz would contextualize the idea within a dialectical frame of analysis. He engaged with the notion of "Aufhebung," as we saw above, and also began conceptualizing the two notions in an altogether new light, where one and the other are integrated, not separate and subsequent, as is made evident in chapter 9, where he speaks of the defence's "offensive character" and refers to the "offensive elements which lie in every defensive battle."[55] In this case, we can see a clear transition from Clausewitz before he engaged with dialectical reasoning, and afterwards: what he once understood as two separate

52 Clausewitz, *Principles of War*, 20.
53 Ibid., 54.
54 Ibid., 58.
55 Clausewitz, *On War*, bk VI, ch. 9, 400.

ideas was thereafter reinvented as a paradoxical dual concept – albeit one that did not fulfill a true Aufhebung in the Hegelian sense.

REAL WAR, ABSOLUTE WAR, AND THE CONTINUATION OF POLICY BY OTHER MEANS

In order to move into an exploration of the use of Aufhebung in *On War*, the one that passes Aron's criteria, we must return to the question of how the real and absolute concepts of war came about. Let us recall how a false consensus was reached among many scholars on the subject of the order in which Clausewitz developed the two concepts, i.e. that a mature Clausewitz toned down the theory of his youth and added in the dichotomous real war to moderate his initial, extreme idea. In chapter 5, we turned this argument around and showed the opposite reality, that the absolute is what came last and forced Clausewitz to reconsider his concept of real war altogether, turning it into much more fluid idea that moves about depending on context.

Having uncovered the "lateness" of the absolute concept of war, this allows us to ask ourselves if the quest to unlock the underlying meaning of its relation to real war was in fact a continuation of his Kantian or Fichtean influence, or if in fact something new and far more potent was on his mind, a "Eureka!" moment where the attempt to reconcile the two in fact brings us closer to Hegelian dialectics.

Real war and absolute war were originally conceived in reference to a Kantian system of categories. However, in order for Clausewitz to begin reconciling them into the continuation of policy, he could not do so using Kantian methodology. The reconciliation depended first and foremost on building the dichotomy in such a way that it could be reconciled in the first place. And this process required an approach that was closer in spirit to Hegel's work. In a Kantian system, one would perceive the absolute and the real embodiments of war as being inherently and thoroughly distinct in nature, mutually exclusive, and suspended in stasis. This is not the case in a Hegelian dialectic, where the stasis is broken and rendered dynamic, that is, the two poles are naturally opposed and distinct but nonetheless contain something of the other within them, a universality that is the root of their Aufhebung. Or, as Hegel explained in his exploration of sense certainty, seeing emerges from having seen and then not having seeing, a universally valid outcome that results from the sublation of the opposition.

Before attempting to reconcile the two, Clausewitz does some groundwork first, by identifying examples of inherent elements of universality that belong to both concepts of war, which he develops in Book VIII, chapter 3. First, he explains that "results" (or "success" in the Howard/Paret translation) in war can also be understood as having an absolute form and a real form, which are perceived as either the larger goals of war or the pursuit of minor advantages.[56] The second is the "use of force," which once again would lead to maximum use in the absolute, but is historically demonstrated to be always limited – more at some times, less at others. Clausewitz uses these two examples to bring forward the intrinsic (or internal) coherence – *innerer Zusammenhang* – that exists between the two categories of war. The term serves as the title of this section and again is a very telling word choice, which is lost in translation. Hegel was the first to try to demonstrate this concept, innerer Zusammenhang, as it exists in history[57] – that is to say as something dynamic, not static.

If we were to use Aron's criteria as our basis upon which to gauge the similarities between Hegel and Clausewitz's dialectical reconciliation, we would find that the way in which the real and absolute dichotomy leads to the demonstration that war is the "continuation of policy by other means" passes the test easily. In attempting to reconcile the two, Clausewitz makes a dialectical advance where "what has been surpassed is also preserved" – or, as Aron proposed, where the second term would negate the first, and the third term would represent a superior conceptual or historical plateau upon which a new conceptual plateau can emerge.[58] By arriving at the conclusion that "war is nothing but a continuation of political intercourse, with a mixture of other means,"[59] Clausewitz found that in both absolute and real war this same idea remains valid, without invalidating the notions inherent to either of the previous constructs nor those features that are inherent to both. This very contradiction and resolution did in fact generate a new plateau: the unitary truth of war conceptualized as an "instrument of policy" that "neutralizes" the contradiction. Here we are moving from the nature of war to the logic, ethics, and reason for war:

HAVING made the requisite examination on both sides of that state of antagonism in which the nature of war stands with relation to other interests of men individually and of the bond of society, in order not to neglect any of the opposing elements, – an antagonism which is founded in our own nature, and which, therefore, no philosophy can unravel, – we shall now look for that unity into

56 Ibid., bk VIII, ch. 3A, 646–8.
57 Engels, "Review of *Critique of Political Economy*."
58 Aron, *Penser la guerre*, 363–4.
59 Clausewitz, *On War*, bk VIII, ch. 6B, 674.

which, in practical life, these antagonistic elements combine themselves by partly neutralising each other. We should have brought forward this unity at the very commencement, if it had not been necessary to bring out this contradiction very plainly, and also to look at the different elements separately. Now, this unity is the conception that war is only a part of political intercourse, therefore by no means an independent thing in itself.[60]

This is not merely an end in the philosophical exploration, but also the beginning: it completes or brings to a close the ontological aspects of war and its categorization, and moves the reader into a distinct realm, that of ethics, which in this case is clearly alluded to in the term "practical life." The ethics emerge from the ontological analysis while also encompassing it: it is a *higher* realm. Indeed, while understanding war as absolute or real implies a mechanical understanding regarding what wars are, and how wars are fought, the continuation of policy leads us to new questions regarding why wars are fought, and more importantly, on what grounds they are ethically anchored. This notion clearly marks the emergence of a higher conceptual plateau, as Aron expected, since entering the realm of ethics, from the ontological, allows further contradictions to become apparent, as we will explore further below. For the exact same reason that the dialectical construct of defence-attack failed to pass Aron's test, Clausewitz's absolute/real dichotomy rendering the idea of war as a continuation of policy must pass. It brings together two contradictory concepts upon which a new, higher conceptual plateau is edified in a distinct realm of analysis – in this case ethics.

INTELLIGENCE OF THE PERSONIFIED STATE

Though the reconciliation of real and absolute war as the continuation of policy by other means did come to Clausewitz late in his life, one must not presume that this means, as some have argued,[61] that Clausewitz introduced the question of war's political nature in the final four years of writing *On War*. Nothing could be further from the truth. From very early on, Clausewitz wrote about the *problématique* of war's relation to the political; it was not a struggle that appeared later in life.[62] That was not the problem. The difficulty was to find an appropriate way to formulate this underpinning into a coherent part of his theory. And this only

60 Ibid.

61 See for example Heuser, *Reading Clausewitz*, 41.

62 Clausewitz, *Schriften, Aufsätze, Studien, Briefe*, vol. I, 63. Cited in Honig, "Early Modern Warfare," 29–48.

happened much later. Having set himself the challenge of establishing a theory that did not base itself on presuppositions, but on objective fact, he could not simply assert the political nature of war as a given; instead he hoped to demonstrate it by extracting his impression from observation. The question followed him throughout his life. Though part of his solution would be to move away from the idea of the state towards using instead the concept of politics, the question remained intact: was the "political" the soul of war, or did it merely give life to war?[63] What was the true relationship between war and politics?

In the oldest text known to have been penned by Clausewitz we find him writing in a broken French and making the argument that one needed to distance oneself either from the "principles of the art of war" or the "natural interests of states," and that given the choice, he preferred sticking with the latter since forgoing the first would imply losing the perfection in the form, whereas forgoing the second would deprive the student of war's "soul."

"Il faut ici s'éloigner un peu ou des principes de l'art de guerre ou de l'intérêt naturel des États; et j'aime mieux le premier [orig. deleted: 'dernier'] puisque ce n'est que la perfection de la forme, qui souffre par-là, tandis qu'en s'éloignant de l'intérêt naturel des états on prive les opérations de leur âme, de cette force qui doit leur donner la vie. L'histoire confirme bien cette opinion."[64] Here, we can clearly distinguish romantic more than idealist tendencies in young Clausewitz's conception of the state as having a "soul" or personal unity.[65] However imbued with the new German intellectual currents from the start, Clausewitz's concept of statehood nonetheless surpassed its initial form and grew over time, away from the "soul" and towards something far closer to the concept being developed concurrently by Hegel in the *Philosophy of Right*, where the state is understood as materialized rationality.

In the final edit of Book I, a mature Clausewitz explained that "policy we regard as the intelligence of the personified state."[66] In this case, it is indeed essential that we stick with the Graham translation, since Howard/Paret translate the original "Denn betrachtet man die Politik wie die Intelligenz des personifizierten Staates"[67] very liberally as "If the state is thought as a person, and policy as the product of its brain."[68] What is

63 Ibid.

64 Clausewitz, "Considérations sur la manière de faire la guerre à la France' February 1801–October 1805." Cited in Honig, "Clausewitz," 1–2.

65 Aron, *Penser la guerre*, vol. 2, 227.

66 Clausewitz, *On War*, bk I, ch. 1, 18.

67 Clausewitz, *Vom Kriege*, Buch I, Kapitel 1.

68 Clausewitz, *On War*, bk I, ch. 1, 88.

strikingly Hegelian in Clausewitz's formulation cannot be understood from the Howard/Paret translation because where they attempt to turn the idea into a mere bodily metaphor, Clausewitz's sentence, which is metaphorical as well in some ways, escapes the mere analogy with the body. The words have a far greater significance when they are taken at face value. Knowing how careful and systematic Clausewitz usually was in his word choice, it is best to translate him without the type of deviation attempted by Howard/Paret, as they add the words brain and person to a text where these words do not appear in the first place.

The intelligence of the personified state appears in the later works of Clausewitz, not the early ones, and it corresponds closely to some of the mid- to late works of Hegel as well. If we turn to Hegel's *Philosophy of Right*, we find that the terms are similarly constructed, though not identical. "Policy" and "intelligence" are swapped for "wisdom": "The wisdom (Weisheit) of the government, the abstract intelligence (Verstand) of the universal will, in the fulfilling of itself. The government is itself nothing else but the self-established focus, or the individuality of the universal will ... it excludes all other individuals from its act, and on the other hand, it thereby constitutes itself a government that is a specific will."[69]

One may be tempted to argue that since Clausewitz was of the opinion that states are the sum of various competing intelligences,[70] he could not share the idea that the state is the "individuality of the universal will." However, this point is not inconsistent with Hegel's position, as the paragraph quoted above goes on to discuss how the singular will rises to universality, but in effect generates factions within the state as a result.[71]

Whereas the young Clausewitz's concept of state has nothing particularly Hegelian to it, his mature concept of policy as the intelligence of the personified state does. Knowing just how central this topic was to Aron's interpretation of Clausewitz, as Murielle Cozette aptly shows,[72] it is indeed all the more striking that Aron should have omitted the important Hegelian resonance. Aron does not provide himself with the necessary tool to perceive the full-scale reversal, because he does not make a clear distinction between the younger and the older Clausewitz. Early on in Clausewitz's writing, the notion of the state is built on a metaphysical and emotional basis, this romantic idea of the soul. However, the later concept is freed from emotion, anchored in pure reason, and heavily imbued with the notion of a materialized rationality: this is distinctly Hegelian.

69 Hegel, *Phenomenology of Spirit*, #591, 360.
70 Clausewitz, *On War*, bk VIII, ch. 2, 643.
71 Hegel, *Phenomenology of Spirit*, #591, 360.
72 Cozette, "Reading Clausewitz," 126.

While the goal here is not to pinpoint direct and irrevocable influence between Hegel and Clausewitz, what this convergence allows us to do is read Clausewitz from a certain perspective that can illuminate aspects of his work that might otherwise not be as clear or intelligible otherwise. Understanding the similarities between Hegel and Clausewitz allows us to appreciate why certain systems of logic found in Clausewitz make sense and come together in the way that they do. This logic, which has been explained in the works of Hegel and in chapter 8, helps us clarify how Clausewitz's system sustains paradoxes logically.

Herberg-Rothe reminds us that Clausewitz made the point that "theory and reality correspond to one another"[73] – and this is indeed a significant aspect of Clausewitz's intellectual predisposition. Like Hegel, Clausewitz meant to bring together the real world and the world of ideas, rather than leaving them apart and in stasis. The fluidity of how the idea of absolute war becomes materialized in varying manifestations of real war is precisely how his dialectical system shows itself to be somewhat post-Kantian. This same process of bridging the gap between the ideal and its actuality occurs again in Clausewitz's new conceptualization of the state as a personified intelligence. In both cases, we are perceiving a convergence with Hegel's idea that *what is rational is actual and what is actual is rational*, and we find ourselves positioning Clausewitz on the same side as Hegel with regard to the latter's argument against Kant, mentioned earlier, that the abstract world of ideas, since it must first be posited in *actual* thought, is not external to the real world.

73 Herberg-Rothe, *Clausewitz's Puzzle*, 77.

10

Clausewitz and Hegel: The Convergence Peaks in On War*'s Book I, Chapter 1, as the Divergence on Ethics Sharpens*[1]

AS WAS MENTIONED EARLIER, what is surprising in the way Hegel and Clausewitz overlap is that even though this overlap becomes increasingly apparent as we move from reading a younger to an older Clausewitz, it is in the end that the two arrive at their greatest disagreement. In this chapter, in order to appreciate the extent to which there are conceptual similarities, we will study the ideas developed in the very last sections that Clausewitz wrote and edited in *On War* relative to the works of Hegel. However, we will be forced to notice that as the resemblances become altogether uncanny, something is still missing. There is a final leap that Clausewitz does not make in his approach, and it is this that leads him to opposite conclusions on ethics. The problem is that the two authors understood the terms "subjectivity" and "objectivity" differently, and this caused an impasse between what each concluded from what they observed. While this could be explained by the fact that Clausewitz made an informed and deliberate decision not to be in agreement with Hegel, one other possibility worth noting is that he simply did not have the right philosophical understanding of objectivity and subjectivity to arrive at the same end point as Hegel did.

This discussion will once and for all crystalize the ethical divide between the two authors and also provide us with the logic that shaped both alternative answers to a single question. Having done this, we will

1 The final section of this chapter, appearing in an earlier version of chapter 9, was previously published in Y. Cormier, "Clausewitz & Hegel: Convergence on Method, Divergence on Ethics," *International History Review* 36, no. 1 (2014): 419–42.

consider, as we did previously in the chapter regarding Hegel's concept of right, what limitations may exist with regard to Clausewitz's idea of instrumentality – especially at the threshold of modern technology and revolutionary warfare, where it appears to develop cracks in sustaining its logic. The chapter will ask: how far can we take instrumentality as a justification for war before its inner logic begins to crumble upon itself? From this point it will be possible, in the subsequent chapter, to consider both the critiques of Clausewitz's instrumentality and Hegel's right in a parallel critical analysis in history.

BOOK I, CHAPTER 1 AND THE WONDROUS TRINITY

One of the frustrations scholars might come across when they attempt to demonstrate the influence of Hegel on Clausewitz is that if there was a learning curve leading to the crisis of the late 1820s, it should be most apparent in Book I, chapter 1 of *On War*, since it was the culmination of the new ideas that Clausewitz had in mind in revising his entire opus. For the most part, however, this does not happen – at least not on the surface. Book I, chapter 1 is not constructed as a dialectical exploration. There is nothing particularly Hegelian in its form with regard to methodology. This section of *On War* is not an argumentative one, but an assertive one. It front-loads all of Clausewitz's major conclusions, but these will not be explained and demonstrated until we read the other seven books. To perceive a convergence with the ideas of Hegel, one cannot merely look to the conclusions found in Book I, chapter 1, because what makes them similar to Hegel is not what they posit, but how Clausewitz got there in his argument, and the place to truly see this happen is in Books VI and VIII.

That being said, even if the method and style of the chapter are of little help, what is significant to the argument for a convergence between the ideas of the two authors is that all four observations in the previous chapter do in fact come together side by side in Book I, chapter 1: the ideas of inner connection and Spirit from the editorial note; a distancing from Montesquieu; a conception of politics as materialized reason or the personification of intelligence; the relationship between real and absolute war merging as the continuation of politics by other means. These ideas, as we shall consider in more detail below, are all reciprocated elsewhere in the final books of *On War*. They are not conceived for the first time in Book I, chapter 1, but are in fact ideas that we come across in Books VI and VIII, which Clausewitz presents in his introduction, without fully spelling out in these early pages the logic by which he arrives at them.

There is however one important exception to this connection between the two last books, the late editorial notes, and the introduction. One idea brought forward in Book I, chapter 1 is set there alone, and it does not reappear anywhere else in *On War*. This could well be the very last thing Clausewitz wrote – since it is the concluding subsection of this first chapter of *On War* – before sealing the draft and heading off to what would be his last mission for the Prussian Army. In fact, the last known draft of Book 1, chapter 1 is almost identical to the published version, but it did not contain this passage[2] – further evidence that this was perhaps indeed the very last addition. The passage in question is so significant to Clausewitz that he refers to it, and only it, as his *Consequences for Theory*, though for most readers it has become known not by this header, but for its description of war as a "wondrous trinity."[3]

The purpose of showing similarities in the concepts and constructs of Clausewitz's trinity and the work of Hegel, will help us explain what meaning can be drawn when we contextualize this part of *On War*, within the metaphysical debates. It will become clear that the use of a reference to godliness in his discussion of war's nature is part of a larger frame of analysis where a holistic method is drawn in, which encapsulates and brings greater meaning to the role of "pure reason" in its strained, but necessary relation with the blind instincts of violence. Placing a Hegelian lens to our analysis of the trinity clarifies the relationships between its three parts, which cease to appear as a subjective set of assumptions made by Clausewitz, to a more objective exploration of his topic. Most importantly, it will contribute to solving a controversy with regard to whether the Trinity "supersedes Clausewitz's political argument."[4] Looking at this from a Hegelian perspective, there is no such contradiction: the Trinity is the notion … it is in fact this very political argument.

In this chapter, I stand in agreement with Waldman who reminds his reader of the importance of understanding the trinity as a "unity" as opposed to its three parts.[5] This idea of unity (Einheit) is in fact also spelled out by Clausewitz in later sections of *On War* that set up the trajectory that leads him to the trinity. What this chapter attempts to do is uncover

2 Herberg-Rothe, *Clausewitz's Puzzle*, 95.

3 Many variations of this translation exist. Clausewitz wrote "wunderliche," which in English has been rendered as "remarkable" and "paradoxical" by Paret, "wonderful" by Graham, and "fascinating" by Bassford. I have chosen to side with Herberg-Rothe on the matter and use "wondrous." Bassford, "Primacy of Policy," 79; Herberg-Rothe, "'Wondrous Trinity' as a Coordinate System," 204–19.

4 Fleming, *Clausewitz's Timeless Trinity*, 3.

5 Waldman, *War, Clausewitz and the Trinity*, 178.

why this unity is in fact possible. What makes it logical to consider three concepts as one? What is the underlying logic? It is not so much that these are three unrelated concepts floating in parallel. In fact the three build up on one another, and in the very order in which Clausewitz wrote them. They are a synthetical construct and to expose this is to clarify the meaning of this very unity.

Before moving into this standalone trinity, let us first take the time to show how the other four ideas come together in Book I, chapter 1, which confirms what would be expected from the last section written by Clausewitz. This forms the basis of a compromise between those who are seeking a Hegelian influence but who are disappointed by not finding the clues of it where it should be most evident, the culmination of Clausewitz's work, and those who deny the influence on this very basis. The reality is not so categorical. Hegelian methodology is not necessary in Book I chapter 1 to speak of converging ideas between the two, insofar as the other half of each of the suggestive ideas is actually developed within such a methodological framework elsewhere in *On War.*

With regard to the ideas developed in the editorial note, the very first sentence of *On War* recalls some of the language we find in it, as well as the themes that recur in the works of Hegel, with regard to "inner connections" and relation of the whole to the particular. Like Hegel, Clausewitz set his sight on the whole, but intended to build it up from the simple to the complex, as a progression of connections. Clausewitz wrote: "We propose to consider first the single elements of our subject, then each branch or part, and, last of all, the whole, in all its relations (inneren Zusammenhange) – therefore to advance from the simple to the complex. But it is necessary for us to commence with a glance at the nature of the whole (das Wesen des Ganzen anzufangen), because it is particularly necessary that in the consideration of any of the parts the whole should be kept constantly in view."

This passage relates closely to the ideas cited in the editorial note, but more so to the two paragraphs that precede the excerpt chosen above, in which Clausewitz explained that generals planning war have the hardest time in determining the proper course of action, because of war's dual concepts, which send contradicting signals. At times this leads generals to choose actions out of merging the diverging opinions at either extreme, and this winds up producing "a middle-course without any real value."[6] His solution to this problem is, unsurprisingly, to establish "clear conceptions" of these inner connections.[7]

6 Clausewitz, editorial note, *On War*, xxxix.

7 Ibid. Note: Graham uses the words "inner relations" in this particular case.

Only in this context can Clausewitz speak of the intelligence of the personified state, which appears in this phrase in Book I, chapter 1, as the definition upon which to ground later discussions of the political nature of war. "If we regard the state policy as the intelligence of the personified state, then amongst all the constellations in the political sky which it has to compute, those must be included which arise when the nature of its relations imposes the necessity of a great war."[8] If the difficulty of determining a logical course of action in war is the result of the tensions between war's real and absolute forms, leading to contradicting signals and bad decisions, it explains why Clausewitz would hope or expect that the state should be infused with the enough rationality and intelligence to comprehend the matter and "compute" good policy in the face of great wars. His problem statement leads directly to his solution.

With regard to the tensions in war's dual concepts, again we find that Book I, chapter 1 has integrated the later conception of the absolute and the real, which places the absolute squarely in the realm of the *totally conceptual*:

> If we should seek to deduce from the pure conception of war an absolute point for the aim which we shall propose and for the means which we shall apply, this constant reciprocal action would involve us in extremes, which would be nothing but a play of ideas produced by an almost invisible train of logical subtleties. If adhering closely to the absolute, we try to avoid all difficulties by a stroke of the pen, and insist with logical strictness that in every case the extreme must be the object, and the utmost effort must be exerted in that direction, such a stroke of the pen would be a mere paper law, not by any means adapted to the real world.[9]

Moving from the simple to the complex, from the particular to the whole, as promised in the opening paragraph, Book I, chapter 1 builds up the argument until the dual concepts of war culminates into the formula "war is the continuation of policy by other means." While this might be perceived as a sufficiently holistic concept for war, because it encompasses the inner logic of war as the reciprocation of extremes and its instrumentalization in policy, Clausewitz does not end his introduction here, but having put forward policy as a product of intelligence, he ends on war's subjugation to "pure reason" itself, and frames this in a most holistic fashion, ending on what appears to be an analogy that draws in the divine with his wondrous trinity. When we contextualize this idea within its dialectical methodology, the choice of words ceases to

8 Clausewitz, *On War*, bk I, ch. 1, 18.

9 Ibid., 5.

be a superficial analogy, but actually fits within a system of logic where the progression of the simple to the complex is never complete until it has encompassed the universal absolute: god. The holistic methodology can only end in the divine, and unsurprisingly – for Christians like Hegel and Clausewitz – this divinity is constructed in a Trinitarian tradition. The trinity thus appears as "a unified, comprehensive concept from Clausewitz's different and in part contradictory definitions, terms and formula."[10]

This coming together of contradictions in the trinity is Clausewitz's attempt at a holistic, yet compressed, representation of war. Three ideas stand out: war's human element, its interactive dynamics, and the centrality of fighting, which showcases the importance of war's psychological, sociological, and material dimensions.[11] He describes war as the sum and interrelations of three sides: "the original violence of its elements, hatred and animosity, which may be looked upon as blind instinct; the play of probabilities and chance, which make it a free activity of the soul; and the subordinate nature of a political instrument, by which it belongs purely to reason."[12] Clausewitz explains that "the first of these three phases concerns more the people, the second, more the General and his Army; the third, more the Government."[13] The third element of the trinity, Strachan argues "became particularly important to Clausewitz's mental baggage, in that it both supplied the unifying purpose to *On War* and restrained absolute war."[14] It might be more appropriate not to say "it became," but rather that it had been latent and on Clausewitz's mind for many years, and now Clausewitz had finally discovered the best language and method to express his idea. What is crucial in Strachan's observation is unifying the whole while also containing the absolute. This represents the difficulty with holism, and the means by which both Hegel and Clausewitz attempt to resolve it is to channel the divine in their work. If the trinity converges with Hegelian thought in such general ways, what is surprising is just how precisely it also does so in its presentation, its ordering, and its word choices, all of which seem to come together as a culmination of the same holistic method for which Hegel has been both praised and scorned.

10 Herberg-Rothe, "Clausewitz's 'Wondrous Trinity,'" 49.

11 Waldman, *War, Clausewitz and the Trinity*, 7.

12 Clausewitz, *On War*, 19. Note: for clarity, I have removed the word "of," which precedes each of the three clauses; also, the Graham translation ends on "pure to the reason," and here the word "the" is superfluous and perhaps even slightly misleading, since Clausewitz uses the word "Verstand" which is not a specific reason but rather "Reason" itself.

13 Clausewitz, *On War*, bk I, ch. 1, 19.

14 Strachan, "Essay and Reflection," 343.

In his article on the trinity, Herberg-Rothe also turns to Hegel to guide his reflections on the matter. But before doing this he offers readers of the trinity a interesting problem to consider; he states that "it is not easy to explain how Clausewitz, in his wondrous trinity, can on the one hand repeat the primacy of politics in war, while simultaneously stressing that this primacy is just one facet of three tendencies, from which every war in its own particular way and mcans is composed. The problem lies with how to reconcile the purposive rationality of war ("pure reason") with the first tendency – the primordial violence of war that is to be regarded as a blind natural force."[15]

Herberg-Rothe argues that while one might attempt to solve this problem by imposing a strict hierarchy on the trinity, this would contradict Clausewitz's picture, while the second option, to seek a solution as the opposition between the real and the absolute (Aron, Heuser, Gat) leads to the "unpleasant consequence" of rejecting Clausewitz's "ideal conception" of war, and, at least in the case of Aron, awarding validity exclusively to Book I, chapter 1, at the expense of the rest of *On War*. Herberg-Rothe offers an interesting third way forward, which consists of understanding the trinity as a "methodological starting point." This allows him to avoid contradictions,[16] as he pursues his objective to deduce from the trinity a "differentiated coordinate system."[17]

While Herberg-Rothe's proposed system for understanding and applying the trinity is useful, and his alternative assumption that the trinity represents a "starting point" is a far better approach to the two problems he describes, it is not without problems. What we should instead consider is not a fourth way forward, but rather a single way backward, to the origin of the idea. In the process this would in fact replace all three approaches with a single logic that appears closer in spirit to what Clausewitz wrote, for one simple reason: the trinity was not presented by Clausewitz as a "beginning" at all. It is the end point of his reflection, the culmination of his idea. Far from wanting it to be easily broken down into coordinates and parts, or dichotomies, Clausewitz's trinity is meant to embody the *whole*. It is unbreakable and complete.

The trouble is that Herberg-Rothe is right to look to Hegel for answers, but he does not turn to the right area of Hegel's works to uncover the key to the wondrous trinity's secrets. It is not enough to show that there are contradictions, or that every statement requires a counter-statement, or weights and counter-weights, which is how Herberg-Rothe

15 Herberg-Rothe, "Clausewitz's 'Wondrous Trinity,'" 52.

16 Ibid.

17 Ibid., 67.

introduces a similarity with Hegel.[18] Contradictions are indeed a feature of dialectical thinking, but they are not ends in themselves: they serve a purpose forward. In the case of Hegel, what distinguishes his dialectical methods from all others is precisely this: that his system is not mere contradiction, but rather allows for the dynamic element whereby contradictions are overcome, which instead of producing various halves that are isolated and in stasis, generates a whole that is in constant flux.[19]

It is not enough to notice that the wondrous trinity is similar to Hegel's work merely because it has contradictions. What connects the two is that both authors use a system that contains three moments that build themselves as a process of sublimating each preceding part, from a subjective chaos, to its objective ordering, to its self-reflection (objectivity as the result of the subjective reflecting the subjective) and integration into "pure reason" in the case of Clausewtiz, or "Geist" in the words of Hegel.

To be clear, Hegel was quite adamant about the importance of splitting apart the appearance of contradictions from contradictory outcomes or ends. "It is a mistake," Hegel explained, "to think that it is reason which is in contradiction with itself; it does not recognize that the contradiction is precisely the rising of reason above the limitations of understanding and the resolving of them."[20] Hegel's three-way process is best developed in the *Science of Logic*, where each chapter builds up in this way towards the final chapter, entitled "The Notion" (Begriff), which is the whole of history reflected, the completion of spirit – god. When Clausewitz wrote his trinity using a nearly identical sequence of triadic logic he also described it, perhaps unsurprisingly, as "The Notion of War" (Begriff vom Krieg).[21]

In both Hegel and Clausewitz, references to Begriff encompass or bring forth the subject of divinity. This is because such references emerge from a perspective that does not allow for a world of ideas to exist outside the real realm – as was mentioned earlier in our discussion of Gat's work on the question. Therefore, to engage in a holistic argument, they must consider the materiality of the divine. When we study how the metaphysics influenced war studies, we are always confronted with a return to theological arguments. Interestingly, what comes to the front, as

18 Ibid., 56.

19 It should be noted in passing that Hegel's dialectics are not always constructed in the form that bridges a dichotomy to its sublation. In many cases, Hegel will posit dichotomies that do not have a convergence or resolution at all but are instead left "hanging." However, the triadic form is one that he developed and it can be most directly identified as the original element of his thought.

20 Hegel, *The Science of Logic*, 46.

21 Clausewitz, *On War*, bk I, ch. 1, 19.

we explore Clausewitz's divinity is that it is built up methodologically in ways that are identical to what Hegel developed in his *Lectures on the Philosophy of History*, given at the University of Berlin during the years 1822, 1828, and 1830. Concurrently, Hegel was also delivering his *Lectures on the Philosophy of Religion* in 1821, 1824, 1827, and 1831.

The problem with turning to the *Philosophy of History* to argue a link with Clausewitz is that it is not particularly convincing, for the simple reason that the book itself wasn't published until six years after both philosophers died. That being said, these lectures were without a doubt the talk of town in Berlin's academic circles throughout most of the thirteen years that Clausewitz spent as commander of the War College. Hegel's lectures were well attended and many copies of detailed notes taken by students were in circulation – indeed several of these were integrated into the first publication of Hegel's lecturing notes.[22] These were Hegel's glory years: he was appointed Rector of the University of Berlin as a result of these lectures and was soon thereafter also decorated by the King for services rendered to the nation.[23]

Did Clausewitz attend any of these lectures? Would that explain in part the "rupture" that occurs in the late 1820s? One can only speculate. Did Clausewitz discuss the topics with colleagues and friends? Did he come across the notes? While this remains uncertain, what we do know is that one of the students at the War Academy while Clausewitz was commander, and according to Creusinger a friend of Clausewitz's – Gustav von Griesheim – was given permission to audit Hegel's lectures at the University of Berlin. Hegel himself commended the student for the accuracy of his notes, and to this day they serve as the basis for some of the editions of these lectures.[24]

To be clear, the intention here is not to claim that Clausewitz read the notes or attended the event, but it is clear that had he wanted to, he would have had easy access to them. Rather, it is for the sake of clarity that it is useful to show the converging elements between Clausewitz's work and the ideas found in the *Lectures on the Philosophy of History*, because while the central tenets were written elsewhere and earlier in Hegel's works, it is here that they are easiest to grasp. The incursion into the *Philosophy of History* can be taken as a heuristic tool, to help explain the method that leads Hegel to also build a trinity that consists of natural passions, war, and historical events, subsumed in pure reason, in this very same order, like the structures and ideas as they appear in Clausewitz's trinity. If indeed the origin of the converging ideas was Clausewitz actually

22 Beiser, introduction to *Lectures*.

23 Duquette, "Biography of Hegel."

24 Herberg-Rothe, "Clausewitz und Hegel," 54–8.

reading Hegel's published work rather than the unpublished notes taken by Greisheim, then we would have to turn our attention to another, earlier book. The *Science of Logic* contains many of the ideas put forward in the *Philosophy of History*. These passages were published years earlier in 1812. All the methodological underpinnings of the triadic moments that make up the divine, which Hegel later drew out in *Philosophy of History*, were already established in the *Science of Logic*.

That being said, before anyone gets too excited about seeing "threes" everywhere, and jumps on a sudden urge to claim convergence between Hegel and Clausewitz, it is important to stress that a mere number, and a fairly commonly used number at that, is clearly not sufficient to draw parallels. Christopher Bassford is right to point us away from any numerological interpretation that posits Clausewitz was obsessed, as others have been, with the number three in generating his trinity.[25] This part of *On War* is far too entwined with pure reason to find itself suddenly sullied by magic and superstition. That being said, when we consider the source of dialectical reasoning in the metaphysical debates of the Enlightenment, it may be a bit rash to toss away too quickly the mystical root of the trinity. Bassford argues that viewing the "trinity as evidence of mysticism" is a fault caused by traditional, linear thought, people who have a "Newtonian world view, who are baffled by Clausewitz's obsession with chance, unpredictability, and disproportionality in the cause-effect relationship."[26] Contextualizing the trinity in relation to similar methods found in Hegel suggests rather that the references to spirit, god, or providence are central, not because of something magical to it, but quite the opposite, because rationality is understood as this spirit actualizing itself, making itself material in the world. The trinity is a means to anchor the argument in a holistic philosophical system, where pure reason gives meaning and vitality to events in history such as war. Pure reason attempts to direct and guide war towards its purpose, but is ultimately confronted with the very passions it attempts to frame, which ultimately offers resistance to rationality. As Bassford explains, the trinity in Clausewitz can be described, in more abstract terms, as a triad representing "irrationality/non-rationality/rationality," for which it is important to note that the final term "bloßen Verstande" must be understood as "pure reason" and not, as Howard and Paret wrote, "only reason,"[27] which loses entirely its philosophical connotation in the German philosophical tradition.

25 Bassford, "'Trinity' in Clausewitz's Mature Thought," 79.
26 Ibid.
27 Ibid., 80.

The fact that the trinity is presented directly after, and in counterpose to, the description of war as a "chameleon" is important, because this sequence allows Clausewitz to spell out, first, the fact that wars seem highly adaptable and constantly changing, yet likewise also that these changes are superficial, mere skin colour changes, and in reality the core is unchanging. Clausewitz's trinity is the complete opposite of this: it represents a universal and absolute configuration for the nature of war that allows for continual fluctuations within a system that is itself unchanging. The chameleon is a manifestation of variable forms, but the trinity is the true essence and its underlying material form. It is "all-inclusive and universal,"[28] containing within it all the shades and colours that the chameleon has taken before, can take today, and might take tomorrow.

It is important to recall that the study of god in the post-Kantian context, and in particular in Hegel, sets itself on a completely different plane of analysis than what was found among the earlier empiricists and theologians who sought out demonstration in deducing the divine – the Causa Prima – from the observation of god's effect in the world. In his introduction to the *Philosophy of History* Hegel presents the divine as a god who "governs the world, where the actual working of his government – the carrying out of his plan – is the History of the World."[29] In the same way, Clausewitz's deity is also expressed as one that gives laws or governs: "these three tendencies, which appear like so many different lawgivers."[30] For Hegel, god is described in these words: "This essential being is the union of the subjective with the rational Will: it is the moral Whole, the State, which is that form of reality in which the individual has and enjoys his freedom; but on the condition of his recognizing, believing in, and willing that which is common to the Whole."[31] Hegel's god is understood as progression of the universe from *irrationality*, to *non-rationality*, to *rationality*, as a historical process consisting of the following three moments:

1 The abstract characteristics of the nature of Spirit
2 What means Spirit uses in order to realize its Idea
3 Lastly, we must consider the shape that the perfect embodiment of Spirit assumes[32]

28 Ibid., 90.
29 Hegel, *Philosophy of History*, 36.
30 Clausewitz, *On War*, bk I, ch. 1, 19.
31 Hegel, *Philosophy of History*, 38.
32 Ibid., 17.

We can right away identify a preliminary similarity between this and Clausewitz's trinity, since the latter also integrates first what is latent, to how it is utilized, to how it is integrated and subsumed in pure reason or Spirit. However, we must go deeper into each of the three parts in order to uncover the extent to which the above three are parallel to Clausewitz's trinity not only as a whole but also in each individual part. Hegel understood the passions of man as the means through which reason actualizes itself in history,[33] and indeed, this forms the first of the three moments, "abstract characteristics": "The state of nature is therefore, predominantly that of injustice and violence, of untamed natural impulses (Naturtrieb), of inhuman deeds and feelings. Limitation is certainly produced by society and the state, but it is a limitation of the mere brute emotions and rude instincts; as also in a more advanced stage of culture, of the premeditated self-will of caprice and passion. This kind of constraint is part of the instrumentality by which only, the consciousness of Freedom and the desire for its attainment, in its true – that is rational and ideal form – can be obtained."[34]

When Clausewitz described the first "side" in his own trinity, he also used the term "Naturtrieb" and spoke of this aspect of war as being composed of blind passions and violence.[35] There is something animal and inhuman about the first moments of the triads in the divinities that both Hegel and Clausewitz describe, but ultimately this animal behaviour will fall prey to reason (bloßen Verstande anheimfällt),[36] and in fact gets instrumentalized in the process. The same finality is at the heart of Clausewitz's trinity, but beyond this end, the means to achieving it also converge.

Before reaching their third moment, in which reason instrumentalizes these passions, both Clausewitz and Hegel present war itself and its generals as the objectification or ordering mechanism that emerges from the chaos of passions. Whereas Clausewitz's second moment is presented as the place of armies and generals in the equation, Hegel's second moment is the section of the *Philosophy of History* in which he describes the role played by "world-historical people" such as Alexander, Caesar, and Napoleon.[37] Their roles are presented as a disciplining of passions, the means by which Spirit attains its aims. "Passion," Hegel writes, "is regarded as a thing of sinister aspect, as more or less immoral. Man is required

33 Avineri, "Instrumentality of Passion," 390.
34 Hegel, *Philosophy of History*, 40–1.
35 Clausewitz, *On War*, bk I, ch. 1, 19.
36 Ibid.
37 Hegel, *Philosophy of History*, 31.

to have no passions."[38] By negating passions and structuring violence teleologically, it becomes possible to imagine how pure reason could in fact instrumentalize it. For it would be impossible for reason to impose itself simply on the chaos of passions, these passions must be structured before reason can make anything of them. The third moment could not possibly exist in either Hegel or Clausewitz's trinities were it not for this second moment that renders passions "manageable" in the first place. But there could be no managing of violence if it were not for its "latent"[39] existence that is the first moment. The three moments are indeed inseparable. This process of instrumentalization is what Hegel refers to as the "cunning of reason,"[40] because it seems counterintuitive that events that appear irrational, like war and blind passionate violence, could be contributing to manifesting reason to the world. What Hegel meant by this is that "history fulfils its ulterior rational designs in an indirect and sly manor. It does so by calling into play the irrational element in human nature, the passions."[41]

Thanks to the presence of the term "cunning of reason" in the *Philosophy of History* we can clearly recognize its direct reference to the *Science of Logic*,[42] in which Hegel uses the term in his chapter on teleology, which has as its purpose to determine whether or not the "absolute determines itself in accordance with ends."[43] In the first phrase of the chapter, Hegel explains that "where purposiveness is discerned, an intelligence (Verstand) is assumed as its author, and for the end we therefore demand the Notion's own free Existence."[44] In Clausewitz, this freedom of spirit theme also appears, when in the second moment of his trinity he describes war as the "free activity of the soul."[45]

If the *Philosophy of History* provides us easier comparison in order to grasp the similarities between Clausewitz's and Hegel's trinities, it remains essential for us to return to the *Science of Logic* to appreciate the way Book I, chapter 1 does in fact take on a Hegelian form, not generally, but near the end when it leads into the final section *Consequences for Theory*. Interestingly, the final segment right before Hegel reaches his own trinity has yet another particularity that may surprise readers who

38 Ibid.
39 Clausewitz, *On War*, bk I, ch. 1, 19.
40 Hegel, *Philosophy of History*, 33.
41 Tucker, "Cunning of Reason," 269.
42 Hegel, *Science of Logic*, 734.
43 Ibid., 746; Hegel, *Philosophy of History*, 33.
44 Hegel, *Science of Logic*, 734.
45 Clausewitz, *On War*, bk I, ch. 1, 19.

are familiar with Clausewitz's famous quote with regard to war's grammar and logic. Though it does not appear directly in Book I, chapter 1, there is an indirect link to it at the very place where we would most expect it. Before Clausewitz jumps into his trinity, his last order of business in the introduction is to define war as the continuation of policy. The chapter in *On War* that deals with this particular subject, "War Is an Instrument of Policy" (Book VIII, chapter 6B), is where Clausewitz brings up the topic of logic and grammar. He wrote: "Is not war merely another kind of writing and language for political thoughts? It has certainly a grammar of its own, but its logic is not peculiar to itself. Accordingly, war can never be separated from political intercourse, and if, in the consideration of the matter, this is done in any way, all the threads of the different relations are, to a certain extent, broken, and we have before us a senseless thing without an object."[46]

By "logic," Clausewitz meant the "set of rules that govern reasoning ... likened to the accepted set of imperatives, principles, or customs governing political intercourse, all of which shape the conceptual limits of strategy."[47] As for the "grammar," which are rules regarding oral and written communications, Echevarria explains that these should be understood as the "military principles, rules, or procedures that govern the use of armed force."[48]

The final two pages of the introduction to the *Science of Logic*, before breaking off into a final sub-header in which he introduced Begriff in the form of a trinity, Hegel differentiated between logic and grammar and settled their relationship to one another as follows:

> He who begins with the study of grammar finds in its form an isolated collection of definitions and terms which exhibit only the value and significance of what is implied in their immediate meaning; there is nothing to be known in them other than themselves ... Through the grammar, he can recognize the expression of mind (Geist) as such, that is, logic ... The first acquaintance with logic confines its significance to itself alone; its content passes only for a detached occupation with the determinations of thought, *alongside* which other scientific activities possess on their own account a matter and content of their own, on which logic may have a formal influence, though an influence which comes only from itself and which if necessary can of course also be dispensed with so far as the scientific structure and its study are concerned.[49]

46 Ibid., bk VIII, ch. 6B, 675.
47 Echevarria, "Reconsidering War's Logic."
48 Ibid.
49 Hegel, *Science of Logic*, 57–8.

More significantly, though, as we read on we uncover in the introduction to the *Science of Logic* that Hegel also builds his argument up to similar ends. In the final subsection of the introduction, right after having discussed the grammar and logic, but before developing the triadic Notion, he brings in the divine into the equation, which is then developed in its detail in the upcoming section entitled "General Division of Logic." Hegel arrives at the same ultimate result as Clausewitz, dividing his "Notion" into three interconnected, syllogical moments – but not without first by contextualizing this trinity in divine terminology, "the soul, the world, and god,"[50] which he then breaks down into three moments of development:

1 The logic of being
2 The logic of essence, and
3 The logic of the Notion[51]

Together, the three form a forward relationship from the latent and subjective, through its objective realization, and finally incorporated and self-reflected as pure reason. This movement is well described by Duquette, who explains these three parts: i.e. "the subjective notion, the objective notion, and the idea which articulates the unity of subjective and objective."[52]

> The first part, the subjective notion, contains three "moments" or functional parts: universality, particularity, and individuality (¶ 163ff). These are particularly important as Hegel will show how the functional parts of the state operate according to a progressive "dialectical" movement from the first to the third moments and how the state as a whole, as a functioning and integrated totality, gives expression to the concept of individuality (in ¶198 Hegel refers to the state as "a system of three syllogisms"). Hegel treats these relationships as logical judgments and syllogisms but they do not merely articulate how the mind must operate (subjectivity) but also explain actual relationships in reality (objectivity).[53]

Clausewitz's trinity is precisely this, a system of three syllogisms, which is to say, three distinct conclusions or inferences, built into internal contradictions or oppositions, which exist in parallel and reinforce one another or build upon one another. In this context, the state as an individual

50 Ibid., 63.
51 Ibid., 64.
52 Duquette, "Biography of Hegel."
53 Ibid.

actor can indeed be "personified" – but more importantly, it achieves this end only because it is "animated by Spirit"[54] in the first place. Such a system of syllogisms is necessarily a relational thing, rather than a set of three fixed items floating independently from one another. As Hegel explains: "According to the relation by which the subjective end is united with objectivity, both premises alike – the relation of the object determined as means to the still external object, and the relation of the subjective end to the object which is made means – are immediate relations."[55]

Both Hegel and Clausewitz perceive their trinities as relational rather than as standalone ideas. Clausewitz refers to this twice as he introduces his discussion of the trinity. He writes that "war is … as a whole, in relation to the predominant tendencies which are in it, a wonderful trinity." This is followed up later, in the concluding remarks by the following argument: "any arbitrary relation between them, would immediately become involved in such a contradiction with the reality, that it might be regarded as destroyed at once by that alone."[56]

These relations between the three moments clarify the process of instrumentalization for which the "Teleology" chapter in the *Science of Logic* is the core argument. Here Hegel understands teleology as the very process by which "we make our ascent to the Absolute Idea"[57] – which is in effect the end goal of the book. It is the whole; it is the Soul of the world. If the first moment, as we saw, represented what nature has dealt us, subjectively, and the second, how this was negated into objectivity through its instrumentalization, the third moment, in which pure reason is self-reflected in the process, is also in itself the neutralization of the instrument – the fact that the instrument cannot exist alone.

> The means has no power of resistance against the end, as it has in the first instance against another immediate object … it is a neutral and also as a different object, no longer self-subsistent. Its lack of self-subsistence consists precisely in its being only *in itself* the totality of the Notion, but the latter is a being-for-itself. Consequently the object has the character of being powerless against the end and of serving it; the end is the object's subjectivity or soul, that has in the object its external side.
>
> The object, being in this manner *immediately* subjected to the end, is not an extreme of the syllogism; but this relation constitutes one of its premises. But the means has also a side from which it still has self-subsistence as against the end.

54 Hegel, *Philosophy of History*, 50.
55 Hegel, *Science of Logic*, 749.
56 Clausewitz, *On War*, bk I, ch. 1, 19.
57 Findlay, "Hegel's Use of Teleology," 8.

The objectivity that is connected with the end in the means is still external to it, because it is only immediately so connected; and therefore the *presupposition* still persists. The activity of the end through the means is for that reason still directed against this presupposition, and the end is activity and no longer merely an urge and a striving, precisely because the moment of objectivity is posited in the means in its determinateness as something external, and the simple unity (Einheit) of the Notion now has this objectivity *as such* in itself.[58]

These two paragraphs are the final parts of Hegel's second moment in the "Teleology" chapter. The instrument itself exists at the middle ground between the blind passions of the first moment, and the pure reason of the third. In Clausewitz, this is the instrumental part of his trinity as well, the play of chances and the roles of generals and armies. When we consider that at the end of his "Teleology" chapter, Hegel arrives almost exactly at the same conclusion as Clausewitz, who wrote in the Trinity that war was the "subordinate,"[59] but more strikingly, in his discussion of "War as an Instrument of Policy" (Book VII, ch 6B), reaffirms that this "unity" (Einheit) or the reconciliation of absolute and real war as lacking independence and being subdued despite its power: "This unity (Einheit) is the conception that war is only a part of political intercourse, therefore by no means an independent thing in itself … policy makes out of the all-overpowering element of war a mere instrument."[60]

Finding such overlap between concepts in the "Teleology" and *On War* is highly significant because "The teleology of Hegel's thought differentiates him from all the philosophers."[61] What this suggests in our study of Hegel and Clausewitz is that the only way for Clausewitz to have achieved similar thinking is to have come up with it himself, because he would not have found this anywhere else in philosophical literature. Either Clausewitz was directly influenced by Hegel, or else he was developing his own, highly similar pattern of thinking. Either way, the logical constructs, when we understand them in this light, provide us with a more complete understanding not only of their meaning, but in what sense they are internally coherent, because they imply a process of Aufhebung that leads from the irrational to the rational, which is in fact the experience of pure reason manifested.

Herberg-Rothe is absolutely right to refer to the trinity as Clausewitz's "real legacy," but it is worth asking if he is right to point out that it should

58 Hegel, *Science of Logic*, 745.
59 Clausewitz, *On War*, bk I, ch. 1, 19.
60 Ibid., bk VIII, ch. 6B, 674.
61 Findlay, "Hegel's Use of Teleology," 1.

be understood as representing a "real beginning" to the book.[62] Though Clausewitz presents his trinity in the introduction of *On War*, it is rather put forward as the theory's end point. The reason why it concludes his introduction is that Clausewitz's trinity represents the culmination of the holistic "concept" (Begriff). The trinity sheds light on the beginning, in self-reflection, but more importantly it calls out forward to what the theory seeks to achieve. The divine is both the end and the beginning. Is Clausewitz's word choice the "first ray of light" not a clear demonstration of this?[63] It recalls the first commands spoken by god in the bible: god's very first act of creation: "Fiat Lux!" If we understand the trinity in its convergence with a Hegelian approach, we can understand it from a holistic perspective that arrives at the divine conclusion, but only insofar as the conceptual premise of this divine is built into the Aufhebung of the progressive moments in a teleological trinity.

Why does this matter in the end? The immediate reason is that this approach to understanding the trinity relativizes it. From this perspective, we can escape the interpretation of the trinity in its "secondary form," where the actors suggested in the trinity are split away: the people, the army, the government. This alternative trinity is fixed and rigid, and allows very limited space for conceptualizing war as a whole and in its various chameleon-like skin colours. Clausewitz mentioned these three actors as examples, but did not suggest that they were the exclusive embodiments of the relationships in the trinity, he described the trinity as being "mainly"[64] embodied by them, but not absolutely. Pulling them out and proclaiming the three as the trinity itself is a gross error, because it defines and imposes a model for what war is, and what is external to it suddenly becomes difficult to understand, and can easily lead to questionable claims regarding the fact that multilateral forces and non-state actors render Clausewitzian thought somehow less applicable or altogether inapplicable.

By presenting the trinity as the culmination of a holistic methodology, as was done above, we can transition from a discussion that would attempt unconvincing refutations of this whole based on poking holes here and there, but without ever engaging in a way that properly encroaches on or dismantles the edifice. As we move into the final pages of this book, the argument will take a different shape altogether, in that we will consider what limits are inherent to this whole, which in effect will legitimize certain ethical features of both the Hegelian and the

62 Herberg-Rothe, prologue to *The Clausewitz Puzzle*.

63 Clausewitz, *On War*, bk I, ch. 1, 19.

64 Ibid.

Clausewitzian theories of war, but will also in the process strip them of the absoluteness and their universality – in effect limiting the *divine aura* of their trinities and the distinct concepts of "good" that emerge from worshipping one or the other.

While there is a clear methodological convergence in the two trinities, what distinguishes them most is the interplay between Hegel emphasizing the relationship between the subjective world, the process of making it objective as a process, and then the reflection of this objectivity back onto itself as finality. This finality or holism at the intersection of the subjective and the object is alluded to in Clausewitz's Book I, chapter 1, but always indirectly. In the trinity, the first element, the subjective end, is the blind natural instincts; the second, the objective means, is war's mechanisms and deployment; and the third represents the objectivity of subjectivity recognizing itself as such – this is the finality that explains how the first two sides of the trinity interact with pure reason and are ultimately relegated below it and instrumentalized by it. Clausewitz is in effect presenting us with subjective and objective concepts, but not referring to them as such. And in the end, unlike Hegel, he does not claim that the third moment in fact succeeds in "cunningly" encompassing the two others, or that war achieves an objective end. Instead Clausewitz builds up towards this argument, but stops short near the very end. When he places this conclusion in the trinity, unlike Hegel he does not place this "pure reason" as properly resolving the other two. The linearity functions one way, from the subjective to the objective to the final end, but it is not self-reflected; pure reason is not given reign over the other two parts of the trinity, even if it instrumentalizes them. Clausewitz is apparently suggesting that this instrumentalization is imperfect, which is why the three coexist and influence one another.

This can mean one of two things. Either Clausewitz had all the methodological tools needed to reach that end, but he chose not to, or else he did not have the necessary understanding of the relationship between the concepts of subjectivity and objectivity to reach the same conclusion as Hegel. Either possibility is tenable. If it was a deliberate choice to part from Hegel, it might have been for the simple reason that being more experienced and perhaps also less naïve about war, he understood that the passions and the machinery of war could in fact undermine its rational ends. His wondrous trinity is more of a floating triad than a linear one, and it allows Clausewitz to showcase the fact that "a complete reduction of war to an instrument of policy would be a contradiction."[65] In

65 Herberg-Rothe, *Clausewitz's Puzzle*, 115

Hegel's teleology, this is not the case – the perfect instrumentality of war goes unquestioned and unaddressed, which allows Hegel to edify war as a right that is contained within the idea of pure reason's manifestation – by whichever means it has at its disposal. His "cunning of reason" effectively becomes his underlying excuse for justifying war as a right. Were it not for this perfect instrumentality, then such a right could not emerge, since there is no such thing as an imperfect right. It is an absolute concept. That being said, Clausewitz's more careful take on instrumentality does not require that we go so far as to claim, as Herberg-Rothe does, that the three tendencies are of "equal importance."[66] Clausewitz does not tell us this, nor does he make it implicit. Clausewitz's imperfect instrumentality nonetheless starts with primordial violence and ends with pure reason, which is the order in which he placed these items. The linear relation between the three nonetheless exists by virtue of the fact that pure reason is meant to preside over the other two – albeit only to the best of its ability, since the other two continually undermine its ability to control them and instrumentalize them, in the Hegelian sense. There is a distinction between the two, but it is not so clear-cut. It is possible that Clausewitz refused to take a leap of faith, and stopped one short of Hegel for this reason, as a way to be more realistic about instrumentality. Alternatively, it is possible that Clausewitz simply did not possess the necessary knowledge of Hegel in order to extract the same conclusion. Since we cannot prove the first, let us explore the latter, and once that has been done it will be up to the reader to choose which of the two is more likely. Either way, it is at this threshold that the convergence between Hegel and Clausewtiz comes to an end, and the ethical divergence appears.

SUBJECTIVITY AND OBJECTIVITY: THE SOURCE OF AN ETHICAL DIVERGENCE?

While one might get away with using concepts in an ad hoc way and according to their immediate utility for some authors, the use of Hegelian concepts in such a manner becomes far more problematic, because the Hegelian system is exactly that – a system. Its parts do not stand alone. When Clausewitz worked in ideas from Kant and Montesquieu, it could more easily be done – and the integrations were therefore more effective. Trying to apply the whole to particular items, or vice versa, in the way Clausewitz was attempting could very likely lead to the kind of crisis that

66 Ibid., 116.

he experienced in the late 1820s. It is a serious and difficult conundrum. As we saw in chapter 8, the most basic form of Hegelian thought, sense-certainty, is premised on the possibility of there being an overarching Geist. The system does not have gaps; it is a continuum. It may be useful, as Taylor and Frost have argued,[67] to focus in on the mid-section that lies between the grand cosmic scale and the minute perceptual scale, but only insofar as we do not forget where this midsection is coming from in the first place.

From the moment Clausewitz applied Hegelian ideas as mere ad hoc tools of analysis, he began generating the root of a contradiction between the two dialecticians: a distinct and incompatible understanding of objectivity and subjectivity, which in some ways betrays Clausewitz's slightly more modest understanding of philosophy in general. Objectivity and subjectivity are a longstanding conundrum of philosophy. For subjectivity to exist, it must result from the existence of consciousness, or there being a subject in the first place. If consciousness alone exists in relation to unconscious objects, then all thoughts would necessarily be subjective, thereby condemning all thought to exist outside objectivity. Without objectivity, there could be no truth.

So central was the question of subjectivity and objectivity to the purpose of his system that Hegel decided to make it his first order of business, in the introduction to the *Phenomenology*. This is the discussion, which was briefly mentioned in chapter 8, where Hegel is describing the problem of whether systematizing our knowledge of the world means seeing it through a medium, or shaping it with an instrument. In either case, the truth is devoid of objectivity, it is dependent on some external factor. Hegel wrote:

> For, if cognition is the instrument for getting hold of absolute being, it is obvious that the use of an instrument on a thing certainly does not let it be what it is for itself, but rather sets out to reshape and alter it. If, on the other hand, cognition is not an instrument of our activity but a more or less passive medium through which the light of truth reaches us, then again we do not receive the truth as it is in itself, but only as it exists through and in this medium. Either way we employ a means which immediately brings about the opposite of its own end; or rather, what is really absurd is that we should make use of a means at all.[68]

67 See Frost, *Towards a Normative Theory*, 168. Taylor also argues that even though the central spiritual and ontological thesis is dead, Hegel nonetheless remains relevant. *Hegel*, 538–9.

68 Hegel, *Phenomenology of Spirit*, #73, 46.

Hegel's solution to this impasse is his method in itself. His dialectical system is not an instrument meant to break down the world into various dichotomies and then rebuild it in parts until it forms the whole. Nor is it a medium through which we see an otherwise non-dialectical world appear to us in a way it is not in itself. He rejects the duality that gives rise to the problem in the first place, and replaces it with the method itself: objectivity is the overcoming of subjectivity in becoming self-aware of it. Hegel explains the possibility of unity between objectivity and subjectivity: "The coming-to-be of Spirit was indicated in the immediately preceding movement in which the object of consciousness, the pure category, rose to be the Notion of Reason. In Reason as observer, this pure unity of the I and being, of being for itself and being in itself, is determined as the in-itself or as being, and the consciousness of Reason finds itself."[69]

If Clausewitz learned a few tricks from Hegel regarding how to reconcile oppositions, he did not integrate any of Hegel's ideas into how he understood the words objective and subjective. To Clausewitz, the terms are used in their colloquial significance, as we might say in a sentence "subjectively speaking," or "objectively speaking," which is more adequately understood as meaning not verifiable or verifiable. Even in his final edits of Book I, chapter 1, there is no sign of this concept having been elevated in any way. For example, he will use the terms in discussing how war's objective nature is that it is a calculation of probabilities, and that its subjective nature is that it is played out like a game (Spiel) (H/P translation "gamble").[70] Elsewhere, in Book II, chapter 2, Clausewitz refers to the "objective form of knowledge," which he opposes to "subjective … skill in action." His use of these terms is therefore quite distinct from how Hegel would have understood them. In the Hegelian system, one cannot split action away from knowledge in this way and suggest that one is the objective element and the other subjective.

Furthermore, knowledge is not considered objective in itself, but objective only insofar as it has come to terms with its subjectivity. In Hegel, one could not split up action from knowledge nor subjectivity from objectivity – and therefore even less split up the former by integrating the latter to it, as Clausewitz did. For Hegel, Geist is precisely this process of reconciling the ideal to the real, knowledge and action combined as subjectivity making itself objective in the world.

Where the divergence becomes most apparent and also has the most impact is the way in which Clausewitz applies dialectical reconciliation to

69 Ibid., #438, 263.

70 Clausewitz, *On War*, bk I, ch. 1, 14.

the real/absolute dichotomy. Though we recognized above that it was Hegelian in its form, we must now analyze in what way it was nonetheless an imperfect attempt at a Hegelian reconciliation, because it was tainted by the problem of subjectivity/objectivity as it is described in the first pages of the *Phenomenology*. That the authors were not using the terms in the same way explains how this problem might surface in the first place. But perhaps more importantly, it stems from the fact that Clausewitz had an idea since his youth, regarding the role of politics and war, but his solution came to him slowly and in increments. As such, in the end he had found an instrument with which he could fix his problem, and thus did he fall squarely into the trap described by Hegel: moulding and altering the object.

To compare, Clausewitz's reconciliation of the absolute and real incarnations of war does not achieve the hands-off objectivity that is made evident in Hegel's discussion of sense-certainty. The actions of "seeing a tree" or "not seeing a tree" are thoroughly mutually exclusive, though either one recalls the other's absence in being posited. When we reach the universal of sight as a new conceptual plateau, we do not have to seek out the items within the two first phases that would justify the third, or bring out similarities within them that could be aspects of the transcendence. The universal emerges in and of itself; its objectivity becomes intuitively self-evident as a result of the Aufhebung.

Clausewitz's reconciliation roughly copies the Hegelian system, or perhaps even forces it a bit onto his argument, and as a result, it is not fully successful. His conclusion does not emerge to the reader as self-evident, as was the case with Hegel's sense-certainty. The various parts of the argument are teased out, tooled in the process. While the mimicry serves as a powerful suggestion of a Hegelian influence, it nonetheless also shows a failure to understand Hegel properly. By applying Hegel in this way, Clausewitz was introducing subjectivity into his theorization by Hegelian standards. The contradiction between the real and the absolute nature of war does not inherently spell out the continuation of policy; this requires modelling both types of war in order to bring out not the completeness of their contradiction, but rather aspects of their coming together. While Hegel's discussion of negation made the unifying universal self-evident, in the case of sight and seeing, Clausewitz starts by teasing out the similarities, namely, in the "results" and the "use of force," as we saw above, before proclaiming a transcendental conclusion. Hence, the conclusion, regardless of how compelling and practical it is, does not emerge entirely objectively.

We could view this to be a failure on the part of Clausewitz, but it would be more adequate to present it as an outcome of his pragmatic style. The reconciliation that he proposes was not completely objective, but it nonetheless generated a useful idea for governments when conceptualizing war and making war plans. Furthermore, such reconciliation provides not simply a self-contained ethic in itself, but a moralistic ethic that imposes responsibility specifically on those in government. By stating that war is subordinated to an outside power, it finds war's ethical essence in its material source, rather than some external or mystical justification. So while Hegel's objectivity generates what one might call spiritual rights for the state, Clausewitz's subjectivity generates an antipodal and material moral responsibility at the state level, thereby serving a purpose, despite not being objective by Hegelian standards. Reciprocally, Hegel's objective notion of war would not have been ethically pragmatic, by Clausewitzian standards.

An interesting anecdote that illustrates perfectly the ethical breakdown between Clausewitz and Hegel concerns their opposite reactions to the defeat at Jena-Auerstedt. Unlike Clausewitz, who was captured and imprisoned in the aftermath of the battle, and whose hatred for Napoleon galvanized, Hegel, who was teaching in Jena when the battle took place, saw the event in a much different light, describing Napoleon far more sympathetically: "I saw the Emperor – this world-soul (diese Weltseele) – riding out of the city on reconnaissance. It is indeed a wonderful sensation to see such an individual, who, concentrated here at a single point, astride a horse, reaches out over the world and masters it. As for the fate of the Prussians, in truth no better prognosis could be given."[71]

Hegel saw in Napoleon the incarnation of the politico-economic reforms required for modernity, or the fulfillment of the modern state, a vehicle of some cosmic destiny. From the opposite perspective, an embittered Clausewitz would write: "Invasion only calls forth resistance, and it is not until there is resistance that there is war. A conqueror is always a lover of peace (as Buonaparte always asserted of himself); he would like to make his entry into our state unopposed."[72] Here the ethical distinction becomes evident: Clausewitz takes a moral stance and *blames* one political actor, whereas Hegel avoids blaming one or the other of the fighting parties, leaving it to history to pass judgment.

If both Hegel and Clausewitz refer to Napoleon in godly terms, what differentiates the two is again what we saw in the above section on the trinity. Clausewitz does not jump naïvely into concepts of perfection, whether it is with regard to instrumentality or to pure reason, and he is

71 Hegel to Niethammer, 13 October 1806, *The Letters.*

72 Clausewitz, *On War,* bk VI, ch. 5, 374.

the same with regard to Napoleon. For Clausewitz, this "god of war" remains imperfect, because war itself is unpredictable and does not allow for perfection. He places Napoleon on par with – or even above – the greatest military geniuses in history, but nonetheless criticizes his actions and describes in detail the strategic "errors" and "true faults"[73] in Napoleon's campaign leading up to his defeat at Waterloo. Clausewitz includes in such errors the "useless" march and counter-march of 20,000 soldiers, which he says amounted to a "capital mistake."[74] In the 1814 campaign, Clausewitz goes so far as to refer to Napoleon's final march towards Paris as "empty," a "supreme risk," the "gravest error of the campaign" – and in its final movement, according to Clausewitz, Napoleon suddenly appeared "in all his ridiculousness."[75] In the end, war is not merely the frustrating cunning of reason pushing forward perfection at great costs along the way, but an imperfect tool even in the hands of history's greatest masters in the craft.

The Hegel-Clausewitz connection is not clear-cut like the one between Kant and Clausewitz, which we explored earlier. One possible explanation for this is that as a young scholar, Clausewitz was less confident in his writing and made far more use of direct borrowing in his attempts to develop his arguments, whereas in his later years, Clausewitz had found his own voice and could borrow ideas less directly, and integrate them into his works in his own words. This may be part of the explanation. Of course, the second element that we have seen above is that while there was clearly a convergence over time between Clausewitz's ideas and the works of Hegel, this incremental convergence remained incomplete in the end. Regardless of how satisfied we are with the level of proximity between the two, it remains nonetheless extremely unsatisfactory to claim that there was no rapprochement.

We find ourselves with a compromise: the Hegelian link is imperfect, it does not take the form of a single citation – a clear and demonstrable influence – but an evolution in thought, a progression in time. Indeed this has revealed itself as a more manageable conclusion than the one found in Aron, who is more categorical, but limits himself to citing the earlier works of Clausewitz to make his point. It is also far less dramatic than in the case of Paret, where the question is brushed aside, the conclusion asserted, and the demonstration never actually made. We find ourselves with a demonstrated convergence, but not a demonstrated

73 Clausewitz, *Campagne de 1815*, 170.

74 Ibid., 98.

75 Clausewitz, *Campagne de 1814*, 82.

influence. It is up to the reader to make the leap from one to the other if they see fit.

CRITIQUE: THE LIMITS OF INSTRUMENTALITY

Though Clausewitz allowed for imperfections in the process or application of "instrumentalizing" violence, he did not present instrumentalization as having inherent problems within its inner logic, and this is the true limit of the concept. The logic that binds Clausewitz's notion that the state or actor is morally responsible for war, and can in fact be *blamed*, is rooted in the instrumentality of war, that is, since war can achieve objectives that may be morally acceptable or not, then it is legitimate to pass judgment on those who make the policy of war. But the entire premise of the relationship depends on two important criteria: first, that the weapons being used can in fact be used instrumentally, that is, they can in fact coerce in the direction of a legitimate policy change. Secondly, if the actor is to be a moral agent, then a second criterion upon which to gauge this morality must be added to the first, that this violence be applied in a sufficiently proportional way for the decision itself to be ethically reasonable (i.e. that it is not genocide or massacre). The strain on these criteria has always existed in some relative way, and indeed, massacres during and after battle – against soldiers and civilians alike – are as old as time, but this strain can become increasingly absolute as war becomes ever more infused with indiscriminate destructive power. This means that to explore the limits of Clausewitz's instrumentality as an ethical foundation, we should temporarily push our analysis forward to a hundred years after it was actually written – because in Clausewitz's time, the machinery of war had not yet seen the impact of industrialization, let alone the nuclear age. In the early 1800s, the most damaging arguments against the logic that binds Clausewitz's ethical system could not yet be made. Though we are breaking away from the central course of the narration so far, this jump forward will eventually form an important grounding element of our discussion of how the limits of Hegelian and Clausewitzian ethics shaped modern secular war and revolution.

The simplest way to illustrate the problem in material terms is to consider how nuclear weapons can turn the strategic element of war upside down. Tactical nuclear weapons would make such minced meat out of any invasion force as to make invading a nuclear power tactically unmanageable, whereas the use of strategic nuclear weapons would make invasion strategically irrelevant, unless one is intent on staking territorial claims in a radioactive fallout area. The instrumentality in this case is not merely disrupted, it is reversed altogether since the instrument no longer shapes or arrives at the end, but destroys the end in its approach. In this reversal, the agent remains responsible for the action but the action itself becomes so counter-intuitive that claims to responsibility, either by the side that launches the strike or by the government that sends its troops to a predictable butchery, is in effect to admit guilt rather than justification. If it were merely a question of disproportionality, then the judgment might be severe, but that is not the question. The apparent uselessness of the action itself leads to a categorical, not merely severe, judgment. That being said, this is only a preliminary thought on the matter, since, as we shall consider in the coming lines, we must also distinguish between actually fighting such a war and threatening to do so.

Some have viewed the problems of instrumentality as a way to brush aside Clausewitz altogether, arguing that his means/ends analysis has become incompatible with the modern world. If nuclear weapons are what made this observation most clear to them, Colin Gray traces back the problem to an earlier time: "The atom has simply served to make unavoidably clear what has been true all along since the day of the introduction of the machine gun and the internal combustion engine into the techniques of warfare ... that modern warfare in the grand manner, pursued by all available means and aimed at the total destruction of the enemy's capacity to resist, is ... of such general destructiveness that it ceases to be useful as an instrument of any coherent political purpose."[76]

Along the same lines, Senator J. William Fulbright would add that the disproportionality of nuclear weapons had "deprived force of its utility as an instrument of national policy," adding that, "so long as there is reason – not virtue, but simply reason – in the foreign policy of great nations, nuclear weapons are not so much an instrument as an inhibition of policy."[77] Hannah Arendt generally agreed, suggesting that "the technological development of the implements of violence have reached the point where no political goal could conceivably correspond to their destructive potential or justify their actual use in armed conflict."[78]

Going so far as to say that Clausewitz's system is no longer applicable or useful in the nuclear age is an overstatement, however, as Moody countered, "Even if it is always irrational to fight nuclear war, it may not be irrational to risk nuclear war."[79] Moody goes so far as to question

76 Gray, *Postmodern War,* 138.

77 Moody, "The Fading Dialectic," 418. Citing J. William Fulbright, "The Foundations of National Security," in *Great Issues of International Politics,* 2nd edition, ed. Morton A. Kaplan (Chicago: Aldine, 1974), 255.

78 Arendt, *On Violence,* 3.

79 Moody, *The Fading Dialectic,* 419.

whether or not Fulbright manages to show a real contradiction: "In Clausewitzian terms, Fulbright is saying that what can be achieved *by* war is negated by the means used *in* war: war no longer pays. But this does not show that Clausewitz is obsolete: it is precisely on Clausewitzian grounds that war is to be avoided."[80] Indeed, nuclear weapons are in some ways the epitome of the Clausewitzian triad: where the absolute concept of war is the annihilation of all mankind, the limited concept of war is the impossible cost or ultimate contradiction of this absolute. And instrumentality is the capacity for the government to calculate a rational course of action, which would guarantee its own self-preservation – in this case, avoiding an all-out nuclear holocaust.

A second way to address Fulbright's thought is to ask whether the existence of new, more potent and awe-inspiring weapons changes and undermines the purposes of violence and the threat of violence in international relations, or rather reaffirms and intensifies the same notions that led nations to seek out traditional armaments. Is it not the same impetus that leads the weaker to enhance their power, and the powerful to sustain the status quo?

The evolution of weapons in war necessarily affects the way in which tactics and strategies are drawn out and implemented. Yet the question of whether or not this implies ontological changes in the nature of war is not as clear-cut as Fulbright, Gray, and others might claim. Actually, Clausewitz's own formulation in many ways addresses the problem that Fulbright is using against him. In Book II, chapter 1 of *On War* Clausewitz wrote: "Fighting has determined everything appertaining to arms and equipment, and these in turn modify the mode of fighting; there is, therefore, a reciprocity of action (*Wechselwirkung*) between the two."[81] This notion of reciprocity of action allows for the principles of war to be defined by weapons only insofar as the weapons themselves come into being in response to the needs of war. Instead of disrupting the theoretical constructs of a dialectical war theory, the weapons and strategies evolve in mutuality, within rather than opposed to the overarching theory. This is also observable in the response, or reciprocity of action between, the evolution of weapons in the past decades, which instead of building ever more powerful weapons brought forth ever more precise ones so as to reaffirm proportionality in warfare.

Those who claimed that the "revolution in military affairs" would undermine Clausewitz's theory by dissipating the friction and fog from

80 Ibid.

81 Clausewitz, *On War*, bk II, ch. 1, 64.

warfare failed to see that in fact this very progress contributes to strengthening Clausewitz's insistence that war should be a rational instrument, by reducing uncertainty and complexity.[82] Modern weapons did not prove Clausewitz wrong: he actually integrated the development of ever more powerful and precise weapons as a central aspect of his theoretical framework of "reciprocity of action" by which the needs of war contribute to the development of its apparatuses, which in turn further reinvents war and requires new innovation. What is more, Clausewitz's insistence that war is game (Spiel) is also crystallized by the fact that these weapons have elevated the game-like aspect of war, where the bluff is key, or as we saw with Moody, there emerges a willingness to risk war, but not necessarily to fight it. In the context of nuclear weapons we went from waging war to wagering war. Strategy is not gone even though the stakes have risen. Arguably, in a wagering rather than a waging of war, there is all the more strategy because there is less of a tactical element. There may have been a relative decline in direct instrumentality, but this has given space to the type of indirect instrumentality we now see. The way we play the game is different; an altered, but nonetheless less real, strategic element remains.

In order to understand the proper conceptual end point to instrumentality, it is better not to let the material question dictate our analysis, but rather to consider an idea of war that builds the end of instrumentality into its very essence. Whereas the doctrine of mutual assured destruction is the epitome of the technology argument against instrumentality, the difference between wagering nuclear war and waging nuclear war shows that it is not an infallible and sacrosanct argument. Actually, the concept of a war to end all wars, depending on how it is constructed, can break down instrumentality in a way that is altogether more significant since it is freed from any external or material cause. To be clear, using the term "war to end all wars," should not be understood as an idea that emerges from hindsight, as was the case with First World War, which was so brutal that a "never again" attitude followed it ... i.e. this *would be the last* such war. The way in which I am about to use the term is rather the other way around, when the idea precedes the war instead of coming after the fact. The war is in fact *declared* as a war to end all wars. Only one such concept of war was ever invented and eventually applied: the communist and anarchist revolution, in which the revolution was posited on the premise that its fulfillment in violence would

82 Mikkel Rasmussen, *The Risk Society at War* (Cambridge: Cambridge University Press, 2006), 43–91. Cited in Fleming, *Clausewitz's Timeless Trinity*, 13.

necessarily put an end to the social structures that generate war in the first place.

The circularity and totality of the proposition is such that it can never achieve its end until there is nothing left to fight. It is as annihilatory in essence as mutual assured destruction, though the capacity may not be there. That is, the war to end all wars is its own inferno and has no conceptual limit, because having been posited as a war that has no end except its own, it must and will always find something to fight, eventually fighting itself internally. It is the nature of social structures and institutions to legitimize their continued raison d'être. The war to end all wars is necessarily self-perpetuating: for the same reason that a hammer must have something to hit to be of use, and cannot be used to hit itself, war that has been posited as instrumental in ending itself as an instrument is logically impossible, because each action produces a counter-action, escalation, reciprocal violence, etc. Thus, even if full victory were eventually *declared* by these warriors, the fact that the victory was built on war and blood – not consensus and evolution – would set into the foundations of society an institutional violence that begets violence and perpetuates a war to end all wars, which by definition never actually ends. The only way it ends is when a counter-force is applied to end the circular perpetuation.

In both the example from modern weapons and the logic of a war to end all wars instrumentality becomes problematic because the tool cannot properly shape its object towards the desired effect. There is a parallel to be drawn here with what we concluded in chapter 8 with regard to Hegel. History has shown limits in the concepts of war as a right and as an instrument: in the former because the relationship between political decay and war could be shown to be reversible, and in the latter because the linearity of instrumentality in war cannot properly cope with weapons that undermine the relationship between cause and effect and concepts of war that are circular in their logic. These limits, however, are not absolute. They do not undermine Hegel's and Clausewitz's theories, though they do impose limits to their otherwise unlimited ethical scopes. And this is particularly observable where modern weaponry combines with revolutionary fervour.

11

Fighting Doctrines and Revolutionary Ethics[1]

AT THE THRESHOLD OF REVOLUTION, Clausewitz encountered the fragility and limits of the absolute war/real war dichotomy on an ontological level. When the communists and anarchists sought to bring forth an "absolute" revolution, they unsuspectingly brought out, in a thoroughly analogous way, the fragility and limits of the instrument/right divide on an ethical level. The reason why they reached this impasse is that their absolute revolution, fought – as Kropotkin claimed – for "absolute freedom, nothing but freedom, all of freedom,"[2] brought their war to the ethical threshold of dialectical war theory, as it intertwined every element discussed in the two above "critique sections" I put forward analyzing the limits of Clausewitz and Hegel. The anti-bourgeois revolution included the circular logic of a war meant to end all wars; it was fought with the intensity of revolutionary fervour and culminated with the integration of modern weapons. Though my objective is to deal with the implications of this threshold of rational ethics in warfare in the upcoming epilogue, before we can fully explore these, we must start by studying dialectical war theory's uptake in the anti-bourgeois revolutions so that we may in fact critically assess the implications of the instrument/right divide in history, and demonstrate where the idea of this impasse coincided with an impasse in history and in the real world.

The anti-bourgeois revolutionary thinkers are indeed an interesting group to consider in our discussion of dialectical war theory, not only because they force the stakes upward in our critical assessment of Clausewitz and Hegel, but also because being among the earliest to discover and integrate Clausewitz and Hegel into a set of fighting doctrines, they were

1 A previous version of this chapter was published in article form as Y. Cormier, "Fighting Doctrines and Revolutionary Ethics," *Journal of Military and Security Studies* 15, no. 1 (2013): 419–42.

2 Kropotkin, "Declaration to the Tribunal."

absorbing the primary sources directly – as opposed to reading tainted secondary interpretations. Furthermore, they also did so as dialecticians themselves, which means they would have appreciated the depth of the method. As a result, we would expect them to best represent what the system of thought leads to when it is applied to human affairs. For that reason alone, we would be justified in going directly to them for our critical assessment, but there is a far better reason to do so. Surprisingly, despite fighting a common enemy and sharing a common ideal for what the world would look like after the revolution, the anarchists and communists integrated dialectical war theory in a most distinctive pattern. They borrowed from either Hegel or Clausewitz very categorically in their respective fighting doctrines: the communists were exclusively Clausewitzian, whereas the anarchists shunned Clausewitz and kept exclusively to Hegel. There was no overlap.

The link between the communists and Clausewitz has often been observed, and in fact there was such a keen appreciation for Clausewitz among them that many Western observers invoked a "Clausewitz connection"[3] to describe the fact that Marx, Engels, Mao, Trotsky, Lenin, and others were all known to cite the opus. The problem with this idea of "Clausewitz connection" is that it suggests a direct, immediate, and natural link between the two, which is not so clear-cut once we actually dive into the details. As dialecticians sharing a common philosophical link to Hegel and Kant, we might indeed have expected that when the Marxists discovered Clausewitz they would be predisposed to appreciate the methodology, because it was so closely intertwined with their own. One might even go so far as to suggest that Marx was to political economy what Clausewitz was to war: the one who, having inherited the modern dialectical method, would be the first to apply it to a specific subject of inquiry – economics and war, respectively. And yet despite this methodological unity the convergence was not immaculately conceived amongst communists, but actually required some tinkering. Moreover it was not Marx and Engels who became devout Clausewitzians, but rather the next generation of communists, Trotsky and Lenin.

With revolution now entering the forefront of the communist experience, the works of Clausewitz did in fact take centre stage. However, what was extracted from the opus was in no way its methodological or dialectical aspects, but a mere distillation for particular strategic gains. With much distortions and cherry picking of ideas, the communist revolutionaries made a very practical and isolated reading of Clausewitz, rather than a comprehensive one.

3 Gat, "Clausewitz and the Marxists," 366.

Meanwhile, in the same family lineage, the fathers of anti-bourgeois anarchist thought Bakunin, Proudhon,[4] and Kropotkin did not deign to make any references to Clausewitz at all.[5] They shunned him altogether. It is indeed surprising, since they too shared in this common methodological background, and would undoubtedly have come across Clausewitz, given that he had been introduced to left-wing circles. Instead, we find that in anarchist thought, there evolved a parallel, distinct, and direct "Hegel connection" in their concept of the revolution and their fighting doctrine. The split between the two factions is clear and total, and once we take the time to understand where it comes from, it is actually quite logical. The breakdown tells us something about how the two groups understood the ethics of political violence as "instrumental" in the Clausewitzian tradition, or as a "right" in the Hegelian tradition. While this distinction complicated the integration of Clausewitz into communist doctrine, it made him altogether irrelevant to anarchist doctrine. Methodological keenness therefore had little to do with the two distinct "connections"; it was rather the ethical dimensions on either side that led one group to identify its fighting doctrines with Clausewitz, while the other chose Hegel.

This historical set of questions is relevant to anyone currently reading Clausewitz or Hegel on the subject of war because uncovering why all this picking and choosing first happened allows us to distinguish and understand the systems of logic found in either of these two founding works in the school of "dialectical war theory," as well as – most importantly – the ethical and strategic implications of these differences. By showcasing the distinction in a parallel study, we gain insight into how overarching, abstract ethical frameworks can and indeed have shaped fighting doctrines in real and concrete ways.

THE COMMUNIST "CLAUSEWITZ CONNECTION"

It is difficult to categorize communism as a single family of revolutionaries and thinkers, and the danger in doing so is to risk finding ourselves with a blanket term that does not quite apply in encompassing all the nuances that one variation on communist thought might have relative to another. That being said, since this question is outside the scope of this

4 I mention Proudhon as another example of where the works of Clausewitz are excluded, but, for the sake of expediency, I will not be using Proudhon's works in this chapter to describe anarchist fighting doctrines.

5 This observation is made possible thanks to keyword searches and the availability of vast archives of works by these authors on the website of the Marxist Internet Archive found here: www.marxists.org.

chapter, it should be specified that the use of the term here refers to those anti-bourgeois revolutionaries who advocated for a political revolution that would *precede* the economic and cultural revolution – which is to say those who believed in the necessity of a revolutionary state to carry out the program of revolution as its policy.

The "Clausewitz connection" refers to the fact that many prominent communists cited him, including Marx and Engels, Mao, Trotsky, and Lenin. One might be tempted to assume that since the two founders are included among the lot of "connectees" it would explain in what sense the remaining followers followed. It is an easy trap to fall into, and the reality is rather that Marx and Engels were actually quite critical of Clausewitz and made little use of him. It was the later revolutionaries who make great use of *On War*, but only in a shallow fashion, by citing a few key snippets that could be easily adapted to Marxist thought.

Indeed, it was necessary to "adapt" Clausewitz to make him relevant to the communists, and provide them with a useful guide in their politico-strategic deployment of the revolution, under the auspices of a revolutionary state. This was achieved by Lenin, and not by Marx and Engels. Lenin was the first who provided the proper basis with which to work out the contradictions and kinks, and integrate Clausewitz's ideas to the revolution. This was no easy problem to resolve, but something quite fundamental: if the state is a central pillar in the works of Hegel and Clausewitz, how can a group intent on attacking and dismantling the state find a coherent logic that balances the use of a statist method against the state itself?

Before we can answer this, it is useful to step back and describe why Clausewitz occupied so little space in Communist thought before this problem was resolved. Marx and Engels discussed Clausewitz in their correspondence on the subject of war between the years 1857–62. That being said, many academics have exaggerated the significance of these short snippets – an exaggeration that is perhaps best exemplified in Sigmund Neumann's writing that not only was Engels "greatly impressed" by Clausewitz, Clausewitz even became "stock-in-trade" for the revolutionaries and "axiomatic" for Engels.[6] Lenin too was convinced that Engels and Marx were fundamentally Clausewitzian, as he alludes to in this commentary: "War is the continuation of politics by other (i.e. violent) means. This famous aphorism was uttered by one of the profoundest writers on the problems of war, Clausewitz. Marxists have always rightly regarded this thesis as the theoretical basis of views concerning

6 Neumann and von Hagen, "Engels and Marx on Revolution," 265–6.

the significance of every given war. It was precisely from this viewpoint that Marx and Engels always regarded different wars."[7]

This paragraph does not make an argument, let alone demonstrate that Marx and Engels were all that influenced by Clausewitz. Instead it takes this for granted. The only conclusion we can draw from such a passage is rather the confirmation that Lenin himself was probably keen on Clausewitz. Lenin was in fact "deeply impressed" by *On War*, referring to it in speeches and texts, after first having commented in the margins of his copy and transcribing sections into his notebook.[8]

Opposing this claim made by Lenin and later by numerous others including Neumann, Azar Gat's *Clausewitz and the Marxists* proposes a more detailed counter-argument, which cuts the legs out from under such an interpretation, by balancing the one aspect of enthusiasm that Marx and Engels showed with regard to the single analogy "Combat is to war what cash payment is to commerce,"[9] relative to their overall appreciation, which lags far behind. Gat notes that before describing this passage as "witty" (witz), Marx's letter first stated that he was "hunting through Clausewitz more or less," which can hardly be considered keenness; in fact, the passage on commerce was cherry-picked by Engels and sent to Marx, knowing that it would be "a piece of picantry in a field which could be of interest to Marx."[10] This makes sense since, as we shall explore further below, Marx was the economist of the two, while warfare was Engels's area, and his friends even called him "The General" for it.[11] Regarding the word "Witz" it might be worth adding the possibility that while Marx made this compliment with regard to Clausewitz's analogy, he may also have chosen the term for the sake of making a playful jest on the name Clause-*witz*.[12] If that were the case, it would further taper the extent of its significance.

Another example, which Gat also includes in his text, comes from the same series of letters: Engels wrote that *On War* was "per se very good," which again is not a grand compliment – especially given that the words

7 Lenin, "Socialism and War," 295–338.

8 Heuser, *Reading Clausewitz*, 19, 46–7. Azar Gat also notes that Lenin was enthusiastic about all passages that referred to war's historical nature, next to which he repeatedly placed annotations. *History of Military Thought*, 504.

9 Marx, Letter to Engels, 11 January 1858, *Marx/Engels Collected Works*, vol. 40, 241.

10 Gat, *History of Military Thought*, 499. It is worth noting that this chapter entitled "Marxism and Military Theory" is a polished version of Gat's 1992 article "Clausewitz and the Marxists."

11 Ibid., 496.

12 The two correspondents regularly used such friendly banter in their exchanges. Another example of this playfulness is forthcoming.

leading up to it are "Clausewitz has an odd way of philosophizing." In the same exchange Marx complains that he had to "spend so much time reading Clausewitz," which might explain indeed why he wound up reading it only "more or less." That being said, it is impossible to determine, simply in the one line where it appears, whether Marx's mention of the word "witty" is in reply, as Gat suggests, only to the commerce analogy and not a wider reading of Clausewitz.[13] If it had been the only introduction he had to Clausewitz this would be a logical assumption, but as Gat notes himself, Marx had read pieces of *On War* several months earlier. It was indeed Marx and not Engels who had introduced Clausewitz into the correspondence several months earlier.[14]

One must therefore tread carefully. Citing the same passages given above, Gat concludes: "neither Marx or Engels had any special interest in, or appreciation of Clausewitz's work."[15] This might be slightly too strong, at least in the case of Engels. As for Marx, it is not a stretch to say that he showed little or no interest – that was true for him regarding war in general. He was far more interested in economics, and preferred relegating the topic of war to Engels. Marx even went so far as to offer some teasing advice to Engels: "It strikes me that you allow yourself to be influenced by the military aspect of things a little too much. As to the economic stuff, I don't propose to burden you with it on your journey."[16] Knowing this about Marx, it becomes frankly laughable to stand with Vincent Esposito, who wrote: "Marx rejoiced at finding in such an eminent military authority substantiation for his own theory of the relationship between war and politics. Thereafter, Clausewitz became imbedded in revolutionary doctrine."[17] Marx had no such interest at all.

However, given that Marx and Engels worked so closely together, and were at times ghostwriting[18] for one another or co-signing articles and texts, it is not enough to demonstrate that one of the two was not interested, since the two in many ways were but one. In the case of Engels, claiming that he had little or no interest in Clausewitz can only be achieved by elevating some of his comments on the subject at the expense of others. It is the same strategy used by those who argue the opposite viewpoint.

13 Ibid., 499.

14 Ibid., 498.

15 Ibid., 494.

16 Marx, Letter to Engels, 10 September 1862, *Marx/Engels Collected Works*, vol. 40, 415.

17 Esposito, "War as a Continuation," 19–26.

18 See Gat, *History of Military Thought*, 496. Engels wrote articles that appeared under Marx's name in the *Manchester Guardian* and the *Pall Mall Gazette*, for example.

The text that Gat cites to nail his case shut is not an altogether fair assessment of the relationship. It is a letter to J. Weydemeyer from 1853, in which Engels writes, "in the end Jomini gives the best account of the Napoleonic Wars; despite many fine things, I can't really bring myself to like that natural genius, Clausewitz."[19] The fact is that this reaction predates the discussion with Marx by five years, and represents Engels's earliest reading of the text. As late as June 1851 Engels had not yet read Clausewitz, as he explains in a prior letter to Weydemeyer[20]; but soon thereafter, by early 1853, Engels knows *On War* well enough to comment negatively on the whole. The timeframe is relatively precise: we can essentially pinpoint Engels, first reading of Clausewitz within an eighteen-month range, which corresponds well with Gallie's suggestion that an article written for the *New York Daily Tribune* in September 1852 showed a "trace of a hasty first reading of Clausewitz in the opening sentences."[21] This fits exactly where we would expect it.

It is rash to cite such an early reaction by Engels, in arguing a formal dislike of Clausewitz. The fact is anyone who reads *On War* for the first time could in all honesty feel that way. The book turns off many first-time readers. However, upon returning to it for a second or third read students of Clausewitz usually arrive at a complete different take on the matter. Frankly, we could say the very same thing regarding the works of Marx and Engels!

We should focus our attention on the letters that appear after 1858, at which point we know that Engels has become sufficiently well-acquainted with Clausewitz, enough to introduce Marx to a few points of interest, including a reference to war as a science versus an art and the analogy with commerce.[22] Here we find ourselves forced into a middle ground between Gat's stance and those on the other extreme – or rather forced into an off-centre ground that is much closer to Gat's viewpoint. It should have been expected that the subject would have disappeared altogether if, beyond the mere snippets exchanged in the three letters of 1858, neither Engels nor Marx had been influenced by Clausewitz – especially given all the other considerations the two had to keep in mind in their political activism and literary contributions. However, we find rather that Engels at least continued to refer to Clausewitz for years afterwards. Engels used Clausewitz in 1862 in his discussion of the American Civil

19 Engels, Letter to Joseph Weydemeyer, 12 April 1853, *Marx/Engels Collected Works*, vol. 39, 303.

20 Ibid., 19 June 1851, vol. 38, 370.

21 Gallie, *Philosophers of War and Peace*, 82.

22 Engels, Letter to Marx, 7 January 1858, *Marx/Engels Collected Works*, vol. 41, 358.

War, and referred to him again in 1871 on the topic of the Napoleonic Wars. If Clausewitz were as insignificant to him as Gat seems to indicate, why would *On War* still be on Engels's mind roughly twenty years after he first read the book?

That being said, while the "Clausewitz connection" to Marx and Engels was long lasting, it remained somewhat weak and definitely sporadic. Engels's interest in Jomini is well evidenced in Gat's work,[23] and it appears all the more true when one turns Engels's writings on the American Civil War, where three additional examples are striking. Engels uses what Jomini describes as the "fundamental principle"[24] in two distinct ways, first in discussing the need to "cut the secessionists' territory in two and enable the Unionists to beat one part after another,"[25] and later in arguing that the north should sacrifice minor positions in order to strike harder on the decisive points. And finally, in a most damning example of a non-Clausewitzian point of view, Engels completely undermines the moral aspects of war, writing: "The seizure of Richmond and the advance of the Potomac army further south – difficult on account of the many rivers that cut across the line of march – could produce a tremendous moral effect. From a purely military standpoint, they would decide *nothing*."[26] The continued reference to Clausewitz years after Engels first discovered him suggests some affinities, albeit not on the most important of his ideas such as the moral forces as well as *On War*'s highly effective refutation of Jominian positive doctrines. It therefore appears all the more likely that Engels and Marx were not in any serious way devout Clausewitzians, and that Engels, at least, shows much closer ties to Jominian than to Clausewitzian thought. That being said, the fact that Marx and Engels introduced Clausewitz to the communist movement did make its mark, and no doubt contributed to its uptake in communism's revolutionary phase.

In the end, any attempt to pinpoint the views of Engels and Marx on war must inevitably hit the unfortunate realization that it was not actually

23 Gat, *History of Military Thought*, 498–501. Gat's quotations include Clausewitz writing that "Jomini gives the best account of the Napoleonic campaigns" and a reference to Engels's reaction to the Austro-Prussian war of 1866 that sounds like classic Jominian doctrine. In the article form, Gat's text spells out the fact that he is referring to Jomini's idea that one should not divide his forces, but this was dropped from the chapter version.

24 This fundamental principle consists of "bringing forth, through strategic combinations, the bulk of the forces of an army, successively upon decisive points in a theatre of war … and manoeuvring against fractions of the enemy army." Jomini, *Précis de l'art de la guerre*, 158.

25 Engels, *American Civil War*, 186.

26 Ibid.

central to their theorizing on communism. Engels, who was the analytical rather than synthetic mind of the two, was busy contextualizing and understanding conflicts, but did not produce any compelling overall "communist theory of war." And Marx would not either, simply out of general disinterest in these matters. A communist theory of war would emerge logically, and in due time, when it was needed: when communism entered its revolutionary phase.

If war had not been a central pillar of early communist theorizing, eventually Lenin is the one who would "put it there."[27] The main problem was how communists understood statehood and policy as subjective, rather than objective. "Apply Marx and Engels's view to First World War. You will see that for decades, for almost half a century, the governments and the ruling classes of England, and France, and Germany, and Italy, and Austria, and Russia, pursued a policy of plundering colonies, of oppressing other nations, of suppressing the working-class movement. It is this, and only this policy that is being continued in the present war."[28]

The issue of Marx's disagreement with Hegel is alluded to in Gat's discussion of Lenin,[29] but is worth developing it slightly further, in order to see not only how it influenced Lenin's interpretation of Clausewitz, but in a larger sense how this argument complicated the direct or coherent uptake of Clausewitz towards communist doctrine. To appreciate the problem, it is best to go back to the origin, when Marx, in the process of applying a Hegelian methodology to his interrogations on society and economics, eventually found himself in disagreement with Hegel. Marx built a conceptual history of the world in which the proletarian and bourgeoisie were inherently opposed, and historically bound towards a fight to unbind the relationship in a formula quite similar to the master/slave dichotomy presented in Hegel's *Phenomenology of Mind.* This necessary event is understood as the Aufhebung of the dichotomy opposing the two, which, if we recall from the chapter on Hegel above, is described by Hegel as an "abstract negation, not the negation coming from consciousness, which supersedes in such a way as to preserve and maintain what is superseded, and consequently survives its own supersession."[30] In this light, the revolution is understood a necessary reaction to a belief that the bourgeoisie exists only insofar as it subjugates the proletariat (much as there can be no master without a slave). And maybe here we might see the "cunning of reason" at work, in that the more the bourgeois

27 Kipp, "Lenin and Clausewitz," 184.
28 Lenin, "Socialism and War," 295–338.
29 Gat, *History of Military Thought*, 505–6.
30 Hegel, *Phenomenology of Spirit*, #188, 114–15.

class exploits and organizes the proletariat to maximize its efficiency and wealth-productiveness, the more it empowers it with the capacity to overthrow the capitalist order of production and provides it reasons for doing so. Since the reciprocation at work is a product of the state and its policies, the end point to this revolution is anti-political in nature, in that once the revolution is achieved only stateless, free, classless men and women remain. To reach this end goal, however, can be seen as a political process, a policy-making initiative that dictates warfare *towards* building the socio-economic and cultural bases of an anti-political society. Ultimately, what remains of the proletarian and bourgeois class is merely their history, their moment in leading towards a classless human existence – their Aufhebung.

Marx explains in *Capital* that while his methodology is Hegelian in spirit, he was in fact challenging the system as a whole, referring to his own work as Hegel's "direct opposite," turning the methodology onto itself and "standing it on its head."[31] Years earlier, Marx had also written in his doctoral thesis that he disagreed with Hegel about the threshold that separates the mystical from the political. In Hegel, the state is understood as a "vehicle of cosmic spirit"[32] – that is, rationality making itself manifest in the world as the progression of history. The concept of the state in Hegel is understood as a necessary, natural, and rational development of freely constituted peoples, inherently embodying their collective greater good. This poses a problem for Marx, who, seeing an entire class of exploited people having become the means of production, without having either access to the decision-making bodies or even the fruit of their own labour, wonders if these men are indeed free. And are they in fact freely constituted, or have they inherited an authority structure that coerces them into a dehumanizing role in society?

For Marx, the state is not an end in itself or a means to a higher spiritual end, and thus not a universal, objective idea, but rather an instrument that would generate and maintain a subjective idea, in this case, capitalism, and its usurpation of political power towards its own ends. As the paragraph below explains, the state is a subjective idea that attempts, strives to pass itself off as objective:

> The fact is that the state issues from the mass of men existing as members of families and of civil society; but speculative philosophy[33] expresses this fact as an achievement of the Idea, not the idea of the mass, but rather as the deed of an

31 Marx, afterword to *Capital*, vol. 1.
32 Taylor, *Hegel*, 119.
33 Speculative philosophy is the term Hegel uses to describe his own writings.

Idea-Subject which is differentiated from the fact itself) in such a way that the function assigned to the individual (earlier the discussion was only of the assignment of individuals to the spheres of family and civil society) is visibly mediated by circumstances, caprice, etc. Thus empirical actuality is admitted just as it is and is also said to be rational; but not rational because of its own reason, but because the empirical fact in its empirical existence has a significance which is other than it itself. The fact, which is the starting point, is not conceived to be such but rather to be the mystical result. The actual becomes phenomenon, but the Idea has no other content than this phenomenon. Moreover, the idea has no other than the logical aim, namely, to become explicit as infinite actual mind.[34]

Since the Marxists question from the very onset the idea that states possess an objective universality, it would be impossible for them to come to terms directly with Clausewitz's "intelligence of the personified state"[35] or his continuation of policy by other means.[36] They would be asking questions like, "the intelligence of whose state?" and "the policy of which class?" In more concrete terms, one place to look to in order to find the crux of this disagreement is the fact that while Hegel identified the bureaucracy as the "universal" class in society, Marx reserved this universality to the proletariat class.[37]

The link from the communists to Clausewitz was not at all direct, but required modifications to be logical. It is actually formed out of a careful addition of words. The first step for Lenin to develop coherence between Clausewitz and communism was to begin reflecting on the subject of the causes of war: "It seems to me that the most important thing that is usually overlooked in the question of war, a key issue to which insufficient attention is paid and over which there is so much dispute useless, hopeless, idle dispute, I should say is the question of the class character of the war: what caused that war, what classes are waging it, and what historical and historico-economic conditions gave rise to it."[38]

Upon this analysis, he would come to the conclusion that that imperialism and capitalist states made war inevitable, and only an armed struggle of the working class could eliminate war.[39] The formulation of war as the continuation of policy becomes very significant in this context, because Lenin had uncovered what seems to be opposing policies or ideas

34 Marx, "State as Manifestation."
35 Clausewitz, *On War*, bk I, ch. 1, 18.
36 Ibid., 17.
37 Avineri, "Hegelian Origins," 39–42.
38 Lenin, "War and Revolution," 398–421.
39 Kipp, *Lenin and Clausewitz*, 184–91.

existing not merely in the state itself, but even at the juncture that explains the causes of war. Using this formula alone would have been problematic in serving this purpose. In the Hegelian sense especially, and the Clausewitzian sense depending on one's reading of it, the state represents a single focal point of policy, a universal policy that is either representative of the people's political greater good, or is essentially the people's will and freedom, materialized in-itself-and-for-itself. Therefore, to embark on the state-toppling adventure would be a self-defeating project, an attack against one's own institutions. Before Marxists could fully adopt the terminology of war as "a continuation of policy by other means," they needed to clarify and distinguish this "policy" from that of the enemy, the state. Instead of being a universally objective thing, or in Hegel's words, the "actuality of concrete freedom"[40] of those who make it up, the state would come to be presented as a subjective entity, an instrument of the bourgeoisie, and its policy as opposed to the higher outlook imagined by Hegel, but the opposite, the very reason for revolt: the antagonism between bourgeois policy versus proletariat policy. From this point of view, like all facets of the bourgeois state, even its wars represent one of the many forms that the exploitation of the proletariat can take. One class is sent off to fight imperial wars for the enrichment of another class. Lenin had in fact stumbled upon the fundamental problem that pitted the concept of war as a continuation of policy against the objectives of Marxism – this formula assumes that there can be a *single universal policy*, when in fact many (or at least two, in this case) particular policies are struggling against one another. He writes: "How, then, can we disclose and define the 'substance' of a war? War is the continuation of policy. Consequently, we must examine the policy pursued prior to the war, the policy that led to and brought about the First World War. If it was an imperialist policy, i.e., one designed to safeguard the interests of finance capital and rob and oppress colonies and foreign countries, then the war stemming from that policy is imperialist. If it was a national liberation policy, i.e., one expressive of the mass movement against national oppression, then the war stemming from that policy is a war of national liberation."[41]

If the continuation of policy was at first contrary and destabilizing to the idea of a revolution against the state, Lenin's argument had turned it into its absolute opposite: an ultimate justification for the revolution. In part, because it helped to identify the enemy more clearly – not merely the more abstract notion of a bourgeois class – but more concretely,

40 Hegel, *Philosophy of Right*, #260, 160–1.

41 Lenin, "Marxist Attitude Towards War," 29–35.

the institutions it had usurped. By distinguishing the policy of the state as a usurpation of political power, a process by which the bourgeois has anchored firmly in its authority by creating as state in its own image, it became possible for the communist to see an attack on the state as an attack on the bourgeoisie itself. The pursuit of an alternative policy, a policy of the proletariat, and conceptualizing the war as a continuation of *this* policy – as opposed to an objective and universal concept of policy – further anchored the premise of communism's justification for the revolutionary state. Clausewitz's formula was in effect reinforcing the communist doctrine.

That is why there should be no surprise to find just how important and well cited this idea of continuation of policy becomes amongst the revolutionary communists. It dominates all other quotes from Clausewitz. Lenin cites it regularly including three times in a single text.[42] Trotsky made use of the term 116 times altogether,[43] and it also appears in repetition at times. Eventually, this idea also found its way into the dark and poetic, dichotomous interpretation proclaimed by Mao, "Politics is war without bloodshed; war is politics with bloodshed."[44]

Whereas we might have expected that methodological affinities would explain why the Clausewitz connection took form, what we find instead is that on the one hand, the founders of the Marxist methodology were not all that interested in Clausewitz, and those later Marxists, who were very Clausewitzian, were fond of only a few maxims and simple concepts they could distill, not bothering at all with Clausewitz's methodology or larger analyses. The revolutionaries were very practical and choosy in their reading. They cited Clausewitz, often, very often, but did not cite him widely or in depth. Only a pocketful of ideas made it through the communist distillation – and only those that were particularly *strategic* in solving specific problems or achieving specific gains.

One specific case, which Gat discusses at length, is that of Trotsky, who made much use of *On War* during a brief period of strife between the ranks, while he was serving as minister of defence. A disagreement emerged on the question of defining war plans and tactics within the communist movement. Trotsky referred extensively to Clausewitz in attempting to ward off a group of young military officials (Frunze, Gusev, Tukhachevsky, and others) who sought the creation of a "Unified Military

42 Lenin, "War and Revolution," 398–421.

43 This observation is based on a search of the archives of the works of Leon Trotsky available on www.marxists.org. It can be assumed that more citations would be found if the search was extended beyond this archive and into other languages as well.

44 Mao, "On Protracted War," 152–3.

Doctrine" that would spell out the character of a communist revolutionary fighting force.[45] In order to quell their ambitions, Trotsky referred to Clausewitz's discussion of positive doctrines, rejecting the notion that there existed a science of war, based on internal principles.[46] "There is not and there never has been a military 'science,'" argued Trotsky. "What is commonly called the theory of war or military science represents not a totality of scientific laws explaining objective events but an aggregate of practical usages, methods of adaptation and proficiencies."[47]

As this discussion regarding the science of war emerged, it brought to light other connected questions on the subject, such as moral forces in war and the historical conditioning of war. Thus, Trotsky also referred to these other features of Clausewitzian thought in order to deepen and strengthen his argument against the "Unified Military Doctrine." In this case, he was completely turning his back on Engels's viewpoint, which was to pay little heed to the role of moral factors in war:

> War is a specific form of relations between men. In consequence, war methods and war usages depend upon the anatomical and psychical qualities of individuals, upon the form of organization of the collective man, upon his technology, his physical or cultural-historical environment, and so on. The usages and methods of warfare are thus determined by changing circumstances and, therefore, they themselves can in no-wise be eternal ... An army leader requires the knowledge of a whole number of sciences in order to feel himself fully equipped for his art. But military science does not exist; there does exist a military craft which can be raised to the level of a military art.[48]

Of greater interest to our overall examination regarding why communists adopted Clausewitz and anarchists did not has little to do with whether or not there could be a scientific combat doctrine for the revolutionary state and its forces, but rather with the overarching, abstract doctrine framing the whole – that is, the meaning and definition of tactics, strategy, objectives, and victory. This turned out to be of grave consequence because, on the one hand, it brought forward the revolutionary fervour, the concept of "absolute war," which both Fichte and Clausewitz understood as being a product of revolution. As we saw above, when Fichte coined the term he was describing how a people rises up against a tyrant, which is to say that their political objective is absolute, because no

45 Gat, *History of Military Thought*, 507.
46 Ibid.
47 Ibid., 508.
48 Trotsky, "Speech at the Meeting of the Military Science Society," 118–19.

truce or compromise is possible when the goal is to dethrone a prince and found a new government.[49] The revolutionaries entertained this idea of absoluteness in their war, a political objective to which there was no compromise, and for which the linear movement to this end could justify the means, and render them ever more unlimited. This clarified both the instrumentality of their war, as well as idea that the war could not be won until the other duellist was overthrown, through a series of engagements leading to a victory that is total: the opponent has been altogether annihilated politically. As Trotsky wrote: "If we consider that the purpose of our action is the overthrow of the autocracy, then, of course, we have not attained that aim .... But our tactics, comrades, are not at all based on that model of protesting and striking. Our actions are a series of consecutive battles ... Understand this: in discussing whether or not we should continue the strike, we are in substance discussing whether to retain the demonstrative nature of the strike or to turn it into a decisive struggle, that is, to continue it to the point of total victory or defeat. We are not afraid of battles or defeats. Our defeats are but steps to our victory."[50]

From this paragraph, we can see that Trotsky fully adopted Clausewitz's view on the relationship between tactics and strategy, where the former consists of how one wins a battle and the latter represents how one uses successive battles towards a final outcome.[51] The logic of this sequence allowed him to imagine the notion of a total victory or total defeat for the revolution, based on the earlier premise that the two opposing factions or classes are in a gruesome, existential duel: failure to dismantle the bourgeois state would imply the failure to achieve the revolutionary, given that one was perceived as the complete opposite and negation of the other.

This strategic understanding of war as a linear sequence of battles towards gains against the opponent is precisely the conceptual frame that explains the Clausewitz connection among communists. The communist movement is organized in this strategic, linear fashion as well. As a political party, a revolutionary movement and then the inheritor of the apparatus of statehold, the movement represents a centralized approach to policy making that takes possession of war towards the ends that it has defined for it and for which it thereafter takes full responsibility. This responsibility explains why it can lay claim to the spoils of war, which in this case is statehood itself. The idea that war is an instrument of policy

49 Fichte, *Machiavel et autres écrits*, 56–7.
50 Trotsky, "November Strike."
51 Clausewitz, *On War*, bk II, ch. 1, 65.

is only intelligible insofar as there is agency, some entity to incarnate this "intelligence of the personified state"[52] to act as both the policy-maker and the executor of its will: war is to the communist state what the hammer and sickle are to the carpenter and a farmer. The insignia itself is a reminder of the underlying logic of the communist movement, which is a linear relationship between means and ends.

THE ANARCHIST "HEGEL CONNECTION"?

Despite the similarities between the communist and anarchist project to topple the bourgeois states by applying violence, the early anarchists snubbed Clausewitz altogether. Proudhon, Bakunin, and Kropotkin made no references to Clausewitz even though they were writing at a time when his works were already quite renowned, especially within left-wing circles. In exchange, anarchist ideas about war, most strikingly in the works of Bakunin, were strictly Hegelian. Having seen what Clausewitz had to offer the communists, what made the anarchists exclude him? Not only was war as an instrument not ethically in line with the anarchist project, it was altogether unintelligible within their *non-linear, anti-political* concept of revolution.

Indeed, the distinct doctrines of the communists and anarchists were each shaped by their understanding of the political element of revolution, especially the goods and evils of the *revolutionary state.* Bakunin perceived the state as an anti-revolutionary and repressive institution by definition, which must not be maintained for a single instant, once the revolution is accomplished, no matter what pretext.[53] "Bourgeois socialists" is the term Bakunin used to describe those who advocated that a political revolution should precede the social revolution as well as the economic revolution, which necessarily included all those who advocated for a revolutionary state to politically engender the remaining two facets of the revolution.[54] Bakunin explained:

> equality should be established in the world by a spontaneous organization of labor and collective property, by the free organization of producers' associations into communes, and free federation of communes – but nowise by means of the supreme tutelary action of the State ... It is this point which mainly divides the Socialists or revolutionary collectivists from the authoritarian Communists, the partisans of the absolute initiative of the State. The goal of both is the same ...

52 Ibid., bk I, ch. 1, 18.
53 Preposiet, *Histoire de l'anarchisme*, 247.
54 Hodges, "Bakunin's Controversy with Marx," 261.

Only the Communists imagine that they can attain through development and organization of the political power of the working classes, and chiefly of the city proletariat, aided by bourgeois radicalism – whereas the revolutionary Socialists, the enemies of all ambiguous alliances, believe, on the contrary, that this common goal can be attained not through the political but through the social (and therefore anti-political) organization and power of the working masses of the cities and villages.[55]

This provides us with an important clue into Clausewitz's absence from anarchist thought. If the revolution is to be "anti-political," as Bakunin wrote, what is the use of conceptualizing the revolution and the war between classes as Clausewitz did, subjected to the political? If the whole revolution did not have to be preceded by political revolution, but could instead be achieved as simultaneous processes of socio-cultural and politico-economic liberation, what would this revolution look like? How could violence rise to the purpose of revolution without taking the shape of a linear policy – nor, for that matter, the policy of a revolutionary state? According to Bakunin and those who were committing targeted acts, it was possible for violence to serve this purpose, insofar as these acts were coherent in themselves and with the project. They did not need to be organized in the Clausewitizian tradition as a sequence of tactics, adding up to the pursuit of strategic goals, because violent revolutionary acts could inspire the revolution and serve as a show of strength. This would lead to the psychological emancipation of those who perceived the deeds and admitted their legitimacy, thereby strengthening the base of the resistance and the wider appeal of the movement.

Hegel is omnipresent in this perception of violence as having within itself the capacity to "awaken" the people. Beneath it lies another idea interconnected to the concept of "Geist": that the revolution is not an end, but a process. There is no revolutionary state required because the revolution is itself this Spirit. Borrowing heavily from ideas in the *Phenomenology* and the *Philosophy of Right*, Bakunin suggested that

Civil war, so destructive to the power of states, is, on the contrary, and because of this very fact, always favourable to the awakening of popular initiative and to the intellectual, moral, and even the material interests of the populace. And for this very simple reason: civil war upsets and shakes the masses out of their sheepish state, a condition very dear to all governments, a condition which turns peoples into herds to be utilized and shorn at the whims of their shepherds. Civil war

55 Bakunin, "Stateless Socialism."

breaks through the brutalizing monotony of men's daily existence, and arrests that mechanistic routine which robs them of creative thought.[56]

The revolution and its violence referred to in this passage reminds us of Hegel's notion that "the ethical health of peoples is preserved in their indifference to the stabilisation of finite institutions; just as the blowing of the winds preserves the sea from the foulness which would be the result of a prolonged calm, so also corruption in nations would be the product of prolonged, let alone 'perpetual peace,'"[57] where the idea of self-justification resides in the act itself, and for this reason, Hegel can also maintain the argument that "war is not to be regarded as an absolute evil and as a purely external accident."[58] Indeed, the above statement from Bakunin strikes deeply Hegelian chords and appears very much in line with this passage in Hegel's *Phenomenology*: "In order not to let (the citizens) become rooted and set in their isolation thereby breaking up the whole and letting the (communal) spirit evaporate, government has from time to time to shake them to their core by war ... Spirit, by thus throwing into the melting pot the stable existence of these systems, checks their tendency to fall away from ethical order, and to be submerged in a (merely) natural existence; and it preserves and raises conscious self into freedom and its own power."[59]

If war must indeed shake the masses, as Hegel and Bakunin seem to agree on, then the methods of war should inspire this motion. Indeed, this is the central aspect of the anarchist fighting doctrine, the propaganda of the deed, whereby the idea is infused directly into the action. Though the phrase "propaganda of the deed" was first coined by the Italian Carlo Pisacane,[60] Bakunin was amongst the first to foster the idea as a key component of anarchist doctrine. In fact, in the same letter quoted above, Bakunin also wrote: "We must spread our principles, not with words but with deeds, for this is the most popular, the most potent, and the most irresistible form of propaganda."[61]

What shape would these revolutionary actions take? It is an aspect of history that is perhaps too often forgotten in the mainstream today, but the anarchists of the late nineteenth and early twentieth century succeeded in carrying out many high-profile acts of terror: the Wall Street

56 Bakunin, "Letters to a Frenchman," 186.
57 Hegel, *Philosophy of Right*, #324, 210.
58 Ibid., 209–10.
59 Hegel, *Phenomenology of Spirit*, #455, 272–3.
60 Feruta, *Scrittori politici dell'Ottocento*, 1:1249–52.
61 Bakunin, "Letters to a Frenchman," 186.

Bombing of 1920, as well as the assassination of an American president, two Spanish prime ministers, a French president, a Russian tsar, a king of Greece, an empress of Austria, an heir to the Austro-Hungarian empire, and many other high-ranking officials and prominent nobles. Kropotkin argued that political assassinations were ethical even on the grounds that normally should exclude murder altogether, the Golden Rule itself: that one should treat others as one wishes to be treated. To this he replied, "To kill not only a tyrant, but a mere viper. Yes, certainly! Because any man with a heart asks beforehand that he may be slain, if ever he becomes venomous; that a dagger may be plunged into his heart, if ever he should take the place of a dethroned tyrant."[62] For anarchists, the choice of targets – attacking symbolic figures and never aiming at allies, peasants, or proletarians – was in fact the justification for the act, embodied in the action itself.

Anarchists had no need for Clausewitz. They were not seeking a policy to guide their war, nor were they even institutionalized in a way that would allow them to frame and generate centralized policy in the first place. What they sought was justification not via a potential, eventual outcome but instead in the act itself. So powerful was this principle that each element of the revolution had to be internally coherent, and justified in-itself. Kropotkin, for example, maintained that he would rather be killed than to kill someone who had done him no harm.[63] By making this exclusion, the anarchists were able to infuse violence with right directly, and by excluding the principle of instrumentality, they reached a conceptual end point to their ethical claims.

The problem that emerged is that the anarchists were in fact transposing the ethical logic that defines war as a right of peoples into a legitimization of the purified violence itself. The process itself was the revolution, having overcome the formula of means to an end. Eventually, this implied that the revolution was in itself violence and only violence, that is, unlike the communists who could delineate between the violence of the revolution and the outcomes or other policies of the revolution, the anarchists, having so closely intertwined violence and revolution into a single set of self-justified acts and an internally coherent whole, could not distance themselves from the violence. New targets necessarily emerged each time one was put down, because there could be no deliberation to establish, frame, or limit this preconceived form of violence.

62 Novak, "Anarchism and Individual Terrorism," 177.

63 Clausewitz, *On War*, bk I, ch. 1, 2–3.

Both the anarchists' understanding of violence as an objective right and the communists' of violence as the instrument of policy of the subjective revolutionary state (against the subjective bourgeois state) must eventually attain an impasse in the hearts and minds of any free citizen, or citizen aspiring to political emancipation. In the former case, attempting to justify violence in itself necessarily breeds criticism, resentment, and fear since it implies that violence has been proclaimed directly, in itself as a right. This is inconsistent with Hegel's understanding of war as a right of the state, since it foregoes an important condition of this right. The link between violence and right is indirect in Hegel in that the right to wage war was not inherent to the state, but rest on the logos of actualized freedom: a voice of reason that forms in the confines of the state and frames its own ethos upon the development and constitution of the individual through phases of development in the family, civil society, and the state. However, the anarchist's notion of a right to violence is not built and constituted, it is assumed, and it is not deliberated upon and rendered a manifestation of reason or collective intelligence, but acts silently, and according to its preordained logic, a designed war. It is the opposite of enacting war as a legitimate and free activity of citizens. As such its violence does not include the citizen, but excludes him – and this exclusion destroys the notion of right, since this very right is derived from inclusion in the ethical realm that the political community generates in the process of making policy manifest. Without this right, any application of force calls for resistance, because eventually the exclusion catches up, calling into question even the most basic anarchist assumption, that monarchs, bourgeois statesmen, and other perceived usurpers are necessarily legitimate targets. But this self-proclaimed legitimacy of violence is itself a product of usurpation, since it is a right belonging to constituted citizens, which has been extracted and detached via their exclusion from deliberation, and attached to pre-conceived notions of who the enemy is and what should be done to punish him. When war is not an instrument of policy, it eventually reaches an end point in its legitimacy and uptake amongst citizens, since their exclusion from policy is in effect a form of tyranny – in this case, tyranny of an immutable idea.

In the case of the communists, even though they claimed to frame instrumentality in policy they nonetheless arrived at the very same impasse. Their pre-ordained revolution may have been instrumental, it may have been a "continuation of policy," but the mistake was to think that the project was in fact policy. There is no true policy without free and open deliberation. The communists were implementing the continuation of ideology by other means – not a continuation of policy. Both groups were therefore condemned to exerting violence to sustain their inner logic, because there existed no means for policy-based checks and balances to this violence: the only possible containment or possibility of limiting their use of force was to meet it with a counter-force, an observation that Clausewitz had indeed made.[64]

Their opposite fighting doctrines, coupled with the fact that the communists and anarchists were entirely consumed by and dependent on violence to exert their ideology, led to disastrous relations between the two. Despite seeking the same revolutionary outcomes and fighting the same enemy, the two factions regularly failed to cooperate and broke out into serious infighting, because the ethical impasse was so tough and violence was the only tool at the disposal of either side. The communists held a deep distrust of the anarchists because they thought their methods "disarmed" the proletariat and "prepared the ground for the politics of the enemy class."[65] Meanwhile, the anarchists rejected the consolidation of state power in the hands of the communists – going so far as to attack, on one particular occasion, the Communist Headquarters in Moscow during the revolution. Twelve were killed and fifty-five were wounded, including Yuda Roshchin, the one anarchist leader who had tried to reconcile the two factions, but was jeered off as a traitor to the cause.[66] On another occasion, when Kropotkin died, Lenin wished to offer him a state funeral but the family of the late anarchist rejected it and instead 20,000 people marched along his cortège waving placards and banners bearing demands for the release of all anarchists from prison and mottoes such as "Where there is authority there is no freedom" and "The liberation of the working class is the task of the workers themselves."[67]

The instrumentality/right divide depended on different temporal schemes and therefore it did not matter that the anarchists and communists were fighting for the same end purpose. The temporality of communism was sequential and that of the anarchists was simultaneous, and consequently, these two concepts of time being categorically exclusive, the linearity of one group was ethically inconsistent with the holistic vision of the other, since for one it meant the ends justifying the means, and for the other means being self-justifying. If either saw in the other the impossibility of revolutionary success or the dangers of tyranny, it was because they were both right in their apprehensions regarding the

64 Clausewitz, *On War*, bk I, ch. 1, 2–3.

65 Avrich, "Russian Anarchists," 297–8.

66 Ibid.

67 Kropotkin, "Declaration to the Tribunal." It is worth noting that the author of this declaration is actually unknown. Kropotkin is one of the accused.

other – though idealism may have warped their ability to see the fault in their own self-defeating tyranny.

Choosing Clausewitz as a mentor made sense to those who set out to fight a war *towards* their revolution. And choosing Hegel made sense to those who thought they could *embody* the spirit of their revolution in itself. In the end, however, the sheer violence of these partial propositions ultimately killed their universal idols. Both instrumentality and right are only ethical insofar as they are limited in their scope, and submitted to the living ethos of a deliberative population that conceptualizes what the greater good entails, but the revolutionaries had dreamt up an unlimited, absolute war that marched forward regardless of consent: it might have been a war waged for the people, but instead of being achieved by the people, it was achieved by the book. Therefore it could not claim the legitimacy that this by the people clause bestows on political (or anti-political) action.

This book was grounded on a premise firmly rooted in the dialectical tradition: that studying paradoxes, though it is more frustrating, nonetheless leads to a deeper understanding of concepts than merely isolating ideas and studying them without considering their opposites and their internal contradictions. For the same reason, instead of reading Clausewitz, Hegel, and Kant individually, they were considered in parallel and at the intersection of their thought. This allows us to heighten our understanding of how the methodologies found in all three thinkers were conducive to understanding war on three interrelated levels: a limited theory on the methods of war that imposes scepticism on claims that specific strategies and tactics can cause victory; a dual ontological theory regarding war's unbounded reciprocation of extremes and war's embodiment in reality; and finally, a dual ethical theory of war, which clearly distinguishes war's instrumentality from the notion of right. Like dialectics themselves, this book is a balancing act, where the production of three insights into war is only made possible insofar as there is a limit set on how deeply each of three thinkers is explored in detail, so that there is space enough to explore what they achieved collectively.

If the first five chapters focused on the intersection of Kant and Clausewitz, and chapters 6–11 on the intersection of Clausewitz and Hegel, one should not therefore assume that this was in fact the purpose of either of the two parts: to showcase similarities or influences, and to stop there. To appreciate the purpose of both parts, it is best to take a step back to see the larger picture of what we have accomplished throughout this book. Following the history of these ideas, from their genealogy to the exposition of their historical clash, there are two narrations happening in parallel: with regard to war's grammar, and with regard to war's logic, to use Clausewitz's terms.

We considered war's grammar, its interconnections from the simple, the noun or the verb, the building blocks that are the tactics and strategies, into its conceptual forms, the real and the absolute, ending with the question of greater good by which an ethical frame that gives structure and meaning to how these are assembled and put into action. As the story evolved, we followed principally the evolution of fighting doctrines that began in the pseudo-sciences of the Enlightenment, which were negated, refuted, tossed into the abyss of time.

However, it became clear in the process and as we studied the next two moments of dialectical war theory that fighting doctrines could also just as well be attached to not only the tactical and strategic elements of war, but also the ontological and the ethical. That being said, there appeared a false impression that – in the frenzy of nationalism and the two World Wars – total war represented the reconciliation of the real/absolute dichotomy. Even though the spirit of absoluteness inspired the real, material manifestation of the World Wars, this relationship stopped short of Aufhebung, because despite the elevated destructiveness it bred, the conceptual aspect remained grounded by material limits: the difference between the wars we decide to fight versus those we can only dream up and would never wish to fight. It was rather within the realm of the final moment, the ethical moment that it became possible to perceive a proper reconciliation: where attaching fighting doctrines directly to the ethical realm generates an impasse that sets limits to the holistic element and brings forth self-contradictions that cannot be undone, but must in fact transition from the Verstand of intellectualizing the contradiction to Vernunft – making sense of it. For the dialectical ethics of war to bring about real and opposite fighting doctrines presented us with a physical space in which to analyze the scope of the method's parts, the scope of the method's grammar.

This story about the grammar of war as it evolved through time was the source of certain conclusions about the logic proposed by the dialectical theories of war. On the one hand, the goal was to demonstrate that while the problems brought up in chapter 1 regarding the works of Clausewitz and Hegel were of a certain conditional order, there could be a better solution to framing this discussion merely on conditions. Instead of repudiating Hegel's and Clausewitz's conclusions in a wholesale manner, pinning synthetical judgments against analytical arguments, it is more tenable and useful to set limits on the holistic elements, as a means of admitting that there are overarching, final contradictions, without attempting an argument that this implies there are terminal flaws in the theories of both authors. Whereas the grammar had a clear-cut scope, the logic was in fact a continuum, from which more analysis could be extracted (and will further be extracted in the coming epilogue).

By studying how the anarchists and communists integrated Hegel and Clausewitz, we were able to consider the tight relationship between ethics and fighting doctrines, and how these relate regardless of statehood and are in fact more heavily anchored in the question of whether or not the state is perceived as the required tool for the achievement of a societal project. In this context, war is not to be understood exclusively as "war" when it is fought by the state, as was alluded to in refutations of Clausewitz, but we can accept that war takes on very different forms when fought by the state, the state-seeking, or state-fearing. We need not reinvent the entire edifice of war theory in order to manage these differences. By separating between wars of the state, of the state-seeking, and of the state-fearing, we also perceive the underlying ethical relation that defines the war, as opposed to merely the institution that fights it. The perception of a "greater good" within the state, towards the state, or without the state is at least as significant to fighting doctrines as the state itself, if not more so, especially in the context of wars where the fighting doctrines were defined in their relation to war's ethics, as opposed to war's machinery. There was no clear-cut contradiction to be made on state wars and non-state wars to justify the kind of dismissals brought forward against Clausewitz, nor more so against Hegel. The question was far more fluid and complex and framed not on the state as a thing in itself, but as something that is perceived and manifested as relations within, relations outwards, and relations towards. We were forced to consider it as a relative and living concept, rather than an absolute and fixed one.

An important contribution that the dialectical theories of war provided for posterity was grounding war once and for all in the human experience, away from an aesthetic of perfection derived from metaphysics and pre-conceived notions of what is natural or divine. Even though Hegel and Clausewitz did return to this attempted perfection of theory, where they thought they might still get away with it on the one level of analysis where holism appeared legitimate – the ethical realm – this book attempted to take them down from this last pedestal as well.

In effect, what we uncovered in the pages above was that if one turns the dialectic onto itself, if we offer a critique of the critical method, there is room for further analysis that breaks down the logic further and takes down with it its final claim to perfection – its ethical holism. However, this is by no means a point of no return, a mere line drawn in the sand. It is a process forward, because the final contradictions exposed above are perhaps fruitful and reconcilable. The limits set prepare the ground for further analysis, by calming the black and white dismissals of dialectical war theory and highlighting the many tones of grey that appear when we carefully split apart the "how," the "what," and the "why" of war. And these questions cannot be fixed in time, with one grand conclusion on the matter, since the methods of warfare change rapidly, since the ontological basis of war is a balancing act between the wars we fight and the wars we dream up, and since the ethics of war are always set at the "red line" – the threshold of what we are willing to tolerate, and what is to be understood as greater good and lesser evil, which may not be the most volatile of these three factors, but is clearly the most determinant.

Many will not be satisfied with an ethical framework for war that is thus limited, constrained, and contradictory because it requires far more effort to wrap our heads around it than do mere slogans like Kropotkin's absolute freedom, which given the vagueness and scope of its claim amounts to very little when critically assessed. Yet perhaps it is exactly this unsatisfactory concept of ethics, incomplete and uncertain, that is needed to stimulate ourselves into truly personifying "intelligence" when we claim to be acting collectively in the name of reason.

Ultimately, helping to define the scope and limits of justification is perhaps the greatest contribution dialectical reasoning can offer our reflections on war: it clarifies and distinguishes those aspects of war that are conceptually limited and conceptually unlimited. In Hegel and Clausewitz, the dialectics of war purified our understanding of war's nature by stripping the concept to its core, eliminating the external layers such as tradition and convention, and allowing its political ethos to emerge from where it hid, behind the veil of nature and god, as a fixed and unchanging thing over which mankind had no control, to a product of society, a phenomenon that is entirely man's to define and to embody, as a process of reciprocating his relationship with others. War is nothing more than this reciprocation, it is not god's will, it is not a natural instinct, it is only man's creation. As such, Hegel and Clausewitz provided us with a call to secularization and a call to responsibilization.

In their ethics, whether it is directly stated or tacitly implied, both Hegel and Clausewitz presented us with a phenomenologically unlimited ethical frame, which ultimately could be shown to have limits that were not merely conditional, but inherent to the very idea. When both right and instrumentality were pushed to their extreme, in the context of revolutionary war that had universal and absolute goals, absolute weapons, and circular logic to sustain a fragile intellectual balance between war's means and its ends, for which the only solution was to relativize the absolute, we were forced to reclaim the centrality of policy-making and the role of the citizen in generating and embodying political rationality.

Once theological ethics have been replaced with secular ethics, the danger is to fall again into the trap of mystification, where the ideas of what we fight for are abstract and intangible, and detached from the very source of what can make war ethical: the idea that where there is freedom, human rights, good government, and the absence of violence and coercion, the secular conscience in the voice of the people is given the opportunity not only to be heard, but also to be enacted as a process of liberation and human development. In that sense, though one can justify war as a right and as an instrument, this can only be done insofar as two criteria are met, first that this instrumentality and right are firmly grounded in the deliberative process that gives rise to their legitimacy as a greater good, and secondly that this process does indeed generate the expectation that a free and open deliberative process gives rise to reason, intelligence, and Spirit in the real world.

While both authors sought a holistic and nearly divine concept of war ethics, as a trinity in the case of Clausewitz and as part of Geist making itself manifest in the world in the case of Hegel, what we found was that the theories could not perfectly achieve what they set out to. In fact, there were inherent contradictions to the conclusions that war was either a right or an instrument. With regard to right, the problem was that the relationship between political decay and war could be shown to be reversible – in which case the social and ethical relationships that gave right to war could become undermined by forms of warfare that were contrary to the manifestation of these very ethical bonds. With regard to instrumentality, beyond the conditioned problem of weapons that undermine the strategic relationship between cause and effect, there was also the problem of concepts of war constructed in circular logic: the war to end all wars, where the means undermine the end, regardless of the specific form taken by the tool. We found that the holistic approaches of either Hegel or Clausewitz led to problems that were not merely conditioned, but were in fact unconditioned and necessarily implied in the concept.

Even though it took time and historical progress for these problems to show themselves, both as consequences of technology and ideology, they were not external counter-arguments like those that were explored earlier in the first chapter of this book. The arguments about historical inapplicability and self-fulfilling prophecies might have appeared convincing, but their general attempt to undermine the synthetic by providing analytical examples of inapplicability was incomplete. They could demonstrate errors of interpretation quite well. They could show specific weaknesses tied to specific examples, but they could not undo the holistic element. The counter-arguments provided were ambitious in their claims, but systematically hit at the margin because they were replicating the problem of not separating the synthetical from the analytical, and the conditioned from the unconditioned.

What differentiates this book's argument from the examples of refutations provided in chapter 1 is that it has slowed down the process of analysis. By focusing on the development of the dialectical theories of war, it was possible to avoid considering Hegel and Clausewitz's conclusions until they had been framed within – rather than without – their underlying logical constructs. It was precisely this that allowed us to break apart the synthetical from the analytical elements, and the condition from the unconditioned, to tailor the conclusions very carefully to where they applied. Instead of attempting a wholehearted rejection or elevation of Hegel and Clausewitz, the strategy was to set limits to their claims, at the very nexus of where both Hegel and Clausewitz have attempted a limitless, holistic argument on the question of ethics. As was argued in chapter 6, though the concept of goodness may have varied historically, it remains part and parcel with our concept of the divine. And though historical progress brought us to conceive a synthetical, modern, secular concept of goodness, there was no escaping the vestiges of meaning associated to the divine. This relationship explains why considering the political ethics that divide Hegel and Clausewitz could give us such a clear glimpse into the metaphysical aspect of their argument. Ethics and holism go hand in hand, construed as a single divine light, an illumination that guides us like a beacon upon the hill.

It is therefore perhaps fitting that the exploration of the limits of this light was modelled in part on the theory of optics. When waves are placed one atop the other, should their amplitudes and frequencies coincide they may either amplify each other or cancel each other out. At the intersection of right and instrumentality, we could conceive where they came together, united under a single holistic revolutionary project, but they also collapsed onto themselves and neutralized their light in opposition to one another, where the very critique of one relative to the other provided the reasoning needed to set limits on both of their claims. Like the antinomies of reason we uncovered above, it became possible at the intersection of right and instrumentality to uncover once again the problem of conditionality and unconditionality: the validity of either sides of the antinomy was not perfect in itself, but conceived as valid in the negation of its opposite. It was an argumentative construct that was giving the impression that either of the ethics were whole and perfect, in relation to the fault of the other, when in fact, we were being blinded by the light, its imperfections blurred by the halos.

It was indeed here, at the threshold, that we would have expected to find the real manifestation of the limits examined in the two critique sections in chapters 8 and 10, because all the unlimited aspects were aligned: the circular characters of a war to end all wars coupled with the absoluteness of the project itself, on the one hand, aimed – as Kropotkin put it – for "Absolute freedom, nothing but freedom, all of freedom."[68] This in fact added an absolute element to revolution's already absolute concept: the absolute revolution that will not end until its concept of freedom has achieved universality and real manifestation in the world. This, as we shall explore in the epilogue, would not in fact be rationally possible – but that did not stop those who believed it to be.

So it was precisely at this intersection that we should have expected to see the light amplified, or to no longer see the light at all. The analytical breakdown in instrumentality and right could thus be observed empirically, by studying what happens when either concept of ethical justification for war is taken to its logical extreme – that is, when right and instrumentality are proclaimed as ethical concepts in-and-for-themselves, external and unconditioned. It was here that we observed that these lose the very ethical basis upon which they are meant to be drawn … their condition itself: constitution and the public appropriation of political violence via legitimate forms of deliberation that attempt to institutionalize rationality. This root of the ethics of right and instrumentality was entirely built on relativity, on the relationship between citizens and their dialogues. The problem was that through a twist of logic, it appeared reasonable to withdraw the dynamic, relative element – the dialogue – from the equation, and nonetheless make claims regarding absolute, static conclusions that were the product of dialectical reasoning. The ideologues had in fact usurped the vitality of liberation that resides in the action of citizen deliberation and the natural authority that resides in actualized freedom. Insofar as instrumentality and right remained relative rather than absolute concepts they could indeed be validated, but when either was claimed as an absolute this resulted in breakdowns in their logic, and the appearance of absurd or illogical propositions. This being the natural limit of pure reason, so too did it appear as a limit to war ethics proclaimed in its name.

68 Kropotkin, "Declaration to the Tribunal." It is worth noting that the author of this declaration is actually unknown. Kropotkin is one of the accused.

Epilogue

THIS LAST SECTION OF THE BOOK is speculative, which explains why I have chosen to separate it from the rest. Though it follows from the arguments above, it is not a "final chapter" in the sense that it concludes or brings to light arguments that necessarily flow out of what has gone before. The previous chapters culminate in their own internal argument and logic. They are complete. The purpose of this final and external section of the book is to explore the paradoxes of modern war and consider what happens when we take Hegel and Clausewitz beyond the paradoxes they themselves explored. Instead of applying their dialectical method to distinguishing between types of war, this epilogue will frame the question to encompass the higher paradox brought forth by twentieth-century authors, whose knowledge of atomic weapons allowed them insight into the relations between the phenomenon of war itself, "all wars," and the negation of the phenomenon as a whole. While the subject of this epilogue is synthetic in scope, my approach, to use Kant's words, will not take the debate anywhere "beyond mere analysis" – on the one hand for lack of a proper critical analysis to test some of these ideas, but also because these are preliminary thoughts that have not yet been developed fully. My objective is to provide paths of reflection worthy of further study.

The goal set out in the introduction was to explore not only the origins and features of the dialectical method in war theory, but also its relevance to our current era. It was argued that seeking out its validity, or at least its utility, depends on there being a coherent ethical dimension to this form of thinking about war. The problem reached, however, is that the contradiction that opposes war as a right to war as an instrument cannot be undone simply by refuting one and proving the other: each of the two has a legitimate and objective underlying logic to it. Both are internally coherent, but neither is absolute, unconditional, perfect.

If that had been the case, we might have come to terms with there being two perfect ideas in suspense – a dual reality, a coin with two sides. But it is not that simple either. The critique sections of the previous two chapters showed us that understanding war as either a right or as an instrument had limits that certain contexts could demonstrate. Both were conditional to the deliberative process, insofar as this was perceived as a greater collective good, and understood as the process by which rationality can (and is most likely to) emerge in policy-making. Without an unconditional and absolute ethical pillar upon which to set their dialectical ethical theories of war, had Clausewitz and Hegel failed the test set out in the early pages of this text: to frame war ethics rationally?

There are a few key problems to keep in mind at this point. The cracks in both "right" and "instrumentality" were present from the very moment when these arguments were first put forward, but they did not appear historically until modernity set in, with concepts of war that were far more absolute in scope than anything Hegel or Clausewitz could have dreamt up. When history introduced the "war to end all wars" and the "weapons to end all life," we arrived at a place that was quite different from the one our two nineteenth-century thinkers had in mind.

Whereas Hegel and Clausewitz wrote about war as though it was in fact a finality, the last resort of political will, they were historically incapable of framing what a finality to this finality would look like. They could theorize about every type of war from the absolute to the limited, but material history has allowed us to delve into a higher dichotomous problem that integrates and surpasses the former: between *all of war* and the *negation of all war*. This is a point in history when the scope of war's potency (or lack thereof, by virtue of its over-potency which destroys its instrumentality and right) forces us to undo the idea of certain concepts of all-out war and utmost force that once existed in the human spirit. Hegel and Clausewitz's only concept of the "negation of all war" was Kantian in character, the notion of perpetual peace; they considered this a mere fantasy, dreamt up by philanthropists, a paper trail of treaties that would always remain contingent and subordinate to the changing whims and desires of states and peoples. They could not imagine that war could undo itself internally as a concept – through its own undoing, rather than through something external to itself like peace treaties, traditions, and conventions. They did not live at a time when the mere contingency of treaties could be underscored by the truest of necessities: that all sides must avoid escalation to all-out war in order to preserve human existence.

Some twentieth-century theorists went so far as to proclaim war's obsolescence as a result of this new reality. One French general expressed it in the simplest terms: "War Is Dead."[1] However, these ambitious conclusions did not pan out. If the authors were right about parts of their observations, what went wrong in their overall analyses? At the core of this was the idea that the logic of warfare had been turned on its head. As Brodie put it: "Thus far the chief purpose of our military establishment has been to win wars. From now on its chief purpose must be to avert them."[2] Senator Fulbright added, "Nuclear weapons have rendered [*war*] totally obsolete because the instrument of policy is now fully disproportionate to the end in view."[3] If war's internal logic, both with regard to escalation and means-to-ends, had indeed been lost, was war itself to be historically revoked? A few years earlier, in her short essay *On Violence*, Arendt had argued that the continued existence of war, in the third world for example, could not be taken as "proof" of war's non-obsolescence.[4] If violence is to be instrumental, according to Arendt, it is only "rational to the extent that it is effective in reaching the end that must justify it."[5] However, in the end she concluded that there are grave contradictions at hand, which have become inherent to a form of power that is impotent: though we can "send a crew to the moon," she wrote, "the 'allegedly greatest power on earth' is helpless to end a war ... It is as though we have fallen under a fairyland spell which permits us to do the impossible on the condition that we lose the capacity of doing the possible."[6]

What is compelling about these arguments regarding the apparent problems of the modern state's actual potency is that they do not come about from some external feature that would undo war as a phenomenon, but rather from within, as an erosion of the inner logic by which a state chooses – or not – to go to war. If one could imagine a war fought in a way that could achieve no rational political outcome, even though risking it might, and secondly if a war to be fought required the claim to the destruction of mankind as a right, then in either case, and especially if both were concurrent, such a war would indeed be absolutely nonsensical. War's obsolescence in this case would mean that history had generated a situation where the inner logic of war no longer applied – its

1 See for example Claude Leborgne, *La guerre est morte ... mais on ne le sait pas encore* (Paris: Grasset, 1987), and Paul K. Crosser, *War Is Obsolete* (Amsterdam: Grüner, 1972).

2 Brodie, *Absolute Weapon*, 76.

3 Moody, "Fading Dialectic," 418. Citing Fulbright, "Foundations of National Security," 255.

4 Arendt, *On Violence*, 6.

5 Ibid., 79.

6 Ibid., 86.

escalatory logic rendered materially impossible to tolerate, its instrumentality and right debunked, and most importantly, its ability to embody the moral health of peoples revoked by the fact that any such moral health must lie in some form of recognition. But in nihilistic war recognition disappears on all sides, and forever.

If history were merely a linear process, rather than a dialectical one, marked by reciprocation and tension, the problem of potency and instrumentality might indeed have coincided with the end of war. What it actually coincided with wasn't the end of war itself, but rather the end of war as we "knew" it. The reason why the loss of external potency in the political will did not lead to a true end of war has everything to do with the reciprocity at work between reason and the material world. There is no end point to this historical process, even though some things do end while others begin. To be fair, some types of wars, or rather justifications for going to war, have been stricken from history: evangelization, manifest destiny, glory, plunder, debt collection, monarchical successions, formal colonization, and capturing slaves. Such ideas would make us cringe nowadays, but were considered legitimate no more than a few generations ago. War has indeed disappeared from history, in certain forms. A panoply of types of wars have become completely obsolete – but this does not mean all war, nor was it a safe bet to assume it might. There are fewer things that we are willing to fight for (and that does indeed spell a certain amount of social progress), but there remain things that societies *are* willing to fight for, and it is unclear that these can in fact go away very easily.

The new material reality for war simply called upon the intelligence of the personified state to adapt. War was too disproportionate a response to justify certain types of political objectives that could be achieved through other means – economic sanctions, diplomacy, and harmonization of policy to facilitate investment, trade, travel, and multilateral cooperation. Policy became much more of a "chameleon" than war ever was, because the policy-making systems themselves had to be protected from a parallel problem: the possible obsolescence of the state itself. Since the state's very existence as an ethical realm depends on there being, as Arendt expresses it, "a space in which it is valid,"[7] its appropriation of the monopoly of force in the area in which it is manifest is an essence that cannot disappear without the state itself disappearing. Etymologically, it is worth remembering that the word "polis," from which we derive "politics," was by extension understood to mean "city-state," but actually

7 Arendt, *Promise of Politics*, 189–90.

meant only the city walls – the external, surrounding force that, to begin with, made statehood within possible. Were the state to recognize war's obsolescence, it would as a result make itself obsolete. The state is first and foremost a pact of mutual defence, meant to sustain the body politic of its citizens: to demilitarize is to cease to exist, or at the very least to become dependent on other states for defence – even the demilitarized state needs the statehood of allies and neighbours in order to exist as an entity. But how far would we go to sustain the idea of war and violence as the underlying logic upon which the state must exist? Would we tolerate contradictions, paradoxes, and absurdity for the sake of sustaining the state as an institution?

At the beginning of chapter 7, I suggested that even though the concepts of good and evil include necessary vestiges of their mystical origins, the framework that builds up modern ethics can nonetheless be grounded on secular ideals found within human experience rather than external to it. The triadic "Liberté, Égalité, Fraternité" provided us with a secularization process in politics, in the sense that their logic was self-contained, self-ordained, and independent of an external or metaphysical force to qualify or define as good and evil. Together, the three ideas represented a new worldly concept of goodness that occurred without any imitation of the divine.

The three parts of this ethical system are built on internal necessity. None of the three parts can take on a full meaning without being supported conceptually by the other two. Given this, we would expect that this framework for a secular concept of goodness would be present in the justification of the modern republic's wars. Yet something odd appears when we try to transpose all three ethical concepts into war: the three were never equally engaged, they were not equally capable of generating a potent enough promise of "greater good" in order to encompass or justify the evils of war. The modern republics did not go on to fight wars of "equalization" or wars of fraternization but oh-so-many wars of liberation (!!): first as emancipations from absolute monarchs, but later as the fruits of nationalism, communism, decolonization, post-communism, and recent so-called "regime changes." Of the triadic French *dévise*, freedom consumed the other two and emerged triumphant over them. Like a Napoleon or Caesar, the idea of freedom broke apart from the triumvirate and took absolute power upon itself, thereby becoming the justifier and redeemer of war's brutalities.

Regardless of how shallow the idea of freedom may appear, especially when applied to conquest rather than a popular uprising, the word itself possesses – like no other – a depth, a connotation that lends itself to the justification of political violence, be they revolutions born within a country or those delivered from outside its borders. However, if freedom can be perceived as being somewhat shallow, it is nonetheless also imbued with great complexities, paradoxes, and depth. Freedom as such cannot be defined with a single concept. Arguably the problem of freedom could very well be that it has too many competing significances to be of any quality as a concept of study. Each group or institution invests it with its own variants and definitions. That being said, the lack of a specific definition of freedom should not stop us from analyzing how these definitions come about and what form freedom can have, depending on how it is being used in various political roles, whether as a rallying cry or as a justification for actions, etc.

Hannah Arendt noted in her essay *On Revolution* that modernity pushed "freedom" to the centre stage in the rationalization of war and revolution. Arendt, had she been alive today, would certainly not have been shocked and awed to find out that the recent wars in Iraq and Afghanistan were given the mission names "Iraqi Freedom" and "Enduring Freedom." She had made the link decades earlier: "Freedom was introduced into the debate of the war question only after it had become quite obvious that we had reached a stage of technical development where the means of destruction were such as to exclude their rational use. In other words, freedom has appeared in this debate like a deus ex machina to justify what on rational grounds has become unjustifiable."[8]

The depth of this passage is hard at first to ascertain. It is an observation that Arendt does not further explain, but it contains extremely powerful lines of interrogation that warrant another round of consideration. Why "freedom" and not some other ethical concept we hold dear? If freedom is in fact more than a mere superficial rallying call, then what is this powerful, mystical aura surrounding it? And how does it act as a "deus ex machina"? Also, if freedom has the power to justify even the irrational, then should it not be expected that freedom can also rationalize any and all war, since the limit has been withdrawn? Arendt's observation appears to be incomplete.

There is a logical corollary to her statement: freedom's introduction to the debate was not limited to the single effect of justifying war. The reverse effect was also felt: freedom effectively pushed all other justifications out. Prior to the nineteenth century, major wars were fought between states for a long list of reasons deemed acceptable at the time, but which today would be unjustifiable. Though there remain some fringe groups, especially non-state actors, that use such traditional systems of

8 Arendt, *On Revolution*, 4.

justification amongst major powers during the twentieth and twenty-first century – communists and capitalists alike – "freedom" increasingly has come to the fore, sending all other reasons for waging war to the history books. Freedom emerged as, and was increasingly asserted as, a proper and overarching principle of *Jus ad bellum.*

This, however, does not imply that other motivators (perhaps far more powerful ones) were thereby excluded from the actions of nations, or even of individual platoons. For example, vengeance remains a fact of war. American soldiers who engaged in a massacre at My Lai or in the dehumanizing practices at Abu Ghraib acted in a vengeful spirit. That being said, after 9/11, though the US and its allies were quick to engage their weapons in Afghanistan and topple the Taliban regime, they did not call it Operation Afghani Vengeance. That feeling may have been in the hearts of decision-makers, but the legitimate course of action, intellectually, was to "liberate" the Afghans from the Taliban. Freedom is not necessarily the only reason for war, but it increasingly appears to be the only justification: the only reason among reasons that is sufficiently legitimate to be both admissible and admitted loudly and publicly.

With regard to the technological side of Arendt's statement, the modern means of destruction were generally attained as early as the Franco-Prussian war and the American Civil War, with the advent of motorized supply lines, ironclad warships, smokeless powder, and rifles that could be easily reloaded. Yet the two World Wars would take the technological reality of the statement to even greater extremes until the appearance of the atomic bomb. By enhancing the destructiveness of war, the new weapons and methods of combat raised the threshold of justification for going to war in first place. Minor tensions between states that might, in the past, have been settled by minor battles were no longer proportional to the power of warfare, and so would have to be replaced by diplomacy. The centralization or reduction of reasons to go to war, as a result of the modernization of weapons, is logical in itself. It is analogous to how modernity brought with it a greater set of increments in the punishments of law, thus avoiding sentencing minor offenders to the death penalty. That being said, if the technological aspect helps explain why justifications for war should be fewer, it is not so clear how the frightful killing capacity of the modern war machine could become so intertwined with the concept of freedom.

Part of the solution to this can be found in the absoluteness of the weapons and the relationship between revolution and absolute war. As we saw earlier, Clausewitz and Fichte both recognized the tight relationship between war's absolute character and revolution. Until the advent of modern weapons, this relationship operated in one direction: revolution served as the momentum for enhancing the power and absoluteness of war. Yet when technology became powerful enough, its momentum and sheer firepower grew so absolute that all wars became at least partially imbued with a revolutionary essence. While technology made war into a tool of physical annihilation, its potency also led to a new "fight to the finish" mentality: that is, fight to the point where the enemy's political institutions can no longer govern.

By the late nineteenth century, wars had become so destabilizing to the political institutions involved that regimes on the losing side could lose not only the battle but also their institutional claim to, and ability to maintain, national sovereignty – indeed to provide governance altogether. Wars were now unlikely to be settled on a border redrawn, a policy altered, or a province ceded. In making this point, Arendt cites, for example, the Franco-Prussian war, which ended in not only a conquest of land but also the overthrow of the Second Empire in France. In the early twentieth century, the 1905 revolution in Russia started immediately after the Tsarist regime had suffered defeat during the Russo-Japanese war.[9] Even today, wars of "liberation" in Iraq and Afghanistan are framed within this idea, where war is fought with aims that are limited regionally but unlimited politically, and are revolutionary in essence. They are not wars that seek a specific gain or advantage in negotiating new terms of peace, but rather a complete annihilation of the political system in place: the full exclusion of the Taliban and the Ba'ath party from the constitution of the state as well as from holding any executive or legislative power.

Compelling as it is, Arendt's observation nonetheless starts off with a wrong affirmation. Freedom was not introduced after the arrival of modern fighting technology, but nearly a century before it, in the early 1800s, as part and parcel of the rise of dialectical reasoning and the discovery or definition of war's political nature. If the bourgeois revolutions had integrated freedom as one part of its triadic conceptual backbone, it was Hegel directly – as well as Clausewitz indirectly – who provided us with the intellectualization of freedom as the source of legitimacy of war. Technology in warfare simply created the necessary backdrop, so that what had been discovered years before in theory could now come to the forefront and be made more easily observable. This does not pose a problem to the forthcoming analysis, nor does it change this essay's general support of Arendt's observation, but it does legitimize further research into the genesis of the war-freedom relationship. Did freedom somehow become a secular god of war? The Ares of modern times?

9 Ibid., 5.

The rise of freedom towards this role was not the product of an assertion, but an unexpected solution to the paradoxical tension between war as a right versus war as an instrument, as well as an underlying logic that would indeed continue to fuel war beyond the threshold of rationality. An analogy can help clarify this. The notion of an object's obsolescence does not necessarily lead to the disappearance of that which has become obsolete. Even if mobile phones exist, I may yet choose a landline. What obsolescence does is set up a situation where rationalization becomes necessary. In the case of the phone example, the mobile phone having become the standard, one who chooses a landline may suddenly feel compelled to explain himself. Modern war needed to explain itself, so to speak; it needed a powerful tool of rationalization in order to sustain the new contradictions that had emerged in its material history.

Many of the premises found in Kant's perpetual peace are in place today, and they do in fact contribute to peace in very real ways that go beyond the mere contingency that Hegel and Clausewitz feared with regard to international law. The harmonization or universalization of policy through treaty-making and multilateral organizations has lessened the contingency of treaties, by establishing norms and practices that do in fact reduce political violence beyond merely the promise in writing to do so. In Paraguay, for example, a *coup d'état* was thwarted by the pressures of the MERCOSUR trade pact, which includes a democracy clause in its criteria for preferential trade relations, meant to "increase the costs of unconstitutional action."[10] Here, the cost of political violence is internalized into the treaty by tying it to the considerable opportunity cost of lost trade relations. With regard to political violence between states, one can only speculate on the extent to which establishing a worldwide market under the GATT-WTO undermines one of the most significant underlying causes of past wars that were fought for the sake of conquering markets and securing access to resources.

As we saw in the chapter on Hegel, the state's own self-consciousness emerges as a process of perceiving, interacting with, and occasionally fighting other states – but there is no reason to think that this self-consciousness cannot equally be achieved through a reciprocation with a community of states as opposed to one state in particular. Even though states make war as a necessary and inescapable continuation of their policy, a *universal* political will may reciprocate this *particular* policy by necessarily and inescapably making peace as the continuation of its own

10 Valenzuela, "Paraguay," 43–55.

universal policy.[11] And the more it emerges and materializes in ways that are less and less contingent, through international legal harmonization, this reciprocation is enhanced because this emerging will can itself become a self-conscious entity, with institutions and people incarnating its role and purpose in the world. Having accomplished sixty-four operations, ended 172 conflicts with peace settlements, and supported the fulfillment of forty-five different free and fair elections,[12] the United Nations' peacekeeping forces provide a good example of the form such policy takes. That being said, however, even though some forms of political violence may have been thwarted or brought to an end, the worldwide machinery of war has never dematerialized.

The post-1945 world order was grounded in the power of the Second World War's victors, and then in the stasis of the *pax atomica*. However, what binds the *pax atomica* is not derived from any concept from Kant's perpetual peace, but actually has many similarities to Kant's use of categories in the early pages of the *Critique of Pure Reason*. The only way to make rational sense of warfare in the atomic world was to split the concept of war into mutually exclusive categories built on the superposition of two dichotomic pairs: limited/unlimited objectives, and limited/unlimited means. Instead of doing away with war, we did away with the relationship between the ends and the means that tied unlimited objectives to unlimited warfare, and limited objectives to limited warfare. This process had already begun with the early twentieth-century pseudo-Clausewitzians who advocated all-out war, or total war for limited objectives. But this reshuffling was all the more extended in the second half of the twentieth century.

Reshuffling the relationship between means and ends in war was a way for the state to hold on to the idea of coercion as limitless escalation without ever actually having to enact it. We returned to Kant, so to speak, by breaking up war into mutually exclusive conceptual categories representing the cleavages of a new irreconcilability: where limited aims were tied to unlimited means and, more importantly, where unlimited aims were tied to limited means. Among technologically advanced states, this

11 Cormier, "Reclaiming the Dialectic," 107. The emergence of a universal political will as the historical fulfillment of war's end was a stance I defended in my MA thesis at the Royal Military College of Canada; however, this appears to me now as only a partial and not a final level of analysis.

12 United Nations Association in Canada, *Peacekeeping Fact Sheet*, accessed 20 February 2006, http://www.unac.org/peacekeeping/en/un-peacekeeping/fact-sheets/what-is-un-peacekeeping/, and United Nations, *Global Issues: Peace and Security*, accessed 20 February 2006, http://www.un.org/en/globalissues/peacesecurity/.

would reclaim war's rationality, not as something intuitively logical but as something thoroughly manufactured in the mind: a rationalization of that which intuitively should be considered irrational. And as Arendt explained, the justification process that existed at the threshold between the rational and the irrational was intricately tied to the concept of freedom.

While traditional war among minor powers, non-nuclear states, and non-state actors continues to exist on a logic that is of another era, the wars of powerful states and nuclear states are the ones that have shifted. When wars are unleashed in Afghanistan or Iraq, for example, they are limited regionally and limited in potency, in that the fullest escalation or the use of weapons of mass destruction is taken out of the equation. Here, the war is absolute in its aims, as a result of the discrepancy in the power of the two duelists. This is not a war meant to alter policy, it is a war designed to eliminate the source of a policy and replace it altogether; it is a "revolution" against the Taliban or the Ba'ath. And consequently, just as you would expect in a struggle of this scope, the invasions must be anchored in the ideas of emancipation and freedom. Their ethos is liberation, because as wars that tend towards the absolute, they are uncompromising and revolutionary in essence. Thus comes into existence a category of warfare that is defined as a limited war, with absolute aims, carried out in the name of freedom. This type of war could not be conceived in any other way: revolution implies liberation.

Meanwhile, between technologically advanced states the presence of absolute weapons, or war as inherently absolute for material reasons, has been locked into a permanent state of limitedness: deterrence, a passive-aggressive state of being, where both parties are free from aggression insofar as they remain inactive. This represents an altogether different idea of freedom. The Cold War was the most dramatic example but we can also turn to Pakistan and India, where conflict in the Kashmir region is reduced to ongoing scuffles and no escalation proper is attempted on either side. Because the extreme of absolute war with unlimited means is there as a backdrop, the conflict's actual aims are forced to remain forever "limited." The result is not war proper, but bears a certain resemblance to the idea of absolutely impenetrable fortifications.

But where does this leave us? If absolute aims in war have become inherently tied to limited means, and limited aims in war have become inherently absolute in their means, has the very dialectic that opposes absolute war and real war – the very demonstration of war's political nature, according to Clausewitz – been undone or historically transcended? It would seem that war no longer exists as a positive instrument or right in any proper sense, but only as a negative unwillingness to sacrifice the institutions of state and war. Despite the aspects of impotence that

Arendt described, we are nonetheless able to dig through the paradox and unearth those aspects of potency that remain within the state: in its external relations, such as practising regime changes with the weak and tough diplomacy with the strong; and (more significantly) internally to the state, resting the rule of law and democracy on the monopoly of force. We thus sustain warfare as an ever-tighter paradox to manage, but we choose to manage it because the alternative is the end of statehood and the deconstitution of the individual as a citizen – the loss of actualized freedom.

The main flaw in the argument regarding war's obsolescence is the failure to recognize this "obsolescence" as a proposition of Verstand, which could be reciprocated by reinventing the war machine to compartmentalize the logic of political violence in order to sustain its meaning (Vernunft). When institutions came face to face with a tool they could no longer use they developed new tools to project their power, such as formalized diplomatic and trade institutions, and new machinery of war that excluded weapons of mass destruction, while still remaining politically destructive. Instead of trying to exert an ever-greater destructive ability, they would deliver a more precise and individualized one – until we reach the age of drones and smart bombs. If war had achieved obsolescence, this had spurred not demilitarization but the reverse: an accelerated reinvention of what a war machine must look like to continue being relevant beyond that fated threshold of its own end. In fact, the new technologies are such a low-risk proposition to the nations using them that they could in fact contribute to heightening aggressiveness. If war died, it is surprisingly lively in its eternal rest.

Dialectics are all the more relevant to the study of war today because modern war is more paradoxical than ever before. On a first level, we must cope with the problem that in pure reason (Verstand), we are able to conceptualize the final dichotomy between "all of war" and the "negation of all war" as an inherent rather than an external feature of the idea of war. But in actuality, its meaning (Vernunft) and application to practical life (ethics) have shifted dramatically: we have had to denaturalize the concept in order to rationalize it. We've excluded the escalatory logic in order to manage the problem of obsolescence: the way we wrap our head around war is no longer direct, but convoluted. It is not a product of reason itself, but reason self-reflected: Vernunft. On a second level, the rationale for fighting, the actualization of freedom, is no longer straightforward, but also self-reflected. In this double convolution, there appears a space where our mind is tasked with rationalization.

The problem is as follows: war is meant to be a finality in political or anti-political discourse. It represents the thin line that separates what a group is willing to tolerate from what a group is unwilling to tolerate. But what happens when this finality itself becomes impossible to tolerate – when the potency of the weapons that one has at his disposal to confront that which revolts him (e.g., human rights abuses, tyranny, etc.) becomes infinitely more revolting than the object of revolt?

Attempting to answer this question has implications both at the individual and the societal level. It has an impact on how societies choose to fight, when and why they choose to fight, and which means they are willing to put forward in doing so. This, as we saw above is closely connected to our discussion of Hannah Arendt's point, and the exclusion of various other reasons for fighting wars. At the individual level, it affects our concept of heroism in a more abstract way, but also the motivational factors and behaviors of individuals when they take arms, which has far more tangible implications. Of course, the two are deeply related since heroism tends to be an overarching motivational factor that attaches itself to every other motivator.

Where the two coincide is the centrality of freedom, which makes sense, since the only answer to that which is revolting is to free oneself from it. What is freedom but the conceptual offspring of revulsion itself? How can there be a quest for freedom unless something, someone, or some power exerts itself on the self, leading one to experience revulsion and the desire to be free? Sisyphus was disgusted by the fate Zeus gave him. The democrat is disgusted by the tyrant. Revulsion nourishes the quest for freedom and that is when our instincts kick in: when revolted, there is willingness to fight. There is a cyclical aspect to this relationship which is reinforcing: the more revolting a war becomes, the more powerful and dehumanizing its methods, the greater place freedom necessarily occupies within its ethical realm, because while the only way out of revulsion is freedom from that which revolts us, there is indeed a dialectical reverse to this, which is that for freedom we are willing to tolerate revulsion, fight the war, or carry the boulder like Sisyphus. This double-edged equation, however, is a thoroughly exclusive one: to be free from revulsion, we will do what is revolting, but only in the name of freedom and nothing else.

If freedom takes centre stage, it is not clear that it can ever be relegated back to whence it came, because freedom does not appear to have been actually "introduced" into the war debate, as Arendt suggests: it may well have been there all along, and modern war merely extracted from the core concept of war. Freedom is the one principle of justification for war that cannot be undone. It cannot come to pass. It forms within a system of circular logic. There is no inherent limit to freedom's role as a justification for war, because there is no way to free ourselves from that which revolts us, since this changes in time and continually reaffirms a will to be free. The cycle is all the more exacerbated by the fact that the more absurd, repulsive, indignant, frustrating war becomes, the more space the concept of freedom takes within it.

When we superimpose this realization with the ethical purpose of statehood being centralization of force to achieve "actualized freedom," an existential problematic surfaces, because the state has integrated into its machinery of war the possibility of destroying all of life on earth, to sustain an idea – the management of freedom as a paradox that posits a revolting idea in order to eliminate that which revolts us. It is all the more haunting to think that this fragile paradox is closely connected to our fighting instinct, which could mean that the ultimate finality to war would be for humanity to become extinct out of instinct. The question therefore is to see if the human spirit can elevate us beyond this paradox. However, to determine what cognitive path can take us there, we must understand what kind of realm of nihilism we are dealing with, because indeed to speak of extinction is without a doubt the ultimate nihilistic concept that the human spirit can evoke.

To be sure, it is an altogether new realm of nihilism: not the nihilism of a universe that we have found ourselves in, but a nihilism that we have constructed for ourselves. The problem of rationality in this context is not merely a question of living day by day without anyone pushing the fateful button. Rationality involves trying to frame one's mind around this relationship between man and this artificial nihilism. From this perspective, it useful to borrow from the French philosopher and novelist Albert Camus, who provides firm ground upon which to set our exploration of the problem.

In his essay on the myth of Sisyphus, Camus asks whether or not Sisyphus should commit suicide, given his absurd predicament: to punish him, Zeus has forced him to repeatedly push a boulder up a hill and let it roll back down for all of eternity. Faced with an absurd existence, Camus wonders how Sisyphus can justify his own life and decision to go on with it, without choosing suicide as a way out of absurdity. This exploration serves as a backdrop to determine if any individual who recognizes the absurdity of their existence should end it, and Camus identifies the source of mankind's absurd predicament in the silence of the universe: we seek out meaning and purpose, we pray and we call out, but no answer is found, no voice is heard in response. We will a rational universe, but perceive an irrational one.

Camus explains that absurdity is a "divorce." It does not exist in the things we are comparing, but rather in their confrontation.[13] Irrational

13 Camus, *Le mythe de Sisyphe*, 50.

war is not the source of absurdity. Many wars have been fought on irrational grounds: wrong estimates about means and ends, illogical calculations, and most of all, unjustifiable concepts of what is moral or ethical. Irrational and rational wars alike may be absurd. The problem is not the rationality of their propositions, but rather our relation to these propositions. Absurdity is closely tied to how one makes sense of nihilism. As Camus argues, it is neither the world that is absurd, nor mankind that is absurd. What is absurd is our quest for rationality in an irrational universe.[14]

For the individual, the confrontation that leads to suicidal questioning is his or her place in the silent universe, whereas for the collective it is the confrontation with possible suicide that actually generates that universe. There is a reciprocal relationship between the two that allows us to draw from the former problematic to elucidate the logic that composes the latter.

War's inner logic, coupled with twentieth-century technology and science, was a linear path that would naturally lead to the possibility of human annihilation. Whether it was rational to stockpile nuclear weapons as a deterrent, or whether mutual assured destruction could produce a manageable peace, neither a positive or a negative answer to these questions changes the fact that living under this threat forces upon us a concept of nihilism that is altogether new: this is not the universe man has been thrown into, it is entirely his own nihilism, and it is in fact a far more potent nihilistic concept.

The secular wars of the modern state, combined with powerful weapons, have injected war with a double dose of nihilism. The object of war is unholy (i.e., it is social and political) and the method of war encompasses the notion of destroying everything. Modern war brings forth a tense relationship between man's capacity to annihilate his universe and to conceive this apocalypse as the product of the social or political, excluding in effect scripture and god, and opposite this, his psychological and existential revolt in the face of such nihilism. The reason why an individual pondering suicide is analogous with the question of modern war is not only the question of annihilation, but also that to make sense of the problematique philosophically, one must consider it in isolation, thereby excluding the possibility of divine intervention and afterlife. It is in this context that a new principle of justification must emerge: for the individual, one that attempts to justify living, and for the soldier, one that

14 Ibid., 40

justifies dying. Surprisingly, these tend to converge at the ideas of revulsion and freedom.

What is interesting with regard to freedom's relation to war is that different concepts of freedom fuel different concepts of war, and certain concepts of freedom can contribute towards lessening political violence, while others exacerbate it. Depending on how we conceptualize freedom, we frame our political attachment to war differently. The more irrational our concept of freedom, the more irrational the wars we will be willing to wage in its name. How we think about policies and visions that might eliminate war in history, or at least might contribute to further rarefying it, can be closely tied to demystifying the concept of freedom: it is a secularization process in its own right. The question is whether a disappearance of war – to use an analogy borrowed from two competing theories we have of the cosmos – would come as a Big Crush (the Marxist war-to-end-all-wars concept) that would deliver a sudden and ideal freedom in a single blow, or would arrive rather as an infinite and tempered expansion of real freedoms, as counted or numbered, built into political apparatuses instead of being assumed or asserted in theory without a practical basis.

The concept of freedom, in relation to war's progression in history, continued to be central even as the notion of war was being reshuffled and broken up into new categories. These categories reversed the relationship between limited/unlimited objectives and limited/unlimited means. That relationship had been central to the all-out wars of the anti-bourgeois revolutions, even as the resulting wars were irrational in their fundaments. Concepts of war, regardless of whether they are rational or irrational, can be tied ethically to the notion of freedom because freedom provides a loophole in the logic of political violence, a logic that varies depending on how we choose to define freedom.

ABSOLUTE FREEDOM: THE IRRATIONAL JUSTIFICATION FOR "ABSOLUTE REVOLUTION"

"It is a war until death," wrote Bakunin, adding that the revolution "cannot come to an end unless victory is decisive and one side has totally defeated the other."[15] In the minds of the early revolutionaries and theorists, there was no possible compromise to the revolution, because it was framed on the abolition of the existing order altogether. No exchange of territory, political reform, or truce would do. There was no negotiation

15 Bakunin, *Théorie générale*, 341.

to be had, and therefore the idea behind this war was conceived in absolute political terms. There was indeed something inherently absolute and universal to the anti-bourgeois revolutions: to free all of mankind, in all corners of the world, for the rest of time. But what was this freedom that they promised? How far would war have to go in order to destroy the infinite shackles that the revolutionaries perceived? Such an unlimited concept of revolution needed an equally unlimiting principle of justification. Luckily, one such unlimited ethical concept existed at the very theoretical heart of the anti-bourgeois struggle – absolute freedom.

Marx did write at length about freedom, and in fact it appeared as a subject of interest very early in his writing career. His difficulty with framing freedom in a very tangible way was that while he agreed with Hegel that "in a real community the individuals obtain their freedom in and through their association,"[16] he could not reconcile the idea of being a wage earner with having freedom. He explained that competition gave the impression that there was an "accidental character" to the fate of wage earners: "in imagination, individuals seem freer under the dominance of the bourgeoisie than before, because their conditions of life seem accidental; in reality, of course, they are less free, because they are more subjected to the violence of things."[17] Engels took this argument further and argued that wage earners were in fact in a situation of slavery: "The only difference as compared with the old, outspoken slavery is this, that the worker of today seems to be free because he is not sold once for all, but piecemeal by the day, the week, the year, and because no one owner sells him to another, but he is forced to sell himself in this way instead, being the slave of no particular person, but of the whole property-holding class."[18] The problem with this argument as the basis for what constitutes freedom is that it is something highly immaterial to it. On the one hand, if there was no labour required to sustain human life, there would be absolute freedom by this logic, but there would be no human life to enjoy this freedom. Clearly we can assume that this was not what Marx had in mind. The other option is that wealth generates freedom, but again it is not a demonstrable proposition. Are the rich necessarily free of labour? They may have reduced their labour, or certain types of labour; they may have augmented their ability to extract wealth from the labour of others, but there is no necessary correlation between their wealth and their actual freedom. The final question that must be asked is whether or not wage earners are in fact more free than slaves. They have

16 Marx, "German Ideology, Part I."

17 Ibid.

18 Engels, *Condition of the Working Class.*

mobility, property (though not necessarily much), and the potential to improve their lot, if not immediately, at least over time, and especially intergenerationally. They are not locked into their situation as a birthright. Nor are the wealthy free from bankruptcy. The question also arises as to whether a man who is wealthier as a wage earner is more free or less free than a small landowner whose crops fail. Meanwhile, there is the complete opposite perspective offered by Soldzenitsin – that to have nothing that someone can take from you is the ultimate freedom. Freedom should be understood as incremental and variable in shape. Once understood in this more fluid way, there appears a contradiction between reality – the existence of various degrees of freedom – and Marx's expectation that freedom only occurs when a man has completely removed the apparent shackles of working for the wealth of another man. Marx is not framing freedom as an actual concept that is posited, framed, and defined, something one can "possess," but as a promise of what is to come, a negation and an abstraction of the present. Given that ownership was the conceptual enemy of communism, it is rather unsurprising that the notion of "owning one's freedom" would have made little sense. Setting the concept of freedom in a future context rather than a present context, and excluding it from the individual's hands, meant that in the anti-bourgeois tradition, freedom was fundamentally intangible.

"With the anticipated disappearance of real and perceived domination in Marx's classless society," writes Arendt, "'freedom' becomes a meaningless word unless it is conceived in an altogether new sense … Marx, here as elsewhere, did not bother to redefine his term but remained in the conceptual framework of the tradition."[19] This lack of actual form to the concept was actually the strength of the movement. This intangible concept of freedom took all the more significance in the term absolute freedom, an ethical construct so emboldened and spiritual it was acting as an external power incarnated individually in revolutionaries and counter-revolutionaries alike, filling the shoes one occupied by the metatarsi of mystical beings. One could incarnate the quest for absolute freedom, but could it ever be implemented as a reality? What did "Absolute freedom, nothing but freedom, all of freedom,"[20] actually mean? What did it look like in the real world? Arguably, nothing at all.

If freedom could justify on rational grounds what had become unjustifiable, this was further exacerbated by the fact that the notion of freedom that was being fought could itself be irrational: an ideal promise of

19 Arendt, *Promise of Politics*, 77.
20 Kropotkin, "Declaration to the Tribunal."

freedom with no basis in actuality. In such a case there would be no end point to violence since the goal that has been set and for which political violence is called upon to achieve, is unattainable and forever fleeting, thus calling forth a continuation of violence.

REAL FREEDOM: A RATIONAL APPROACH

Freedom and revolt are not only political phenomena; they are also part of a far more complicated *existential problématique*, deeply rooted in the individual psyche, self-awareness, and self-expression, through which the collective is constituted, not in some independent way, but as a relation to the self. Camus alludes to this when he writes, mimicking Descartes's cogito, "I revolt therefore we are."[21] Revolt can legitimately take the form of a replacement existential *Causa Prima*, because choosing to revolt not only generates an identity, it also *results* in life and death consequences – it is an existential "cause" – and this cannot do otherwise but lead to a crisis that impacts identity and action alike, in some cases even reaching the point of overcoming the fear of death itself, to satisfy this thirst that one may feel to free themselves from that which is the source of their revulsion. To overcome the fear of death through a process of revolt is very akin to a religious experience at the individual level. That being said, however, the revolted martyr of liberation faces a paradox which the religious martyr does not: whereas dying for god brings you closer to god, dying for freedom means you shall never enjoy the freedom for which you have fought. Dying for freedom therefore has something personally irrational to it, but something nonetheless heroic, selfless, and consequently, perhaps even more existentially meaningful in the balance. This might explain why, when one revolts, the stakes should be construed in absolute terms, otherwise, how could one be willing to make the absolute sacrifice of giving one's life so that the reward may be enjoyed by others? The justifying idea must be deeply intertwined to an existential concept, and that is why it can indeed appear rational to fight for the irrational, to die for the ideal chimera in the distance: *absolute freedom, nothing but freedom, all of freedom.*

The infinity of freedom which Kropotkin evoked in this phrase was gross and inadequate, because it dispensed with the complexities of the art of creating a state of right and individual freedom, undermining the fact that each individual freedom is particular, it is posited, granted, or mutually assented. Freedom is a relational concept, existing not in

21 Camus, *L'homme révolté*, 36.

someone, or some group, but *between people*: indeed, one's freedom ends where another's begins – it is inherently relational. To demand an absolute freedom, nothing but freedom, all of freedom, is to destroy the very basis of the formation of freedom in the first place, because it undermines this relational aspect of freedom. Beyond this core problem, there is also a numerical problem: freedoms are not infinite, nor could they conceivably be. They are counted: freedom to vote, freedom to run for office, freedom to marry or choose not to, freedom of assembly, freedom of speech, freedom from arbitrary detainment, freedom from cruel and unusual punishments, and freedom from government interference in personal affairs. The list may go on, and each generation may add to it in order to cover new needs and concerns for human development, but it is nonetheless a numbered one, *viz.* it cannot be preceded by the square root of minus one, in the hope to make the numbers imaginary. It exists as an idea – a compact, a constitution, a bill of rights – as well as in a material form – customs, institutions, the power of coercion and protection, etc. Contrary to this, "absolute freedom, nothing but freedom, all of freedom" is not unlike a synthetic a priori proposition – which, as was explained above, comes compressed or contained as to convey its universality in the simplest of form. Like a positive doctrine, the idea of absolute freedom is an elevated form of nothingness, generating the debates and antinomies of reason that gives it credence, despite the emptiness, like the leaking jar and sieve of the Danaïdes.

Freedom has the potential to become a self-fulfilling argument for fighting that forges war and freedom into an ever more tightly intertwined conceptual relation, where the only freedom worth having is the freedom one would accept to fight for and die for; and the only cause worth fighting and dying for is necessarily this very same freedom. This explains why even a freedom that is immaterial and non-committal can nonetheless sustain a system of circular logic that results in political violence – actually the less tangible it is, the more it can serve this purpose. It becomes something to "believe in." Arendt argued that freedom was like a deus ex machina that justified the unjustifiable in war. But the fact is that given "absolute freedom's" divine and metaphysical nature it is not "like" a deus ex machina: it *is* literally a deus ex machina that intervenes and resolves, insofar as individuals and groups have taken it upon themselves to incarnate this divinity, or rather a divinity in the making.

Indeed, there is a Christian undertone to this concept of emancipation and salvation that is at times almost Franciscan in its asceticism. The anarchist project merged self-sacrifice with faith and dedication, best exemplified in the memoirs of Vera Figner, an anarchist involved in the assassination of Tsar Alexander II: "All members becoming solemnly engaged in the forces of the revolution must forget all their linkages, their bloodlines, their personal sympathies, their lovers, their friends, and must give their lives without reservation, abandon all personal belongings, and renounce their individual will."[22]

If detachment and abstraction is a key element to the mystification of the fight for freedom, this gives us an important clue as to why, of the three ethical tenets of the modern state, "Liberté. Fraternité. Égalité," only the first stepped up to the plate as the justifying aspect of war. Equality is numerical and objective. Despite what Orwell ironically hinted at, one cannot be more equal than others, nor can they be more equal than equal. Its effects and its achievements can be tabulated and counted. Meanwhile, fraternity is a sentiment of mutuality that is felt in the immediate. It is either present or absent. Both fraternity and equality can be made physically and intellectually intuitive because equality is perfectly objective, and fraternity is perfectly subjective. We are able to perceive them as a result, and we understand them as either existent in the now, or eventually existent in a future "now."

Contrary to both of these, freedom cannot be properly felt or counted. It does not take on such an unconditional form; freedom depends on the context that gives life to the idea. It is a freedom to do something or a freedom from something: the idea always in a subjective relation to an object. And this cannot constitute a perfectly objective or intuitive idea such as equality and fraternity. That being said, while there are ways to frame and organize freedom within the political community in order to actualize it in laws and institutions, it can easily take on theological or mystical characteristics when it left vaguely defined, because of the relationship between subjectivity and objectivity at the heart of the concept.

Freedom, unlike equality and fraternity, is conceptually embedded with a potential to draw and commit individuals into a system of belief, which is not altogether different from believing in god. Freedom also has what the theologian and philosopher Søren Kierkegaard described as "objective uncertainty," a cognitive impasse solved by a leap of faith, which in the process engages the "leaper" into a set of actions and thoughts that continually increase his or her commitment to the initial premise. If society is built on the notion that freedom is the "principle" that binds society into a coherent whole, would you not hold it as the only concept that would convince you to take arms? But more significantly, once you have fought and killed for freedom, would it not be that much more difficult to go back and question the premise of your

22 Préposiet, *Histoire de l'anarchisme*, 370. My translation.

actions? The premise sets the stage for actions, and the actions reinforce the premise. Once the leap of faith has been acted upon, either for immediate or future freedoms, then each subsequent action makes it harder psychologically to be critical towards the idea itself.

In his quest to understand the personal relation to the universal or god, Kierkegaard argued that "decisiveness is rooted in subjectivity" – that is to say that being committed to anything is closely related to there being an idea that is "objectively uncertain."[23] In his presentation of Kierkegaard, Schufreider adds: "Rational beliefs are those that adhere to ideas which have achieved the highest degree of objective validity. We might go so far as to say that the more objective plausibility an idea enjoys, the greater the degree of rationality involved in holding it as a belief. And this would seem very well to describe even if not the way people make decisions, at least the manner in which they ought to."[24]

However, once an idea achieves certainty there is no longer any room to commit oneself. "If a person says he believes (has decisively committed himself to the claim) that 2 + 2 = 4, we should have to inquire whether or not he did not know it; and if he agreed that he certainly did also know it, it would seem quite proper for us to remind him that insofar as this latter is the case he is to that extent not in a position to have to decide in connection with the matter ... For if it is certain, there is simply no room left for me to make any decision in relationship to it."[25]

Precisely because freedom is objectively uncertain it can, just like belief in god, prophecy, or any metaphysical concept, take on the form of truth, not an objective one, but its exact opposite, a completely subjective one, a personalized one. It is a truth in which the individual can become involved. In fact "the traditional notion of objective truth seemed strangely irrelevant to finding our way to a truth which is 'true for me' in the sense of truth for the subject and its subjectivity."[26] The less objective it is, the more powerful it is as a personal motivating force because the individual has to make a choice, has to take a first step towards the idea. And once this first step is taken they are committed to the end, because otherwise they would be psychologically in contradiction or suffering from what psychologists refer to as cognitive dissonance.

Is there a rational limit to this motivational effect? Arendt points out, with regard to the American revolutionary slogan "Give me Liberty or

23 Schufreider, "Logic of the Absurd," 63.
24 Ibid.
25 Ibid., 64.
26 Ibid.

give me death!," that "in the face of the unprecedented and inconceivable potential of destruction in nuclear warfare is not even hollow; it is downright ridiculous. Indeed it seems so obvious that it is a very different thing to risk one's own life for the life and freedom of one's country and one's posterity from risking the very existence of the human species for the same purpose."[27] It remains unclear whether or not there is a limit, and if there is, it may not be a rational one.

BRAVERY AND SILENCE IN MODERN WARFARE

Even though "Give me Liberty or give me death!" can be a ridiculous and hollow slogan, in the context of modern war it remains a *heroic* thing to cry out. And heroics in our understanding of war and the state must not be too quickly discounted, especially in the context of nihilism and absurdity. If we recall the chapter on Hegel, the relationship that binds citizen to state and state to citizen is essentially the very notion of aggrandizing the individual, so much so that the most sublime form, which the state's actual freedom can take, is the citizen-soldier deployed to the front. There is no greater hero for Hegel than he who has fought bravely for his country, because in the process he has elevated both himself and the very ethical realm that is represented by the relationship between the state and the self. When we are confronted with nihilism and absurdity, the need for aggrandizement is far greater because it can be perceived both as the only thing man has to live for and as the only reason to die. There is no greater reason to seek self-aggrandizement than the perception of universal emptiness.

In modern war, where the divine has been excluded and replaced by a higher belief that is not god, loud heroics give meaning to self-sacrifice, insofar as they help man cope with otherwise insurmountable fears. However, the heroics are different when one dies for freedom as opposed to dying for god. Not so much in the form that they take, the actions they breed, but in their substance. If war is framed by a nihilistic premise, its heroics will be infused by this same nihilism. Indeed, as was mentioned above, whereas dying for god brings someone closer to god, dying for freedom separates him or her from the possibility of ever enjoying this freedom. The idea is necessarily frustrating and contains a certain absurdity, at least, at the individual level, since absurdity is a self-reflection on the relationship between one's will and the impossibility of

27 Arendt, *On Revolution*, 3.

its realization in the world. To fight for freedom is truly to negate the self for others, but if one also fights for an irrational or immaterial concept of freedom then the absurd element is all the more enhanced, since the greatest sacrifice has been offered in exchange for the inexistent.

Whereas in war heroics can make one ready to die even in the absurd context Arendt describes, in Camus's universe heroics are the only thing giving us the courage *to live* in the absurdity of the world. Even Sisyphus himself, the "Hero of absurdity," says Camus, overcomes the absurdity – the infinite punishment, the futility and sterility of pushing a boulder up and down a hill forever and ever – through revulsion and resentment, which free him from the gods and make him happy to go on.[28] In either case, we can appreciate in what sense nihilism is in fact a powerful instrument for producing heroic actions in the individual, whether as a justification for living or as a justification for dying.

Personal heroics of this kind explain how the individual fighting for a mystically endowed and yet non-divine, earthly concept of freedom may logically justify the unjustifiable and rationalize the irrational. Freedom and revolt form an existential crisis at the individual level, and heroics are a means to resolve it. To aggrandize the self is to transcend a nihilistic fear. While Hegel was right to perceive bravery as the sublime moment in the relationship between the state and the individual, this bravery is not exclusive to the state, since rebellion against the state can also produce an impression of self-aggrandizement in the individual, which competes with the state's actualized freedom. In the revolutionary ethic, "I revolt therefore we are," we find in the first clause the moment at which the individual de-constitutes himself, raising himself to sovereignty, as though the ghost of Rousseau's contractarian theory was avenging itself against Hegel's *constitutive* approach. But in the immediate process of doing so – and this is the causal element of the second clause – the act of revolt is a constitutive process in itself, it creates the "us." And within the rebellion, which can be state-like in its constitution, aggrandizement of the individual passes all the more through the bravery of living out the revolt, than what we would expect with regard to the bravery of a citizen of a stable and mature state.

The ultimate problem with such a theory of individual aggrandizement, however, is in the end a technological one, and this is what bridges the gap between freedom and modern warfare, because there is nothing heroic in sudden death. When hundreds of men march into machine gun fire, they fall silently, their heroic screams overcome by explosions

28 Camus, *Le mythe de Sisyphe*, 162, 164, 166.

and fire. Lucien Poirier expressed the *end of heroics* particularly well, also taking the time to integrate the idea of dialogue's end – the silence of dictats:

> An unprecedented rupture. At the half-point of the 20th century, the Bomb did not proclaim the death of god, nor that of Man, but that of Death itself, forever denaturalized. A society built on happiness, it censored death as something of "poor taste." Now a weapon of calculated genocide forced it back into the unhappy consciousness. It substituted personalized death – the exalted kind expressed by Rilke "god, give on to everyone his own death." – with mass death, anonymous; absolute death, gross, playing itself on the largest numbers, and the descent of civilization. This eschatological discourse brought us back to our old condition, though more derisory than ever before. We could engage discussions with god, even question his existence. But there is no dialogue to be had with the Bomb. It dictates its laws.[29]

Arendt also notes that "sheer violence is mute."[30] And this silence, much like the silence of the universe that Camus writes about, is the ultimate insult. Because while Camus's solution to the silence is to revolt against it – Sisyphus may choose to yell out a Zeus and find comfort in hearing his own voice and anger – in the case of modern warfare even revolt or loud heroics are silenced. Modern war is in effect more nihilistic in its expression than man living in the nihilistic universe, because while the latter robs him of his reason for existence, the former robs him of not only this but also his voice, his logos, the expression of his mind. It is even more revolting than the condemnation of Sisyphus.

As a result of this silent death, modern war has created a nihilistic scenario for the human spirit that is *more* revolting than the natural scenario into which we are born – the silent universe. Since revolt and freedom are conceptually inseparable, it should come naturally that in such a context, freedom should be elevated as the idea that is inextricable from modern war, as Arendt observed. This is so because there is nothing left. The intensity of modern means for the application of violence is so extreme that they forced out every other "rational" concept that could attach itself to war, because no other concept could elevate the self in a way that mimicked the divine while also being reinforced by the necessary relationship of ideas that links revulsion to freedom.

29 Lucien Poirier, *Des Stratégies Nucléaires* (Paris: Éditions Complexe, 1988), 9. My translation.

30 Arendt, *Human Condition*, 26.

Ultimately, modern war has centralized and elevated the concept of freedom at the centre of its application and justification. At the societal level, this has been shown to be the case as a result of its sheer firepower and the revolutionary essence that accompanied the introduction of such absolute weapons. At the individual level, we found that the question of heroism became fundamentally altered so that again freedom took centre stage. In both cases, centrality shifts our expectation that we are dealing with a purely rational situation, but rather one that borders on irrationality, instinct, and existential questions regarding life, the self, and the collective. It is unclear that there are any limits left. If freedom is intangible, unlimited and able to justify in war what is unjustifiable and rationalize that which is irrational, are there consequently no limits whatsoever to its potential call to arms? Or can we hope that there is in fact a way to understand the concept of freedom in a way that leads away from violence instead of towards it?

THE MARCH OF REAL FREEDOM

Mystifying freedom might have been necessary in the past, when we had not yet fully taken the time to understand freedom. To relegate its meaning to whatever the individual wanted it to be – an undefined promise open to personal interpretation – was simply a tool borrowed from religion, which facilitated its call to arms without having to bother with the problem of lacking a solid conceptual frame for this very freedom. Thus freedom could be presented and accepted as a mere phantom. To properly frame war through our concept of freedom, with the hope of better applying reason to war, freedom should not be perceived in such a metaphysical light. Instead it must be broken down using a scientific, realistic analysis that allows the individual to define his freedom, but within a frame that makes it applicable and manageable – which is to say, real and relational. Luckily, twentieth-century philosophy has offered some tools with which to pursue the path of a "science of freedom," where the analytical replaces the spiritual. It begins with the question: *what is freedom exactly and how does it take a real and concrete form in everyday life?* The science of freedom is interested not in the promise of freedom, but in its delivery. And in that sense it is a form of secularization that takes an abstract concept of freedom that one can "believe in" to an actual concept of freedom that one can experience.

The first thing, in attempting to be scientific about freedom, is to realize that freedom as we know it is a very modern invention. Though we may find many references to freedom in ancient or medieval texts, it has a collective rather than individual connotation, such as an attempt to ward off an invader, depose a tyrant, or establish a republic. Freedom in this context is merely the sovereignty of the political institutions from external powers or internal corruption that is *free* – not necessarily the universal individual rights and freedoms of those residing within. As such, rebellion and revolt in this previous social context had nothing to do with the notion of individual emancipation, which has become so closely tied to modern revolution.

"Antiquity," explains Arendt, "was well acquainted with political change and the violence that went with change, but neither of them appeared to bring about something altogether new."[31] For example, the ancient Greek statesman Solon might have destroyed the oligarchy, but he would not have undermined the institution of slavery or the traditional laws of the polis. Contrary to this, the modern idea of freedom as it was developed in the context of the bourgeois revolutions represents at least a partial, though at times a complete, break from tradition. That is, individual emancipation whether in the bourgeois or the Marxist traditions of revolution were closely conceptually tied with a dismantling or replacement of far-reaching elements of the state or the monarch's powers. The fall of the communist bureaucracies and state apparatuses in 1989–91 takes on a very similar form as well. In each case, though some laws or institutions may be kept and reformed, no institution of the old system is guaranteed a place in the new system. In the three revolutionary processes – bourgeois, communist, and post-communist alike – while freedom was evoked, there is no reason to believe that its evocation represented a single concept of freedom. Actually, that would be impossible since the very freedoms communism seeks undermines – destroys – those freedoms necessary to generate a market based economy, first and foremost individual property and the ability to enter into binding contracts. The fact that these two conflicting ideals of society existed, pitted one against the other, further confirms the fact that there is no single concept of freedom. Anarchist and communists sought their freedom as the absence of class and state, whereas liberals understood freedom as being part and parcel with the state, which acts as the purveyor of rights and freedoms. So who then possesses the right version? This depends on where we stand vis-à-vis the Rousseau/Hegel debate on the nature of *Rights*.

With regard to freedom, it is better in this case to proceed by some degree of theoretical abstraction, in order to clarify that there is no single, all-encompassing concept of freedom. If the definition of freedom

31 Arendt, *On Revolution*, 13–14.

can vary from one faction to the next, it is also plural at a higher conceptual level. In his essay "Two Concepts of Liberty," Isaiah Berlin convincingly argues that we cannot proclaim a unitary concept called "freedom" since there are in fact two distinct incarnations of freedom which are not only distinct, but can in fact play against one another. Negative freedoms, or "freedoms-from," are conceptualized as those freedoms that create space for the individual to exist free from the interventions of others (e.g. state, neighbours), or as Berlin explains the answer to the question "What is the area within which the subject – a person or a group of persons – is or should be left to do or be what he is able to do or be, without interference by other persons?" On the other hand, positive freedoms are the idea of one's personal or collective ability to posit (freedom to) his or their own definitions of liberty. Here, Berlin's defining question for positive freedoms is "What, or who, is the source of control or interference that can determine someone to do, or be, this rather than that?"[32] By this, we can understand positive freedoms as meaning essentially the right to choose or elect one's government.

While the American Revolution became closely entwined with generating positive freedoms, the French and Russian Revolutions gained popular support by taking on the social question, promising first and foremost "freedom from" toil and poverty.[33] The American Revolution more so than the French, and in complete opposition to the ideals of the Russian Revolution, made good governance its first and only point of business at its inception. The American concept of negative freedom – itemized in the Bill of Rights – focused again on good government and protections from the arbitrary law, tyranny, confiscation, self-incrimination, torture, and freedom of speech and assembly, to name a few. At the complete antipode to this, during the Russian Revolution, the negative freedoms would take centre stage, but not in relation to any concept of good government, but solely in relation to freedom from toil and labour for the benefit of an upper class and freedom from a state apparatus conceived to serve the interest of capital and its holders. Or, as Lenin described it, communism was simply "soviet power plus electrification."[34] Arendt makes the interesting point throughout *On Revolution* that the successes and failures of the revolutionary movements were tied to the types of freedoms at the centre of their cause. If during the American Revolution the continent and its wealth allowed for the social question

32 Berlin, *Liberty*, 169.

33 Arendt, *On Revolution*. This argument cannot be pinpointed to any single page, but is one of the overall theses of the book.

34 Lenin, "Foreign and Domestic Position."

of poverty to be less of a concern, it became possible for the revolution to focus on the creation of positive freedoms. However, during the French and Russian Revolutions, the destitution of the masses was such that the social question, the quest to free people from their poverty, overtook the revolutionary purpose and focused the revolution on material objectives – thus sacrificing certain ideals for the expediency of tyranny and wealth redistribution. Depending on one's definition of freedom, either as positive or negative, the revolution will take a different course. If public spaces and laws alone can provide positive freedoms, many freedoms-from must be gotten, must be extracted or must be coerced into reality: so, while the Americans had their Washington and Jefferson, the French would have their Robespierre and Napoleon, and the Russians, Stalin. It was indeed quite telling that only the American Revolution, fought for and towards positive freedoms would achieve a lasting success in the terms it set for itself, and without falling into tyranny as a means to maintain its power.

If the state could act as either an exploiter or a purveyor of freedoms and rights, or arguably could do both, then the anti-political basis of the anti-bourgeois revolutions essentially threw the baby out with the bathwater. The possibilities for materializing or instituting real individual freedoms and rights having been excluded from the revolution, it was therefore necessary for freedom to take on a more abstract form somewhere between assumptions regarding natural endowment and future or imagined concepts of *what freedom might be.* While the French Revolution may have succumbed to the "social question" or the demands of implementing the safeguard of negative freedoms on account of the state of misery amongst the populace, it nonetheless did have its *Déclaration des droits de l'homme et du citoyen.* Like the American Revolution it did include within its ideology the notion of positive freedoms, though it failed to properly follow up on them. That being said, the communist revolutionaries did not make room for such positive freedoms at all. The end goal being anarchy, and the path towards this end being dictatorship, positive freedom was excluded at every step. Dictatorship excludes positive freedom by definition, and statelessness renders the notion inapplicable and meaningless. Since the anti-bourgeois revolutions were built upon an anti-political foundation, they necessarily excluded the constitutive approach to individual freedom and therefore had to rely exclusively on the contractarian or natural endowment concept of human rights and political freedoms ... and since the rights are assumed to exist in nature, they are not formally institutionalized in society.

Whereas absolute freedom is filled with rage, impossible demands, and martyrs because it is a mere phantom in the distance with a promise of salvation, materializing real freedoms can come about through non-violence and the progression of reforms. Real freedoms can be counted and managed, because they rest on the opposite of martyrdom: the religious or anti-bourgeois martyr necessarily dies for the immaterial, his bravery is the fullest demonstration of the individual's lack of power: sacrifice is his greatest tool, and arguably his only tool, with which to *grasp at the spectre.* He who seeks real freedoms need not necessarily be made a martyr, because each small gain makes him more free and more empowered for the task of acquiring more freedom, whether this is measured in human security, human rights protection, voting rights, and eventually access to markets and to an enhanced role in civil society and the state. Opposite the martyr, his power resides in the fact that he can in fact *grasp for the sceptre.* Each step represents a reason to live, as opposed to a reason to kill and die. But should any form of tyranny hold back this natural march of freedom in history then violence may be inevitable, because those who are not allowed real freedoms naturally begin to dream up absolute freedoms for themselves. And the consequences of this can be grave.

The Marxists and anarchists effectively proved that modern secular war could become metaphysically sublime in the same way that religious crusades had – even more so, because the belief structures that made it anti-political, individual, heroic, and ethically coherent were so existentially potent that they could overcome even the silence of nihilism. The concept of freedom could be channelled like a spirit: it could be called upon to justify war when all other justifications had been relegated to the history books. Since then, if states and other fighting factions that are not anarcho-communist do indeed continue to propagate the logic of their wars in these terms, it is mere mimicry, learned and borrowed from previous use, though equally effective in other contexts. But it resides in a mystification of freedom, an undefined and abstract concept of freedom because it can rationalize the irrational and justify the unjustifiable.

If there ever was an end of war it could only be the product of a universal constitutive process. Freedom is the ideal that puts the constitutive process into motion. While it may not have a clear-cut beginning or end point, it does have a fairly manageable mid-point. As was the case in Hegel's philosophy, which has its most practical implications somewhere halfway between the perceptual and cosmic levels of his system, so too can this be said of our understanding of universal constitution and freedom. These can be attained by the provision of government by the people alongside instated guaranties with regard to human rights and human security. Though Jefferson's famous words *life, liberty, and the pursuit of happiness* might have been assumed as natural rights, in reality they represented the epitome of what a constitutive balance between positive and negative freedoms actually looks like, when implemented in human society.

To end on an example, if ISIS strikes us as a particularly virulent form of extreme political violence, the explanation for this can be found at the intersection of its two parallel justification systems. It is on the one hand religious and doctrinaire in its purpose and internal functioning, but it is also deeply rooted in the ideal of liberation: cultural reaffirmation, exclusion of foreign occupation and influence, this, far more than the religious undertones, is what holds together the group, helps its recruitment efforts, and maintains its base in the community. It should not come as a surprise that their objective is first and foremost constitutive in spirit: ISIS establishes Sharia law wherever it conquers. While this system of law has none of the guarantees regarding human rights and good government provided by modern constitutions, it remains surprisingly popular in the Muslim world according to a Pew Research Center survey, which suggest that in many countries, a majority of Muslims wish to be governed by it (e.g. 91 per cent in Iraq and 99 per cent in Afghanistan).[35] Regardless of whether it is objectively a good political system, in many cases it may nonetheless often represent a lesser evil, compared to the lawlessness of the land many communities have recently experienced under anarchy, war, colonization, and tyranny. Discretionary and unpredictable rule is far more disempowering than even doctrinaire and premodern systems of governance that have not integrated the most basic of human rights and dignity. At least in the latter, one can know the laws and protect themselves from the violent punishments and discrimination written into it. As a result, the constitutive effects of Sharia law cannot be easily offset merely by subjugating those who would have it, since this reaffirms the discretionary rule and lawlessness that leads to cycles of poverty, religious dogmatism, tyranny, and the desire for any alternative form of constitution, including Sharia law. The question is rather if Sharia law can serve as the basis for stabilizing and eventually enhancing prospects for providing systems of law that constitute citizens to political universality, or if its establishment actually leads to an opposite end, a direction for society that further disempowers citizens and leads to poverty, low levels of education, and bad prospects for human development. It is no easy question to resolve.

35 Lipka, "Muslims and Islam."

CONCLUSION: LESSONS FROM HEGEL AND CLAUSEWITZ

Freedom emerged as the bearer of modern war's justification, because it is the only pole of the modern state's ethical triad that could be conceived as objectively uncertain and that could generate a sense of personal belief powerful enough to carry with it the notion of self-sacrifice and heroics both within the state and against the state. It provides the missing mystical pillar in a godless concept of war and state, a demonstration of Voltaire's famous maxim, "Si Dieu n'existait pas, il faudrait l'inventer."[36] Whereas if the gods had whims, these could at least be somewhat guarded against, framed or at least expected and prepared for by referring to scripture, with freedom, however, the danger resides in its inherent limitlessness in scope, meaning, and power to justify. If freedom can justify irrational war and rationalize unjust wars, then it can and will do so indefinitely because there is no way to free ourselves from the concept of freedom. The best one can do is attempt to frame it in concrete, applicable terms so that when revolutionaries claim to fight for some undefined absolute freedom, or states hide colonial wars behind the veil of some undefined notion of liberation, neither are immediately given credence but instead we react to such declarations with critical questioning. These promises of freedom, in trying to embody a sort of undefined "everything," end up being nothing at all.

We generate their illusions of reality through antinomies of reason when we frame our critical response with the question "what freedom?," because therein lies an assumption of unity or singularity to the concept. To avoid the antinomies and create a proper frame for gauging the virtue and value in the promises of freedom, one must ask the more precise question: "which freedoms?"

In Hegel and Clausewitz, the dialectics of war purified our understanding of war's nature by stripping the concept to its core, eliminating the external layers such as tradition and convention, and allowing its political ethos to emerge from where it hid. But as we deepened the dialectic, we found that even this purified internal logic contains an underlying principle. The relationship between freedom and revulsion, which is an inescapable, existential, and individual rather than collective thing, justifies even that which is not necessarily rationally justifiable because it is rooted in a person's emotional psychology and conscience – perhaps even somewhere deeper in the mind than pure rationality itself, as it can

36 Voltaire, *Épître à l'auteur du livre des Trois imposteurs*, 1770, in *Œuvres complètes*, vol. 3, *Poésies*, 382.

be visceral. The mystification of freedom merely serves to enhance the drive and power of politically motivated goals, with no limits to how far, how brutal, and how nihilistic its concept of war may become.

Keeping this in mind, if we return now to the very first chapter of this book regarding Clausewitz and Hegel being considered far and wide as warmongers, we can now better extract the underlying logic of their brutal words. On the one hand, the brutal character of Hegel's writing is directly related to his understanding of the state as a "mortal," "transient" ethical realm that provides, generates, and guarantees the rights and freedoms of individuals. When these are at risk wars must be fought at any cost, because these are – according to Hegel's morality – worth fighting for. Meanwhile, in Clausewitz, the brutality stems from his ontological analysis. He understands that war is a matter of unlimited force, and that any attempt to make it otherwise either fails or leads to even worse outcomes.

> Self-imposed restrictions, almost imperceptible and hardly worth mentioning, termed usages of International Law, accompany it without essentially impairing its power. Violence, that is to say physical force (for there is no moral force without the conception of states and law), is therefore the means; the compulsory submission of the enemy to our will is the ultimate object. In order to attain this object fully, the enemy must be disarmed; and this is, correctly speaking, the real aim of hostilities in theory ... Now, philanthropists may easily imagine there is a skilful method of disarming and overcoming an enemy without causing great bloodshed, and that this is the proper tendency of the art of War. The errors which proceed from a spirit of benevolence are the worst (since) he who uses force unsparingly, without reference to the quantity of bloodshed, must obtain a superiority if his adversary does not act likewise. By such means the former dictates the law to the latter, and both proceed to extremities, to which the only limitations are those imposed by the amount of counteracting force on each side.[37]

The subtle thing here is that as Clausewitz describes war as having essentially no logical limit in the use of force, he is nonetheless implying that force is in itself the limit. The idea of force is unbounded – that is, one can always apply more force. That being said, it is nonetheless bounded in itself: more force, less force, the balance of force, nothing else but force. The benefit of this analysis is that it excludes the idea that war can be framed in ways that are not force. By crystallizing this point of view, Clausewitz is offering posterity a warning: do not expect war to not

37 Clausewitz, *On War*, bk I, ch. 1, 2–3.

get out of hand, don't expect laws and institutions to protect you from the logic of escalation. This form of simplification of the idea of war is a useful tool for policy-makers, in part for its warning, but more so because it demystifies the kind of false expectations regarding war and peace that may in fact serve as prelude to the very worst and explosive wars. One can think of the Peace of Versailles, which Foch abhorred from the start, and ironically, but accurately said, "This is not peace. It is an armistice for 20 years."[38] Similarly, Liddell Hart notes in his history of the Second World War, that had it not been for weakness with which the Western powers allowed Germany to militarize the Rhineland, and take over Austria and Czechoslovakia, followed by sudden and opposite policy in reaction to the invasion of Poland, the war might have been avoided, but the reversal was so abrupt and unexpected that it made war inevitable.[39] In each case, it was this failure to see war as a simple matter of force that led ill-advised statesmen to make policies that, although meant to facilitate peace, wound up actually eroding some of its core premises – such as consistency, trust, and firmness. Though Clausewitz has been blamed for the world wars, arguably these would not necessarily have led to such brutality had the lessons regarding both the risk of escalation and the fact that only counter-aggression or the promise of counter-aggression can put a stop to a nation bent on aggressing its neighbours. The Axis grew in strength and daring, because they were breaking international law and not being checked, countered, or sanctioned outright for doing so.

Though Clausewitz may have suffered great reprimands from readers ever since for having written the pithy and brutal passage above, there is nonetheless an important truth to it that is actually quite beneficial even to pacifists. Understanding war as force, the escalation of force, and only force allows governments to make better policy decisions. Such decisions include how war can be avoided either by counterpoise or by depending on things that are certain and fixed, rather than contingent and changing. The more rationality is materialized in the use of force, the more precise, the less extreme, and the more effective warfare can be.

Trying to isolate freedom and make the argument that it is an inescapable *principle of justification* for war – because it is self-reinforcing and deeply set in a perhaps sub-rational, emotional, and most importantly existential place in the human psyche – does not imply suddenly claiming that freedom has or necessarily will replace all other reasons for war. It is rather legitimacy of war and the eternal element of war that we are after. Fighting tyranny with violence will always be justifiable in the mind

38 Churchill, *Memoirs*, 5.
39 Liddell Hart, *History*, 7.

of true citizens, because tyranny breeds a type of revulsion that allows the counterpoise of violence to be tolerable. Meanwhile, if force is applied in ways that properly enhances human security, human development, and generates spaces in the world where positive freedoms can thrive, then it will be perceived as ethically legitimate. This form of political violence cannot disappear from history as a concept, even though it may be necessary less often as real freedom progresses. As Thomas Jefferson once said, and can now be read on the cupola of his memorial in Washington, "I have sworn upon the altar of god eternal hostility against every form of tyranny over the minds of men." It is indeed an eternal struggle, an eternal vigilance, for which only hostility and force alone can act, because tyranny itself is an act of force that disguises itself in a false legitimacy.

How we understand freedom can enhance the role of reason in the application of political force. It is analogous to how Clausewitz's simplification of war as force and only force can contribute to a clearer perspective on the phenomenon. Freedom and force are similar in that they are both unlimited in scope – they are self-defining and changing – but they nonetheless bring self-limiting or rather intrinsic constraints on war, as opposed to extrinsic ones. With fewer reasons to fight wars, the question therefore becomes: if freedom is becoming increasingly the *only* legitimate reason to fight, how then shall we define freedom itself? As we have seen, freedom frames the concept of war and if the former is unreasonable and immaterial, then the latter is more likely to be extreme because the objective is unbounded and in the distance: the inability to reach it sustains the call to arms indefinitely. But the logical corollary to this should be that war can be more effectively bounded and rendered less extreme by framing its objectives in more rational concepts of freedom. As we learned from Hegel, *what is rational is actual and what is actual is rational*, which is to say that the only actualized freedom in the world is rational freedom. Since chimerical concepts of freedom are built upon internal contradictions, the outcome of antinomies of reason necessarily remains forever immaterial; if the quest for them happens to become violent, then there are no limits to that violence except in counter-force – because the irrational cannot be actualized, it is only conceptual and therefore materially fleeting. On the other hand, a rational concept of freedom can of course be achieved through violence, but perhaps more interestingly, can also be achieved without recourse to violence, but through other exercises in freedom, such as voting, peaceful protest and assembly, speech, etc.

In contrast, the anti-bourgeois revolution, which claimed to be the war to end all wars, turned out to be perhaps one of the greatest cons in human history. Not only did it fail to deliver its promise of freedom, because the freedom it promised did not actually exist outside the imaginary, its promise of peace merely gave mankind the worst wars in history. With hindsight, we can better appreciate this: it could not fulfill its two promises because no ideology, political system, economic system, legal system, or diplomatic system is ever completely free from the spectre of tyranny. "Experience hath shewn," argued Thomas Jefferson, "that even under the best forms of government those entrusted with power have, in time, and by slow operations, perverted it into tyranny."[40] That is why mankind must never lay down its arms nor its vigilance. Beyond it being simply ill-advised to risk guaranteed, mutually recognized freedoms for the hope of achieving some form of naturally endowed freedoms outside the realms of force, coercion, and authority, it would also be existentially dehumanizing, cowardly, and belittling either to stand down before tyranny or to come to terms with one's own slavery or the slavery of others.

The natural propensity to want rights and freedoms exists deep inside the socialized individual. This explains why the war to end all wars – though it sought out and catered to this individual idea, so much so as to allow each a full possession of his or her own personalized, individual concept of freedom – nonetheless failed to overcome and eliminate the quest for freedom. Even though the revolution promised absolute freedom, and this necessarily included the promise of freedom from tyranny, the revolution itself could not guarantee that it would not in the end be tyrannical itself, and thus worthy of being resisted. The first error was to think that a personalized concept of freedom with no structure could replace the institutionalized structures for the provision of freedom. The second error was to expect that by promising the former, the latter might cease to exist as a desire at the centre of the individual's concept of self.

It was an attempt at prophecy built on the premise that a belief in an absolute concept of freedom could serve to reinvent man so that he might submit to an idea of history's end – as opposed to a continued striving to enhance and materialize a progressive concept of freedom that grows and develops in time and is never satisfied but forever marches forward, enhancing its idea and furthering its material reach. Their prophecy belonged to scripture, not to philosophy. The error of absolute freedom was not altogether different from those that caused misinterpretations of Hegel and Clausewitz. It was the impression that a single term – or in some cases two – could possess some grand, external, divine truth to it when in fact these words and explorations were only put on paper to help us compare, analyze, and understand.

40 Jefferson, *Preamble.*

MATURITY AS IRONY, NOT REVOLT

Military power, though it has often destroyed and taken away human security, human rights, human dignity, and freedoms, remains nonetheless the underlying source of them as well. On the one hand, building freedoms into the political community and then enforcing them is like an *insurance policy* protecting us against thc risk that Rousseau was wrong when he asserted the indemonstrable proposition that man is not naturally bad or evil (*méchant*), that society brings out the soldier in him, and that he is born free, but is everywhere in chains.[41] More importantly though, it is a reaction to the realization that in those governments and revolutions where the natural endowment of freedom was assumed, there was in fact a rather predictable failure to institutionalize freedoms, and this led more easily to the rise of tyranny. It was the main difference between the American Revolution on one side, and the French and Russian Revolutions on the other. If human rights and freedoms cannot be objectively demonstrated to be the product of natural endowment, they must be built into the political community as an act of mutual recognition so that they can be guaranteed and enforced. This is ultimately the lesson we must take home from Hegel. It is a proactive alternative to assuming man's natural dispositions, and it furthermore allows us to frame society so that man is born into freedom and set up to live in freedom, rather than naturally born with it, and able to experience it regardless of others. Above all this, it allows man to discover freedom as a *social technology* that can be developed and defined in ways that can exceed any form of freedom which nature alone might provide.

Even though we may arrive at the idea that force destroys and constructs freedom in an equally great way, the problem is in how we should cope with the realization that the enforcement of freedoms can become ensnared in ever more potent weapons, until we find ourselves living under a permanent threat of annihilatory war. If this book had been written at the height of the Cold War, it might simply have reached a conclusion with regard to the unresolved tension between ideological superpowers and argued that mutual fear produced a manageable peace. *The End.* But roughly a quarter of a century after the end of the Cold War, this does not appear to be a sufficient analysis. We are no longer merely in a deadlock but rather in a world that manages the paradox described above, attempting as best we can to maintain and enjoy an era prosperity

41 Rousseau, "État de guerre," "Discours sur l'origine et les fondements de l'inégalité parmi les hommes," and "Du Contrat social," in *Œuvres complètes.*

and peace, albeit at the barrel of an annihilatory gun. The Cold War demonstrated high restraint in the face of grave tension. Such restraint is clearly as important today as it was then, because while the nuclear joust is less tense, it remains with us. However, making sense of the nuclear threat when the reciprocity of revolution is not framing the tension in an easily understandable way requires more than restraint, it requires a special type of maturity that integrates restraint and further understanding.

So what exactly is the root of this maturity? While it might be tempting to mimic Camus's solution to his impasse about suicide and absurdity, this could in fact be a dangerous rather than useful way forward. Camus's logic works to resolve man's relation to the universe he has been thrown into, but it would not resolve man's relation to the universe he built for himself. The first attempt from Camus at a solution to the question of nihilism was "defiance and scorn"[42] – meant to provide a meaningful existence to Sisyphus's hell, because it would allow us to "salvage our dignity … by shaking a fist at the world which is deaf to our pleas, and continuing to live in spite of it."[43] This does not make the impression that one lives in absurdity disappear, even though it may lend us a certain sense of nobility within it.[44] Is nobility necessarily the foremost solution to the torment? Could it not well be a rather immature reaction to it, a longing to escape it? Sisyphus might be revolted in the first thousand years of his sentence, but would it not tire him out in the second or third millennium? In the case of war, one might wonder if being revolted is in fact the right intellectual route, especially knowing that revolt is so closely intertwined to our fighting instincts. There is a second way to frame the question, a superior alternative that does not call upon our spirit of revolt. How we perceive the absurd is comparable to epistemological scepticism, explains Nagel in response to Camus.[45] The very fact of arriving at judging something absurd is a feature of human intellect. He writes: "absurdity is one of the most human things about us: a manifestation of our most advanced and interesting characteristics. Like scepticism in epistemology, it is possible only because we possess a certain kind of insight – this capacity to transcend ourselves in thought … [If] there is no reason to believe that anything matters, then that doesn't matter either and we can approach our absurd lives with irony instead of heroism and despair."[46] Transposed to the question of modern warfare, this reflection reminds us that the very emergence of a concept of war that is

42 Nagel, "The Absurd," 726.
43 Ibid.
44 Ibid.
45 Ibid., 722.
46 Ibid., 727.

absurd presents an opportunity, which past eras did not have with regard to their analyses and understandings of war. Folly can and occasionally does breed lucidity. Was it not for this reason that even amongst the absolute monarchs of Europe, the king's buffoon was the only member of the court who was exempt from the prohibition on mocking the king? Even if there is folly in creating doomsday weapons, the recognition of its absurdity is an intellectual process in its own right, one that has had a fruitful outcome: we brought war to the brink, and it did not die there, it is true. But it nonetheless fulfilled a rationalization of the world system of states. The fear of materializing the absurd risk of self-annihilation, or collective suicide, is precisely what led to a vast project to harmonize policy around the globe, generating a golden age of diplomacy and trade that demonstrates a greater maturity in the human spirit a capacity to materialize rationality on a whole new scale.

We have grown in the process. Like Camus, who concludes that to live in the silent universe and to live an absurd life is no cause for suicide, so too has humanity, insofar as it has upheld a mature political system that does not make use of nuclear weapons, managed a paradox in a way that chooses life over death. We have achieved a far higher level of collective human intellect by finding ways to coexist and organize ourselves with less recourse to the silence of war, and more recourse to dialogue, *the logos of two.* However, this is not necessarily achieved in the way Camus would have expected, as a form of revolt against the absurd, but rather as something slightly more ironic. Even though we carry the burden of war eternally with us like Sisyphus his boulder – as an existential condition – because we cannot undo the existence of human technology, we also have the power to sit on it, observe it, and understand it without necessarily rolling it out continually.

If war and freedom are indeed an inseparable pair, the greater the universalizing of actual or real individual freedoms in the world, the less absolute freedom serves as a call for arms and a call for martyrs, which may ultimately lessen the recourse to political violence. Thus, when we think about war and freedom within the framework of a constitutive analysis of mankind's political and ethical realm, it becomes possible to reverse our concept of perpetual peace – not as something that is posited "in" policy, which is conceptually impossible, but rather as the negation of war as a process of constituting the individual towards political universality, which can be pursued, managed, and orchestrated "as" policy. The end of war would therefore not happen as a mere demilitarization process per se, but rather as a universal constitutive process, whereby the eternal and inescapable justification for war, the *promise of freedom,* is eradicated through the actualization of freedom in the world, and the corresponding erosion of tyranny and oppression from history.

Bibliography

Altizer, Thomas J.J. "Hegel and the Christian God." *Journal of the American Academy of Religion* 59, no. 1 (Spring 1991): 71–91.

Aquinas, St Thomas. *The Summa Theologica*, Second and Revised Edition, literally translated by Fathers of the English Dominican Province, 1920. Accessed 18 May 2016. http://www.newadvent.org/summa/3040.htm.

Arendt, Hannah. *The Human Condition*. Chicago: University of Chicago Press, 1998.

– *La vie de l'esprit*. Paris: Presses universitaires de France, 1992.

– *Lectures on Kant's Political Philosophy*. Chicago: University of Chicago Press, 1982.

– *On Revolution*. New York: Penguin Classics, 1977.

– *On Violence*. New York: Harcourt Brace, 1970.

– *Promise of Politics*. New York: Schocken, 2007.

Aron, Raymond. "Clausewitz et l'État." *Annales. Histoire, Sciences Sociales* 32, no. 6 (November–December 1977).

– *Peace and War: A Theory of International Relations*. London: Transaction, 2003.

– *Penser la guerre*, vols 1–2. Paris: Gallimard, 1976.

– *Sur Clausewitz*. Paris: Éditions Complexe, 1980.

Avineri, Shlomo. "Hegel Revisited." *Journal of Contemporary History* 3, no. 2, Reappraisals (April 1968): 133–47.

– "The Hegelian Origins of Marx's Political Thought." *The Review of Metaphysics* 21, no. 1 (September 1967): 39–42.

– "The Instrumentality of Passion in the World of Reason: Hegel and Marx." *Political Theory* 1, no. 4 (November 1973): 388–98.

– "The Problem of War in Hegel's Thought." *Journal of the History of Ideas* 22, no. 4 (October–December 1961): 463–74.

Avrich, Paul. "Russian Anarchists and the Civil War." *Russian Review* 27, no. 3 (July 1968): 296–306.

Bakunin, Mikhail. "Letters to a Frenchman." In *On Anarchy*, edited and translated by Sam Dolgoff. New York: Knopf, 1971. Accessed 18 May 2016.

https://www.marxists.org/reference/archive/bakunin/works/1870/letter-frenchman.htm.

– "Stateless Socialism: Anarchism." In *The Political Philosophy of Bakunin*, edited by G.P. Maximoff. New York: The Free Press, 1953. Accessed 18 May 2016. https://www.marxists.org/reference/archive/bakunin/works/various/soc-anar.htm.

– *Théorie générale de la révolution.* Paris: Éditions les nuits rouges, 2008.

Ball, Richard A. "The Dialectical Method: Its Application to Social Theory." *Social Forces* 57, no. 3 (March 1979): 785–98.

Bassford, Christopher. *Clausewitz and Jomini: Their Interaction.* Atlanta: State University of Georgia, 1993. Accessed 18 May 2016. http://www.clausewitz.com/readings/Bassford/Jomini/JOMINIX.htm.

– *Clausewitz in English: The Reception of Clausewitz in Britain and America, 1815–1945.* Accessed 18 May 2016. http://www.clausewitz.com/readings/Bassford/CIE/TOC.htm.

– "John Keegan and the Grand Tradition of Trashing Clausewitz." *War and History* 1, no. 3 (November 1994). Accessed 18 May 2016. https://www.clausewitz.com/mobile/keegandelenda.htm.

– "The Primacy of Policy and the 'Trinity' in Clausewitz's Mature Thought." In *Clausewitz and the Twenty-First Century*, edited by Hew Strachan and Andreas Herberg-Rothe, 74–90. Oxford: Oxford University Press, 2007.

Beck, Lewis. *Essays on Kant and Hume.* New Haven: Yale University Press, 1978.

Beiser, Frederick. Introduction to *Lectures on the Philosophy of History.* Lincoln: University of Nebraska Press, 1995.

Benhabib, Seyla. "Obligation, Contract and Exchange." In *The State and Civil Society: Studies in Hegel's Political Philosophy*, edited by Z.A. Pelczynski, 159–77. Cambridge: Cambridge University Press, 1984.

Berkeley, George. "Principles of Human Knowledge." In *The Empiricists*, edited by Richard Taylor, 135–306. Toronto: Anchor Books, 1974.

Berlin, Isaiah. *Liberty.* Edited by Henry Hardy. London: Oxford University Press, 2002.

Black, Edward. "Hegel on War." *The Monist* 57, no. 4, Philosophy of War (October 1973): 570–83.

Bourgeois, Bernard. *Le vocabulaire de Hegel.* Paris: Ellipses, 2011.

Bousquet, Antoine. *The Scientific Way of War.* New York: Columbia University Press, 2009.

Brodie, Bernard. "The Continuing Relevance of *On War.*" In *On War*, edited and translated by Michael Howard and Peter Paret, 45–58. Princeton: Princeton University Press, 1989.

– "On Clausewitz: A Passion for War – Review of *Clausewitz: A Biography* by Roger Parkinson." *World Politics* 25, no. 2 (Jan 1973): 288–308.

– ed. *The Absolute Weapon: Atomic Power and World Order.* New York: Harcourt, Brace and Co., 1946.

Butts, Robert E. "Hume's Scepticism." *Journal of the History of Ideas* 20, no. 3 (June–September 1959): 413–19.

Camus, Albert. *Le mythe de Sisyphe.* Paris: Gallimard, 1942.

– *L'homme révolté.* Paris: Gallimard, 1951.

Carrias, Col. Eugène. *La pensée militaire allemande.* Paris: Presses universitaires de France, 1948.

Charvet, John. *A Critique of Freedom and Equality.* Cambridge: Cambridge University Press, 1981.

Churchill, Winston. *Memoirs of the Second World War.* Cambridge: Riverside Press, 1959.

Clatterbaugh, Kenneth. "Cartesian Causality, Explanation, and Divine Concurrence." *History of Philosophy Quarterly* 12, no. 2, Studies on Descartes (April 1995): 195–207.

Clausewitz, Carl von. *Campagne de 1814.* Translated by G. Duval de Fraville. Paris: Édition Champs Libre, 1973.

– *Campagne de 1815 en France.* Translated by M. Niessel. Paris: Édition Champs Libre, 1973.

– *Historical and Political Writings.* Translated and edited by Peter Paret and Daniel Moran. Princeton: Princeton University Press, 1992.

– Letter to Marie v. Bruhl, 28 January 1807. "Carl und Marie von Clausewitz, Ein Lebensbild." In *Briefen und Tagebuchblättern,* edited by Karl Linnebach. Berlin: Keil Verlag, 1916.

– *On War.* Translated and edited by Michael Howard and Peter Paret. Princeton: Princeton University Press, 1989.

– *On War.* Translated by J.J. Graham. Introduction by Jan Willem Honig. New York: Barnes & Noble, 2004.

– *Principles of War.* Translated by Hans W. Gatzke. New York: Dover, 2003.

– *Schriften, Aufsätze, Studien, Briefe.* Edited by Werner Hahlweg. 2 vols. Göttingen: Vandenhoeck, 1990.

– *Two Letters on Strategy.* Edited by Peter Paret and Daniel Moran. Carlisle: US Army War College, 1984. Accessed 12 April 2016. http://www.clausewitz.com/readings/TwoLetters/TwoLetters.pdf.

– *Vom Kriege.* Edited by Werner Hahlweg. Bonn: Dümmler, 1991. Accessed 18 May 2016. http://clausewitz.com/readings/VomKriege1832/TOC.htm.

Colson, Bruno. "Présentation du Précis de l'art de la guerre." In *Précis de l'art de la guerre,* by Antoine Jomini. Paris: Perrin, 2001.

Cormier, Youri. "Reclaiming the Dialectic in the Study of War." MA thesis, Royal Military College of Canada, 2006.

Coutau-Bégarie, Hervé. *Traité de stratégie,* 2nd edition. Paris: Économica, 1999.

Cozette, Muriel. "Reading Clausewitz: Raymond Aron's Interpretation of *On War.*" In *The State and War,* edited by Andreas Herberg-Rothe, Jan Willem Honig, and Daniel Moran, 109–28. Stuttgart: Staatsdiskurse – Franz Steiner Verlag, 2011.

Delbrück, Hans. *History of the Art of War.* London: Greenwood Press, 1985.

Descartes, René. *Meditations and Selections from "The Principles."* Translated by John Veitch. Chicago: Open Court, 1903.

Dicker, Georges. *Kant's Theory of Knowledge.* London: Oxford University Press, 2004.

Dobry, Michel. "Clausewitz et l'entre-deux, ou de quelques difficultés d'une recherche de paternité légitime." *Revue française de sociologie* 17, no. 4 (October–December 1976): 652–64.

Duffy, Christopher. *The Fortress in the Age of Vauban and Frederick the Great.* London: Routledge, 1985.

Duquette, David A. "Biography of Hegel." *Internet Encyclopedia of Philosophy.* Accessed 19 August 2013. http://www.iep.utm.edu/hegelsoc/.

Echevarria, Antulio J. *After Clausewitz: German Military Thinkers before the Great War.* Lawrence: University Press of Kansas, 2000.

– *Clausewitz and Contemporary War.* London: Oxford University Press, 2007.

– "Reconsidering War's Logic and Grammar." *Infinity Journal* 2 (Spring 2011): 4–7.

Engels, Friedrich. *Condition of the Working Class in England.* Moscow: Panther Edition, 1969. Accessed 18 May 2016. https://www.marxists.org/archive/marx/works/1845/condition-working-class/.

– "Correspondence: Engels to Joseph Weydemeyer in Frankfurt, 19 June 1851." In *Marx/Engels Collected Works,* vol. 38. Moscow, 1934. Accessed 18 May 2016. https://marxists.anu.edu.au/archive/marx/works/1851/letters/51_06_19.htm.

– "Correspondence: Engels to Joseph Weydemeyer in New York, 12 April 1853." In *Marx/Engels Collected Works,* vol. 39. Manchester: 1934. Accessed 18 May 2016. https://marxists.anu.edu.au/archive/marx/works/1853/letters/53_04_12.htm.

– "Correspondence: Engels to Marx in London, 7 January 1858." In *Marx/Engels Collected Works,* vol. 40. Stuttgart: Der Briefwechsel zwischen, 1913. Accessed 18 May 2016. https://marxists.anu.edu.au/archive/marx/works/1858/letters/58_01_07.htm.

– "Correspondence: Engels to Marx in London, 30 July 1862." In *Marx/Engels Collected Works,* vol. 41. Stuttgart: Der Briefwechsel zwischen, 1913. Accessed 18 May 2016. https://marxists.anu.edu.au/archive/marx/works/1862/letters/62_07_30.htm.

– "Review of Marx's *Critique of Political Economy.*" In *Marx/Engels Collected Works,* vol 16. New York: International Publishers, 1983. Accessed 18 May 2016. https://www.marxists.org/archive/marx/works/1859/critique-pol-economy/appx2.htm.

– *The American Civil War.* Vienna: Die Presse, 1862. http://marxists.org/archive/marx/works/1862/american-civil-war.

Esposito, Vincent J. "War as a Continuation of Politics." *Military Affairs* 18, no. 1 (Spring 1954): 19–26.

Fernández Vega, José. *Las guerras de la politica: Clausewitz de Maquiavelo a Perón.* Buenos Aires: Edhasa, 2005.

Feruta, Franco Della, ed. *Scrittori politici dell'Ottocento.* Vol. 1: *Giuseppe Mazzini e i democratici.* Napoli: Ricciardi 1959.

Fichte, Johann Gottlieb. *Machiavel et autres écrits philosophiques et politiques.* Edited and translated by Luc Ferry and Alain Renaut. Paris: Payot, 1981.

Findlay, J.N. "Hegel's Use of Teleology." *The Monist* 48, no. 1 (January 1964): 1–17.

Fleming, Colin M. *Clausewitz's Timeless Trinity: A Framework for Modern War.* Surrey: Ashgate, 2013.

Foch, Ferdinand. *Des Principes de la guerre*, 7th edition. Paris: Berger-Levrault, 1926.

– *Éloge de Napoléon.* Paris: Les îles d'or, 1947.

Foucault, Michel. *History of Sexuality.* Translated by Robert Hurley. New York: Pantheon, 1978.

Freund, Julien. "Guerre et politique de Karl von Clausewitz à Raymond Aron." *Revue française de sociologie* 17, no. 4 (October–December, 1976): 652–64.

Frost, Mervyn. *Towards a Normative Theory of International Relations.* Cambridge: Cambridge University Press, 2009.

Fuller, J.F.C. *The Conduct of War.* London: Eyre & Spottiswoode, 1961.

Gallie, W.B. *Philosophers of War and Peace.* London: Cambridge University Press, 1978.

Garceau, Benoit. "Les travaux de jeunesse de Hegel et l'interpretation de sa philosophie de la religion." *Philosophiques* 1, no. 1 (1974): 21–49.

Gat, Azar. "Clausewitz and the Marxists." *Journal of Contemporary History* 27 (1992): 363–82.

– *A History of Military Thought.* Oxford: Oxford University Press, 2001.

– *The Origins of Military Thought: From the Enlightenment to Clausewitz.* Oxford: Clarendon Press, 1989.

Gaukroger, Stephen. *The Blackwell Guide to Descartes Meditations.* Oxford: Blackwell, 2006.

Gewirtz, Alan. "The Cartesian Circle." *The Philosophical Review* 50, no. 4 (July 1941): 368–95.

Gilson, Etienne, and Thomas Langan. *A History of Philosophy: Modern Philosophy From Descartes to Kant.* New York: Random House, 1963.

Girard, René. *Achèver Clausewitz.* Paris: Carnets Nord, 2007.

Gray, Chris Hables. *Postmodern War: The New Politics of Conflict.* London: Routledge, 1997.

Gray, Colin. *Modern Strategy.* London: Oxford University Press, 2004.

Grene, Marjorie. "Descartes and Skepticism." *The Review of Metaphysics* 52, no. 3 (March 1999): 553–71.
Grier, Michelle. "Kant's Critique of Metaphysics." In *The Stanford Encyclopedia of Philosophy*. Edited by Edward N. Zalta. Summer 2012 edition, accessed 18 May 2016. http://plato.stanford.edu/archives/sum2012/entries/kant-metaphysics.
Guibert, Jacques Antoine Hippolyte de. *Essai general de tactique.* Paris: Magimel, 1805.
Handel, Michael. *Masters of War: Sun Tzu, Clausewitz and Jomini.* London: Frank Kass, 1992.
Hegel, G.W.F. *Hegel: The Letters.* Translated by Clark Butler and Christine Seiler with commentary by Clark Butler. Bloomington: Indiana University Press, 1984.
– *Lectures on the Philosophy of History.* Translated by J. Sibree. New York: Dover, 1956.
– *The Phenomenology of Mind.* Translated by J.B. Baillie. New York: Cosimo, 2005.
– *Phenomenology of Spirit.* Translated by A.V. Miller, with analysis of the text and foreword by J.N. Findlay. Oxford: Oxford University Press, 1977.
– *Hegel's Philosophy of Right.* Translated by T.M. Knox. Oxford: Oxford University Press, 1952.
– *Science of Logic.* Translated by A. Miller, foreword by J.N. Findlay. Amherst: Humanity Books, 1969.
– *Vorlesungen über die Philosophie der Geschichte.* Hamburg: Der Spiegel/ Gutenberg Projekt. Accessed 10 August 2013. http://gutenberg.spiegel.de/buch/1657/1.
Herberg-Rothe, Andreas. *Clausewitz's Puzzle: The Political Theory of War.* Oxford: Oxford University Press, 2007.
– "Clausewitz und Hegel. Ein heurististischer Vergleich." *Forschungen zur brandenburgischen und preußischen Geschichte* 10, no. 1 (2000): 49–84.
– "Clausewitz's 'Wondrous Trinity.'" *Theoria: A Journal of Social and Political Theory* 114, War and Terror (December 2007): 48–73.
– "Clausewitz's 'Wondrous Trinity' as a Coordinate System of War and Violent Conflict." *International Journal of Conflict and Violence* 3, no. 2 (2009): 204–19.
Herberg-Rothe, Andreas, Jan Willem Honig, and Daniel Moran, eds. *Clausewitz: The State and War.* Stuttgart and New York: Franz Steiner, 2011.
Heuser, Beatrice. *Reading Clausewitz.* London: Pimlico, 2002.
Hodges, Donald Clark. "Bakunin's Controversy with Marx: An Analysis of the Tensions within Modern Socialism." *American Journal of Economics and Sociology* 19, no. 3 (April 1960): 259–74.
Honig, Jan Willem. "Clausewitz and the Politics of Early Modern Warfare." In *Clausewitz, the State and War*, edited by Andreas Herberg-Rothe, Jan Willem

Honig, and Daniel Moran, 9–48. Stuttgart and New York: Franz Steiner, 2011.
– "Clausewitz's *On War*: Problems of Text and Translation." In *Clausewitz and the Twenty-First Century*, edited by Hew Strachan and Andreas Herberg-Rothe, 57–73. Oxford: Oxford University Press, 2007.
– "Strategy in a Post-Clausewitzian Setting." In *The Clausewitzian Dictum and the Future of Western Military Strategy*, edited by Gert de Nooy, 109–21. The Hague: Kluwer Law, 1997.
Houlgate, Stephen. Introduction to *Hegel's Philosophy of Right*. Oxford: Oxford University Press, 2008.
Howard, Michael. *Clausewitz: A Very Short Introduction*. Oxford: Oxford University Press, 2002.
– "The Influence of Clausewitz." In *On War*, translated and edited by Michael Howard and Peter Paret, 27–44. Princeton: Princeton University Press, 1989.
Humboldt, Wilhelm von. *Sein Leben und Werken, Dargestellt in Briefen, Tagebüchern und Dokumenten seiner Zeit*. Edited by Rudolf Freese. Darmstadt: Wissenschaftliche Buchgesellschaft, 1986.
Hume, David. *Enquiries Concerning Human Understanding and Concerning the Principles of Morals*, 2nd edition. Oxford: Clarendon, 1902.
Hutchings, Kimberley. *Kant, Critique and Politics*. London: Routledge, 1996.
Jefferson, Thomas. *Preamble to a Bill for the More General Diffusion of Knowledge 1778*. In Thomas Jefferson, *The Papers of Thomas Jefferson*, edited by Julian P. Boyd et al. Princeton: Princeton University Press, 1950. Accessed 18 May 2016. http://press-pubs.uchicago.edu/founders/documents/v1ch18s11.html.
Jomini, Antoine-Henri. *Précis de l'art de la guerre*. Paris: Anselin, 1838.
– *Précis de l'art de la guerre*. Bruxelles: Librairie Militaire de J.B. Petit, 1841.
– *Précis de l'art de la guerre*. Introduction by Bruno Colson. Paris: Perrin, 2001.
– *Traité de la grande tactique*. Paris: Magimel, 1805.
– *Treatise of Grand Tactics*. New York: D. Van Nostrand, 1865.
Kaldor, Mary. *New and Old Wars. Organized Violence in a Global Era*. Stanford: Stanford University Press, 2001.
Kant, Immanuel. *Critique of Pure Reason*. Translated by J.M.D. Meiklejohn. London: George Bell & Sons, 1893.
– *Critique of Pure Reason*. Translated by Weigelt. New York: Penguin, 2007.
– *Kritik der Reinen Vernunft*. Edited by Gerd Bouillon. Chapel Hill: Projekt Gutenberg, 2004.
– *Logic*. Translated by John Richardson. London: Simpkin & Marshall, 1819.
– *Perpetual Peace*. London: Verner and Hood, 1796.
– *Theoretical Philosophy after 1781*. Cambridge: Cambridge University Press, 2004.
Kantonen, T.A. "The Influence of Descartes on Berkeley." *The Philosophical Review* 43, no. 5 (September 1934): 483–500.

Kaufmann, Walter. "The Hegel Myth and Its Method." In *From Shakespeare to Existentialism: Studies in Poetry, Religion, and Philosophy*, 88–119. Boston: Beacon Press, 1959.

Keegan, John. *A History of Warfare.* New York: Alfred A. Knopf, 1994.

Kipp, Jacob W. "Lenin and Clausewitz: The Militarization of Marxism, 1914–1921." *Military Affairs* 49, no. 4 (October 1985): 184–91.

Kropotkin, Peter. *Anarchist Morality.* San Francisco: Free Society, 1898. Accessed 18 May 2016. http://dwardmac.pitzer.edu/Anarchist_Archives/kropotkin/AM/anarchist_moralitytc.html.

– "Anarchist Morality." In *Kropotkin's Revolutionary Pamphlets.* Whitefish: Kessinger Publishing, 2005.

– "Declaration to the Tribunal of Lyons, by the Accused Anarchists." In *Ni Dieu, Ni Maître*, edited by Daniel Guérin. Lausanne: La Cité Editeur, 1969. Accessed 7 May 2016. https://www.marxists.org/reference/archive/kropotkin-peter/1883/lyons-declaration.htm.

Langendorf, Jean-Jacques. *Faire la guerre: Antoine-Henri Jomini*, vol. 2. Geneva: Georg Éditeurs, 2004.

Langsam, Harold. "Kant, Hume, and Our Ordinary Concept of Causation." *Philosophy and Phenomenological Research* 54, no. 3 (September 1994): 625–47.

Lenin, Vladimir Ilyich. "The Marxist Attitude towards War and Defence of the Fatherland." In *Lenin, Collected Works*, vol. 23. Moscow: Progress Publishers, 1964. Accessed 18 May 2016. https://www.marxists.org/archive/lenin/works/1916/carimarx/1.htm.

– "Our Foreign and Domestic Position and Party Tasks." Speech delivered to the Moscow Gubernia Conference of the R.C.P.B. 21 November 1920. In *Lenin, Collected Works*, 4th English edition, 408–26. Moscow: Progress Publishers, 1965. Accessed 18 May 2016. https://www.marxists.org/archive/lenin/works/1920/nov/21.htm.

– "Socialism and War: The Attitude of Socialists towards Wars." In *Lenin, Collected Works*, vol. 21. Peking: Foreign Languages Press, 1970. Accessed 18 May 2016. https://www.marxists.org/archive/lenin/works/1915/s+w/ch01.htm.

– "Socialism and War: The Attitude of the Russian Social-Democratic Labour Party towards the War." In *Lenin, Collected Works*, 4th English edition. Moscow: Progress Publishers, 1964. Accessed 18 May 2016. https://www.marxists.org/archive/lenin/works/1915/s+w/.

– "War and Revolution." Lecture delivered on 14 May 1917. In *Lenin, Collected Works*, vol. 24, translated by Isaacs Bernard. Moscow: Progress Publishers, 1964. Accessed 18 May 2016. https://www.marxists.org/archive/lenin/works/1917/may/14.htm.

Liddell Hart, B.H. *History of the Second World War.* London: Cassell, 1970.

– *The Ghost of Napoleon.* Westport: Greenwood Press, 1980.

Lipka, Michael. "Muslims and Islam: Key Findings in the US and around the World, 2015." *Pew Research Center.* Accessed 24 May 2016. http://www.pewresearch.org/fact-tank/2015/12/07/muslims-and-islam-key-findings-in-the-u-s-and-around-the-world/.

Machiavelli, Niccolò. *The Prince.* Translated by W.K. Marriott. Rockville: Arc Manor, 2007.

Maizeroy, Joly de. *Mémoire sur les opinions qui partage les militaires.* Paris: Claude Antoine Jombert, 1773.

Mao Zedong. "On Protracted War." A lecture given from 26 May to June 3 1938. In *Selected Works,* vol. 2. Peking: Foreign Language Press, 1965. Accessed 18 May 2016. https://www.marxists.org/reference/archive/mao/selected-works/volume-2/mswv2_09.htm.

Marx, Karl. Afterword to the second German edition of *Capital,* vol. 1. Translated by Samuel Moore and Edward Aveling, edited by Frederick Engels. Moscow: Progress Publishers, 1999. Accessed 18 May 2016. https://www.marxists.org/archive/marx/works/1867-c1/p3.htm.

– "Correspondence: Marx to Engels in Manchester, 10 September 1862." In *Marx/Engels Collected Works,* vol. 41. Stuttgart: Der Briefwechsel zwischen, 1913. Accessed 18 May 2016. https://marxists.anu.edu.au/archive/marx/works/1862/letters/62_09_10.htm.

– "The German Ideology, Part I: Feuerbach, Opposition of the Materialist and Idealist Outlook." In *Marx Engels Collected Works,* vol. 5. International Publishers, 1976. Accessed 18 May 2016. https://www.marxists.org/archive/marx/works/1845/german-ideology/ch01a.htm.

– "The State as Manifestation of Idea or Product of Man." In *Critique of Hegel's Philosophy of Right,* edited by Joseph O'Malley. Cambridge: Cambridge University Press, 1970. Accessed 18 May 2016. https://www.marxists.org/archive/marx/works/download/Marx_Critique_of_Hegels_Philosophy_of_Right.pdf.

Meerbote, R., and William L. Harper. *Kant on Causality, Freedom and Objectivity.* Minneapolis: University of Minnesota Press, 1984.

Montecuccoli, Raimondo. *Memoires de Montecuccoli : ou Principes de l'art militaire en général.* Amsterdam: Aux dépends de la Compagnie, 1734.

– *Opere,* 2nd edition. Milan: Giovanni Silvestri, 1831.

Moody, Peter. "The Fading Dialectic." *World Politics* 31, no. 3 (April 1979): 417–33.

Moran, Daniel. *Strategic Theory and the History of War.* Accessed 18 May 2016. http://www.clausewitz.com/readings/Moran-StrategicTheory.pdf.

Nagel, Thomas. "The Absurd." *The Journal of Philosophy* 68, no. 20 (21 October 1971): 716–27.

Neumann, Sigmund, and Mark von Hagen. "Engels and Marx on Revolution." In *Makers of Modern Strategy,* edited by Peter Paret, Gordon A. Craig, and Felix Gilbert. Princeton: Princeton University Press, 1986.

Nietzsche, Friedrich. *The Genealogy of Morals.* Translated by H.B. Samuel. New York: Boni and Liveright, 1887.

Norton, David Fate. *David Hume: Common-Sense Moralist, Sceptical Metaphysician.* Princeton: Princeton University Press, 1982.

Novak, Derry. "Anarchism and Individual Terrorism." *The Canadian Journal of Economics and Political Science* 20, no. 2 (May 1954): 176–84.

Pappas, George. "Berkeley and Scepticism." *Philosophy and Phenomenological Research* 59, no. 1 (March 1999): 133–49.

Paret, Peter. *Clausewitz and the State.* Princeton: Princeton University Press, 1985.

– "Education, Politics and War in the Life of Clausewitz." *Journal of the History of Ideas* 29, no. 3 (July–September 1968): 394–408.

– "The Genesis of *On War.*" In *On War,* translated and edited by Michael Howard and Peter Paret, 3–25. Princeton: Princeton University Press, 1989.

Parkinson, Roger. *Clausewitz, a Biography.* New York: Stein and Day, 1971.

Pelczynski, Z.A., ed. *The State & Civil Society.* Cambridge: Cambridge University Press, 1984.

Peltz, Richard W. "The Logic of the Cogito," *Philosophy and Phenomenological Research* 23, no. 2 (1962): 256–62.

Phillips, Thomas R., ed. *Roots of Strategy.* Harrisburg: The Military Service Publishing Company, 1940.

Pinkard, Terry. "Freedom and Social Categories in Hegel's Ethics." *Philosophy and Phenomenological Research* 47, no. 2 (December 1986): 209–32.

Plamenatz, John. *Man and Society.* London: Longmans, 1963.

Plant, Raymond. *Hegel: An Introduction,* 2nd edition. Oxford: Basil Blackwell, 1983.

Poirier, Lucien. *Les Voix de la stratégie.* Paris: Fayard (Géopolitiques et strategies), 1985.

Préposiet, Jean. *Histoire de l'anarchisme.* Paris: Tallandier, 2002.

Puységur, Louis Pierre de Chastenet de. *L'Art de la guerre par principe et par règles,* vol. 2. Paris: Charles Antoine Jombert, 1749.

Quincy, M. le Marquis de. *L'Art de la guerre.* The Hague: Henri Scheurleer, 1728.

Rapoport, Anatol. Introduction to *On War,* translated by J.J. Graham. Baltimore: Penguin Books, 1968.

Reid, Julian. "Re-appropriating Clausewitz: The Neglected Dimensions of Counter-strategic Thought." In *Classical Theory in International Relations,* edited by Jahn Beate, 5–10. Cambridge: Cambridge University Press, 2004.

Rey, George. "The Analytic/Synthetic Distinction." In *The Stanford Encyclopedia of Philosophy,* edited by Edward N. Zalta. Summer 2012 edition, accessed 7 May 2016. http://plato.stanford.edu/entries/analytic-synthetic.

– *The Analytic/Synthetic Distinction.* First published 14 August 2003; substantive revision 15 August 2008. Accessed 4 April 2016. http://plato.stanford.edu/entries/analytic-synthetic.

Rohlf, Michael. "Immanuel Kant." In *The Stanford Encyclopedia of Philosophy*, edited by Edward N. Zalta. Fall 2010, accessed 7 May 2016. http://plato.stanford.edu/archives/fall2010/entries/kant.

Rousseau, Jean-Jacques. *Œuvres complètes*. Paris: Dalibon, 1826.

Roxborough, Ian. "Clausewitz and the Sociology of War." *The British Journal of Sociology* 45, no. 4 (December 1994): 619–36.

Saxe, Maurice de. *Reveries on the Art of War*. Harrisburg: Military Service Publishing, 1944.

Schufreider, Gregory. "The Logic of the Absurd." *Philosophy and Phenomenological Research* 44, no. 1 (1983): 61–83.

Singer, Peter. "Hegel, Georg Wilhelm Friedrich." In *The Oxford Companion to Philosophy*, edited by Ted Honderich, 339–43. Oxford: Oxford University Press, 1995.

Smith, Constance. "Hegel on War." *Journal of the History of Ideas* 26, no. 2 (April–June 1965): 282–5.

Smith, Steven B. "Hegel on Slavery and Domination." *The Review of Metaphysics* 46, no. 1 (Philosophy Education Society Inc. 1992): 97–124.

– "Hegel's Views on War, the State, and International Relations." *The American Political Science Review* 77, no. 3 (September 1983): 624–32.

– "What Is 'Right' in Hegel's Philosophy of Right?" *The American Political Science Review* 83, no. 1 (March 1989): 3–18.

Strassler, Robert B., ed. *The Landmark Thucydides: A Comprehensive Guide to the Peloponnesian War*. New York: Free Press, 1996.

Strachan, Hew. "Essay and Reflection: On Total War and Modern War." *The International History Review* 22, no. 2 (June 2000): 343.

Strachan, Hew, and Andreas Herberg-Rothe, ed. *Clausewitz in the Twenty-First Century*. Oxford: Oxford University Press, 2007.

Taylor, Charles. *Hegel*. Cambridge: Cambridge University Press, 1975.

Trotsky, Leon. "The November Strike." In *1905*, translated by Anya Bostock, London: Vintage Books, 1972. Accessed 18 May 2016. https://www.marxists.org/archive/trotsky/1907/1905/ch15.htm.

– *The Revolution in Spain*. New York: Pioneer Publishers, 1931. Accessed 18 May 2016. https://www.marxists.org/archive/trotsky/1931/spain/spain04.htm.

– "Speech at the Meeting of the Military Science Society Attached to the Military Academy of the Workers and Peasants, May 8, 1922." In *The Military Writings of Leon Trotsky*, vol. 5: 1921–23. Translated by Brian Pearce. London: New Park Publications, 1973. Accessed 18 May 2016. https://www.marxists.org/archive/trotsky/military-pdf/Military-Writings-Trotsky-v5.pdf.

Tucker, Robert C. "The Cunning of Reason in Hegel and Marx." *The Review of Politics* 18, no. 3 (July 1956): 269–95.

Valenzuela, Arturo. "Paraguay: The Coup That Didn't Happen." *Journal of Democracy* 8, no. 1 (1997): 43–55. https://muse.jhu.edu/. Accessed 18 May, 2016.

van Creveld, Martin. *The Art of War.* London: Cassell, 2000.
– *The Transformation of War.* New York: The Free Press, 1991.
Vauban, Sebastien Le Prestre de. *Les Oisivetés.* Sysse: Champs Valeon, 2007.
– *Œuvres.* Amsterdam: Arkstee & Merkus, 1771.
Vaysse, Jean-Marie. *La stratégie critique de Kant.* Paris: Ellipses, 2005.
– *Le vocabulaire de Kant.* Paris: Ellipses, 2010.
Voltaire. *Candide.* New York: Boni and Liveright, 1918.
– *Œuvres complètes, Poésies.* vol. 3. Paris: P. Didot, 1825.
von Bülow, Dietrich. *Esprit du system de la guerre moderne.* Accessed 18 January 2006. http://www.stratisc.org/partenaires/cfhm/micro/Von_Bülow_Section10.html.
Waldman, Thomas. *War, Clausewitz and the Trinity.* Surrey: Ashgate, 2013.
Wallace, R. Jay. "Practical Reason." In *The Stanford Encyclopedia of Philosophy,* edited by Edward N. Zalta. Summer 2012 edition, accessed 6 May 2016. http://plato.stanford.edu/archives/sum2009/entries/practical-reason.
Westphal, Merold. *Hegel, Freedom and Modernity.* Albany: SUNY Press, 1992.

Index